Extractive Imperialism in the Americas

Studies in Critical Social Sciences Book Series

Haymarket Books is proud to be working with Brill Academic Publishers (www.brill.nl) to republish the *Studies in Critical Social Sciences* book series in paperback editions. This peer-reviewed book series offers insights into our current reality by exploring the content and consequences of power relationships under capitalism, and by considering the spaces of opposition and resistance to these changes that have been defining our new age. Our full catalog of *SCSS* volumes can be viewed at www.haymarketbooks.org/category/scss-series.

EXTRACTIVE IMPERIALISM IN THE AMERICAS

Capitalism's New Frontier

By

JAMES PETRAS
AND HENRY VELTMEYER

WITH CONTRIBUTIONS BY
PAUL BOWLES, DENNIS CANTERBURY,
NORMAN GIRVAN, AND DARCY TETREAULT

Haymarket
Books
Chicago, IL

First published in 2014 by Brill Academic Publishers, The Netherlands.
© 2014 Koninklijke Brill NV, Leiden, The Netherlands

Published in paperback in 2015 by
Haymarket Books
P.O. Box 180165
Chicago, IL 60618
773-583-7884
www.haymarketbooks.org

ISBN: 978-1-60846-494-4

Trade distribution:
In the U.S. through Consortium Book Sales, www.cbsd.com
In the UK, Turnaround Publisher Services, www.turnaround-uk.com
In all other countries by Publishers Group Worldwide, www.pgw.com

Cover design by Ragina Johnson.

This book was published with the generous support of Lannan Foundation
and the Wallace Action Fund.

Library of Congress Cataloging-in-Publication Data is available.

Contents

List of Tables

List of Acronyms

ALBA	Bolivarian Alliance for the Peoples of Our America (*Alianza Bolivariana para los Pueblos de Nuestra América*)
AMLO	Andres Manual López Obredor
BCGI	Bauxite Company Guyana
BRICS	An association of five major emerging national economies: Brazil, Russia, India, China and South Africa
CEPAL	Comisión Económica Para America Latina (ECLAC, in English)
CLOC	Latin American Coordination of Rural Organizations (*Coordinadora Latinoamericana de Organizaciones del Campo*
CSR	Corporate Social Responsibility
CCT	Conditional Cash Transfers
ECLAC	Economic Commission for Latin America and the Caribbean
EI	Extractive Imperialism
FDI	Foreign Direct Investment
FTAA	Free Trade Areas of the Americas
GB & GWU	Guyana Bauxite & General Workers Union
GMOS	Genetically Modified Organisms
GWMA	Guyana Women's Miners Association
IGFMMSD	The Intergovernmental Forum on Mining, Minerals, Metals and Sustainable Development
IMF	International Monetary Fund
MNC(s)	Multinational Corporation(s)
MNCI	National Movement of Indigenous Peasants (*Movimiento Nacional Campesino Indígena*)
MST	Rural Landless Workers Movement (Movimento dos Trabalhadores Rurais Sem Terra)
NAFTA	North American Free Trade Agreement
NBC	Northern British Columbia
NGO(s)	Nongovernmental Organization(s)
NSP	The New Social Policy
OECD	The Organisation for Economic Co-operation and Development
PAN	National Action Party (*Partido de Acción Nacional*)
PT	Workers Party (Partido dos Trabalhadores)
SITMMSSRM	Sindicato Nacional de Trabajadores Mineros, Metalúrgicos, Siderúrgicos y Similares de la República Mexicana
UNCTAD	United Nations Conference on Trade and Development

List of Contributors

Paul Bowles
is Professor of Economics and International Studies at the University of Northern British Columbia in Prince George. This book is part of a larger project funded by the Social Sciences and Humanities Research Council of Canada. Other work from the project includes a co-edited volume (with Gary Wilson) entitled *Globalizing Northern British Columbia: Agency, Contestation and Development in a Resource-dependent Region* (forthcoming). Other recent publications include (with Henry Veltmeyer) *The Answer is Still No. Voices of Resistance to the Enbridge Northern Gateway PipelineCapitalism*; and (with John Harriss) *Globalization and Labour in China and India: Impacts and Responses*, 2010.

Dennis Canterbury
is Associate Professor in the Department of Sociology, Anthropology and SocialWork at Eastern Connecticut State University. His research interests are globalization, labour, development, mining and agriculture. Currently, his research is on the economic partnership agreements between the European Union (EU) and the Africa, Caribbean and Pacific (ACP) group of countries, focusing on the Caribbean Forum (CARIFORUM) and the Economic Community of West African States (ECOWAS), with the Institute of Development Studies (IDS), University of Cape Coast, Ghana. He is the author of European Bloc Imperialism (Brill, 2010).

Norman Girvan
is Professor Emeritus at the Institute of International Relations at the University of the West Indies in Trinidad, and Distinguished Visiting Professor at Saint Mary's University (Halifax, Canada). He was formerly Director of the UN Centre for Transnational Corporations (UNCTC), Chief Technical Director of the National Planning Agency of the Government of Jamaica and Secretary-General of the Association of Caribbean States. He is widely published in the area of globalization and development, particularly in the context of the Caribbean.

James Petras
is Professor Emeritus in Sociology at Binghamton University in New York and Adjunct professor in International Development Studies at Saint Mary's University (Halifax, Canada). He is the author and coeditor of over sixty books

and numerous other writings on the dynamics of world and Latin American developments. Recent publications include *Imperialism and Capitalism in the 21st Century, Beyond Neoliberalism: A World to Win, Social Movements in Latin America: Neoliberalism and Popular Resistance*, and *What's Left in Latin America*. A list and an actual file of his periodical writings and journal articles are maintained and can be accessed at www.rebelion.org/hemeroteca/petras .htm.

Darcy Tetreault

is Research Professor of Development Studies at the Autonomous University of Zacatecas, Mexico, and author of numerous publications in the area of poverty and Latin American development studies, including 'Alternative pathways out of rural poverty in Mexico' in *European Review of Latin American and Caribbean Studies* (2010), and, with Henry Veltmeyer, *Poverty in Latin America: Public policies and development pathways* (2013).

Henry Veltmeyer

is Professor of Development Studies at Saint Mary's University and the Universidad Autónoma de Zacatecas (UAZ) He is author and editor of over 40 books on Latin America and world development, including most recently *Development in an Era of Neoliberal Globalization, Poverty and Development in Latin America, The Critical Development Studies Handbook, Socialism of the 21st Century*; and (with James Petras) *The New Extractivism in Latin America, Imperialism and Capitalism in the 21st Century, Social Movements in Latin America*.

Introduction

Over the past decade, a new form of capitalism has emerged within the framework of a post-Washington Consensus on the need for governments to move beyond the neoliberal policy agenda as well as some epoch-defining changes in the global economy. These changes include the rise of China as an economic power and conditions of a primary commodities boom that have provoked a tsunami of resource-seeking foreign investments in the acquisition of land in developing countries and the extraction of natural resources ranging from fossil- and bio-fuels, industrial minerals and precious metals, and agro-food products. Of particular note in this land—and resource-grabbing process is the role played by the multinational corporations as the operating agencies of the world capitalist system, and the actions taken by the powerful states at the centre of the system to advance and in support of this 'resource seeking' or extractivist capital.

The operations of these corporations in advancing what we might term extractive capital, and the facilitating actions and support of the imperial state, have generated a new dynamic of capitalist development and unleashed powerful forces both in support of this process and in resistance. As for the forces behind the advances of extractive capitalism they are engineered and led by a few powerful states with a vested interest in the expected outcome—reactivation of the economic development process within their national boundaries. To ensure this outcome, and to maximize their ability and freedom to manoeuvre within the confines of the world market, the agencies and agents of the imperial state have mobilized the diverse powers available to them in constructing an economic model designed to advance the 'forces of economic freedom' (private property, capital, the market) in the global economy, and the multinational companies within the 'private sector', assigning to them the role of catalyst in the process of sustainable resource development.

However, the relevant model (the private sector as the catalyst of 'inclusive growth' or 'inclusionary state activism') and its institutional and policy framework (free market capitalism vs. the regulated market) have been hotly contested, giving rise to an alternative model based on the inclusionary activism of the post-neoliberal state in the resource-rich countries of the global south on the periphery of the system, as well as an alternative system for organizing the global trade in commodities. This book analyses the dynamics of this conflict, as well as the forces brought into play by a system that is fast approaching the limits of its capacity to expand the forces of production within the institutional framework and workings of the world capitalist system. The system has evidenced a propensity towards crisis, the multiple dimensions of which—production and financial, energy and food, environmental—reflect the built-in contradictions of the capitalist system and generate powerful forces that have the potential of forcing all sorts of policy adjustments and institutional reforms on the system in order to save it from itself.

As for the forces of resistance, they are wielded by the organizations and communities that are negatively affected by the destructive socioenvironmental operations of extractive capital in its development of the forces of production and its latest assault on people's livelihoods, their health, communities and social conditions, as well as the environment on which economic activity and life itself depends. In this context the resistance is taking multiple form, including the struggle of dispossessed or small landholding peasant farmers and their communities to secure their access to and protect their territorial rights regarding the global commons of land, water and the natural resources to which they have a customary and at times ancestral claim. The resistance in these conditions also involves a struggle for survival against the negative socioenvironmental impacts and destructive operations of extractive capital, and opposition to the policymakers and public policies that facilitate these operations.

The stakes in this struggle are high. At stake on the side of capital are the enormous profits to be made in the extractive process of natural resource development. Extractivism is highly profitable due to the enormous rents generated on a world scale and appropriated in large measure by the transnational corporations and the commodity traders that dominate the system. But it also results in enormous social and environmental costs, deemed by mainsteam economists to be 'external diseconomies', that are transferred to local populations and society at large. Furthermore, the external effects and social and environmental costs inherent in extractivism and the associated process of 'accumulation by dispossession' have increased the power of large producers as well as corporate profitability and resource rents.

At stake for the communities of small-scale agricultural producers, and the masses of dispossessed rural landless workers and peasant farmers, are their livelihoods and their communities as well as their right to live in social solidarity and harmony with the land and nature. As for the State the stakes are also high. For the imperial states at issue is the power to secure their geoeconomic and geopolitical interests and to impose order, rules of engagement for capital and labour, and the system, that will secure these interests. For the resource-rich developing country states, which are either forced or all too willing to play the host to foreign investments and extractive capital what is at issue is a share of the resource rents extracted by capital from the export and sale—plunder, to put it succinctly—and an additional source of fiscal revenues for financing their economic and social development projects.

The expansion of extractive capitalism and the turn towards extractivism over the past decade has been generally explained as the response of capital and the state to the 'economic opportunities' presented by the growing global demand for energy, minerals and other 'natural resources', and the global primary commodities boom (see, for example, the studies in Veltmeyer & Petras, 2014). However, there are broader and deeper economic and political forces involved. A considered explanation of the current dynamics of extractive capitalism and imperialism must also take into account the geoeconomics and politics of a system in crisis—a crisis that reaches well beyond the institutional and policy dynamics of the so-called 'global financial crisis' into the very foundation of the system.[1] As was the case with the global financial crisis the epicentre of this crisis is in the United States, still the biggest economy of the capitalist world. The US economy, as it turns out, is in the throes of a major economic crisis brought about by a major reconfiguration of global capitalism over the past four decades and the financialization of capitalist development.[2]

One result of the financialization of capitalist development, and the associated hegemony of financial capital, has been a weakening of several key pillars of the US economy (industry, in particular) and the destruction of forces of production that had built up over half a century. Another result has been the deepening of a major social divide in the distribution of wealth and income, a divide that has not only reached the proportions of a social crisis but that has

---

1 The 'global crisis' has deepened with the passing of the years, weakening the institutions of the central powers of the imperialist state system, breaking down the economic and cultural patterns that united these societies, and exposing an irreversible process in which the system is fast reaching its limits, exhausting its ability to expand the forces of global production.

2 Financialization has meant the expansion of fictitious capital and parasitical forms of speculative investments, as well as the dominance of financial capital over industrial capital in the system of global production. It is estimated that by the end of the 1990s less than five percent of global transactions on the world's capital markets had any productive function or connection to the real economy. It is estimated that by the end of the 1990s transactions based on speculative investments (derivatives, etc.), a clear reflection of the financialization of development, amounted to about 2.4 times the nominal value of global economic production. By 2002 it was 4.3 times and by the end of 2006 8.5 times. In 2008, in a the midst of a speculative frenzy that took form as a 'global financial crisis' the value of total transactions based on fictituous capital reached as high as 11.7 times the value of global production. Since then (by mid-2013) it had fallen to 8.6 (Bank for international Settlements. http://www.bis.org/statistics/derstats.htm).

emerged as a major contradiction of capitalist development, a contradiction that sociologists have described as the 'hollowing out of the middle class' in American society, viz. the inability of a growing number of citizens to meaningfully participate in the capitalist development process as producers or consumers. This means closing down of what has been a major motor of economic growth for the US economy.

A third outcome of the forces now operating on the American economy (financialization, deindustrialization, underconsumption, etc.) is the inability of the economy to sustain the built-in and rapidly growing costs of maintaining the global empire. Some analysts have described this as 'imperial overreach', implying the need for the US to cut back on its military adventures overseas. Others have asked themselves and debated how many wars that the US can afford to wage simultaneously, or have been in the forefront of pushing the US administration to demand of its European and other allies that they pay a much greater share in the global effort and growing costs of keeping the world safe from the forces of evil and terror. However, it is increasingly evident that the issue (the relation between economic and political power) is much more serious—and systemic—than understood by these analysts.

For one thing, the weakening of the economy (via financialization and deindustrialization) and the double face of US imperialism (economic and social decay, military expansion) suggests that the current global military apparatus of the empire is totally unsustainable. If we include in addition to the Defense Department fixed and procurement costs and related expenditures of other agencies (Department of State, Energy, NASA, etc.), and interest payments on the military debt, expenditures on this apparatus and global military operations currently cost the US government 1.3 trillion dollars. This figure represents in 2013 budget terms 100 percent of all personal tax revenues collected by the government or 140 percent of the projected budget deficit (Beinstein, 2013: 3). Some economists stress the contributions of these expenditures to the economy (it is estimated that the military apparatus includes up to one third of the GDP and one-fifth of the labourforce), but there is no question that the costs of maintaining the military apparatus of the empire will only increase, while the capacity of the economy to sustain them will be further eroded. On this there is a virtual consensus. The current massive inflow of foreign direct and portfolio investments in treasury bonds and real estate, especially, by Chinese investors and banks, as well as the massive operations of US financial capital, can help the economy stay afloat in the short term, but in the long-term the prognosis is poor, if not dire.

In this context of an impending economic and fiscal crisis, and the new geo-economics of global capital, the turn of both governments and corporations toward a strategy of natural resource extraction makes sense. At issue is not only the opportunity for boosting capital accumulation, plunder and personal enrichment, and for the governments involved to extract resource rents and boost revenues, but the possibility of at least a partial solution to a situation of systemic crisis. The world system has not yet reached its limits or exhausted its capacity to expand the forces of production on a global scale. The dynamism of the 'emerging' economies and markets in Asia, and even in Africa, suggests otherwise. However, the crisis is evidently deepening at the centre of the system, both in the US and Europe, and the only way out is an expanded cycle of capital accumulation and the mobilization of the forces of global production. This requires productive investment in technological innovation and the exploitation of labourpower, as well as the global expansion of industrial capital. However—and this the irony of current efforts at capitalist development—neither financial capital, not extractive capital, has the capacity to pull the system out of its current and imminent crisis. The problem is that these two forms of capital, both in command *as it were* of the forces of production, are oriented towards an immediate and short-term response to the crisis rather than a long-term solution that would require a major restructuring, if not an overhaul, of the system.

Natural resource extraction, or extractivism, is not the only form taken by capitalism and imperialism in the current conjuncture. In fact, the entire arsenal of weapons and tactics used over the past five decades of US imperialism (on this see Petras & Veltmeyer, 2004, 2005b, 2011) in the exercise of imperial state power has been brought into play as circumstances require. Thus, as illustrated in several of our case studies in the South American theatre of the struggle the imperial state has engaged a variety of strategies in the projection of state power—from funding oppositional groups in electoral contests where its interests are at issue (in Venezuela, for example) to diplomatic pressure, funding of community development projects, and bribery of state officials, to the imposition of a supportive economic order or policy regime, and the subjection of progressive regimes to the rules of the neoliberal world order and the interests of empire. In other contexts, of course, the arsenal and mechanisms of imperial power include armed force. In the case of imperial Canada, discussed in Chapter 9, the state has even placed its program of international cooperation for development at the service of the Canadian companies that dominate the mining sector of the extractive industry both in Latin America and Africa.

In the South American frame of these developments—the extraction of natural resources—for development and profit, the focus of the book is on the policy dynamics of the 'new extractivism' and the post-neoliberal state. Our focus on agrarian extractivism in this context is on Argentina and Brazil. In these countries extractivism applies particularly to the production of biofuels and the soy agribusiness model of development in which production is based on the use of transgenic seeds provided by Monsanto and other transnationals and new technologies that bring into question the sustainability of development. This constitutes a new characteristic of present-day agriculture that historically was sustainable for millennia. Humanity would not have subsisted in the long term if agriculture had not been sustainable; that is, if agriculture did not have the capacity for reproducing itself and thus producing the food required for increased populations.[3]

Structure of the Argument

The book is organized in two parts. Part I explores the diverse dynamics of capitalist development in the current context of extractive capital and extractive imperialism. The aim of the six chapters in this part of the book is to put these dynamics in both a theoretical and historical context. Part II takes the form of a number of country case studies into the contemporary dynamics of extractive imperialism.

Chapter 1 provides a framework for understanding the contemporary dynamics of extractive capital and imperialism in the context of the Americas—in Latin America and the Caribbean—and in Canada, where the state has been clearly placed at the service of extractive capital in its diverse capitalist development projects at home and abroad.

At issue in these rather complex dynamics, summarized in the form of ten theses on extractivism and imperialism, is what we might term the new geo-economics of capital and the geopolitics of the state. As regards capital the fundamental issue is the form taken by the productive investment of global capital in the development of the forces of production in the various societies that make up the Americas. Here it is argued that a primary commodities boom in the world market has accentuated a trend towards the development of 'resource-seeking' capital, with significant economic, social and political

---

3 The prospect for maintaining sustainability is probably a reaction against new technologies and models—the so-called hybrid and the more recent transgenic seed revolutions—that involve new organizational forms of agribusiness. Although farmers throughout history have used a wide range of technologies and practices that we can today call sustainable it is only in recent decades that the concepts associated with sustainability have come into more common use (Altieri, 2004).

repercussions that are elaborated and discussed in other chapters of the book. As regards the state the chapter highlights the role of the state in relation to, and in support of, extractive capital—what we term extractive imperialism.

As we see it there are essentially three modalities of the state at issue. One is in regard to the active engagement and support provided by the Canadian state and the US to American and Canadian mining and energy companies operating in different countries and regions of the Americas. Here we have what we might well term an *imperialist state*, with reference to the geopolitical strategy pursued by officials and agents of this state in support of US and Canadian capital. A second issue relates to the economic model used by state officials and policymakers to make public policy in the area of economic development. Here we identify various permutations of a *neoliberal state* (where the government continues to toe the line of the Washington Consensus regarding the virtues of free market capitalism) and a *post-neoliberal state*, which has emerged in South America in response to a widepread disaffection and rejection if neoliberalism as an economic doctrine and political ideology.

One of the most important developments in Latin America in the last decade has been the emergence of this post-neoliberal state in what has been described as a 'red' or 'pink' tide of centre-left 'progressive' regimes under conditions of a regionwide movement to abandon neoliberalism and the emergence of a primary commodities boom. The central question addressed in the chapter is whether the model used by policymakers and officials of the so-called post-neoliberal state, a state characterized by 'inclusionary activism' (in regard to the social distribution of resource rents), serves (or could serve) as a pathway to a sustainable form of economic and social development, or whether instead we should view it as a new political ideology—to replace the defunct or tarnished neoliberal model. The model is constructed on two pillars: a new development paradigm based on a post-Washington Consensus on the need for inclusive development and poverty reduction (the 'new developmentalism') and a national development strategy ('the new extractivism') based on the extraction of natural resources, their export in primary commodity form, and a policy of social inclusion in regard to the distribution of the resource rents collected in the development process.

Chapter 2 provides a historical context for understanding the contemporary dynamics of extractivist imperialism. The argument advanced by Norman Girvan is that a pillage of natural resources has always been a defining feature of capitalism and imperialism—as much so as the exploitation of labour emphasized in Marx's theory of capitalist development. Girvan traces out the history of extractive imperialism in the context of the Caribbean. Girvan reflects on the question as to what lessons can be drawn from this history? To this end he distinguishes five broad historical periods since Europeans arrived in the Americas: the age of conquest and colonisation; the age of commercial capitalism; the first industrial revolution; the emergence of monopoly capitalism; and the contemporary age of global finance capitalism.

To facilitate an analysis of the changing dynamics of capitalist development and extractive imperialism over the course of this historical process, he also constructs an analytical scheme focused on seven factors that assume particular characteristics in each age: (i) key resource commodities; (ii) labour; (iii) capital; (iv) the state; (v) ideology; (vi) resource rents; and (vii) contradictions. The first six factors taken together constitute a kind of 'regime' that corresponds to each historical period—a regime of power, ideology and distribution of resource rents. The seventh relates to the nature of contradictions that result in changes over time. The changes occur within an existing regime; and, less frequently, they replace one regime with another—regime change (as is taking place today in South America).

With Chapter 3 the book delves into what has been theorized as the 'agrarian question'—with reference to the role of agriculture in the capitalist development process, and the dynamics of productive and social transformation that has accompanied this process. The argument here advanced is that the contemporary dynamics of extractive capitalism in the agricultural sector replicate under different conditions the historical process of 'accumulation by dispossession'—dispossessing the small-scale agricultural producer or peasant farmers from the land and their means of production as a source of capital accumulation. In the current context this process takes the form of landgrabbing for the purpose of 'natural resource development'; reducing or closing off access to the global commons of land, water and natural resources; and environmental degradation.[4] The chapter identifies and describes the forces engaged in this process, making the point that the operations of agricultural

---

4 Several authors have suggested that mining practices in Latin America typify what David Harvey (2003) calls 'accumulation by dispossession'. On the contemporary dynamics of 'primitive accumulation' (Marx) and accumulation by dispossession, see Borras et al. (2012) and Sosa & Zwarteveen (2012). In Marx's classical formulation, this process of capitalist development and social transformation concerned agriculture (that is, the conversion of peasants into a proletariat) and entailed the enclosures of the land, leading to a protracted land struggle. In more recent studies of this process, the enclosure of the commons is expanded to include both water and sub-soil resources, leading not only to land grabbing but water grabbing as well as a major resource grab (Kay & Franco, 2012).

extractivism, in regard to both global capital and the state, have activated the forces of resistance to extractivist imperialism—a resistance movement led by peasants (in Latin America) and indigenous communities (both in the South and North).

Chapter 4 elaborates on the forces engaged in the capitalist development process in the current context of extractivist imperialism, with particular reference to the economic model used to guide public policy, govern international relations of trade, and advance the development process. The argument advanced in this chapter can be summed up in the proposition that the capitalist development process in the Americas has resulted in the construction of three alternative economic models, each used to mobilize forces of change in one direction or the other, each associated with a particular type of polity and policy regime, and a particular system for arranging and managing trade and investments as well as relations with US power and the agencies of global capital.

The argument is constructed as follows. First we outline the contours of capitalist development within the institutional and policy framework of the neoliberal world order, with a focus on the economic model used by governments as a template and script for the structural reforms mandated by the Washington Consensus. Here it is argued that the structural reforms implemented in accordance with the neoliberal agenda (privatization, financial and trade liberalisation, market deregulation, administrative decentralization) resulted in a massive inflow of global capital liberated from the regulatory constraints of the developmental state. This capital took the predominant form of foreign direct investment (FDI) directed towards non-traditional or modern manufacturing, high-tech information-rich services, and natural resource extraction. Other outcomes included the project of a free trade regime designed to deepen and extend the financial and trade liberalization process, and a process of uneven capitalist development that was materialized in the construction of a model to promote development (inclusive growth: boosting economic growth while reducing extreme poverty) and conduct international relations of trade and investment within the policy framework of the new world order.

In Chapter 5 we turn away from an analysis of the dynamics associated with the economic model of capitalist development towards the class struggle associated with these dynamics. The aim here is to provide a framework for understanding and conducting an analysis of the forces engaged in the class struggle. The main argument advanced in the chapter is that the class struggle under current conditions assumes multiple forms, including a struggle over land, ownership of natural resources and improved access to the global commons, as well as opposition to the model used to organize production. One model is based on large-scale corporate capitalist production (with inputs of imported capital and advanced modern technology) and geared to a development strategy based on large-scale foreign investment in land, natural resource extraction, and the formation of joint venture partnerships between the private sector (multinational corporations that provide both capital and technology) and the state in a new association with capital. In opposition to this corporate model, the resistance movement is oriented towards small-scale local production and alternative non-capitalist forms of development and trade. A second argument advanced in the chapter is that the resistance has generated a continental network of social movements concerned about the destructive social and environmental impacts of extractivism, but that most of these movements are not yet prepared to abandon the operative capitalist system.

With Chapter 6 the book turns towards a series of case studies into the dynamics of extractive capitalism and the resistance to it. The chapter, contributed by Dennis Canterbury, features the dynamics of capitalist development and the resistance in Guyana. The main conclusions drawn by Canterbury from his analysis of these dynamics are that:

1.   the state is being relied on to play an increasing role in the economic development process via the mechanism of joint ventures;

2.   mining is playing an increasing role in the Guyana economy in terms of its contribution to the GDP and attraction of foreign direct investment into the country;

3.   capital from the emerging economies is playing an increasing role in production in the extractive industries, while capital from the advanced capitalist countries is engaged more in exploration and financial speculation;

4.   the state of Guyana is actively collaborating with capital from the 'emerging economies', which are dominant in the bauxite industry in Guyana, particularly in regard to anti-working class activities such as union busting;

5.   the prevalence of criminal activities, including money laundering, gold smuggling, foreigners illegally mining for gold, corruption, murder, rape, etc., are other dimensions of the dynamics of extractive capitalism in Guyana;

6.   the current extractive phase of capitalist development is characterized by landgrabbing in which foreign companies are acquiring large stretches of lands to explore for uranium and rare earth minerals;

7. mining, as well as the landgrabbing phenomenon, has a particularly destructive impact on the livelihoods of indigenous peoples and their communities; and

8. in the Guyanese context the labour movement, such as it is, is playing an important part in the resistance to extractive imperialism, i.e. the actions of the state in support of extractive capital.

Chapter 7 turns the spotlight on Brazil, which, until recently was widely regarded as an emerging regional power and an 'emerging economy' with the potential of joining China, Russia and India as the new powerhouses of the global economy and the world capitalist system. But with the virtual collapse of industrial production and exports in 2012 the picture has radically changed. It appears that the country has succumbed to the 'resource curse' that has plagued so many developing countries in the past in their efforts to bring about economic development on the basis of extractivism.[5]

In any case, although the jury is still out, we argue that under the current Worker's party (PT) regime Brazil is well under way towards transitioning from a potential industrial powerhouse to an exporter of primary commodities, reverting from a dynamic nationalist-industrializing economy to a vulnerable imperial-driven agro-mineral extractive dependency. The chapter reviews and documents key moments of this 'great reversal', and reconstructs the political and policy dynamics involved.

A major feature of these dynamics is the emergence of a new wave of mass protests against the current PT regime and its policies. While the class struggle for land, higher wages and better working conditions has declined precipitously over the past quarter of a century of neoliberal reforms, the regime's policies in favour of extractive capital have spawned a new wave of mass social movements that has placed both the regime and the extractive model under siege. The main point of political confrontation in Brazil today can be found not in the workplace but in the streets as well as in Amazonia and other sites on the new frontier of capitalist development—extractivism. The

---

5   The idea of a 'resource curse' is an expansion of the idea of the Dutch disease, first coined by *The Economist* magazine in 1977 to refer to how the Dutch discovery of oil in the North Sea precipitated its industrial decline. While the Dutch disease focuses attention on foreign exchange rate dynamics, the resource curse thesis, as first stated by Richard Auty (1993), emphasises the role of conflict, corruption, political instability and price volatility in explaining how countries rich in natural resources have failed to climb the ladder of development. While many of these factors help explain the resource curse, they are merely manifestations of the underlying dynamics of imperialism and capitalism.

organizational independence and autonomy of the organizations involved in the popular movement underline the deeper challenge to the entire neoliberal extractive model. Even though no national organizations or leadership of these mass movements has emerged to elaborate an alternative the struggle continues.

Chapter 8 profiles the case of Mexico, which, unlike Brazil, continues to adhere to the neoliberal model of free market capitalism rejected by Brazil in favour of 'inclusionary state activism' and the 'new developmentalism' regarding the belief in the need for a more inclusionary form of development (Bresser-Pereira, 2009).[6] In this chapter the book moves from a paradigmatic case of the 'new' or 'progressive' extractivism (Brazil) to a paradigmatic case of extractivism in the neoliberal mould. Although Mexico does not fit the profile of an extractivist state in recent years the government has increasingly turned towards the extractive industry for its development strategy, particularly in regard to the mining of precious metals such as silver and gold, of which it is one of the world's biggest producers. This is to make up for the lack of dynamism in the industrial sector, which in 2013 hit a new low in the volume and value of production (a 0.7 percentage decline).

The Mexican government in this context has focused on resource extraction as a catalyst for national development, taking advantage of the primary commodities boom in the world market and the growing and sustained demand for energy, minerals and metals, as well as for agro-food products. However, as Tetreault explains, within the framework of the neoliberal model used by the government over the last three decades, the end result has been the pillage and looting of the country's wealth of mineral resources at an enormous environmental and social cost, borne directly and disproportionately by the country's indigenous communities. Having ceded over a quarter of the national territory to transnational companies for exploration and their extractive operations, the government has furnished these companies with the freedom and opportunity to make significant profits on their investments and to transfer those profits out of the country, with precious little to show in return in terms of national development—except for the extraction of scarce and non-renewable resources and the degradation of the environment and the livelihoods and health of the communities that are contiguous to the mines. The chapter's central focus is

---

6 Regarding the role of the state in this post-neoliberal strategy—dubbed "inclusionary state activism" by Arbix and Martin (2010) and a feature of the new developmentalism (Bresser-Pereira (2007, 2009)—it is based on the idea that rather than constituting a curse, the exploitation of resources such as minerals and hydrocarbons or fossil fuels generate easily taxable rents that can finance social development (Stijns, 2006).

INTRODUCTION 13

on the nature and the dynamics of the resistance to extractive capital and its operations—the social and environmental movements generated by these operations.

Chapter 9 turns from the resistance in Mexico to the resistance of indigenous and non-indigenous communities to the building of a oil pipeline to transport bitumen from the tarsands of Alberta to the coast of North British Colombia and from there to Asian markets. What is significant about the findings of this case study—another case of extractivism pursued by a regime committed to neoliberalism (private sector-led inclusive growth and sustainable resource development, in the discourse of the Canadian government)—is the similarity in the political dynamics of the resistance on the new frontier of extractive capital in both Brazil and Mexico.

The chapter has two aims. The first is to provide a theoretical framework in which extractivism can be understood globally and within which specific country and regional debates can be situated. The second is to analyse resistance to a specific form of extractivism, that of oil pipelines in Northern British Columbia, and to illustrate how it can be understood within the context of the turn of many countries towards natural resource extraction as a model of national development. While resistance to extractivism has been the subject of much analysis in the Latin American context much less is available on resistance in the global north (Canada in this case). This chapter seeks to fill this void and, in doing so, demonstrates the similarities in extractivist resistance in both the north and the south. Canada provides a good case study for exploring such similarities since the government engages in 'extractivist imperialism' abroad at the same time as the natural resource development on the unceded territory of indigenous groups in Canada represents a form of neo-colonialism, not unlike the situation in Brazil, Mexico and other countries in the America with a significant indigenous population.

The Chapters 10–12 turn away from the specifities of extractive imperialism towards a more general evaluation and report on US imperialism at home and abroad. The reason for this is that the US has assumed the responsibility of leading the 'forces of economic and political freedom' in the defense of world capitalism and remains the hegemonic power in the system notwithstanding growing evidence of its decline.

Chapter 10 brings into focus the relationship of the US to Venezuela, where the government, although extractivist in form (no country in the region is as reliant as Venezuela on the extraction and export of natural resources for its development) is leading the struggle against both capitalism and imperialism.

Relations of the US with Venezuela illustrate the specific mechanisms with which an imperial power seeks to sustain client states and overthrow independent nationalist governments. By examining US strategic goals and its tactical measures in regard to Venezuela the chapter sets forth several propositions regarding the nature and instruments of imperial politics in Venezuela; the shifting context and contingencies that influence the successes and failures of specific policies; and the importance of regional and global political alignments and priorities.

The chapter employs a comparative historical approach to highlight the different policies, contexts and outcomes of imperial policies during two distinct Presidential periods: the ascendancy of neoliberal US client regimes in the late 1980s through 1998, when the *Caracazo* challenged the legitimacy of the neoliberal model, and the rise and consolidation of a nationalist populist government under President Hugo Chávez who turned the country towards the 'Socialism of the 21st century'.

US-Venezuela relations are characterized by the hostility of the US government, in defence of its geo-political and economic interests, and both capitalism and the empire. The chapter examines this relationship of political conflict, with one government acting in defence of imperialism and the other to attack it, at three levels. At the country level, Venezuela marks out a new development paradigm that features public ownership over the free market, social welfare over multi-national oil profits and popular power over class dominance and elite rule. At the regional level Venezuela promotes Latin American integration over US-centred Latin American Free Trade Agreements, anti-imperialism over 'pan-Americanism', foreign aid based on reciprocal economic interests and non-intervention as opposed to US military pacts, narco-military collusion and military bases. At the world level Venezuela has rejected the US invasions of Afghanistan and Iraq, ignored US trade sanctions against Iran, opposed Washington and NATO's bombing of Libya and the proxy invasion of Syria. Venezuela condemns Israel's colonization and annexation of Palestine. In other words, Venezuela upholds national self-determination against US military-driven imperialism.[7]

In Chapter 11 we turn towards an analysis of the contemporary dynamics of US imperialism. The configuration of 21st century imperialism combines patterns of exploitation from the past as well as new features which are essential to understanding the contemporary forms of plunder, pillage and mass impoverishment. In this chapter we will highlight the relatively new forms of imperial exploitation, reflecting the rise and consolidation of an international

7   Interview, President Chávez Caracas, November 7, 2006.

ruling class, the centrality of military power, large scale long-term criminality as a key component of the process of capital accumulation, the centrality of domestic collaborator classes and political elites in sustaining the US–EU empire and the new forms of class and anti-imperialist struggles.

Imperialism is about political domination, economic exploitation, cultural penetration via military conquest, economic coercion, political destabilization, separatist movements and via domestic collaborators. Imperial aims, today as in the past, are about securing markets, seizing raw materials, exploiting cheap labor in order to enhance profits, accumulate capital and enlarge the scope and depth of political domination. Today the mechanisms by which global profits are enhanced have gone far beyond the exploitation of markets, resources and labour; they embrace entire nations, peoples and the public treasuries, not only of regions of Africa, Asia and Latin America but include the so-called 'debtor countries of Europe', Ireland, Greece, Spain, Portugal and Iceland, among others.

Today the imperial powers of Europe and the United States are re-enacting the 'scramble for the riches of Africa, Asia and Latin America' via direct colonial wars accompanying a rising tide of militarism abroad and police state rule at home. The problem of empire building is that, given popular anti-imperialist resistance abroad and economic crisis at home, imperial policymakers require far-reaching expenditures and dependence on collaborator rulers and classes in the countries and regions targeted for imperial exploitation.

Chapter 12 provides some concluding reflections on the nature and dynamics of US imperialism today, as well as an assessment of its defeats, forced retreats, advances and victories.

PART 1

Imperialism and Class Struggle Dynamics

∴

CHAPTER 1

A New Model or a New Form of Imperialism?

Capitalist development and imperialism today in the Americas can best be described in terms of what economists have termed 'extractivism' (economic development based on the extraction of natural resources such as fossil and biofuels, minerals and agro-food products extracted in a process of 'large-scale investment in land acquisition' (or, in the discourse of critical agrarian studies, 'landgrabbing').[1]

As noted in the introduction to the book there is nothing new about this. Both extractivism and the associated strategy of primary commodity exports have long played an important if inglorious role in the history of capitalism and imperialism, which has always meant pillage—the plunder and looting of a society's wealth of natural resources, and the transfer of this wealth to the centre of the system for the purpose of capital accumulation or simply to enrich the holders of power. Capitalism and imperialism have always relied on the prerogatives of private property, as well as the enclosure and privatization of the commons and the dispossession of direct producers, not to mention the exploitation of both natural resources and labour, and the exercise of class and state power in the interests of capital. However, after the end of World War II in conditions of a collapsing British empire and the system of colonial rule, governments in both the north and the south (the development state) turned towards a new development strategy of economic growth based on import substitution industrialization and the exploitation of the unlimited supplies of rural surplus labour generated by the capitalist development of agriculture. To facilitate and advance this process, the theorists and architects of capitalist development elaborated a strategy to encourage the proletarianized and impoverished peasant farmers (the rural poor, as they are termed in development discourse) to abandon agriculture and migrate to the cities in the search for work—to capacitate them for entry into the urban labour market and to integrate them into the modernizing process of capitalist development.

---

1 The term 'land grabbing' (large-scale investments in land) re-emerged on the international stage in the context of a spike in global food prices in 2007/2008. But since then the discourse has begun to merge with the literature on 'water grabs' and the 'resource grabs' of extractive capital (Sosa & Zwarteveen, 2012; White et al., 2012).

This state-led development strategy was pursued for several decades (the so-called golden age of capitalism in the 1950s and 1960s) until market constraints and a crisis of the states at the centre of the system led to a major paradigmatic shift in development thought in the direction of free market capitalism and a fiscal crisis of the states at the centre of the system, which brought a new generation of social conservatives and economic neoliberals to power. Through a strategy of armed force in the form of military coups and juntas, and a new world order based on free market capitalism and the financialization of global production, a new neoliberal model of 'structural reforms' in macro-economic policy became the dominant paradigm (neoliberal globalization).

However, several cycles of neoliberal policies and 'structural reforms' that led to the destruction of the forces of production in both agriculture and industry on the periphery of the system also brought about a powerful resistance movement and forces of change in the neoliberal model of free market capitalism. In the vortex of these forces government after government in Latin America, both those with a continuing commitment to the 'Washington consensus' on the virtues of free market capitalism and those that rejected neoliberalism, turned towards natural resource extraction as a strategy of economic development—the 'new extractivism', as it is termed in Latin America, with reference to the 'inclusionary activism' of the postneoliberal state formed under these conditions. Both 'inclusive development' and 'extractivism' emerged as a fundamental pillar of the economic model constructed in the changing conditions of the new millennium, and pursued by an increasing number of governments—especially in South America—in their national development strategy and policies.[2]

The conclusions that we draw from our research into the dynamics of the new extractivism associated with this new model, and our reflections on the country case studies in this book, are here presented in the form of ten theses.

---

2 According to Claudio Katz, an important Argentinean Marxist economist, the model put into place throughout Latin America over the past two decades has five pillars: agricultural exports, open pit mining, large-scale resource extraction, the maquilla manufacturing system, and tourism and remittances, as a correlate of forced migration (Minga Informativa de Movimientos Sociales, 17 May, 2013). We would agree with Katz's assessment except that it fails to include one of two key pillars of this model, namely, the 'new developmentalism', a strategy of poverty reduction designed to bring about a more inclusive form of (capitalist) development.

Thesis 1

The New Geoeconomics of Capital in Latin America

Although global flows of capital over the past three decades of neoliberal globalization have become increasingly speculative in form and disconnected
from the production process[3] it is nevertheless revealing to trace out the
changing pattern of capital flows, especially in regard to north-south flows of
FDI and 'resource-seeking' capital, which have increased dramatically in
recent years. A review of these flows (see Table 1.1) shows that over the past
decade, and especially since 2005, they have moved away from manufacturing
and high-tech information-rich services towards the extraction of natural
resources, both renewable and non-renewable, including fossil and biofuels
for energy, precious metals and industrial minerals, as well as agrofood products and the 'large-scale acquisition of land' for the purpose of accessing these
resources directly (as opposed to trading them)—or, in regard to the governments involved, the food and energy security needs of some countries.

A close look at these flows of resource-seeking capital points towards a
major shift in their destination—in the geoeconomics of their global distribution. Not only has Latin America, especially Brazil, been the recipient or destination for much of this capital but the changing pattern of capital flows reveals
a major reconfiguration in the structure of global production, a structure modified by the continuous but changing flows of capital.

TABLE 1.1   *FDI in South America and Mexico (1990–2011, annual average flows in USD billions)*

	1990–1994	1995–2000	2000–2005	2006–2010	2011
Sth America	8.9	47.2	37.9	69.1	n/d
Brazil	1.7	21.8	19.2	34.6	66.7
Argentina	2.9	10.7	4.3	6.4	6.3
Chile	1.2	5.1	5.0	12.6	17.6
Colombia	0.8	2.6	3.7	8.0	14.4
Peru	0.8	2.0	1.6	5.8	7.9
Venezuela	0.8	3.4	2.5	-3.7	n/d
Mexico	5.4	11.3	22.7	21.7	17.9

SOURCE: CEPAL (2010: 45); UNCTAD (2012); ZIBECHI (2012).

---

3   It has been estimated that less than five per cent of the capital accumulated today and in
    recent decades has a productive function, i.e. is used to finance the growth of the economy.

The so-called 'global financial crisis' triggered by the 2007 sub-prime debacle in the US served as a sort of watershed in this regard but the process can be traced back to the early 2000s and the 'primary commodities boom' provoked by the growing demand for precious metals and by China and other 'emerging markets' for energy, industrial minerals and agrofood products (Cypher, 2010). In 2010, for the first time since UNCTAD kept records, i.e. since 1970, developed countries in the global north received less than half of global FDI flows (until the late 1980s they attracted 97 percent of investments). In 2005, developing and emerging economies in the global south attracted only 12 percent of global flows of productive capital (FDI) but in 2010, against a background of a sharp decline in capital flows in the world, these economies in the aggregate overcame the 50 percent barrier (CEPAL, 2010). Looking more closely at the geopolitics of these capital flows, it is evident that South America was the destination of choice, and this because, as Raúl Zibechi (2012) argues, FDI was evidently attracted to the huge reserves of natural resources (metals and industrial minerals, hydrocarbons or fossil fuels, soy and other forms of biofuels, and agrofood products) that the governments of the day were anxious to open up for exploitation by foreign investors in order to take maximum advantage of the economic opportunities provided in the form of additional fiscal revenues.

Under these conditions Latin America changed from being a relatively marginal location for north-south capital flows (about five percent of the world total) into an important and dynamic destination. Between 2000 and 2005 Latin America received an annual average of USD 66 billion that grew exponentially up to USD 216 billion in 2011, which meant that it was able to attract 15 percent of all global flows of productive capital over this period (CEPAL, 2010: 45).

The main datum here is the pattern of continued growth of investment flows to the region, which in the case of South America reached USD 150 billion in 2011, fifteen times greater in absolute figures than in the early 1990s. However, not all countries participated equally in these flows, a function of geopolitics as much as geoeconomics. Indeed it would seem that some countries— Venezuela, Argentina and Ecuador in particular, but also and less understandably, Mexico—have been 'punished' by capital. In the case of Venezuela the explanation is very simple: Hugo Chávez's nationalization policy was at the base of a massive emigration of capital that has not been offset by the relatively large investments originating in China and the much lower investments of Brazilian capital. As for Argentina the mood of capital changed from euphoria under the Menem regime to substantial caution in the wake of the Kirchner regime's default in 2002 and its reluctance to heed the dictates of the

IMF regarding debt repayment and restructuring in the context of the worst crisis in the country's history.[4] At the beginning of its sharp turn towards neoliberalism in the early 1990s Argentina received twice the investments that Brazil received and in the second half of the 1990s FDI inflows equalled those of Mexico, even though both economies are much larger than Argentina. After the 2001 crisis foreign investors began to beat a retreat although not to the same scale and speed as in Venezuela, and Brazilian capita—and to a lesser degree Chinese and Canadian capital—entered into the vacuum left by the retreating US and European investors.

The case of Mexico is very curious in that the government is clearly aligned with both the neoliberal policy agenda and US imperialism—and it has one of the most *entreguista* regimes in all Latin America, particularly as regards mining capital (no royalties, and an effective tax rate of 1.2 percent (Bárcenas, 2012). At the time of the inception of NAFTA in January 1994 Mexico received up to 60 percent of FDI destined for Latin America. The subsequent withdrawal of capital from Mexico, or the evident reluctance to invest in a highly liberalised economy vis-à-vis US capital, evidently relates to the changing structure of investment capital—for example, the dominance of resource-seeking rather than efficiency- or market-seeking capital—as well as political instability in that the withdrawal of capital quickened as of 2008 when the state began its dirty war against drug trafficking.

The Latin American countries that today are the most attractive to capital include Brazil, the biggest economy in the region and very much open to business as far as foreign investments go, particularly as regards to what we term 'agro-imperialism' or agrarian extractivism (see Chapter 4), Colombia, the linchpin of US imperialism in the region and long a supporter of extractive capitalism, and Chile, which continued to hoe the line of natural resource extraction and primary commodity exports, and free market capitalism, when other countries turned towards protectionism and regulationism. The attraction of Chile to capital is probably a matter of geopolitics as much as geoeconomics, i.e. a matter of legal security provided by the state to the private property interests of foreign investors. However, the attraction of foreign investors to Colombia is more difficult to explain, particularly given the low intensity but long-standing class

---

4   Argentina began a process of debt restructuring in 2005, three years into a solid recovery from the worst of the crisis, which allowed it to resume payment on the majority of the USD 82 billion in sovereign bonds on which it defaulted in 2002. A second debt restructuring in 2010, after six years of uninterrupted growth based on a primary commodities boom, brought the percentage of bonds out of default to 93%, although ongoing disputes with holdouts remain.

warfare and the high level of internal insecurity related to the protection of private property and the operations of extractive capital in the country. Notwithstanding the high level of political insecurity in the country Colombia in recent years has displaced Argentina as a favourite destination point for foreign investment and has begun to approach the level of foreign investments in Chile and Mexico, even though the latter's economy is three times the size of Colombia's. Only a closer look than what we have undertaken will allow us understand the reasons for this extraordinary interest of capital in Colombia, starting with the Uribe regime and jumping under the current administration of Juan Manuel Santos. Again, the answer is as likely to be found in the geopolitics as the geoeconomics of capital.

Brazil illustrates the success of the geopolitical project to convert the country into a global power and the interest of foreign investors in an economy that has been able in just a decade to incorporate close to 40 million people into the market. Receiving only half of the investments that Mexico attracted two decades ago today the volume of FDI inflows is four times that of Mexico even though the two economies are comparable in size. However, what distinguishes the Brazilian case is not the growth of FDI, which currently positions it as the fourth largest destination point for FDI after the US, China, Hong Kong and the UK, but the quality of those investments. Until 2005, capital inflows had three basic locations: industry, which absorbed from 50 to 30 percent of total FDI inflows; services, which absorbed 50–60 percent; and mining and agriculture, which accounted for less than ten percent of total FDI inflows (SOBEET, 2011). However, several trends and 'developments' in recent years have dramatically changed this pattern. The strong demand for primary commodities on the world market, the expansion of large-scale foreign investments in land for the purpose of agro-food extraction and the production of biofuels, and the rampant speculation in food and minerals as well as land, have wrought a profound change in the structure of FDI inflows: FDI in services have fallen from around half of total investments to 30 percent; the share of industry, where exports have lagged in recent years (partly as a result of the so-called 'Dutch disease'), has fallen to 35 percent; while mining and agribusiness have tripled their share of FDI flow to 30 percent (Zibechi, 2012).

Thesis 2

Extractivism a Defining Feature of the New Economic Model
The economic model used today by South American policymakers in current conditions (a reconfiguration of global economic power, a primary commodities

boom, the decline of neoliberalism, the emergence of left-leaning 'progressive' policy regimes) has two fundamental pillars: a focus on natural resource extraction and primary commodity exports as a strategy of national development (economic growth), and a new development paradigm focused on poverty reduction and what has been termed 'inclusionary state activism'. As Eduardo Gudynas (2009) has pointed out in his summary of the South American version of this model (the 'new extractivism' and 'new developmentalism') it subscribes to the classical ideas of development as economic growth, modernity and material progress. But, he observes, it is a hybrid that has gone back to and revived an extractivist approach to capitalist development as well as a more inclusionary form of state activism: 'progressive extractivism' The resulting reconfigured mix of old and new ideas includes a belief in the comparative advantage of primary commodity exports, the private sector (foreign direct investment, the multinational corporation) as a catalyst of economic growth, a consensus on the need for 'inclusive growth' (a more inclusive form of development), and a belief in the need to bring the state back into the development process—to regulate the private sector operations of extractive capital and thus provide for a more equitable and progressive distribution of the social product as well as the socially and environmentally responsible behaviour of the corporations that run these operations.[5] This mix of old and new ideas regarding development and natural resource extraction explains the commonalities between the approach towards development used by the new postneoliberal regimes and their neoliberal predecessors. What unites them is a belief in capitalism as the operating system (although in need of reform) combined with a concern to achieve a better balance between the market and the state than had been the case in the era of state-led development and the subsequent neoliberal era. This balance, it is believed, is secured by means of a judicious dose of foreign direct investment and a mix of market-friendly capitalist development, insertion of the local economy into

---

5   The latter has take form in the doctrine of 'corporate social responsibility' (CSR), a platform of ethical principles elaborated by UN-based policy advisors in six UN agencies as part of a 'global compact' designed as a means of incorporating the 'private sector' (profit-oriented enterprises) into the development process and ensuring their adherence to sustainable development practices. The United Nations Global Compact, also known as the Compact or UNGC, is a United Nations initiative to encourage businesses worldwide to adopt sustainable and socially responsible policies, and to report on their implementation. The Global Compact is a principle-based framework for corporations, to bring them together with UN agencies, labour groups and civil society in a policy of corporate self-regulation (as an alternative to state regulation). The Compact was announced by the then UN Secretary-General Kofi Annan in an address to The World Economic Forum on January 31, 1999, and was officially launched at UN Headquarters in New York on July 26, 2000.

globalized production circuits and value chains, corporate social and environmental responsibility, and a measure of nationalism and state activism. In other words, a mix of capitalism at the level of the economy and 'socialism' at the level of the state. Socialism in this specific context is understood to mean resource nationalism, state regulation, a new development paradigm, and the active engagement of both communities and civil society in the development process.

Thesis 3

From Classical to the New Extractivism
Gudynas in his take on the new extractivism notes that an extractivist approach towards national development is shared by both neoliberal and postneoliberal regimes in the region. But, as he notes and we emphasize this extractivism takes two different forms: one, exemplified by Colombia and Mexico, where the governing regime continues to follow a neoliberal path towards national development within the orbit of the Washington Consensus and US imperialism; the other, represented by South American regimes such as Argentina, Brazil, Bolivia and Ecuador that have been described in terms of 'progressive extractivism' and 'post-neoliberal developmentalism'. However, here a distinction should be made between cases such as Argentina, Brazil and Chile, where public policy is geared to a model that could be described as 'pragmatic neoliberalism' (a moderate and pragmatic form of post-neoliberal regulationism and progressive extractivism), and Bolivia and Ecuador, which, together with Venezuela, exemplify a more radical form of progressive extractivism, oriented towards what is understood by some as the 'socialism of the 21st century' (Petras & Veltmeyer, 2009).

   In this regard it is difficult to place Peru, which, under the current Humala regime, is taking a path and implementing policies that is closer to neoliberalism than post-neoliberalism. Jan Lust (2014) in this regard describes the regime as 'neoliberalism with state intervention', but then this might also apply to Argentina (and Brazil and Chile), as well as Bolivia and Ecuador. The one difference between the latter two post-neoliberal regimes and Peru under Humala is in the case of Bolivia the partial reversion of an entrenched neoliberal policy of privatization in the direction of nationalization and the socialization of consumption if not production—or, in the parlance of the new developmentalism, social inclusion. Another difference is that unlike Correa in Ecuador and Morales in Bolivia Humala makes no pretence of seeking to advance 'socialism' in any form, a stance that separates his regime from Bolivia, Ecuador and Venezuela, where governments have rallied around an anti-imperialist alternative trade alliance (ALBA). In addition, Peru has been drawn into the 'Pacific Alliance', a grouping of countries that are now locked into an imperialist trade regime via a series of bilateral trade agreements with the US and Canada. In any case, what defines post-neoliberalism (regardless of what form), in addition to a policy of 'inclusionary state activism', is a new form of association with global capital, together with a mild and limited dose of nationalization, and a continuing reliance on foreign direct investment as a source of capital.

Thesis 4

Contradictions of the New-Extractivism

The advent of a post-neoliberal state and construction of a new development model have generated a new and as yet unsettled debate about 'extractivism'—as to whether like classical extractivism it is a curse rather than a blessing and implies a development trap, or whether, as argued by economists at the World Bank—that it implies an 'economic opportunity' that governments in the 'resource-rich' developing countries should take advantage of in a management regime that combines good governance with corporate social and environmental responsibility. Our own view is that extractive capitalism is fraught with contradictions that militate against and will prevent the achievement of even modest progress in the direction of a more socially inclusive, equitable form of capitalist development that is sustainable at the level of both the environment and livelihoods.

Most governments in the region, whether neoliberal or post-neoliberal in orientation, evidently share the belief of World Bank economists that an extractivist strategy provides an unsurpassed if not unique economic opportunity, and that it provides a viable new model as long as the operations of extractive capital are properly regulated in the public interest under a policy regime that ensures for the State a fair share of corporate profits and that protects both society and the environment. The shared idea is that on behalf of the people whose interests they represent they can strike a better deal with extractive capital than their predecessors were able to. However, case studies in Veltmeyer & Petras (2014) as well as this book suggest that even the new 'progressive' extractivism is unable to overcome the inherent contradictions of capitalist development based on the plunder of natural resources and the exploitation of labour, and the problems associated with a reliance for this development on foreign investment. These contradictions and associated problems relate to what has been conventionally described as a 'resource curse' (Auty, 1993; Sachs & Warner, 2001). The notion of a resource curse feeds on evidence that many resource-rich countries in seeking to take advantage of their comparative advantage in an abundance of natural resources by exporting them as primary commodities have ended up among the poorest of countries, while so many resource-poor countries have success-fully navigated the tortuous path of advanced national development by manu-facturing their wealth and investing in human resource development—human capital in the form of knowledge, skills and social technology (UNU-IHDP & UNEP, 2012).[6]

Our position, and the central argument of his book, is that the new extrac-tivism is more of a curse than a blessing or a fortuitous economic opportunity. The argument can be summarized as follows. First, the most successful devel-opment pathway evidently is not the extraction of natural resources and pri-mary commodity exports, but rather the exploitation of the 'unlimited supplies of labour' that are generated in the capitalist development process, and an industrialization strategy based on investments in economic and social infra-structure and human resource development.[7] From this perspective without industrialization there can be no development (of the forces of production and in terms of an improvement in the social conditions)—at least not on a national or global scale.

Second, development based on natural resource extraction is necessarily localized in enclaves with linkages to the global market but with very few to the rest of the economy, thus preventing the formation of a more balanced and extended form of economic and social development.

Third, extractive capital is characterized by a high organic composition of capital and a very low propensity to use labour in the production process, with the result that labour in the extractive sector is apportioned a very low share of the social product. Even in Bolivia, where the government has 'nationalized' the country's reserves of fossil fuels and sub-soil mineral resources, it is esti-mated that labour receives less than ten percent of the world market value of

6   The one Latin American country that has proved to be the exception of the rule (that reliance on the export of natural resources with little value added via processing is a recipe for under-development) is Chile. It is the only Latin American country that has managed to develop the country's forces of production to a relatively advanced state (as a high middle income coun-try in the World Bank's ranking).

7   Evidence or support for the idea of a natural resource curse is provided by a UN report on Inclusive Wealth published in 2012. It places wealth into three categories—natural, manufac-tured and human—and suggests that the most advanced countries (in terms of capitalist development) are those in which natural resource wealth is but a relatively small proportion of total wealth.

exported minerals—six percent in the case of Argentina and Chile (Solanas, 2007: 2) and as little as 1.2 percent in the case of Mexico.[8] And evidently workers have not benefited in the least from the extraction of minerals and primary commodity exports (Cypher, 2013). ECLAC (2007: Table A-28) on this point reports that after four years of booming exports (from 2002 to 2006) the index of the value of real wages in the formal sector had grown by less than 0.5 percent. This is in contrast with the well-established pattern of cumulative wage increases in the era of state-led development based on the operations of 'labour-seeking' FDI and industrial development based on the exploitation of labour. In the context of these developments, the share of labour (wages and salaries) in the social product (in the income derived from the production process) had settled at a much higher rate—as much as 60 percent—with undeniably positive (although contradictory) development outcomes and implications.

A fourth view of this cursed development path, i.e. the fact that the reliance of resource-rich countries on the export of commodities more often than not results in underdevelopment rather than development, is an evidently long-term trend towards a deterioration in the terms of trade for commodity exporting countries vis-à-vis the importation of manufactured goods, leading to 'development' at the centre of the system and 'underdevelopment' and poverty on the 'periphery' (Prebisch, 1950). In the context of the current primary commodities export boom, which has sustained the robust economic growth of the extractivist regimes of South America, most of these regimes over the past decade have received record prices for their natural resources with terms of trade that favour commodity exports. But economists at ECLAC argue that

---

8   In some cases in the mining sector as in Mexico and Peru, where the government is very open to extractive capital, there are no royalty payments at all and the tax rate is extraordinarily low, less than 2% (1.2%) in the case of Mexico. In other situations (the post-neoliberalism) the state is able to extract a greater share of resource rents in terms of a negotiated or legislated royalty rate and a higher tax rate, but even in the best case scenario for the government, which is in Bolivia where the government has nationalized its wealth of natural resources including its strategic hydrocarbon reserves, among the largest in the region, in the mining industry the government's share of the resource rent in the mining sector is only 6%, not much more than the regional average from 3–5%; in the strategic hydrocarbon (fossil fuels) sector it has been able to increase its share of resource rent to 50% (18% royalty + 32% tax rate). But at the same time the government has been obliged to increase an exportation-production subsidy provided to the foreign companies that dominate production from $10 a barrel to $40 a barrel; and it is estimated that the government's share of world price received by the companies for its exports of oil and gas, and minerals, is only 19%, which means enormous profits for the companies.

sooner or later the terms of trade will turn against the exporters of raw materials and primary commodities. It is too early to tell when this might occur or whether the market for commodity exports can be sustained in the medium to long-term, but the prognosis derived from a review of the history of capitalism is not favourable (Cypher, 2013).

A fifth and related understanding of what has been described as a resource curse is that extractivism and primarization implicates a boom-bust cycle in which what goes up (prices) inevitably come down, exposing the economy to conditions over which policymakers have no control. In the past a commodity boom would always eventually go bust, usually in a relatively short cycle that would leave the country dependent on volatile commodity exports exposed to fluctuating prices. Some argue that conditions today are different and that the demand for resources will be sustained at least into the medium- if not long-term. Nevertheless few countries have succeeded in developing their forces of production without breaking out of the dependence on the export of a few commodities and a reliance (and dependency regarding) on FDI.

Another possible explanation of the resource curse is that primary commodity exports have a negative impact on the exchange rate vis-à-vis the export of products in other sectors of the economy—an impact described as the 'Dutch disease'. An example would be the dilemma faced by the current government of Brazil. Until 2010 Brazil was a major destination of industry-focused FDI—and one of the 'emerging' markets' (together with China, India and Russia) driving the world market in terms of the pent-up demand of the growing world middle class). However, in recent years (since 2008) both FDI and the government have increasingly turned towards natural resource extraction. Over the past five years Brazil, together with Colombia and Chile, has been converted into the major destination for 'resource seeking' FDI in Latin America—large-scale investments in the extraction and production of fossil and biofuels, and minerals as well as agro-food products. The result—from a Dutch disease perspective—has been a significant reduction in the rate of economic growth. Having averaged a growth rate of over five percent a year from 2003 to 2010, Brazil's overall rate of economic growth in 2012 was only 0.9 percent. By the government's own assessment this slowdown is not just related to the reduced market for its products resulting from the repercussions of the 'global financial crisis'. It reflects a significant appreciation in the exchange rate of the *real*, due in part to increased exports of primary commodities.

A seventh idea mooted in regard a purported resource curse relates to the restricted social base for natural resource extraction and the associated skewed social structure of income distribution. The argument here is that when

resource extraction is dependent on FDI it inhibits domestic capital formation; it has a narrow social base that excludes many from participating in the
benefits of economic growth; and it tends towards an extreme form of social
inequality in which the benefits accrue to a small stratum of foreign investors
and multinational corporations—while the costs, both social and environmental, are externalized, borne disproportionately by small landholders and
indigenous communities that are dispossessed of their territorial rights regarding land, water and other natural resources.

In addition to these arguments focused on or related to the notion of a
resource curse our case studies suggest that the policy dynamics of resource
extraction prevents the broadening of the economy's productive base and thus
inhibiting a more equitable distribution of wealth, and an increased share of
labour in national income, which an increasing number of economists view as
the key for unlocking the door of economic growth. Hence the fallacy described
by Dávalos and Albuja (2014) in the case of Ecuador. Even though the windfall
rents collected by progressive governments within the policy framework of the
new extractivism has allowed some of them, notably Brazil, Bolivia and
Ecuador, and of course Venezuela, to significantly reduce the incidence of
poverty if not the structure of social inequality,[9] it is evident that the gains
made on this front on the basis of the primary commodities boom cannot be
sustained with a policy of social inclusion and economic assistance to the
poor. Nor can these gains be sustained by a reliance of the state on resource
rents to finance a process of economic and social development, a fundamental
characteristic of the new extractivism. The reduction of social inequalities in
land ownership and the distribution of income require structural change,
which in turn requires a confrontation with economic and political power.

As Dávalos and Albúja show in the case of Ecuador the argument made by
ECLAC and World Bank economists, and reported on by Gudynas (2009)—that
a resource extraction and primary export approach towards development provides additional fiscal resources that can be used to generate a more inclusive
and equitable form of development—is fallacious. For one thing, they show

---

9 The 'structure of social inequality', as the UN (ECLAC, 2010) describes it, is measured in terms
   of the distribution of income—not land ownership, which would show no improvement in
   the direction of greater equality. In these terms, by means of a policy of conditional cash
   transfers, which automatically reduces or even eradicates the incidence of extreme poverty
   as defined by economists at the World Bank (via $1.25/day threshold), Brazil has managed
   to reduce noth the poverty rate and its ranking on the Gini Coefficient index. In the case of
   Chile, however, notwithstanding the progress made on the anti-poverty front the structure
   of social inequality it would seem has deepened.

that in the case of Ecuador resource rents and revenues derived from booming commodity prices and oil exports are structured in such a way that they cannot be used to finance social programs. Furthermore, the authors argue, because of the way that tax revenues are collected it is the poor that end up paying for the increased social expenditures. Thus they conclude that the link established by the government in its political discourse between extractive rents and social expenditures and poverty reduction is not at all what it seems. In fact, increased social expenditures on health and education and public works (infrastructure, etc.) under Correa's *Alianza País* regime serve primarily and above all as a means of justifying and lending legitimacy to its extractivist policies.

Another conclusion reached by Dávalos and Albúja in their analysis of the Ecuadorian government's political discourse is that a sustainable process of economic and social development would require an intervention of the state that not only moves beyond neoliberalism but post-neoliberalism and progressive extractivism as well. It would require abandoning capitalism—a strategy of substantive social change and structural transformation. And both this and other case studies of the new extractivism suggest that the agency for this transformation is unlikely to be the state, and also that without a deepened program of nationalizations, nationalizing and socializing production, progressive extractivism is *not* the solution. On the contrary. Substantive social change and structural transformation requires the mobilization of the forces of resistance in the direction of socialism. It will require the agency of the social movements united in opposition not only to neoliberalism but also in rejection of the underlying capitalist system. We elaborate on this point below.

Thesis 5

Continued Reliance on Foreign Investment is a Development Trap
A key argument advanced in this book is that an economic model based on the extraction of natural resources and primary commodity exports, even under the new regulatory regimes of South America, is a development trap. This is because of the relation of dependency between capital and the state, and a reliance of this model on large-scale foreign investment and the operations of extractive capital that are extremely destructive albeit very lucrative, generating in the process enormous profits on invested capital that are for the most part expatriated, as suggested by *The Financial Times* in an article (April 18, 2013) that documented the fact that traders in commodities—at or near the top of the surplus value extraction chain—have accumulated large

reserves of capital and huge fortunes in the context of the primary commodities boom. As the author of the article observes: "The world's top commodities traders have pocketed nearly 250 billion over the last decade, making the individuals and families that control the largely privately-owned sector big beneficiaries of the rise of China and other emerging countries"—and, we might add, beneficiaries of the turn or return towards extractivism and export primarization. In 2000 the companies and traders in the sector made USD 2.1 billion in profits but in 2012 USD 33.5 billion. And while some traders enjoyed returns in excess of 50–60 percent in the mid-2000s today, in the context of a 'global financial crisis' and a downturn in some commodity process, they are still averaging 20–30 percent, huge by any business standard.[10]

Of course, post-neoliberal regimes such as Morales' in Bolivia and Correa's in Ecuador, in turning towards the new extractivism have sought to reduce their dependence on global capital and to overcome the obstacles of this dependency by nationalizing to some extent the country's wealth of natural resources. However, except for Venezuela no country has managed yet to escape its reliance on FDI and global extractive capital. Thus, under the conditions of such dependency both Presidents Morales and Correa have been obliged to form an association with global extractive capital that clearly reflects the power of the latter, and to strike a deal with concessions that have seriously negative economic consequences and that are undoubtedly detrimental to the country's plans for sustainable natural resource development. The case studies presented in Veltmeyer & Petras (2014) illustrate this point clearly.

Political regimes such as Colombia and Mexico that embrace neoliberalism and have stayed the neoliberal course, and opened wide to foreign capital, provide the foreign mining companies and extractive capital every facility to penetrate or bypass any obstacle in their path with minimal regulation, leaving them to regulate themselves under a regime of corporate social and environmental responsibility. The consequence, as we have shown, is windfall profits for the corporations, additional fiscal revenues for the government, increased health risks and deteriorating working conditions for the workers, and a degraded environment for the communities located near the mega-mining and extractivist projects. As for the left-leaning progressive regimes in the region they might very well have managed to secure additional fiscal revenues

---

10   The net income of the largest trading houses since 2003 surpasses that of the mighty Wall Street banks Goldman Sachs, JPMorgan Chase and Morgan Stanley combined, or that of an industrial giant like General Electric. Indeed these commodity traders made more money than Toyota, Volkswagen, Ford Motor, BMW and Renault combined.

by squeezing capital for a greater share of resource rents, but they have done so at an exceedingly high economic and social cost, which, like the environmental cost of natural resource extraction, is disproportionately borne by the indigenous and farming communities and a rural proletariat of dispossessed peasants and mine workers. As for the economic and social costs they can be measured in terms of the consequences of allowing the companies to pillage the country's stock of natural resources without them having to pay for it anywhere near their value or assume the enormous externalized environmental and social costs of their extraction.

Another conclusion that we draw from our case studies is that the costs of the new extractivism are not only socioeconomic and environmental. They entail a political cost as well. In every case the Executive makes decisions without consulting the electorate or the legislature. MNC-State agreements erode democratic processes and are upheld and enforced through violent repression of citizen protests. These political costs derive from and relate to a continuing reliance and dependence of the governments on FDI, which explains the evident propensity of these governments, even in the case of those with a nationalist orientation and a post-neoliberal progressive policy stance, to side with capital against the communities and the social movements in the conflict generated in the extraction process. Examples here can be found in Argentina and Peru, cases of more moderate and pragmatic post-neoliberalism, but also Bolivia and Ecuador, which have adopted a more radical nationalist or populist stance.

The reason why even the most 'progressive' post-neoliberal regimes in the region tend to side with the mining companies in their relation of conflict with the communities and the social movements has two dimensions. One is because the governments have banked on and mortgaged the country's future with an extractivist development strategy. The second is the coincidence of economic interests that flows from this strategy, namely profits for the corporations and resource rents for the governments. This coincidence has led Ecuador President Correa, for example, to brand opponents of the government's extractivist strategy and policies as 'environmental extremists' opposed to extractivism in any form and under any conditions, no matter necessary or how favourable. As for Bolivia and Peru we need but look at Vice-President García Linera's (2013) denunciations of protesting miners and public employees and Jan Lust's analysis of the dynamics of extractive capital in Peru (Lust, 2014).

Other problems of FDI dependence include vulnerability in regard not only to wildly fluctuating and an inevitable fall in commodity prices but to the machinations of the imperialist state—Canada the prime example—in the effort of the agents of this state to turn the governments of the FDI-recipient countries against the nationalization and socialization of production (nationalism, socialism) and to have them adopt a private sector model of inclusive growth.

Thesis 6

The Idea That Extractive Rents Can Finance a Process of Inclusive Development is Fallacious

Are resource rents necessary to finance development? What kind of development emerges from the operations of extractive capital? How does extractivism mesh with social investment? Are official arguments concerning extractive rents as necessary (an alternative) for income redistribution and social spending correct? What are the real dynamics being generated under the guise of the discourse that promotes extractivism in the name of development, equity and social justice?

These questions, raised by Dávalos and Albuja (2014) in their study of Ecuador, relate to the argument advanced by governments in the region (especially those with a 'progressive' PNL regime) to explain and justify their extractivist approach to national development. As Dávalos and Albuja construct it the Ecuadorian government's nationalist discourse on extractivism and development takes the form of six arguments conveyed through political speeches and public discourse. First, we have the argument that the fiscal revenues provided by extractive rent (ER) can be used to finance social spending, especially on health and education, largely neglected in neoliberal times. Second, the government's political and development discourse links ER revenues to public investment, economic development and economic growth. Third, this discourse links ER revenues to income redistribution policies, especially in regard to subsidies provided to the poor. Fourth, the discourse has an ideological function in serving to connect ER revenues to a vision of national sovereignty, and using these rents as a weapon in the government's confrontation with transnational capital, especially American capitalism. Fifth, the creation of domestic or national mining companies (as opposed to nationalizing or renationalizing the private sector firms operating in the extractivist sphere of the economy) is constructed to mean a significant change vis-à-vis 'entreguismo'— opening up to and giving in to the demands and pressures exerted by neoliberals. And sixth, the discourse of progressive extractivism advances the idea of extractivism as a transitional phase in a modernization process that leads to the formation of a 'production matrix' in a capital-intensive economy, which can and eventually will add value to the country's natural resources before exporting them.

The conclusion drawn by Dávalos and Albuja—replicated by Giarracca and Teubal (2014) in their case study of Argentina, and Lust (2014) in the case of Peru—is that the political discourse of the progressive PNL regimes in the region tends to mask rather than describe or explain the pitfalls of extractive capital and monocultural growth models. In actual fact, the inclusionary and extractivist policies pursued by governments under the mantle of post-neoliberalism and the new developmentalism serve more as an ideology than an economic model—to obfuscate the play of naked economic interest and corporate greed involved in the new extractivism, disguise the elitist nature of the deal reached with extractive capitalist and their imperial back-ers, to placate and pacify the victims of capitalist development with temporary handouts, and to subdue any fires of revolutionary ferment. In this regard the extractivist discourse serves the same purpose as the Corporate Social Responsibility (CSR) strategy does—to justify the governments' provid-ing mining companies a social license to conduct their extractivist operations in social and environmentally sensitive areas. The only difference is in the form of regulation and the nature of the regulatory agency (state regulation vs. corporate self-regulation). In practice it makes little to no difference: even neoliberal extractivist regimes (Colombia, Mexico) require mining companies to consult with and respect the human and territorial rights of those affected by their operations, and to protect the environment via the assessment of possible risks and the impact of extractive operations. And they also conform to the new developmentalist consensus regarding a policy of social inclusion and direct assistance to the poor.

Thesis 7

The Costs of Extractive Capitalism Exceed Actual and Potential Benefits

The operations of extractive capital, especially where and when based on open pit mining, have extraordinarily negative social and environmental (as well as economic and political) impacts that have generated widespread resistance. One dimension of this resistance is that the perceived or actual benefits derived from resource extraction are highly concentrated and for the most part appropriated by out-of-country interests (labour receiving only six to nine per-cent of the social product in this sector, while the state captures around ten percent in the form of resource rents) while the costs are widespread and disproportionately borne by groups and communities that receive very few if any of the benefits. The empirical evidence of this development, accumulated in recent years and presented and analysed in the case studies above, is compelling. It also substantiates the point made by Gudynas (2013) regarding the propensity of both corporations and governments to externalize the social and environmental costs of extractive capitalism so as to increase profits and rents—and coincidentally transfer these costs to communities and workers in the wider society.

The impacts of extractivism can be put into several categories, particularly socioeconomic and environmental. The environmental impacts relate to the degradation of the environments in which increasingly indigenous and farming communities of small-scale producers have to live and work, operate their enterprises and sustain their livelihoods. The case studies above illustrate some very few of these impacts, which have been very well documented, giving rise to a large number of detailed scientific studies that have corroborated the endless charges and claims and concerns of the populations and communities negatively affected by the operations of extractive capital, particularly but by no means restricted to open-pit mining. As for the negative social impacts of extractivism they have to do with jobs and livelihoods, and the health of community members and mine workers, as well as new forms of social inequality. And, according to several contributors to this volume they also have to do with what Harvey described as 'accumulation by dispossession', i.e. enclosure of the commons of land and water, separating the direct producers from their means of production to the purpose of extracting and exploiting—and profiting from—the human and natural resources mobilized in the process. In conditions of the new extractivism the 'enclosure' and the 'dispossession' dynamics of the capital accumulation process take and is taking the form of privatizing access to and commodifying both the commons of land and water and the extracted sub-soil resources, degrading the environment (polluting the air and water), and undermining the livelihoods of the direct producers in their communities.

Thesis 8

The Superiority of Class Analysis to Neoclassical Cost-Benefit Analysis

The case studies in this book point to the growing forces of resistance and opposition to the operations of extractive capitalism and the economic model that sustains them. Unfortunately, in the burgeoning literature on the new extractivism the social and environmental impacts of extractive capital, and associated 'tensions' and 'pressures', are viewed not from a class struggle perspective (as the inevitable consequence of capitalist development) but from a limited social and environmental perspective based on a cost-benefit calculus.

From this perspective, the issue is not the correlation of class forces in the resistance against extractive capitalism, but the social and environmental costs of extractivism, which, although possibly mitigated and the country's resources prudently 'managed', have to be balanced against the anticipated or purported benefits of natural resource extraction. Thus, rather than establishing the class division associated with the costs and benefits of extractivism—the former borne by workers, small landholding peasants, family farmers and indigenous communities; the latter appropriated by capitalists and rentiers—the contemporary discourse on extractivism (and the environmental movement, which is rooted in 'civil society' rather than the class structure) is not in the least concerned with issues of class. Rather it is concerned with the question as to whether the social and environmental costs of extractivism are acceptable and manageable, and also the question of the appropriate governance regime, an issue regarding which two basic models have been advanced. One, based on corporate self-regulation, or corporate social responsibility, has been constructed and is advanced within the framework of the 'inclusive growth' model (sustainable resource development, as it is termed by the Canadian government under the conservative Harper regime).[11] The other, based on state regulation as per the post-Washington consensus, is presented as the neostructuralist model of 'inclusive development' predicated on achieving a better balance between the state and market than had been achieved under the Washington Consensus.

The proponents of 'inclusive growth' argue that the 'private sector' (=the MNCs) is the 'driver of inclusive growth' (economic growth + poverty reduction) and that the optimum condition of national development is

---

11   There are diverse permutations of this model, which has been constructed within the framework of a global network of neoliberal think tanks such as the Washington-based Heritage Foundation and Canada's Fraser Institute, and presented at diverse international policy forums such as IGFMMSD (the Intergovernmental Forum on Mining, Minerals, Metals and Sustainable Development, which includes Canada, nine Latin American and 19 African countries as well as the BRIC minus China). For a notable exemplar of this model we can do no better than to turn towards the report *Driving Inclusive Growth*, tabled in March 2012 by the Standing Committee on Foreign Affairs and International Development of Canada's lower parliamentary chamber, the House of Commons.

achieved under a regime of corporate self-regulation; a partnership approach towards natural resource extraction, including the contribution of mining companies to local development efforts, can create mutual benefits and lead to an inclusionary form of economic growth without government intervention in the market. This differs from the model of inclusive development constructed by the architects of the 'new developmentalism', which holds that profit-seeking capitalist corporations in the private sector have to be regulated in the public interest and that some form of nationalization is called for in the formation of joint ventures with capital as well as in some circumstances state enterprises.

The case studies presented in Veltmeyer & Petras (2014) and in this book suggest that the progressive extractivism model of inclusionary state activism has achieved better results than the private sector-led inclusive growth model in allowing the government to strike a better deal with capital, in achieving a higher rate of poverty reduction and social inclusion in the development process. For example, Venezuela, as well as Brazil—and in recent years both Bolivia and Ecuador—have achieved a impressive level of reduction in both the incidence of poverty and structure of social inequality, an achievement that stands in sharp contrast to Mexico, the paragon of a neoliberal approach towards national development. However, our own research suggests that the new developmentalist model adopted and used by the post-neoliberal regimes in South America does not enable the country to escape the contradictions of capitalist development or the pitfalls of extractivism. Indeed, as Gudynas has shown, the environmental and social impacts of extractivism in these cases are maintained, and in some cases have worsened under the post-neoliberal progressive extractivist regimes.

Another issue in debate on extractivism surrounds the question of measurement and a full accounting of its social and environmental costs, with environmentalists arguing that environmental costs have to be 'internalized' and fully accounted for in balancing out relative costs and benefits. Indeed it appears that much of the opposition of the global environmental movement to extractivism relates to this concern for the magnitude of environmental damage, the internalization of environmental costs in national economic development planning, and sustainable resource management. That is, the issue is neither neoliberalism nor capitalism as such, but rather the lack of environmental regulation and proper community-based resource management. However, the case studies in this book shows that the environmental impacts and costs of the new extractivism, as Giarracca and Teubal (2014) argue, 'have nothing to do with the prospects for development heralded by local, provincial and national governmental sources'. These studies, as well as our own research, show that the concerns of workers and communities that are negatively impacted by the destructive operations of extractive capital run much deeper than the concern for the environment—with correspondingly greater political implications and engagement in the class struggle (see the brief discussion below).

The discourse on the environmental, social and territorial impacts of extractivism inside the progressive regimes of the post-neoliberal state is described by Gudynas as 'opaque', reflecting as it does an evident contradiction between the government's professed concern for the 'national interest' and the effective deal struck with the operating agents of capitalism and the imperial state. As for the environmental dimension of the conflicts that surround extractivism on some occasions their existence is denied or minimized, and in other cases these conflicts are presented as a fight over competing economic interests or political views, the expression of hidden agendas and partisan politics. Rafael Correa has gone so far as to accuse the indigenous communities and their supporters in 'civil society' (opponents of extractivism) as 'environmental extremists', opposed to natural resource extraction under any conditions and in total disregard to the national interest in economic and social development—in the need of the country to exploit and take advantage of its natural resource wealth in seeking to escape the cycle of poverty that has dogged the country for so long, allowing the government to take the country down a sustainable development path.

Thesis 9

The Resistance is United on Extractivism, Divided on Capitalism
There are two ways of understanding the dynamics of resistance in conditions of the new extractivism. One is as in terms of the response to the negative socioeconomic and environmental impacts of extractivism and the agency of the social and environmental movements formed on the social base of the indigenous and farming communities contiguous to the mines and extractive operations (Svampa, 2012).[12] Through the political ecology lens used by these authors the resistance movement today is, as Tetreault (2014) phrases it, 'on the cutting edge of a search for an alternative modernity...impl[ying] greater participation in decision making, local control over local natural resources...and a rationale that draws attention and emphasizes the importance of the matrix of environmental, social and cultural factors'.

---

12   See Toledo (2000) and Tetreault (2014) in regard to the dynamics of this resistance in
      Mexico, and Bebbington (2011) regarding Peru and elsewhere in the Andes.

Exponents of this political ecology approach emphasize the negative impacts of extractive capital and mega-mining projects such as open pit mining—one of the world's most polluting, devastating and dangerous industrial activities—on the environment and the habitat of indigenous and farming communities, particularly as relates to access to clean or potable water. Examples of these impacts and associated struggles abound.

Another way of understanding these resistance movements and explaining their dynamics is in terms of their connection to the class struggle. Lust (2014) in the case of Peru, and Sankey (2014) in the case of Colombia, take this approach in coming to the conclusion that the forces engaged in the struggle, and the social base of the social movements formed in the resistance movement, constitute in effect a new proletariat composed of wage workers and miners, communities of peasant farmers and semi-proletarianized rural land-less workers surplus to the requirements of extractive capital, and, most significantly, indigenous communities concerned with retaining access to their share of the global commons, securing their livelihoods and protecting their territorial rights and way of living. As Sankey argues in the Colombian context the social and political struggles that surround resource extraction, and the associated upsurge in the forces of resistance, have 'been accompanied by the entrance of new actors onto the scene'. While wage workers continued to play an important role in the class struggle and the broader resistance movement—in fact, accounting for close to one half of the collective acts of protest resistance since 2005—at least 25 percent of the collective actions of protest had to do with the communities negatively affected by the operations of extractive capital, and these communities were the major driving force of a growing resistance movement, as they clearly are in Mexico.

Looking more closely at the forces engaged in the class struggle it is possible to identify the contours of a new class system or social structure. First, we have the social groupings that share what Svampa (2012) terms 'the commodity consensus' (*Consenso de los Commodities*). This includes elements of the middle class, including those that take the form of an associational-type social organization, or nongovernmental organization, which for the most part have been formed within the urban middle class.

Notwithstanding the environmental concerns of many—the middle class can best be defined not in terms of the relation of individuals within this class to production but to consumption—the middle class to a significant degree is complicit in the operations of extractive capital, with a rather mild or muted opposition and resistance to the environmental implications of unregulated resource extraction and social justice considerations regarding issues of class and excessive social inequalities in the distribution of wealth and income.

These forces constitute the centre-left of the ideological and political spectrum and are readily accommodated to both capitalism and extractivism via a reformist program that combines extractivism with the new developmentalism.

Another major 'actor' in the resistance to extractive capitalism is the community, which relates to the indigenous and other communities located close to (and negatively impacted by) the operations of extractive capital and associated megaprojects. These forces tend to be anti-imperialist and anti-capitalist as well as anti- or post-neoliberal in their political orientation. They (correctly) distinguish between corporate capitalism, which they oppose, and small-scale production in the private sector, which they support. They include certain sectors of organized labour but are predominantly made up of proletarianized and semi-proletarianized rural landless or near-landless workers, or small-landholding family farmers and peasants concerned for their livelihoods based on access to land, and indigenous communities concerned to protect their territorial rights to water and the land, and to secure their freedom from both exploitation and the degradation of the environment as well as their relationship to nature. On this broad social base the forces of resistance predominantly take the form of social movements opposed not so much to extractivism as extractive capitalism, or the neoliberal model of public policy as well as the underlying system.

For many in this social and political sector 'socialism' is not understood as an economic system but as a matter of principle (equality and social justice), which can be actualized in different ways, even accommodated to capitalism in the form of local development in the local spaces of the power structure formed within and on the basis of the broader capitalist system. In this context, some elements of the resistance movement are simply looking for a bigger piece of the pie, on both the local level (greater monetary compensation and investment in community development) and the national level (higher taxes and royalties for the mining companies for social redistribution). Furthermore, inasmuch as these movements are anti-capitalist it does not necessarily imply that they seek to conserve anachronistic social and production relations, but nor does it mean that they mean to overthrow the dominant capitalist system; it simply means a project to distribute more equitably and share the wealth.

In addition to these two forces of resistance, one located in the urban middle class and taking form as an environmental movement and a 'civil society' of social organizations, the other located in the indigenous communities of proletarianized peasant farmers, the resistance to corporate capital and extractive capital, and to government policy in the service of capital (capitalism) and the empire (imperialism), is once again taking the form of organized labour. An example of this is the anti-capitalist coalition of diverse social forces, including columns of exploited organized mine workers, that have come together to engage the class struggle against extractive capital, agri-business operators and the agrarian elite, an oligarchy of big landowners. In many contexts (Brazil, for example) these groups and classes constitute a ruling class, in firm control of the state (even when having to contest state power).

Several conclusions can be drawn from this brief sketch of the class struggle in Latin America today. One is that the class struggle under current conditions assumes multiple forms, including a struggle over land and the model used to organize agricultural production—one based on the corporate model of large-scale capitalist production (with inputs of imported capital and advanced modern technology) and oriented towards the world market, the other based on small-scale production and geared to the domestic market and an agroeco-logical revolution protecting the environment from the ravages of large-scale capital- and technology-intensive production); a mega-project development strategy based on large-scale foreign investment in land, natural resource extraction, and the formation of joint venture partnerships between the private sector (multinational corporations that provide both capital and technology) and the state in a new association with capital; the enclosure and privatization of the commons for the purpose of natural resource extraction, and the resistance of the indigenous and farming communities negatively affected by the operations of extractive capital. A third conclusion is that a large part of the resistance movement is anti-neoliberal and anti-imperialist but not anti-capitalist.

The characterization of the resistance movements discussed in Veltmeyer & Petras (2014) as anti-capitalist and anti-imperialist (as well as anti-neoliberal) is shared by the network ('articulation') of social movements that has congealed around Hugo Chávez's proposed model of an alternative (non-neoliberal) system of international trade network—the *Alianza Bolivariana para Nuestras Américas* (ALBA). From the 16 to the 20th of May, 2013, over 200 social movement delegates from 22 countries met to debate a continent-wide Plan of Action constructed around the principles of this alliance, which include the need 'to do battle against the transnational corporations and the processes of privatization' and 'to defend the rights of mother earth and to live well' [in harmony with nature and social solidarity] as well as 'international solidarity' (*Minga Informativa de Movimientos Sociales*). At this 'founding assembly' of a continental social movements network (Social Movements for ALBA), the antisystemic nature of this network[13] was articulated in the declaration of the need to mobilize and unify the diverse sectors of the popular movement— the indigenous communities, organizations of the peasant farmers, the organized working class, the rural landless workers, the proletarianized rural poor, the semi-proletariat of informal sector street workers, the middle class (intellectuals and professionals, university students and the youth, small business operator) and a civil society of nongovernmental organizations—around a program of opposition to capitalism and imperialism (the 'voracidad capitalista, imperialista y patriarcal') in a struggle for 'authentic emancipation with socialism on its horizon'.

However, neither the formation of this continental network of social movements, nor the formation of a resistance movement in each country where extractive capital has made major inroads, means the end of capitalism. For one thing, while the resistance movement is generally opposed to the dominant extractivist development model and its destructive effects on both the environment and livelihoods very few are prepared to abandon the operative capitalist system.

Thesis 10

The Issue is Post-Capitalism, Not Post-Neoliberalism

There are three models at issue in the current debate on the new extractivism. One has taken form in the search for 'inclusive growth' based on large-scale foreign investment, private sector development, and active state support, what we have termed imperialism. This model is based on the Washington (now the Davos) consensus on the virtues of free market capitalism and private sector-led development. It has been given diverse forms, most notably in the Canadian House of Commons report *Driving Inclusive Growth*.

A second neo-structuralist model has been constructed by the economists at ECLAC in the form of progressive extractivism and inclusive development (resource nationalism, inclusionary state activism). This model is based on a

---

13   In 2007, during its 5th Summit in Tintorero, Venezuela ALBA was institutionalized at the level of both governments in the region (Venezuela, Bolivia, Ecuador, Cuba) and a Council of Social Movements (CMS). In this context the social organizations and movements in support of ALBA Consejo de Movimientos Sociales (CMS) committed themselves to expand ALBA in a project of regional integration based on an anti-neoliberal and anti-imperialism stand.

post-Washington Consensus on the need to 'bring the state back in', to establish thereby 'a better balance between the state and the market' so as to bring about a more inclusive form of development (the 'new developmentalism') concerned with and focused on the reduction of extreme poverty. The 'new developmentalism' is designed to empower the poor to act for themselves and for the state to assume the responsibility for social development, to facilitate the development process, together with international cooperation and social participation—engaging civil society in the development process. But even so, grassroots organizations and the social movements continue to be excluded from government and decision-making processes, a situation that the advocates of an emerging radical consensus—of the need to move not only beyond neoliberalism but also beyond capitalism—seek to change.

A third model has been constructed—or rather, is under construction—by advocates of more radical change, i.e. of the need to abandon capitalism as well as moving beyond neoliberalism. This model is yet to be given a definitive form, existing only as a set of agreed-upon principles, but it is geared to the nationalization and socialization of large-scale export-oriented production combined with the organization of small-scale production oriented towards the domestic market. This model (the socialism of the 21st century, in Hugo Chávez's formulation) is based on an emerging radical consensus on the need to move beyond capitalism at the level of the state and large-scale corporate enterprise, and to combine socialism—the nationalization and socialization of production—with an alternative system of trade relations (ALBA) and small-scale non-capitalist production for local markets, and to engage the agro-ecological revolution, a concern for food sovereignty, as well as a process of community-based development 'from below' based on 'participatory democracy'.

Conclusion

The illusion of development driven by the 'forces of economic freedom' (free markets, the private sector) or the 'mining locomotive', as President Manuel Santos of Colombia prefers to call it, has crashed head on with the continued repatriation by the mining companies of their enormous profits, the weak enforcement by most governments of what are already lax regulations, the absence of a broad development dynamic based on structural transformation, and the enormous costs, both socioeconomic and environmental, that exceed by far the purported benefits of economic growth that tend to be concentrated in a few sectors.

The argument advanced in the literature regarding this capitalist development dynamic is fairly conclusive, substantiated as it is with evidence derived from so many diverse case studies. This argument can be summed up very clearly as follows:

> An abundance of natural resources, together with other endogenous processes of a pathological character, distorts the allocation of economic resources in the region, resulting in a negative redistribution of national income, the concentration of wealth in a few hands, and widespread poverty and recurrent economic crises, while consolidating a 'rentier' mentality, further weakening an already weak institutional framework, encouraging corruption and damaging the environment.
> JAÜRGEN SHULDT & ALBERTO ACOSTA

Others, however, including ourselves, argue that the major issue is not so much uneven and unequal development, or environmental and social insecurity, as a propensity of capitalism towards class conflict: that resource extraction tends to pit mining companies against local communities in a class struggle, and because of a coincidence of economic interest (profits for the company, resource rents for the government) the state tends to side with the company against the community in the resulting class struggle. Along these lines, the so-called 'resource wars' can be seen not only as one more political obstacle to sustainable development, adding to the insurmountable macro-economic and environmental problems that afflict excessive reliance on natural resource extraction, but as a class struggle against the latest offensive of capitalism in the relentless and pathological search for profit.

Our own research in this regard can be summed up as a number of propositions, to wit:

1. Regardless of the form taken by extractivism today it is generally reliant on the investment and extractive operations of global capital, and thus given to problems and subject to conditions that are not only inherent in capitalism but that take a particularly damaging and violent form in the extractive sector.

2. This reliance has sown the seeds of a fundamental relation of dependency between government and global capital, a relation in which the government's aims and concerns, and strategy, are inevitably subordinated to the interests of capital—a new relation of 'dependency' that reinforces the logic of submission of the national economy to globalized finance and the imperial state.

3. Here the mining companies, as major operating units of extractive capital, are able to maintain control over the key decisions related to production, with the dependent state reduced to the residual role of regulator and guarantor of private property rights, including the right to repatriate profits.

4. Under these conditions, the mining companies are in a position to exact favourable terms, with a license to operate under legislation and a favourable regulatory regime that means enormous profits for the companies.

5. Because of the coincidence of economic interests between the state and capital (resource rents for the governments, profits for the companies) governments in the region—even those oriented towards a policy of anti-imperialist resource nationalism—are led to advance the interests of capital, and in the conflict between the company and the communities directly affected the operations of extractive capital these governments tend to side with capital against the communities. Thus, the officials of the rentier or extractivist state, including those with a post-neoliberal or new developmentalist policy regime, have turned out to be effective functionaries of extractive capital, agents of an emerging new form of capitalism.

6. Apart from the economic problems of extractivism as a strategy of economic development it is destructive of both the environment and livelihoods, and the operations of extractive capital have extraordinarily high costs, both socioeconomic and environmental.

7. The resistance to extractive capital in the current conjuncture of capitalist development is led by the communities most directly affected by its destructive operations and by the new proletariat formed in a process of 'accumulation by dispossession' and in conditions of labour exploitation.

8. While the negative impacts arguably can be managed or mitigated, and the costs can be compensated for or balanced against anticipated benefits, the costs are nevertheless too high and are disproportionately borne by the indigenous communities and what we have described as the new proletariat.

9. Rather than serving as a new economic model the new extractivism, vis-à-vis the notion of 'corporate social responsibility' or, to be precise, corporate self-regulation, represents a new political ideology, which is designed in a process of calculated deception as a means of enlarging the scope of the private sector in the development process and reducing the public sphere, replacing the defunct idea of 'globalization' in its neoliberal form.

10. An alternative model for bringing about genuine progress and a sustainable development process requires more than institutional reform (a post-neoliberal policy regime) and 'inclusionary state activism' (the new developmentalism—inclusive development). It requires radical change or systemic transformation and mobilized class activism, empowering the working class in its diverse social formations to make public policy and act in the collective interest.

CHAPTER 2

Extractive Imperialism in Historical Perspective

Norman Girvan

When Columbus landed in the Caribbean he thanked God and enquired urgently after gold. Nowadays the investors arrive by jet clipper. They thank the Minister of Pioneer Industries and enquire after bauxite (Lloyd Best, *Independent Thought and Caribbean Freedom*, 1997)

As the quotation suggests, the history of Extractive Imperialism (EI) in the Caribbean, and more generally in the Americas, shows both continuity and change. My purpose here is to reflect on the question: what lessons can we draw from this history? To this end I distinguish five broad historical periods since Europeans arrived in the Americas: the age of conquest and colonisation; the age of commercial capitalism; the first industrial revolution; the emergence of monopoly capitalism; and the contemporary age of global finance capitalism. My analytical scheme focuses on seven factors that assume particular characteristics in each age: (i) key resource commodities; (ii) labour; (iii) capital; (iv) the state; (v) ideology; (vi) resource rents; and (vii) contradictions

The first six factors, taken as a whole, constitute a kind of 'regime' that corresponds to each historical period—a regime of power, ideology and distribution of resource rents. The seventh relates to the nature of contradictions that result in changes over time. The changes occur within an existing regime; and, less frequently, they replace one regime with another—regime change.

Conquest and Colonisation (c. 1500–1700)

When Columbus enquired urgently after gold and looked with growing excitement at the evidence of its use made by the Taíno people, the encounter dramatized a fundamental difference in the role of the metal in the two cultures. Arguably, this was to lead to one of the first instances on a massive scale in human history; of a clash between the 'use value' of a thing and its 'exchange value'—or more precisely, its value as an element in a system of economy in which relationships of market exchange predominate. The Taínos and other First Peoples of the Americas used gold and silver to create objects of adornment, status and beauty; and especially of religious and spiritual significance. In the Europe of emerging capitalism, these metals were assuming the functions of money in an exchange economy—i.e. a means of exchange, a measure of value and a store of wealth. The First People probably never fully understood the greed, lust and ruthlessness with which the newcomers pursued the metals, it must have seemed to be a strange form of mental disorder. Yet in the end whole civilizations were destroyed, and their populations decimated, by the madness. It's been conservatively estimated that the demographic shock in the Americas amounted to a ninety percent decline in the aboriginal population in the first two centuries following the Conquest. This was undoubtedly due mainly to the impact of epidemics of unfamiliar diseases; but massacres, suicides, infanticide, and accelerated mortality due to starvation and general social disorganisation were significant contributors to the virtual elimination of the Taíno peoples from the islands of the Greater Antilles.

The labour regime and the ideological system instituted for the purpose was anticipated by Columbus when he wrote in his Diary that the people he encountered in October 1492 'ought to make good and skilled servants, for they repeat very quickly whatever we say to them. I think they can very easily be made Christians, for they seem to have no religion. If it pleases our Lord, I will take six of them to Your Highnesses when I depart, in order that they may learn our language'.[1] He added that 'I could conquer the whole of them with 50 men, and govern them as I pleased' (Fusion, 1992). Hence the key features would be subjugation by force, enslavement, abduction, transmission of language and religious indoctrination. The initial methods of extraction were taxation and extortion from the indigenous people, which developed into alluvial (gold) and underground (silver) mining by enslaved or semi-enslaved indigenous and African labourers.

Columbus' expedition had been outfitted courtesy of Italian investors and by the sovereigns of Aragon and Castile. The condition was that, if his trip succeeded, Columbus would be entitled to one-tenth of the revenues from new lands, one-eighth of the profits from associated commercial ventures, and an assortment of titles. Hence the role of the state and of private capital, the distribution of risk, and the division of the rents from initial resource extraction in the Americas were all negotiated before Columbus even set sail. The rule that was eventually establishment was that 20 percent of the booty of Conquest went to the Crown—the quintetwith the rest divided mainly between conquistadors, *encomenderos,* settlers, the Church, the shippers and the merchants.

Do we see here certain historical precedents for the subsequent evolution of the role of foreign capital and the colonial or imperialist state in the

---

1   Wikipedia, http://en.wikipedia.org/wiki/Population_history_of_indigenous_peoples_of_the
    _Americas.

hemisphere? Arguably, the 'original sin' of EI was set in the summer of 1491 in the Court of Ferdinand and Isabella—a place far removed from the object of the enterprise; and at a time when neither perpetrator nor victim even knew of each other's existence. It's also of interest that the battles over the spoils of EI were present from the outset. Columbus and his royal sponsors had a falling out and his descendants reportedly carried on their legal battles with the Spanish crown over their entitlements for centuries. There were also many contradictions: between Crown and colonists; between colonists and governors; between governors and contrabandists eager to circumvent imperial monopoly; between pirates and the Spanish Empire; and between the enslaved and their oppressors.

It is estimated that over a 300-year period 2.5 billion pesos (Pieces of Eight, 25 grams) of silver were shipped to Europe from America; and another 1.1 million pesos shipped to Asia (Walton, 2002). There can be little doubt that by enormously increasing the supply of precious metals used for coinage, the specie of the Americas fertilised and accelerated the transition to full-blown commercial capitalism in Europe. Paradoxically, it was not the Spanish economy that ultimately reaped the benefits of this bonanza of monetary wealth. The vast inflow of specie fuelled inflation at home; financed huge trade deficits with the rest of Europe and with Asia; and encouraged Spanish monarchs to over-borrow and foreign creditors to over-lend. Spanish extractive capitalism retained the backward character of an essentially tributary system, with the atrophy of its basic agricultural and industrial development; showing symptoms not unlike the latter-day Dutch disease. The complacency and extravagance of the Hapsburgs who ruled Spain in the 16–17th centuries were to become legendary.

Commercial Capitalism (c. 1650–1850)

The nations that came to dominate the Atlantic mercantile economy that flourished in the 17–18th centuries were those that specialised in trade, production and naval warfare. France, the Netherlands and England became the centre of the new Imperial Europe. National wealth was still equated with possession of specie; but this was to be accumulated by means of a surplus on the balance of trade. The key commodities in the trade were tropical products and the slaves used in their production in the plantations of Middle America. At the centre of the trade was sugar, a luxury good in scarce supply and commanding premium prices. Was this Extractive Imperialism or not? This is a matter of definition, but arguably it satisfied several of the criteria. It extracted

wealth from a particular kind of natural resource that only occurred in certain
localities and was the object of violent rivalries; and the land and labour
required for turning it into profit were, from an economic point of view, wast-
ing assets. Slaves were worked to death; land was worked to the point of
exhaustion. Fresh supplies of slaves were continually imported to replace
those who died; fresh land was brought into cultivation.

> The average survival rate of a mining slave during the great 18th-century
> gold rush in Minas Gerais, Brazil, was no more than two years; the sur-
> vival rate of a field hand in the sugar plantations of northeastern Brazil
> was only about seven years. Prior to 1800, slave-mortality rates in the
> Portuguese, British, French and Dutch colonies of Latin America and the
> Caribbean were so high that only the continued importation of more and
> more Africans kept the colonial economies thriving.
> MORGANTHAU, 1991

The Caribbean islands were cleared of valuable forest cover and strenuous
efforts had to be maintained over time to sustain the productivity of the soil.
Extension of the land frontier within and between islands led to the pattern of
'shifting terrain' noted in the theory of Plantation Economy by Lloyd Best and
Kari Polanyi Levitt (Best & Kari Polanyi Levitt, 2009). The model addresses the
questions of agency and of distribution of the surplus. The surplus was divided
between Crown, merchant capitalist and planter; but the strategic position of
the merchant capitalist as provider of supplies and credit and as handler of
final sale meant that he was able to 'recover his costs and claim his share of the
surplus, leaving the planter to bear the full risk of the enterprise' (p.16). As the
authors note, the state is in a similar position today vis-à-vis the multinational
corporation (MNC) in a resource industry; which can manipulate transfer pric-
ing, management and marketing contracts and financing arrangements to
secure assured returns; while government revenues fluctuate.

The ideology that underpinned racial chattel slavery was the doctrine of
white and European superiority and of black and African inferiority (Girvan,
1976). It was as a direct consequence of this that the 'white' and 'negro' races
were invented, arguably around the 17th century (Perry, 2013). The social consequences of 400 years of racial slavery outlived the formal system and endure
to this day in the disadvantaged condition of African-descendants in American
societies.

Local economic development, as we now understand the term, was an alien
concept in mercantile plantation economy. The purpose of the system was to
enrich the dominant and emerging classes in the metropolis. As far as Africa

was concerned, the system was disastrous. Walter Rodney's classic *How Europe Underdeveloped Africa* tells the story of depopulation, fratricidal wars, destruction of indigenous agriculture and handicrafts, and social and political disorganisation consequent on slave trading. These consequences were anticipated in a famous letter written in 1526 by the King of Dahomey, a Catholic convert, to his fellow Catholic sovereign the King of Portugal as follows:

> Each day the traders are kidnapping our people and children of this country, sons of our nobles and vassals, even people of our own family. This corruption and depravity are so widespread that our land is entirely depopulated. We need in this kingdom only priests and schoolteachers, and no merchandise, unless it is wine and flour for Mass. It is our wish that this Kingdom not be a place for the trade or transport of slaves.
>
> Many of our subjects eagerly lust after Portuguese merchandise that your subjects have brought into our domains. To satisfy this inordinate appetite, they seize many of our black free subjects.... They sell them. After having taken these prisoners [to the coast] secretly or at night.... As soon as the captives are in the hands of white men they are branded with a red-hot iron.[2]

Here again, the words of a contemporary sum up the principal features of the relationships that were to be established: external agency, local intermediation, asymmetrical power relations, imported culture of consumption, social disorganisation and human degradation.

First Industrial Revolution and Free Trade Imperialism (c. 1800–1914)

The plantations of Brazil and the French and British West Indies generated huge profits for their owners and stimulated shipping and allied industries, helping to lay the basis of the First Industrial Revolution. For the most part, this was based on resource commodities endogenous to the early industrializers—coal and iron. With the onset of Free Trade Imperialism in the second half of the 19th century, the resources of Latin America was increasingly brought into play to help feed and clothe the growing urban populations of industrial Europe and to supply its factories. Wheat and other cereals,

---

2   http://www.sources.com/SSR/Docs/SSRW-Atlantic_Slave_Trade.htm.

coffee, tea, cotton, wool, rubber and palm oil, were some of the commodities in demand. Production of tropical resource commodities was organised by local landowning elites; with infrastructure financed by foreign—mainly British—capital and transported in the merchant marine of the leading European powers. In the last half-century before the First World War, Britain's earnings on foreign investment and services more than financed its deficit on merchandise trade. It was another kind of tributary system; one based on debt.

On the ground in the Americas, a new round of accumulation by dispossession began, most notably in the temperate zones; where First People and mestizos lost ground to European and Asian immigrants. According to Arthur Lewis, wage rates in the export sector were kept low by the low productivity and earnings of labour in the traditional agricultural sector (Lewis, 1978). But this was not because of the impersonal logic of the market. Landowners controlled the state; they ensured that peasants were deprived of good land, credit, and technology. They made good money even if the international terms of trade turned against the products they exported to Europe. The main beneficiaries, however, were the traders, shippers and especially the financiers of Britain and the other Western European nations.

Spanish American elites had to throw off the Spanish yoke in order to negotiate the new dispensation with European capital. In Africa, the opposite happened: local resistance had to be overcome to open up the resources of the continent needed for European industry. Colonisation of Africa followed hard on the heels of decolonisation in Spanish America. Samir Amin has shown that colonial economic structures in Black Africa took three main forms (Amin, 1973). Resource extraction was the essential goal of all three, but different forms of labour exploitation were devised according to the particularities of the geo-demographic structure in different regions and the kind of resource products desired.

In the first, the 'Africa of the colonial economy' including most of West Africa; the game was about tropical agricultural commodities and the forms were mainly establishment of monopsonistic relations with peasant farmers by means of colonial trading companies. In the second, the 'Africa of the Concession-owing companies', which is the area surrounding the Congo River Basin, the goal was to secure mineral commodities and the resources of the forest. Mines using African wage labour were established; and in other instances, notably King Leopold's Congo, Africans were made to deliver commodities (rubber) harvested from the wild on pain of whipping, maiming and death. The human death toll of King Leopold's project of extractive imperialism in the Congo between 1884 and 1908 is normally estimated to be at least 10 million; Leopold himself amassed a personal fortune worth over $1 billion in today's terms.[3] The third macro-region is mainly eastern and southern Africa, the 'Africa of the labour reserves'. Africans were dispossessed of their land and made to work for European settlers, European plantations and European-owned mines. Amin's point is that, whatever the form, returns to labour remained low and stagnating, laying the basis of contemporary African underdevelopment.

The Scramble for Africa took place in the last quarter of the 19th century. The way was paved by the monstrous firepower of the Gatling machine gun, first employed in the American Civil War. In a bizarre example of doublespeak, the barbarity of European imperialism was cloaked in the language of Civilizing Mission and White Man's Burden (on the other side of the Atlantic, the American ruling class was discovering its 'Manifest Destiny'). The doctrine of racial superiority was given a pseudo-scientific status by the new science of evolutionary biology. In 1853–1855 the French writer Joseph Arthur Comte de Gobineau published his *Essay on the Inequality of the Human Races,* to critical acclaim, a book proclaiming the inherent superiority of the 'white' race, with the 'Aryans' at the top of the pile. The Haitian writer Anténor Firmin trashed Gatineau's theories in his 1885 book *The Equality of the Races*; followed by many others since; but the thinking continued to influence dominant Western cosmologies. As pointed out by Aimé Césaire in his *Discourse on Colonialism* (1955), the road to the Holocaust in Nazi Germany originated with the thinking and the practices of the European imperialist project in Africa.

With the Imperialist states as their agents and the colonial and neocolonial states as their servants, Extractive Capital secured concessions in the peripheries of world capitalism that assured them of the lion's share of the rents derived from the exploitation of the resource commodities associated with the massive expansion of international trade in the late 19th century. The pattern continued with the new resource commodities demanded by the so-called 'Second Industrial Revolution'—commodities like petroleum, petrochemicals and metallic minerals including copper, bauxite and aluminium, lead, zinc and uranium. From 1870 to 1945 virtually all of what is now called the Global South fell victim to this predatory form of capitalism. Workers were paid the barest minimum, trade unions were banned, social benefits were minimal, racism was rampant; linkages with the domestic economy were practically non-existent and surpluses were repatriated to foreign shareholders instead of being invested in the all-round development of the local economy. The inevitable consequence was the rise of national liberation and socialist movements

---

3   King Leopold II and the Congo; http://www.enotes.com/king-leopold-ii-congo-reference/king-leopold-ii-congo.

in the Global South; fed also by the two great intra-imperialist wars of the first half of the 20th century and the great capitalist crisis of the 1930s.

Monopoly Capitalism (c. 1870–1980)

The transition from competitive capitalism to monopoly capitalism coincides with the era of Free Trade Imperialism and the Second Industrial Revolution. Vertically integrated monopolies or oligopolies emerged and spread to become multinational oligopolies, prefigured by the organisation of Rockefeller's Standard Oil in the 1870s, predecessor of Exxon Mobil. This in turn led to the transnational conglomerate, vertically integrated from raw material to finished product and horizontally integrated across several lines of business. Approximately 95 of the world's 150 largest entities today are corporations; 55 are countries. The purpose of the transnational mega-corporation is to replace the market with internalised transactions across national boundaries and to deploy oligopolistic and oligopsonistic power against employees, suppliers, customers, regulators and governments. Direct ownership of operations can be supplemented, or even replaced, with outsourcing relations through global commodity chains in which suppliers assume the risk and the corporations garner the benefits.

Most important of all, the rise of finance capital to dominance over productive capital originally flagged by Lenin a century ago, has become the dominant feature of contemporary capitalism. Ever-increasing sums of money have to be mobilised in order to finance resource investments, due to resource depletion and the need to extract and process lower grades of raw material, the increasing scale of operation and the increasing complexity of technology. Financial consortia mobilise huge amounts of money, while spreading the sovereign debt risk and relying on the IMF to ensure repayment; and shifting the business risk to the peripheral state via the TNCS responsible for resource development.

After World War II the balance of bargaining power in resource industries shifted to the newly independent states; which found in the spirit of Bandung and in prevailing developmentalist thinking the rationale for policies of resource nationalism; buttressed by the existence of the Soviet Union. Led by OPEC and a series of oil nationalisations in the 1960s and 1970s, the new thinking was that surpluses from resource commodities should be put to the service of national economic development. The high point was reached in the early 1970s with the OPEC price hikes and the UN Declarations on the Establishment of the New International Economic Order and the Economic Rights and Duties of States. Nationalisations and increased taxes on profits almost certainly shifted the distribution of resource rents to the resource exporting states in the 1970s.

Global Finance Capitalism (c. 1980-Present)

The new dispensation was not to last. Recycling of petrodollars by Western banks to much of the Global South led to a steep increase in indebtedness. The emergence of stagflation in the North helped to discredit Keynesianism and to create the climate for growing acceptance among policy elites of the neoliberal ideology that had been systematically promoted by Hayek and his allies in the Mont Pelerin society since the 1940s (Polanyi Levitt, 2013). This was backed by big money doled out to think tanks, intellectuals, politicians, journalists and others in the policy elites. The Volker interest rate shock of 1982 ultimately precipitated the Third World debt crisis and brought the IMF and the World Bank into the driver's seat of policymaking in most of the Global South. The Empire had struck back. The Washington Doctrine—misrepresented as a 'Consensus'—privileged concessions to foreign investors as part of the package of liberalisation, deregulation and privatisation.

The WTO agreement, NAFTA, the US-Central America Free Trade Agreement (CAFTA-DR), the EU's Economic Partnership Agreements, bilateral FTAs and bilateral investment agreements all operate to limit the policy space of the peripheral states of Latin America, the Caribbean and Africa for policies to foster national agricultural and industrial development and to regulate foreign investors in the interest of local businesses and local consumers. In sub-Saharan Africa, thirteen countries in IMF programmes at the end of the 1990s had an average of 114 policy and governance conditionalities per programme. Three Latin American countries had an average of 78; and four East Asian countries had an average of 84.[4] Approximately 3000 Bilateral Investment Treaties are now in existence involving more than 170 countries; generally these limit government regulation and allow foreign direct investors access to international investor-state arbitration to settle disputes before using national courts. US and EU Bilateral Free Trade Agreements with developing countries customarily cover services, capital flows, investment, government

---

4 'The average number of (IMF) conditions rose from about six in the 1970s to ten in the 1980s. In the (case of the World Bank) the average number of conditions rose from thirty two in 1980–3 to fifty six by the decade's end' (Kapur & Webb, 2000: 3–4; Table 5). *See also* Buira (2003).

procurement, economic structures (competition policy) and regulations, labour and environment policies; the US has now signed ten of these globally and the EU 21 (Bilaterals.org).

The effect of all this is to create a framework of conditioned policies and of international treaty law and a set of accepted 'best practices' that is mutually reinforcing; and reproduces many of the features of the previously existing colonial set-up. In place of direct colonial administration we now have the discipline of the threat of financial blockade and of trade sanctions. The government of a peripheral state that defies the system runs the risk of being economically—and hence politically—undermined within its own domestic space. In addition, buttressed by the fall of the Soviet Union and the subsequent ideological offensive accompanying neoliberal globalisation, the Washington doctrine captured the policy elites of much of the Global North and South in the 1980–1990s. Its influence became especially strong in central banks, finance ministries, trade ministries, development agencies and the business pages of the mainstream media. University Economics departments trashed Development Economics; and a whole generation of policy functionaries came of age trained in economic abstractions devoid of historical and institutional context and innocent of their countries own intellectual history. As Columbus had hinted in his journal entry 500 years ago, once the language is properly taught; the rest will follow.

Furthermore, resort to direct military force always remained within the policy arsenal of the core imperialist states. Errant regimes are often destabilised and overthrown by means of the promotion of coups d'état and direct military action under the cloak of humanitarian intervention and the newly invented doctrine of responsibility to protect. Witness the cases of Venezuela 2002, Honduras 2009, the first and second wars against Iraq, and Libya 2011. The so-called wars on terror and on drugs serve as covers for security agreements that give the core states access to the physical territory, intelligence and security personnel of the peripheral countries, ready to be mobilised at a moment's notice.

However, the shift to neoliberal orthodoxy of the 1980s–1990s was not sustainable. The Washington Doctrine had held that foreign acquisition of state-owned enterprises would reduce the debt burden, cut the fiscal deficit, and power a new round of export expansion. In fact, it served to power a round of reprimarisation and of renewed denationalisation over much of Latin America and of Africa; with the bulk of resource rents at the margin going to the multinationals. Latin Americans had been promised dramatic growth and poverty reduction to accompany the fall of military dictatorships in the 1980s and their embrace of outward-looking, market-friendly policies. Instead growth was modest, poverty continued to increase and distribution of income worsened in many countries.

The backlash came in the 1990s, led by the dramatic rise in anti-globalisation social movements in the continent and internationally. Beginning with Venezuela in 1998, progressive governments have been elected over much of the continent prioritising policies of income redistribution and the assertion of national sovereignty vis-à-vis foreign investors. Venezuela and Bolivia have nationalised hydrocarbons and used the rents to fund social programmes. Ecuador has sought to increase the take from its petroleum industry. Argentina and Brazil privilege state-owned enterprises in their hydrocarbons industries. The new approach has not yet reached the countries of the Caricom Caribbean. In Jamaica, for instance, the take from the bauxite industry is a fraction of what it was during the resource nationalism years of the 1970s. At the same time, the rise of what is called the New Extractivism has brought many 'progressive regimes' into conflict with local communities which have traditional land rights in areas wanted for mineral industry development. In each of these countries, the class character of the state varies from case to case; as does the constellation of political forces that underpins the relation of the state with transnational capital and the imperialist states.

China has become a new player in extractive industry in Latin America and in Africa. To the extent that Chinese SOEs in extractive industry investments behave like Western capitalist enterprises, then they are becoming part of the general phenomenon of extractive imperialism. This would be the case, for instance, if Chinese SOEs extract raw materials for processing in China; engage in minimal technology transfer; generate few local linkages and garner the bulk of resource rents. Further research remains to be done on this.

The contemporary setting for Extractive Imperialism involves several actors and overlapping processes: the ideological framework, the core states, the military, China, finance capital, the transnational resource corporations, international law, debt dependency, the IFIs, the peripheral states, local elites, local communities; and the associated the division of resource rents and its uses.

Conclusion

What then, can we learn from history? First, the drive for resource commodities under EI and resulting conflicts with local/ communities is a particular manifestation of a general *contradiction between use value and exchange value* in the development of capitalism. The contradiction which was dramatized from the first encounters of Columbus with the Taínos is arguably manifested today as the state, acting on behalf of extractive capitalism, which demands access to mineral resources in the subsoil of land wanted for 'development'.

Secondly, *class matters*. The relations involved in Extractive Imperialism are not adequately captured by a straightforward extractive capital/peripheral state frame of analytical reference. This tends to overlook the specificities of class and group make-up of the elites controlling the state; and that of the other local groups and class forces involved in contestations for state power and policy influence. The extension of class analysis and elite analysis—the two are not necessarily the same to the relationships involved within the sphere of extractive imperialism will also be necessary to explain the particularities of the relationship assumed in any particular setting. In particular, *extractive imperialism cannot function, and has never functioned, without the presence of a local intermediary class or group whose role is to organise and facilitate access to resources*. Whereas agency in EI is always external, by definition, agency often represents itself as a local force in the form of the local state and its agencies, and/or a local elite or even a national bourgeoisie.

Third, *state violence is integral to EI*. From an historical point of view, the use of state violence has more often than not set the basic political, social and legal framework within which relationships for resource access are played out. In relations between technologically advanced and less advanced societies, instances of peaceful negotiation for provision of initial access to resources are nowhere to be found. One reason for this is that this is the stage where the clash between exchange values and use values is sharpest; with the balance of military power lying always with the society in which exchange values have become firmly implanted.

Fourth *ideology is power*. Ideology conditions the behaviour, attitudes and assumptions of the major players in resource political economy. Historically, it has rationalised racial and class-based hierarchies of power and prescribed the roles and responsibilities of different groups to ensure the stability of relations initially instituted by violence. Contemporaneously, it prescribes what is acceptable and what is not, what is seen as feasible or unfeasible; and what is established as a commonly accepted guide to good practice within which negotiations over the division of resource rents take place. The role of the committed scholar therefore becomes very important, as s/he is uniquely placed to investigate underlying ontologies, epistemologies and cosmologies that condition approaches to resource use and the associated interplay of class relations.

Fifth, *law and institutions are established within specific political and ideological parameters*. Constitutions, laws, international treaties and trade agreements set the stage within which state-state, state-MNC and intra-state class relations are played out; but behind these lie a structure that is almost always set by violence and is buttressed by a specific ideological framework. Over time within any given regime of EI, there is a tendency for increased reliance on ideology, law and institutions; while reliance on violence is relaxed and less frequent. Crucially, class power is obscured by ideology, law and institutions, while the claims of use value are dismissed as 'archaic' and 'anti-developmental'.

Sixth, *money talks*, meaning that the role of finance capital is crucial to understanding where power lies; in identifying the distribution of risks and explaining the distribution of resource rents. Decomposition and analysis of the specific arrangements made for the financing of resource projects and related infrastructure is vital.

Seventh, the peripheral state is *an arena of contestation* among elites over the distribution of resource rents. Contestation takes place within the ruling elites; between them and extractive capital; between elites and the core imperialist states that act on behalf of extractive capital; and between the elites and local communities with claims to the resources.

Eighth, *watch technology*. Technological changes render resources obsolete in terms of exchange values, or valuable; they change the relative attractiveness of different physical locations; they create new possibilities for use values of known and unknown resources. A peripheral state needs therefore to develop its technological capabilities to monitor global trends and to create new use values. It must seek always to stay on top in terms of knowledge.

A ninth lesson concerns the question of whether resource-based development is, or can be, an 'alternative' to neoliberalism. The lesson is that this is not a useful way to pose the question. In short, whether resources are part of an alternative development depends on the context. We need to examine the ideological framework, the national development strategy and constellation of national political forces, including class forces, within which resource-based development takes place. The key questions are therefore, the division of resource rents, the use of resource rents domestically, and relations established with local communities with traditional claims to the land.

CHAPTER 3

Agro-Extractivism
The Agrarian Question of the 21st Century

A salient feature of global capitalism over the past decade has been the emergence of a trend towards the rapid expansion of foreign investment in the acquisition of land, dubbed 'landgrabbing' by the exponents of 'critical agrarian studies' (Borras & Franco, 2010), who view the trend as part of a broader transition into a new phase of capitalist development based on agrarian change.[1] In this chapter we overview the dynamics of change associated with this transition in both the 20th century and today—the 'agrarian question' then and now. In the early decades of the 20th century the 'agrarian question' involved different national paths of development of capitalism in the countryside and its contributions to industrialization (Bernstein, 1997). Later in the decade the transition took the form of the construction of a world market/economy with a centre and periphery, while in the current context the agrarian question is taking shape as a new form of colonialism (landgrabbing) and extractive imperialism, viz. the imperial state in its active support of extractive capital in its diverse operations in the global south.

The Global Land Grab: Neocolonialism in Action?

It is 2012. Hundreds of rural communities in Africa, parts of Asia and Latin America, are confronted with dispossession or loss of their livelihoods and lands that they customarily presume to be their own. These lands are reallocated by administrative fiat to mainly foreign investors to the tune of an estimated 220 million hectares since 2007, and still rising.[1] Large-scale deals for hundreds of thousands of hectares dominate the process, but deals for smaller areas are not uncommon (World Bank, 2010).

---

1 Foreign investors in recent years have accelerated this process of landgrabbing, buying or leasing vast amounts of farmland in developing countries to profit from the surging demand for food and biofuels. By a number of accounts the process is widespread and deepening, affecting countries in Africa, South America, Asia and Eastern Europe. In the case of Liberia 100% of arable land is now under foreign control, while close to one-half of farmland in the Philippines is owned by foreign investors and US corporations have secured over one third of Ukraine's farmland.

At issue in this development process is a veritable global land rush, triggered in part by crises in oil and food markets over the last decade, and in part by the opportunity to make extraordinary profits by extracting and selling primary commodities for which there is strong demand on the world market. In addition, the financialization of these markets has provided lucrative new investment opportunities to sovereign wealth funds, hedge funds and global agribusiness, the new entrepreneurs with 'accumulated capital burning holes in their owners' pockets'.

In this process global shifts in economic power are evident. While northern and western actors (corporations, investors, governments) continue to dominate as investors and land grabbers, the BRICS (Brazil, Russia, India, China) and food-insecure Middle Eastern oil states are active competitors. A regional bias is beginning to show; China and Malaysia dominate land acquisition in Asia while South Africa shows signs of future dominance in Africa. Two South African farmer enclaves already exist in Nigeria, and Congo Brazzaville has granted 88,000 hectares with promises of up to ten million hectares to follow.

One hundred percent of arable farmland is now in the hands of foreign investors, and negotiations for the acquisition of large-scale landholdings and farmland are ongoing in at least 20 other African states. What foreign governments such as China and other investors primarily seek are lands to meet their security need for agrofood products and energy, while multinational corporations in the extractive sector of the global economy are primarily concerned to feed the lucrative biofuel market by producing oil palm, sugar cane (for ethanol) and soya, increasingly the crop of choice for the conversion of farmland for food into the production of energy to feed the growing appetite for biofuel. Another motivation for the global landgrab is to produce food crops and livestock for home economies, bypassing unreliable and expensive international food markets. Additionally, investors are now seeking to launch lucrative carbon credit schemes. For all this cheap deals are needed: cheap land (US$0.50 per hectare in many cases) as well as duty-free import of their equipment, duty-free export of their products, tax-free status for their staff and production, and low-interest loans, often acquired from local banks on the basis of the new land titles they receive.

This rush for land, and the associated plunder of the host country's wealth of natural resources,' is not restricted to the extraction of agrofood products and mining for gold and industrial minerals. Local banks, communications, infrastructural projects, tourism ventures and local industry are also being bought up in a frenzy of privatizations. These ventures are keen to take advantage of the new market liberalization and other 'structural reforms' that the governments of resource-rich but poor countries on the periphery of world capitalism have been pushed into by international financial institutions such as the World Bank as a means of allowing them to benefit from the resulting 'economic opportunities'. For host governments, foreign investment in land and the extraction of natural resources is the new catalyst of 'inclusive economic growth' and sustainable development, here replacing foreign aid—and, it would seem, international trade.[2] While the governments that host this foreign investment in the process collect ground and resource rents, as well as bribes, the promise of jobs is more or less the only immediate benefit to national populations, in exchange for the heavy social and environmental costs (as discussed in other chapters).

But where are the poor and the commons (land, water, natural resources) in all this? The answer is evident. Much of the land being sold or leased to entrepreneurs are commons, lands that are used by the 'commoners' but to which they have no title. This is not surprising because land defined as 'commons' in the contemporary development discourse generally exclude permanent farms and settlements. Governments and investors prefer to avoid privately-owned or settled lands as their dispossession is most likely to provoke resistance. They also want to avoid having to pay compensation for huts and standing crops, or for relocation. Only the unfarmed commons—the forest/woodlands, rangelands and wetlands, can supply the thousands of hectares large-scale investors want. But most of all, as Borras and associates (2011) point out, the commons are deemed 'vacant and available'. This is because the laws of most host lessor states still treat all customarily owned lands and unfarmed lands in particular as unowned, unoccupied and idle. As such they remain the property of the state.

In fact as Borras et al. have emphasized the commons are neither unutilized or idle, nor unowned. On the contrary, under local tenure norms virtually no land is, or ever has been, unowned, and this remains the case despite the century-long subordination of such customary rights as no more than permissive possession (occupancy and use of vacant lands or lands owned by the state). In practice, customary ownership is nested in spatial domains, the territory of one community extending to the boundaries of the next. While the exact location of intercommunity boundaries are routinely challenged and contested,

---

2   Chapter 1 (Table 1) provides a graphic representation of north–south 'international resource flows'. It shows that until well into the 1990s Africa was dependent on the 'official' inflows of financial resources in the form of 'aid', while Latin America shifted from the massive inflow of private capital in the form of bank loans towards even greater inflows of FDI in the 1990s. Africa continued its dependence on 'aid' until the new millennium, when the primary commodities boom created new opportunities for both foreign investors and governments to benefit from the growing demand for land and natural resources.

Liz Wiley (2013: 5) notes that there is little doubt in the locality as to which community owns and controls which area. Within each of these domains property rights are complex and various'. The most usual distinction drawn today, the author adds, 'is between rights over permanent house and farm plots, and rights over the residual commons' (p. 5). And she continues: '[r]ights over the former are increasingly absolute in the hands of families, and increasingly alienable. Rights over commons are collective, held in undivided shares, and while they exist in perpetuity are generally inalienable'.

The implications of the continuing denial that property ownership exists except as recognized by 'imported' European laws are evident that not just the commons but occupied farms and houses are routinely lost as investors, ownership or concessions to mine or harvest the natural resources in hand, move in while villagers and farmers are either forcibly relocated or forced to abandon their land and communities as the result of the negative socioenvironmental impacts of the extractive activities that ensue. In some contexts (see the discussion below) communities are merely dramatically squeezed, retaining houses and farms but losing their woodlands and rangelands—a variation of the 'classic' pattern of enclosures described by Marx in his analysis of the dynamics of 'primitive accumulation' in England.

Sometimes villagers tentatively welcome investors in the belief that jobs, services, education and opportunities will compensate for the loss of traditional lands and livelihoods. In such cases—at least in the African context—traditional leaders and local elites are often facilitators of deals, making money on the side at the expense of their communities. Reports abound of chiefs or local elites in Ghana, Zambia, Nigeria and Mozambique persuading communities of the benefits of releasing their commons to investors, and even reinterpreting their trusteeship as entailing their right to sell and benefit from those sales. As in the case of North British Colombia discussed in Chapter 9, government officials, politicians and corporate 'entrepreneurs' (energy and mining companies, in the Case of Canada) are routinely on hand to back them up. Such accounts are repeated throughout Africa, and in some Asian states as well as the Americas. Everywhere the story is more or less the same: territorial and communal rights are ignored and disrespected, farming systems upturned, livelihoods decimated, and water use and environments changed in ways that undermine the sustainability of both the environment and livelihoods.

Evidently, possession in the form of customary use is no more sufficient today than it was for the English villagers of the 17th and 18th centuries enclosures. Only legal recognition of commons as the communal property of communities can afford real protection. A number of states in Latin America (Bolivia, Ecuador) have taken this step, setting aside formal registration as prerequisites to admission as real property as well as enshrining in the Constitution ancestral territorial rights and ownership by the people of the country's resource wealth. The global land rush reduced the likelihood of such reforms coming to pass but it also raises concern that fragile reformist trends in this direction will not be sustained. Because of the coincidence of economic interests (extraordinary profits for the companies, resource rents/additional fiscal resources for the governments) governing regimes find selling or leasing their citizens' land too lucrative to themselves and the class and elites aligned with them, and too advantageous to market-friendly routes of growth, to let justice or the benefits of the commons, or the forces of organized resistance, stand in their way.

Dynamics of Primitive Accumulation: Capitalist Development as Dispossession

From a world-historical standpoint the history of capitalism begins with a process of accumulation originating with the dispossession of the direct small-holding agricultural producers, or peasants, from the land and thus their means of production. Under conditions of this development, secured by diverse means ranging from enclosure of the commons to forceful eviction or expropriation by legal means or by administrative fiat under colonial rule, the capitalist development of the forces of production proceeded apace, and with it a process of productive and social transformation—historically the conversion of an agrarian society based on a precapitalist relations of production and a traditional communalist culture into a modern industrial capitalist system in which relations of direct production are replaced by the capital-labour relation (an exchange of labour power for a wage).

Within the framework of development economics this transformation or transition towards capitalism was theorised as a process of structural change—modernisation and industrialisation—based on the exploitation of the 'unlimited supply of surplus labour' generated by the capitalist development of agriculture.[3] But within a Marxist political economy framework the transition

---

3 Within the framework of 'modernization theory', the dominant paradigm in development economics, the development process has been theorized to be the result of a process of long-term social change in three dimensions, each the source of a distinct theoretical perspective and a 'narrative' based on it: There are essentially three dimensions of this transformation, each giving rise to a meta-theory and a historical narrative based on this theory: *industrialization*—the productive transformation of an agrarian economy and society into

towards capitalism was conceptualized as the 'agrarian question', in which reference is made to the following processes:

1. The commodification of land and labour;
2. The concentration of property in landholdings and capital, with fewer and larger landholdings and units of production at one pole and the proletarianization of the small peasant farmers at the other, converting them into a class for hire or proletariat (Marx, 1979: 5054);
3. The internal differentiation of the peasantry, with the conversion of some medium-sized peasant landholders into rich peasants and capitalist farmers, and the impoverishment of large numbers of medium—and small-landholding peasant farmers;
4. The transition, by diverse paths, towards capitalist agriculture based on the exploitation of the countryside by capital in cities;[4]
5. The proletarianization and impoverishment of increasing numbers of small agricultural producers and poor peasant farmers—what Marx in his theory of the General law of Capital Accumulation (GLCA) conceived as the 'multiplication of the proletariat'; and;
6. A process of industrialization and modernisation based on the exploitation of surplus agricultural labour and its incorporation into the capitalist development process.

----

an industrial form based on an extended division of labour and the social construction of a dis-embedded market; *modernization*—transformation of a traditional form of society based on a relatively simple form of technology and a communalist culture into a modern culture oriented towards individualism—based on the modern values of individual freedom and achievement (the search for individual self-realization and advancement) and the expansion of choice; and *capitalist development*—transformation of a pre-capitalist form of society and economy into a system based on the capitalist mode of production, and with it the conversion of a society and economy of direct producers on the land into a proletariat, a class of individuals that dispossessed of any means of production are forced into a relation of wage-labour with capital.

4   In Marxist theory the systematic exploitation of the countryside by the city and the monopolization of industrial development by cities leads to a pattern of uneven development and dependency, in which the 'purely industrial character of labour' in the cities 'corresponds to the purely agricultural character' of labour in the countryside (Marx 1967: 633). The exploitation of the countryside by capital in cities results in a net outflow of value from the rural to the urban, which is accomplished by (i) financialization leading to the systematic incurring of debt by farmers by 'regular flows of capitalist credit': (ii) ground-rents and absentee landlordism as the land-owning classes become more urbanized: and (iii) taxes, as urban development imposes taxation in money terms on the countryside, a 'driving force behind the development of production for direct consumption to production of commodities' (Kautsky, 1988: 212–213).

This process unfolded with different permutations more or less as theorized from both a development economics and a political economy perspective, leading large numbers of dispossessed peasants—viewed by the agencies of 'development assistance' as the 'rural poor'—to abandon both their rural communities and agriculture, a process that was facilitated by several pathways out of rural poverty—labour and migration—opened by the agencies of development (World Bank, 2008). While some of the 'rural poor', mostly dispossessed peasant farmers and rural landless workers, initially (in the 1960s and 1970s) took up arms in the land struggle and others were cajoled by the agents of 'development' to stay on their farms with assistance provided through programs of integrated rural development, others in large numbers migrated to the cities and urban centres in search for work, fuelling a process of rapid urbanization and capitalist development of the forces of production, and with it the depopulation of the rural communities and the capitalist development of agriculture. By the end of the first decade into the new millennium this process had resulted in the urbanization of most of the population—now over 70 percent.

This entire process unfolded if not quite according to the planning models of development theorists then more or less as theorized by development economists such as Walt Rostow who saw as the end point of the modernization process the creation of prosperous centres of modern capitalist industry and middle class societies of high income earners and mass consumption (Rostow, 1960). But in the 1980s on the periphery of the system—in Latin America, for example—the capitalist development process began to unfold in quite if not an entirely different form. Behind or at the base of this peripheral capitalist development process was the installation of a new world order, a new set of rules used to govern international relations of trade and the flow of investment capital. The new rules required governments to implement a program of 'structural reforms' (privatization, deregulation, liberalization, decentralization) designed to open up the economy to the forces of 'economic freedom' (the market liberated from regulatory constraint, capitalist enterprise in the private sector, and the flow of private capital), to unleash thereby a process of 'economic growth' and 'prosperity'. However, the outcome was rather different than theorised or expected.

Opening up local and national economies in peripheral regions to the 'forces of economic freedom' resulted not in economic growth but in the destruction of the productive forces in both industry and agriculture—as well as a decade 'lost to development' marked by economic stagnation, increased social inequalities in the distribution of wealth and income, new forms of poverty (urban rather than rural), and the emergence in the urban economies of an informal[5] sector in which rural migrants were forced to work on their own account on the streets rather than in factories and industrial plants, and offices, for wages (Klein and Tokman, 2000).

As for the rural economy and society the capitalist development process continued to generate what development economists conceptualized as 'unlimited supplies of surplus labour' for the urban labour market, and what Marxists viewed similarly as 'proletarianization' (the transformation of small-scale impoverished agricultural producers or peasants into an industrial proletariat or working class), with its 'industrial reserve army' of proletarianized peasants whose labour is surplus to the requirements of capital.[6] On this process in the Latin American context see Nun (1969) and Quijano (1974). Regarding the associated process of social transformation there emerged a major debate in Latin America between the 'peasantists' (Esteva, 1983) and 'the proletarianists' (Bartra, 1976) as to the fate of the peasantry. At issue in this debate was whether the forces of change unleashed by the capitalist development of agriculture would result in the disappearance of the peasantry.[7] Roger Bartra and other proletarianists argued that the forces of capitalist development would lead to the disappearance of the peasantry and any form of pre-capitalist forms of production just as it had in manufacturing and other sectors. On the other hand 'peasantists' argued that there were limits to the capitalist development process in its capacity to subsume the labour of the direct producers and that the economy of small-scale agriculture could survive within the interstices of the capitalist system.

The debate took place in the 1970s, but it would take 'developments' in the 1980s to more or less settle it. The 'development' that advanced if not settled the debate was the emergence of an urban proletariat of informal street workers and a large rural semi-proletariat of near-landless rural workers with one

---

5 According to Klein and Tokman (2000: 17), the informal sector accounted for 100% of all new jobs created in 1989, towards the end of a decade 'lost to development'. Over the next decade (from 1990 to 1998) for every 100 new jobs in the urban economy 30 took the form of a micro-enterprises in the informal sector and 29 others were based on self-employment. In effect 59% of all new jobs did not entail an exchange of labour for wages or engage the recognised formal labour market (Klein and Tokman, 2000).

6 Marx theorized this process of capitalist development (and productive and social transformation) in Capital, Volume 1, in terms of the 'general law of capital accumulation', which specified a twofold tendency, on the one hand towards the concentration of (and centralization) of capital, and, on the other, the 'multiplication of the proletariat'.

7 On more recent contributions to a renewed form of this debate see Petras & Veltmeyer (2001a) and Otero (1999).

foot as it were in the urban labour market and the other in the rural communities and agriculture.

It was not until well into the 1990s that mainstream development economists took cognizance of this 'development'—the emergence of a dualist two-sector economic structure, each with its own structural features and social conditions—by adapting their development strategy vis-à-vis the rural poor, and adjusting the theory used to inform this strategy. Up to this point the theorists and practitioners of development encouraged the outmigration of the rural poor, encouraging them to abandon agriculture in favour of labour in one form or the other—to take the labour and migration pathways out of rural poverty. The role assigned to the state, or the government, in this process was to facilitate the process by capacitating the poor to take advantage of the opportunities available to them in the urban labour markets—to provide the services and programs (education, health, social welfare) designed to this end, and to generate or strengthen the human capital of the poor.

But by the mid-1990s and the turn into the 21st century it was evident that the operating theory of economic development (modernization, industrialization, capitalism), as well as the associated strategy and policies, had to be 'adjusted' to prevailing conditions. For one thing, neoliberal policies based on free market capitalism or the Washington Consensus were simply not working—they neither delivered on the anticipated economic growth, and led to excessive inequalities in the access to productive resources and the distribution of income, and with these inequalities a worsening of poverty and the emergence of social discontent that threatened to undermine and destabilize the system. Also it was evident that both labour and migration had begun to reach if not exhaust their limits in the capacity to expand the forces of production.

With an increasingly restrictive labour market for employment in the private or public sector—up to 80 percent of jobs in the 1980s were generated in the informal sector—and the limited capacity of the informal sector to generate productive forms of self-employment, labour no longer was the pathway out of poverty that it had been theorized to be.[8] Not only did the expanding urban economies generate unsustainable levels of employment, but they featured high levels of un—and under-employment, low income, social

---

8   This phenomenon of an informal sector and an associated 'planet of slums' is by no means specific to Latin America. In 'high growth' Asia the figure for informal employment as a percent of total employment is 78.2 percent (Westra, 2012: 23). This in turn feeds into a burgeoning 'shadow economy', of which the informal economy is a part, that in Asia, Latin America and Africa is equal to 34.9%, 39.7% and 40% respectively of GDP (FN .22)

disorganization and crime, not to mention the 'planet of have' that bred these conditions (Davis, 2006).[9]

Under these conditions[10] of modernity and deindustrialization several new social categories of individuals emerged in peripheral social formations: an urban proletariat of street workers and large numbers of youth who neither studied nor worked.[11] The reason for this was the contradictory dynamic of uneven capitalist development based on the town-countryside relation: at some point the system will exhaust its capacity to absorb the masses of surplus

---

9   In 2007 the absolute number of people living in urban centres worldwide overtook the
        number of people living in the countryside for the first time ever, and it is estimated that
        by 2010 the rural world will be 3.3 billion with another 3.5 billion living in urban commu-
        nities (Borras & Franco, 2010: 3). This dramatic shift in the rural–urban balance is fairly
        recent, the result of a process of uneven rural–urban development (or arrested industrial
        development, urbanization without industrialization). Of the total world population of a
        mere 3.7 billion people in 1970, 2.4 billion were rural dwellers and 1.3 billion were urban.
        The change in the agricultural/non-agricultural population was even more dramatic dur-
        ing the same period. In 1970, the agricultural population stood at 2.0 billion people and
        the non-agricultural population at 1.7 billion. By 2010, this is expected to radically reverse,
        with a 2.6 billion agricultural population versus 4.2 billion non-agricultural. Yet even as
        the urban population overtakes the rural, the absolute number of rural dwellers remains
        significant.

10   What has been described as a 'frightening scenario' relates to the flooding of humanity
        into titanic urban agglomerations, with a consequent expansion of thus 'planet of (urban)
        slums'. The UN estimates that by 2050, seven out of 10 people in the world will be living in
        these 'mega-cities' and possibly one billion people living in them are destined to inhabit
        the ever-expanding urban slums! Such rates of urbanization as are commonplace in the
        developing world—notwithstanding recent efforts of the 'international development
        community' (economists at the World Bank, etc.) to slow down the rural–urban migra-
        tion process—outstrip those of the industrial revolution heyday and in many places
        exceed rates of economic growth to the point that the UN itself labels the urban flood as
        'pathological' (United Nations Secretariat, 2008). What is also disconcerting is the way in
        which these urban slums emerge as 'the nodal point where the melding of informal and
        formal employment occurs across the non-developed world' (Westra, 2012). This is where
        what the business and development literature refers to as 'global value chains' of the
        major non-financial multinational corporations that prey on what this literature dubs
        'vulnerable' workers, the 'vulnerable poor'.

11   The informal sector is characterized by 'petty informal bourgeoisie' and an 'informal pro-
        letariat' who are forced into 'working on their own account' on the streets or to embrace
        entrepreneurship due to the shrinkage of the formal sector. Employees in the informal
        sector, whether paid or unpaid, directly or indirectly work for the 'petty informal bour-
        geoisie' who exploit them due to the absence of formal contracts, rights, regulations and
        bargaining power in the informal sector (Davis, 2006: 178–181).

workers, the rural proletariat of landless or near-landless rural workers (or from another perspective, the 'rural poor'), expelled from the countryside and forced to migrate in the search for work. At the same time, even international migration was reaching or had evidently exceeded its capacity to absorb surplus labour.

The result of these contradictory 'developments'[12] was a shift in thinking among development economists and policymakers in the direction of seeking to slow down rather than encourage rural outmigration—to look for ways to keep the rural poor in their communities. This led to or played into the ongoing search for a new development paradigm—for a more inclusive and participatory form of development based on what rural sociologists would conceptualize as the 'new rurality' (Kay, 2009). This 'new rurality' made reference to the response of the rural semiproletariat and the poor to the forces of capitalist development and social change operating on them, which was to seek to diversify their sources of household income. Other responses included an adjustment to these forces in the form of outmigration in the search for greater opportunities and improved conditions in the world of work. This remained the strategy of a large number of rural households. But another response was to resist rather than adjust to the forces of change by forming or joining a social movement designed and aimed at mobilising the resistance against the policies that released these forces and resulting conditions, and to take direct collective action against them.[13]

This was a major response of the dispossessed peasantry and rural proletariat to the forces of peripheral capitalist development in the 1960s and 1970s, and again in the 1990s, when the indigenous communities in a number of countries joined the rural semiproletariat in the class struggle for land reform. In both contexts the guardians of the prevailing social and economic order turned towards 'development' as a way of dampening the fires of revolutionary

---

12   Marx's first systematic review of the literature on the history of society and the emerging science of economics (political economy) led him to conclude (on this see his *Economic & Philosophical Manuscripts* and *The German Ideology*) that the social division between town and countryside, the urban–rural divide, was one of the most fundamental contradictions of capitalist development.

13   Under the policy conditions of capitalist development in its latest phase of neoliberal globalization—privatization, deregulation, liberalization, democratization—the peasantry in its diverse forms had but two options: to absorb and adjust to the forces of change (industrialization, urbanization, modernization, capitalism, globalization) or to resist them. The political dynamics of social movement formation in the 1980s and the 1990s can be understood in these terms.

ferment—to provide the rural poor a less confrontational and alternative agency and form of social change. In the 1990s, however, this development process took a different form. Rather than a program of state-led rural development micro-projects (based on a strategy of 'integrated rural development') 'development' in the 1990s increasingly took the form of local development in which the active agent was the 'community'—community-based organisations run by the poor themselves, by those among the poor who were empowered to act for themselves with 'international cooperation' and 'social participation' (the mediation of NGOs funded by international donors or the government). Development in this form was geared to diverse efforts, and the 'project' of ensuring that the inhabitants of rural society are able to subsist and stay in their communities and not be forced to migrate. The solution: a strategy of diversifying sources of household income.

Evidently (from a World Bank perspective) agriculture is not a development pathway out of rural poverty, given that peasant agriculture is deemed to be the structural source of rural poverty (low productivity) and that very few 'peasants' have the capacity or the wherewithal to be transformed into a capitalist entrepreneur—to access the needed capital, modern technology and markets. However, it behoves the near-landless rural proletariat and semiproletariat to retain access to some agriculture, if only for self-subsistent food production. But the sustainability of rural households is predicated on accessing alternative and additional sources of income, particularly derived from labour—working off-farm or for some household members to migrate week-days, or seasonally, or for longer periods. Sociological studies into household income have determined that today, and as of the mid-1990s, over half of the income available to rural households in the region is derived from one form of labour or the other. However, food gardening and labour/migration by themselves would not relieve the pressure on the 'rural poor' to migrate and abandon their communities. Additional sources of household income, facilitated by state-supported 'development' and international cooperation, today include migrant remittances and conditional direct income transfers to the poor, as well as income-and employment generating development micro-projects.

This rural household survival strategy and associated conditions of community-based development (the 'new rurality') constituted the reality lived by much of the rural proletariat on the periphery of world capitalism at the turn into the 21st century. But conditions would soon change as these rural communities were swept by the changing tides of capitalist development—with the penetration of resource-seeking foreign investments and the expanded operations of extractive capitalism.

The New Geoeconomics of Capital and Associated Dynamics of Agrarian Change

As already noted the 21st century opened up with changes in the global economy driven by the growing demand for natural resources, both fossil fuels and other sources of energy, industrial minerals and precious metals, but also agro-food products. This demand not only led to a primary commodities boom, as governments in resource-rich countries responded to this demand by increasing their exports of these commodities, but to a global land- and resource-grab in the search for improved direct access to these resources.

An important but as yet not well-documented by-product of this expansion of foreign investments into land and agribusiness, as well as the mining of fossil fuels and industrial minerals, has been the concentration of capital in the natural resource sector (metal mining, oil and gas, agriculture)[14] as well as increased foreign land ownership (Borras et al., 2011: 9)—what FAO prefers to term 'large-scale land acquisitions'—and also the rapid expansion of extractive industries that require the capture or control of lands.[15]

By a number of accounts and any measure the scale of these foreign investments in both the acquisition of land and natural resource assets, and the rights to explore and extract these resources, is enormous. At the macro-level it is reflected in a significant shift in the 'sectoral distribution of foreign investments'.[16] While resource-seeking investments (in land and natural resource development) constituted only ten percent of FDI flows into Latin America in 2000 by 2010 it represented over 30 percent (Arellano, 2010).

By some accounts the change in the sectoral distribution of FDI has been even greater in Africa, with a larger proportion of these investments being in

---

14   The degree of concentration in the metal mining industries increased significantly between 1995 and 2005 (UNCTAD, 2011: 110–111). The degree of concentration rose the fastest in gold mining (from 38% to 47%), an area in which Canadian capital has been particularly active.

15   Borras et al. (2011) document this as a process of capitalist development across the globe. As for Latin America and the Caribbean, they write that 'there has been a significant increase in [foreign] investments in land and agriculture during the past decade. The level of these investments', it is noted, 'is high for nearly all seventeen countries' studied in the region (p. 10).

16   Across the globe as a whole, particularly taking account of change in the non-developed countries (generally referred to as 'developing' or 'emerging markets'), mass population shifts from around 2006 onwards have not been out of agriculture into industry as characterizing the past two centuries of capitalist development. Rather, the movement has been out of agriculture and into services.

the acquisition of land rather than in investing in the extraction of natural resources. In either case, the outcome has been the same—a process described by Harvey (2003) as 'accumulation by dispossession'.

One outcome and a major feature of this global land grab has been increased foreign ownership of land as well as the concentration of capital in the agricultural sector (UNCTAD, 2011: 110–111), adding another twist to the century-long land struggle. Other dimensions of the landgrabbing process include:

1. The privatization and commodification of land, and with it the transformation of a system of customary rights in regard to land usage into legal and written titles to land ownership;
2. The rationalization of the use of such demarcated landed property as a form of capital (land as a commodity) at the service of 'original' and expanded capital accumulation;
3. The proletarianization of the direct agricultural producers in the form of rural outmigration—by reducing nonmarket access to food and self-sustenance and creating a mobile global proletariat concentrated in the urban centres of what has become the world economy (Araghi 2010); and, more specifically in regard to extractive capitalism,
4. The forced displacement of inhabitants of the rural communities contiguous to the major sources of natural resources by the negative impacts of extractivist operations—damaging the health, and destroying the environment and livelihoods of the inhabitants of these rural communities.[17]

Under contemporary conditions of this 'great transition'—i.e. within the new world order of neoliberal globalization[18]—peasants have been and are,

---

17 The complex global history of this process of commodification of land rights, according to Araghi (2009) can be divided into four historical periods: primitive accumulation, colonialism, developmentalism, and neoliberal globalization. We concur, but we can now add another: extractive imperialism.

18 With the transition from a development state to the neoliberal state, the globalization process has unfolded in four phases: (i) a series of strategic responses to a crisis in the capitalist system of global production, and a cycle of 'structural reforms' implemented by the military-authoritarian state in the southern cone; (ii) a second cycle of neoliberal reform (privatization, deregulation, liberalization, decentralization and democratization) in the 1980s; (iii) a third cycle of neoliberal reform based on a model of 'sustainable human development'—adding to neoliberal 'pro-growth' policies a new social policy and a decentralized and localized form of participatory development and politics (good

so to speak or write, 'on the move' in three different senses. One is in the form of spatial relocation—migration from diverse rural localities and communities to the urban metropolis and beyond. The dynamics of this well-documented response to the forces of capitalist development are much in evidence, manifest in the uprooting and displacement from the countryside of huge numbers of landless producers, their families and their households.[19] The vast majority of these migrants are absorbed into the urban economy at the level of work or economic activity as a mass of informal workers, working 'on their own account' on the streets, rather than for wages in industrial plants and factories, in private and public sector offices, or in transportation or construction. At the level of living and residence, these rural migrants and landless workers are incorporated into what Mike Davis has dubbed 'a planet of slums'.

Migration is a well-defined response of the rural proletariat to the forces of social change generated in the capitalist development process and the social antagonism between the city and the countryside is present in all societies that have developed under the capitalist mode of production.[20] The World Bank in its 2008 *World Development Report* conceives of this response as a 'pathway out of rural poverty'. Another option available to the rural proletariat—also conceived by World Bank economists as a 'pathway out of poverty'—is 'labour': basically an exchange of labour-power for a living wage. Responses along this line, also understood as a matter of individual decision-making, are

------

governance); and (iv) the demise of neoliberalism brought on by the accumulated forces of resistance in the 1990s and regime change.

19   The significance and enormous dimensions of migration in the process of productive and social transformation is represented by developments in Brazil and Mexico. In Brazil, the 1986 rural census estimated the rural population as 23.4 million people. By 1995, the rural population had declined to 18 million, pointing to an exodus of over five million people. In addition, IBGE (the Brazilian Institute of Geography and Statistics) estimates that another two million landless or near-landless workers and their families abandoned the countryside from 1995 to 1999. In Mexico between 1990 and 2002 the annual rate of the rural exodus rose from 11 to 15% while the rate of rural outmigration to the US by individuals doubled, rising from 7 to 14%. The cumulative effect of this outmigration and that of previous decades is that today, according to ECLAC (2002) over 30% of the Mexican population, representing a mass of some 40 million workers, today lives in the US.

20   The contradiction between town and country is the decisive geographical relation of all patterns of capitalist development, whereby the surplus produced in the countryside is mostly consumed in cities and access to the important natural resources of the countryside is monopolized by capital based in cities; both relations are a prerequisite for the accumulation of capital and industry in the cities.

represented in the resulting process of social transformation, which for the individual small-scale agricultural producer or 'peasant' means entry into a relation of work or labour under whatever conditions might be available.

This type of response or pathway out of poverty has resulted in the formation of a sizeable semiproletariat with links to both land and wage-labour, allowing peasants to secure the livelihood of their households; and, at a different level, to constitute what Marx in a different context termed an 'industrial reserve army' of workers whose labour is held in reserve without capital having to assume the costs of its reproduction (Veltmeyer, 1983).[21] As for the World Bank's interpretation of this response it is reflected in the category of 'labour-oriented household' that has adopted 'labour' (wage-labour in agriculture and industry, self-employment) as a strategic pathway out of rural poverty—from 45 percent of all households in predominantly rural/agriculture-based societies such as Nicaragua to 53 percent of households in societies such as Ecuador considered to be 'urbanized' or 'transforming' (World Bank, 2008: 76).[22]

---

21   The main source of this 'industrial reserve army' are the peasant farmers and other groups dispossessed from their means of production by the forces released in the capitalist development of agriculture. However, the formation of an 'informal sector' in the urban economies of developing societies on the periphery of the world capitalism led to another major 'supply of surplus labour', namely the informal workers who, in the absence of opportunities for paid work in the urban labour market, were forced to find work 'on their own account' on the streets. The functioning of these informal sector workers as an 'industrial reserve army' is evident by the effect of having such a large reserve of workers in the cities and urban centres on the wages of workers in the formal sector. The relatively low level of wages and labour remuneration in the formal sector—from one-seventh to one-tenth of equivalent rates in more developed socieities without such a large reserve army (in developed societies the IRA can be measured as the rate of unemployment, which is much lower than the rate of informalization)—undoubtedly reflects the depressant effect on wages caused by the existence of a large number of workers whose labour is held in reserve.

22   Migration and labour constitute the primary sources of household income and the dominant form of productive and social transformation—or (from the World Bank's perspective) pathway out of rural poverty. However, the resulting pattern does not conform to the theory constructed in this regard within the mainstream of sociological and development studies. In theory urban-based industry is expected to absorb the surplus labour released by the force of capitalist development, resulting in a process of productive and social transformation—converting on a progressively growing scale the direct agricultural small producer into a proletariat (the 'multiplication of the proletariat' in Marx's original formulation of the General Law of Capital Accumulation). In practice, however, i.e. under conditions of peripheral capitalism and neoliberal globalization, industry, at the centre of

The economists behind the 2008 *World Development Report* on Agriculture
for Development identify 'farming' as the third strategic response of the
rural poor to the forces of social change.[23] This pathway out of rural poverty
is predicated on the modernization of agriculture and the capitalist development of production. But a more consequential strategic response, not identified by the World Bank given its ideological focus on possible forms of
structural adjustment, takes a 'political' rather than a 'structural' form (the
outcome of economic decisions made by countless individuals). It is to organize a social movement as a means of mobilizing the forces of resistance
within agrarian society against the processes of primitive accumulation and
proletarianization—against the loss of land and the destruction of their livelihoods, against forced migration and the subsumption and exploitation of
labour, against the depredations of global capital and imperialism, against the
policies of the neoliberal state and its governing body in the global economy
('the international bourgeoisie').[24]

the so-called 'expanding capitalist nucleus', has been unable to absorb this surplus labour,
with the resulting appearance in the rural society of a large semiproletariat of rural workers who manage to retain access to some land as a means of sustaining the livelihoods of
their households and reproducing family labour. As for the burgeoning urban centres, the
displaced surplus labour is absorbed and the rural migrant is incorporated into the ubiq-
uitous 'informal sector' and into the planet of slums that Davis (2006) writes of so
eloquently.

23   The 2008 *World Development Report* identifies three strategic responses of peasant small-
holders to the forces of capitalist development, forces that are viewed as progressive or
liberating—opening up new opportunities for self-advancement and an escape out of
poverty. But this third response ('farming') is also one of 'structural adjustment' to changing conditions and new opportunities—economic (decision as to source of livelihood)
rather than political (the construction of a social movement) as the third pathway out of
rural poverty. One reason for a trend towards poverty reduction in some societies classified as 'agricultural-based' is that in these countries agriculture is affording increased
opportunities for hired labour. Indeed, the World Bank has detected a trend in this direction. As the Bank sees it, 'the worldwide share of wage-labour' in agricultural employment
'is rising in many countries'.

24   The diverse regional and international organizations formed by the peasant movement in
the 1990s are quite consistent in their vision of an alternative future and a better society
as regards its organizational principles, institutional framework and underlying system
(socialism—'a society without exploiters and exploited'). See, for example, the *iv Congreso*
of the Latin American Coordination of Countryside Organizations (CLOC) on 11 October
2005, with the participation of 178 delegates representing 88 peasant and indigenous
organizations from 25 countries.

In a sense, both sides of the argument regarding the process of capitalist development and agrarian transformation are supported by some of the 'facts' and thus able to explain some of the changes taking place in the Latin American countryside, on the periphery of the expanding capitalist nucleus in the urban centres. This is because, under conditions of what some have conceptualized as 'peripheral capitalism', the peasantry is being transformed in part but not completely, emerging as what we have described as a 'semiproletariat' of near-landless rural workers or landless peasants. Under these conditions rather than the 'disappearance of the peasantry' what we have is its reproduction in diverse forms. Many self-defined 'peasants' or family farmers in these circumstances emerge as a rural semiproletariat of landless workers forced to combine direct production on the land with wage-labour—working off-farm to secure the livelihood of their households and families; and an urban proletariat of workers in the informal sector of the urban economy, to work 'on their own account' in the streets and live in the slums formed on the periphery of this economy.

There is little 'new' about this process. Its diverse permutations can be traced out in the dynamics of productive and social transformation all over the world in different geographical and historical contexts. But what is new or distinctive about the transition towards capitalism in this context is that the associated process of productive and social transformation process has been arrested or stalled in its tracks as it were, with both modernity and capitalism taking a distinct peripheral form in the formation of a semiproletariat of rural landless workers forced into seasonal or irregular forms of wage-labour. Under these conditions, together with the politics of resistance against the neoliberal 'structural reform' agenda responsible for them, there is no question of the peasantry disappearing into the dustbins of history as predicted by structuralists in both the development economics and Marxist camps. The problem is to determine the particular form taken by the class struggle under these conditions and under the new conditions that have emerged over the past decade of extractive capitalism and extractivist imperialism.

The devastating and painful consequences of this process are reflected in the detritus of grinding poverty left behind in the countryside as well as the negative socioenvironmental impacts of extractive capitalism. As for the issue of poverty the concerted efforts of the international organizations engaged in the fight against 'global poverty' and those governments that have embraced the post-Washington Consensus and the 'new developmentalist' policy agenda appear to have succeeded in reducing the incidence of poverty—at least in some cases (Brazil, Chile, Venezuela) and in these cases by as much as 40 percent. Nevertheless, notwithstanding these advances on the anti-poverty front, and notwithstanding the emergence in the 1990s of poverty as an urban phenomenon, 75 percent of the world's poor today still live in the rural areas.[25]

In this connection, the century-long class struggle for land has been transformed into a broader struggle for sustainable livelihoods and for maintaining a 'traditional' way of life and culture associated with small-scale agricultural production. This struggle, as well as the struggle by organized labour for improved wages and working condition, has also been broadened and transformed into resistance against the policies of the neoliberal state and the forces of 'globalization'—integration into a global economy in which the forces of 'economic freedom' (investment capital, trade in goods and services) have been liberated from the regulatory constraints of the development-welfare state. And in the new millennium, as discussed below, a new phase in the capitalist development of the forces of production on a global scale—extractivist imperialism—would bring about another major change in both the form taken by the forces of resistance and the correlation of forces in the broader struggle.

Food vs. Energy: The Political Economy of Biofuels Capitalism

Agricultural extractivism rakes a number of forms, but in the current context what has dominated the debate—apart from the dynamics of landgrabbing— has been what we might term the political economy of biofuels capitalism: the conversion of farmland and agriculture for food production into the production of biofuels. What set off the debate was the change in land use in Brazil in the use of corn from a food and feedlot product into ethanol. However, what sparked the current debate has been the large-scale change in the use of

---

25   This is a methodological construct, the result of measuring poverty in terms of income for which there is a greater need in urban centres when it comes to households and individuals meeting their basic needs. By the same token, the reported advances in the fight against global poverty depend on an income measure for the poverty line ($2.50 a day, or $1.25 a day for extreme poverty). It is very unrealistic to set the poverty line at $2.50 when it comes to urban society. In most cases even setting the poverty line at $5.00 a day, more or less the average minimum wage rate for most countries in Latin America, which ranges from 40 to 80 cents an hour, would not be unrealistic. However, it would immediately wipe out the reported gains on the fight against poverty over the past decade. For example, in Chile, one of the leaders and a successful case in this fight, it is estimated that up to 25% of the population can be found just above the poverty line and well below 'middle class' socioeconomic status measured in terms of consumption capacity.

farmland to convert it from food production into the production of soy as a biofuel form of energy. It would appear that biofuels production and related financial speculation is a major impetus behind landgrabbing, particularly in Argentina and Brazil, where enormous swathes of farmland have been given over to soy production.

The conversion of agriculture (sugarcane and soya) production of food into energy evidently drives agrarian change in countries such as Argentina and Brazil.[26] However, as emphasized by Novo et al. (2010) regarding Brazil, biofuels production must be understood in the broader context of the new geoeconomics of capital (extractive capitalism), not just than in terms of the recent expanded global demand for energy. Agrarian change in this context includes not only increased large-scale land grabs and a process of accumulation by dispossession, but a process of economic concentration[27] in addition to changes in land use[28] and the destruction of traditional economies that have

---

26 Borras et al. (2011: 4) note that because of its analytic framework and rather narrow definition of landgrabbing FAO (2011), in its case study of 17 Latin American countries, concludes that 'land grabbing' exists *only* in two countries in the region, namely Argentina and Brazil. The authors themselves, however, argue with evidence that landgrabbing is much more widespread in the region. For example, 43% of soya production in Bolivia is in the hands of non-Bolivians (p.27).

27 This economic concentration not only occurs at the level of land ownership but also in the structure of production. For example, Novo et al. (2010) argue that the turn towards the production of biofuels in the case of Brazil led to a process of fast concentration in the dairy industry. The main targets of this concentration by corporate acquisition were the national, medium scale and family-administrated dairy industries that were bought by transnational groups. For example, the Italian group Parmalat pushed aggressively the concentration of industry by acquisitions in several regions that resulted in the disappearance of more than 50% of dairy firms from 1988 to 1997 (Jank et al., 1999). A similar process of concentration took place in the distribution sector, by acquisitions and mergers of supermarkets. In fact, the distribution and supermarket networks became much more powerful than the dairy industry sector (Neves, 2006).

28 Changes in land use have to do with the displacement of existing producers or traditional activities with practices that are deemed by the advocates of agrarian change to be more efficient in the application of modern technologies that result in productivity growth, increased productive capacity and access to global markets, and sustainable development (e.g. reduced carbon emissions and thus climate warming)—in a word 'progress'. But others argue that there is no evidence whatsoever for these claims, and that what we see instead is environmental degradation, displacement of populations and loss of viable livelihoods. Novo et al. (2010) in this regard show that the expansion of sugarcane production is associated with an almost equivalent reduction in pasture areas and a decrease in number of cows and milk production, with no tangible overall benefit.

sustained generations of farming families and local food markets, the destruction of the livelihoods of millions of small landholding producers for local food
markets, and, more broadly a sharp rise in the price of food and with it the
onset of a global food crisis.[29]

Environmentalists have criticized the massive conversion of forestland and
other yet non-arable land into biofuel production, and have called into question its supposed environmental efficiencies and the overall effect of biofuels
on reducing greenhouse gas emissions.[30] But development-oriented arguments have suggested that the biofuel agenda in rich countries, supported with
heavy government subsidies, were driving up food prices and competing with
other forms of land use, and also when biofuel production is planned on sup-
posedly 'marginal' lands, because these are often important for the livelihoods
of the poor (OXFAM, 2008). These arguments have shifted views within some
decision-making bodies of the EU and the FAO. The FAO (2008), for example,
has concluded that the rise of food prices is indeed an effect of the expansion
of biofuel production and that whether biofuels will help to reduce or increase
greenhouse gas emissions depends on the precise conditions. But to date, there
seem to be few empirical studies of competing claims on land use, even though
these seem to be central to the biofuel controversy.

In the controversial debate about biofuels, the case of Brazil is pivotal in
that it is the second largest liquid biofuel producer in the world with a complete biofuel social-technical configuration and a full chain from producing
sugarcane and ethanol to flex-fuel[31] cars that run on biofuels, supported by

---

29   The economic, social and environmental impacts of biofuels production have been heav-
      ily debated, with some analysts emphasizing the positive outcome such as a greater effi-
      ciencies in transportation systems and supplies to the global market for energy, and a
      significant reduction of global greenhouse gas emissions.

30   The Swiss Federal Laboratories for Materials Science and Technology (Empa) released the
      results of an extensive new study on the full life-cycle impact of biofuels, which found
      that few biofuels were more environmentally friendly than petrol. Rainer Zah, head of the
      Empa study, explained to swissinfo.ch that 'if you are producing biofuels on productive
      land, you are usually inducing higher environmental impacts then those caused by fossil
      fuels'. After analyzing 17 years of data to settle the food versus fuel debate Michigan
      State University scientists concluded that using productive farmland to grow crops for
      food instead of fuel is 36% more energy efficient http://www.soyatech.com/news_story
      .php?id=18194.

31   Landgrabbing, according to Borras et al. (2011: 6) occurs not only within the context of the
      search for more food production. It also occurs within the emerging food-feed-fuel com-
      plex involving what they term 'flex crops' (crops that have multiple and/or flexible uses in
      the '3-in-1' complex) as well as in non-food sectors such as industrial tree plantation and

government subsidies, a regulatory system, technical research and finance arrangements (Novo et al. 2010). Another such case is Argentina, where the government has actively promoted opening up the country to large-scale investments in the production of soy to fuel both the domestic and the global economy. Next we will briefly explore this case of biofuels capitalism. The Brazilian case is briefly discussed in Chapter 7.

The Soy Model of Extractive Capitalism in Agriculture: The Case of Argentina[32]

One of various contradictory features of capitalist development is the expanded capacity of the system for food production and the growing incapacity of the masses of the rural poor, forced to migrate to the urban centres, to access food because of its conversion into a commodity, and the spike in the price of agrofood products, brought on in part by the conversion of agriculture for food production into a source of energy, for which there is a greater demand in the world market.[33] This dynamic has turned out to be a defining feature of world capitalism on the agrarian front in the first decade of the 21st century. It implicates the emergence and rapid growth in recent decades of new agribusinesses such as the production of soy for export based on transgenic seeds, that according to the Argentine government, a booster of expanded soy production for exports as a strategy of national development have the potential to grow significantly in the near future.

---

large-scale conservation. As for flex-fuel technology it involves car motors running on gasoline, ethanol, or mixtures. It was considered a breakthrough since it allowed for purchasing the cheapest type of fuel available.

32   This section closely follows Giarraca and Teubal (2004).

33   Expansion of biofuel production in the United States, Europe, and South America has coincided with sharp increases in the world market in prices for food grains, feed grains, oilseeds, and vegetable oils. The percentage of rural *poor* people continues to be higher than the urban poor. Although the world population today is more than 50% urban, three-quarters of the world's poor today live and work in the countryside. Poverty is often associated with hunger, and in 2008 there were an estimated one-billion hungry people in the world. At the height of the recent food price crisis, FAO (2008) announced that in order to meet the world's growing needs food production would have to double by 2050, with the required increase mainly in developing countries, where the majority of the world's rural poor live. However, what FAO failed to recognize is that the crisis consists not in the scale of production but in the price of food.

This strategy, together with the emergence of soy production based on transgenetic seeds as a key sector of the global food regime, relates to and reflects the dramatic expansion in recent years of foreign investment in the large-scale acquisition of land, or landgrabbing, and the importance gained by large transnational corporations in controlling key segments of extractivist processes, not to mention the application of new technologies promoted by neoliberal policies implemented throughout the continent.

The soy model[34] implemented in Argentina is based on transgenic seeds that are resistant to glyphosate, an agrochemical that kills off weeds and brushwood remaining in the field after the 'no tillage' system is applied, but that does not kill the transgenic seed itself. While the cost of labour and the use of fossil fuels are substantially reduced under the soy model, the system causes enormous environmental and social degradation, leading to the concentration of land ownership and massive rural unemployment, particularly in the small cities in the country's interior, as a result of the disappearance of regional crops due in part to the labour-saving technologies involved in soy production (Domínguez & Sabatino, 2006).

Throughout the 20th century, Argentina, as well as countries such as Australia, Canada and even the US, was an important supplier of meat and grain to the world economy. These exports—including beef, wheat, corn and sunflowers—were also basic foods consumed domestically. Production was concentrated in the Pampas while other regions focused on traditional industrial crops for domestic consumption: sugar cane in Tucumán and Salta; cotton and yerba mate in Chaco and Misiones respectively; apples and pears in the Río Negro valley in the Patagonia; and vineyards and wine production in Mendoza and San Juan. Originally oriented towards the domestic market, some of this production was exported (apples, for example). Argentina was historically self-sufficient in food; the bulk of food consumed domestically was produced locally, except for some tropical products such as coffee or palm hearts. Furthermore, the country was considered one of the breadbaskets of the world, capable of providing food for a population several times that of Argentina (Giarracca & Teubal, 2014).

This production potential was based in large part on small- and medium-sized family farms that constituted an important component of Argentine agriculture. According to census data 'medium and large multi-family farms' (basically large estates) occupied over half of Argentina's farmland and production back in 1960 (in Brazil, Chile, Ecuador and Guatemala this proportion

---

34   Discussion of this model is based on Giarracca & Teubal (2014).

was higher). At the same time 'family farms', or 'small and medium producers', occupied 45 per cent of agricultural land and accounted for 47 per cent of total output, a larger proportion in both cases than in other Latin American countries where land ownership was even more concentrated but where local food markets were predominantly served by the peasant economy, the *minifundios* or small landholdings of the peasant economy, which occupied only three per cent of the land in Argentina, compared with 17 percent in Ecuador and 14 per cent in Guatemala (Feder, 1975: Table 18, 102).

In the 1970s, new grain and oilseed varieties were introduced in the Pampas. Farmers began harvesting two crops a year instead of alternating crop and livestock production. New crop varieties allowed a 'secondary' crop to be sown in combination with wheat. The boom in soybean production began at this time, with the introduction of a Mexican germplasm in wheat that gave rise to the wheat–soybean dual cropping that spread rapidly throughout the Pampas, especially in the sub-region where corn was mainly produced. This dual cropping partially supplanted corn and sorghum as well as livestock production, which traditionally formed part of a mixed production system. The essence of this new agriculturization of the Argentine countryside was based on soybeans and the accompanying technological package they required. It expanded largely at the expense of livestock production and other traditional grains and foods.

Neoliberal policies and institutions established in the 1990s under the Menem regime had a significant impact on Argentina's agricultural 'development'. First, the institutions that had traditionally regulated agriculture were eliminated or privatized. The 'structural reform' or 'deregulation decree' of 1991—which compares to similar legislation regarding the 'modernization' of agriculture implemented in Mexico and elsewhere in the region around the same time (from 1991 to 1993)—dissolved the marketing boards that had regulated agricultural production since the 1930s. This included the *Junta Nacional de Carnes* (National Meat Board), the *Junta Nacional de Granos* (National Grain Board) and the *Dirección Nacional del Azúcar* (National Sugar Directorate). The elimination of the National Grain Board gave greater power to the large grain and oilseed exporters, and leverage over key segments of the economy. These measures were combined with the flexibilization of contracts, setting aside the tenancy laws that had been in place since the 1940s.

In the process, large properties were consolidated and the disappearance of medium-sized and small farms intensified. The resulting pressures on small landholding family farmers, and the possibility of losing their lands, led to the wives and women farmers to protest the auctioning of their farms due to their ballooning indebtedness and to organize the *Movimiento de Mujeres*

Agropecuarias en Lucha (Farm Women's Agrarian Struggles Movement), which managed to halt the process, stopping the auctioning of more than 500 farms (Giarracca & Teubal, 2010).

The institutional changes that underlie the agribusiness system have permitted large transnational corporations to take control of key sections of the agro-food sector, including the provision of seeds and inputs, purchase of land in certain regions, industrial processing of agricultural produce, and the domestic and international marketing of production. These new agribusinesses engaged a logic that was very different from that of former agro-industries. As Giarracca (2008) has pointed out: 'this used to be a country of *chacareros* (family farmers), cooperatives, and national industries, [important agroindustrial complexes formed by local industries based on national capital, all or which] were doing well'. While some of these former industries exported part of their output, food production was mostly oriented to the domestic market. But with the wholesale transfer of local industries to transnational capital, export commodities increased and a new stratum of very large agricultural producers was formed to serve the world market for agrofood products and commodities such as wheat and meat.

These changes can be traced back to the years of the military dictatorship (1976–83), when, within the framework of the 'new world order' of neoliberal globalization, finance capital became dominant and there emerged a new regime of accumulation for agriculture and the agro-food system as a whole—what Friedmann (1987) and McMichael (2009) term 'the global food regime'.[35] As part of this system, large multinational or transnationalized corporations came to determine key aspects of agricultural policy. These processes continued under subsequent democratically elected governments. An important landmark was the deregulation decree of 1991 (mentioned above); suddenly, Argentine agriculture became one of the most deregulated in the world, subject to the vagaries of world markets like no other nation's agricultural sector. It was transformed into a system that mainly produced commodities for export, based on advanced technologies and dominated by transnational corporations.

---

35   The neoliberal era is traced back by many observers to the conservative counterrevolution and the installation in the early 1980s of what was touted as a 'new world order'. However, the 'structural reforms' (the 'structural adjustment program') introduced within the institutional and policy framework of this world order and a cycle of democratic regimes formed in the 1980s were anticipated by the neoliberal policies introduced in the 1970s with the military regimes formed in the Southern cone—Chile, Argentina, Uruguay and Bolivia (Veltmeyer & Petras, 1997, 2000).

Further, during the military dictatorship, the seed banks developed by the National Institute for Agricultural Technology (Instituto Nacional de Tecnología Agropecuaria or INTA) were dismantled and the accumulated knowledge was transferred to transnationals likely to invest in the local economy. Thus, local genetic banks that sustained biodiversity were shared with the transnationals and new technologies, hybrid seeds and transgenics were increasingly dominated by companies such as Monsanto that invested heavily in the acquisition of land for agricultural production, while agricultural producers were induced or obliged to purchase their seeds year after year from the transnational seed corporations.

As Giarracca and Teubal note this did away with a traditional feature of agriculture: the prospect farmers had of using and reproducing their own seeds. These sterile transgenic seeds required new agricultural practices—a system of direct sowing and the spraying of large quantities of agrochemicals to kill off weeds and any agricultural material not required. In 1997, transgenic seeds were 'liberated' to the market and farmers began planting Monsanto's trademark soybean seed, Roundup Ready, a commercial brand of glyphosate and is the herbicide to which the genetically modified soybean seed is resistant. A new technological package combined this seed with glyphosate in a 'no tillage' system that required no plowing of the land, which implied the need for special machinery not generally accessible to local medium—or small-scale farmers.

Within this framework, a handful of large transnational seed corporations such as Monsanto and Novartis induced farmers to incorporate a technological package they controlled by providing them with seeds that are resistant to glyphosate and with the agrochemicals that producers are obliged to purchase when they plant the genetically modified seed. Farmers became increasingly dependent, not only on agro-industry and supplies of agrochemical products, but also on the companies that provide transgenic seeds. At present, more than 95 percent of soybean seeds used by farmers in Argentina are transgenic and are provided by transnational corporations or their licensees.

This process took place alongside the flexibilization of tenant and rental laws, which permitted rental of land for one harvest (renewable ad infinitum). As a consequence, a new social actor, the *contratista* (contractor)—now an important factor in the rental of land—materialized. In addition, ports and silos were privatized and agro-export complexes dominated by large transnational exporters increased in importance. New very large producers emerged as significant social actors on the stage of agricultural development, some of them combining with their own seed pools or financial trusts to dominate a large part of the local agricultural scene. They also took on an important role in the rental of land by contractors, their finance coming from many sources, not only agriculture. The agro-food system as a whole, including local industry, supermarkets and other service industries, was increasingly dominated by transnational corporations.

Production and Land Use under the Soy Model

Soy production began in the 1970s. In 1980, 3.7 tons were produced, accounting for 10.6 per cent of Argentina's total grain output. Production increased to 11 million tons in 1996–97, when transgenics were 'liberated' to the market, and to 46.6 million tons in 2007–08. The soy harvest of 2012–13 is estimated at 50 million tons, representing more than half of Argentina's total grain output.

The land area dedicated to soy also increased substantially. In 1996, soy production covered 20 per cent of the total land used for grain. In 2011–12, 18 million hectares were allocated to soy, while in the present crop year (2012–13) more than 19.5 million hectares were used for soy production, more than half of Argentina's total grainland. These data (Giarracca & Teubal, 2014: 54–55) reflect a trend towards monoculture in soy production and the export of grains, soy and soy oil and biofuels.

Large multinational corporations that dominate the global market are the main exporters of these commodities. Exporters include Cargill, Noble Argentina, ADM Argentina, Bunge Argentina, LDC (Dreyfus), A.C. Toepfer and Nidera. Together these companies exported 83.5 percent of Argentina's cereal and oilseed exports (including soy). As for soy oil nearly 83 percent was exported by just five firms and a total of 90 percent of soy sub-products was exported by six exporters (Giarracca & Teubal, 2014: 55). Among the twenty most important exporters in Argentina, eleven exported agricultural products and their derivatives, five were producers of gas and petroleum products and one, Minera Alumbrera, was the main company that extracted and exported copper and gold, among other metals. Only two manufacturing companies— Siderca (iron tubes) and Ford Argentina (automobiles and parts)—were important exporters, a situation that denotes the importance that extractive activities have acquired in the export structure of Argentina. According to ECLAC (2012) about 70 percent of Argentina's total exports take the form of primary commodities (71.2 percent in 2004, 68.3 percent in 2011). This compares to 95.5 percent in the case of Bolivia and Venezuela in 2011, 89.2 percent in the case of Chile and Peru, and a low of 29.3 percent in the case of Mexico, and a regional average of 60.9 percent.

In recent years, large companies and landowners have increased their operations in agriculture. As family farmers and rural producers of food for the local market were forced out of business and to sell or rent their land, many of them turned over management of their land to firms or investors, with technological packages that included transgenics (Domínguez & Sabatino, 2006: 21).

The Socioenvironmental Costs and 'External Effects' of Soy Production

Soy production is very profitable for Argentine farmers. However, this profitability does not take into account what economists view as 'externalities' or 'external effects', which can be very pernicious. The first negative impact of this type of agriculture is that it is based almost exclusively on the production of soy, with no regard to other agricultural products. This implies a monoculture, with soy becoming one of Argentina's main exports—a fact that denotes its vulnerability to price and demand changes on international commodity markets.

The trend towards a specialization in soy is fraught with risks and dangers. The emerging monoculture implies a loss of biodiversity and less production of other crops, including those providing for the food needs of the local population. This excessive specialization also inhibits rotation with livestock production, which traditionally contributed to the maintenance and sustainability of agriculture. These factors have led to a debate relating to the government's foreign trade policies, on the one hand, and local production policies on the other.

It is worth considering the views of Vía Campesina, a global movement of peasant and small family farmers, on this matter. Vía Campesina points out that free trade contributes to a worsening of the crisis affecting the rural areas of the world. The liberalization of markets for agricultural produce in third world countries and the corresponding limitless competition to which these countries are subjected are detrimental to the interests of the peasantry throughout the world. Free trade tends to favor agribusiness and damage the interests of the peasantry, as well as of populations inhabiting rural areas. Liberalization of agricultural markets, opening them up to external competition via reductions in tariffs and trade controls, has subjected the peasantry to a global competitive system whose main beneficiaries are agribusiness multinationals and their stockholders. These trends are also instrumental in the present world food crisis.

As noted above, the share of land used for soy production has increased systematically since the 1970s while the proportion of other crops in the total output has fallen. Furthermore, the number of dairy farms were reduced while the size of those remaining in operation increased; also, livestock and meat production in general, together with agrofood products designed to the needs of the local population, has fallen substantially, raising serious questions about food security, particularly in the context of rising prices, which in some countries (Mexico, for example) have assumed crisis proportions. While Argentina continues to be generally self-sufficient in food, and to date has managed to avert the crisis in the production and marketing of agrofood products—the food crisis—that has beset other countries and regions in recent years, it is evident that the country has not averted the propensity of the capitalist system towards crisis. Indeed, the soy model of agricultural production, and the extractivist strategy pursued by the government guarantees that Argentina will go down this road.

In this connection several 'external effects' of the soy model deserve consideration. Throughout the 20th century, deforestation increased, mainly as a consequence of the expansion of agriculture. But deforestation was intensified due to soy expansion in the north—Santiago del Estero, Chaco, Salta and Jujuy— which not only led to the violent expulsion of peasant and indigenous communities from the land but an intensification of the trend towards deforestation, which, together with widespread degradation of the environment, can be viewed as one more way of enclosing the commons.

According to Giarracca and Teubal (2014: 58) soy also expanded over the native woodland and the Yungas, particularly in the north. According to the 1937 Censo Agropecuario Nacional (National Agriculture and Livestock Census), native forests covered 37.5 million hectares, while in 1987 forest areas had been reduced to 33.1 million hectares. From 1998 to 2002 some 230,000 hectares of native forestland were lost every year.

It is also important to note that these forests are part of territories inhabited by thousands of small communities of peasants, indigenous populations and *criollos*, who depend upon the forests for their livelihoods. This is not just a livelihoods issue but also a political issue in that the call for action by some indigenous communities dependent on the forest for their livelihood has resulted in a new law for the protection of native forests. However, in many situations and cases the law has not been enforced because of powerful interests working against the law.

Another major impact on the indigenous communities in the direct path of extractive capital in the agricultural frontier of capitalist development (the production of biofuels) has to do with the negative impact of the chemicals mobilized in the production process on the health of the inhabitants of the rural communities located near the soy plantation fields where glyphosate fumigations by air are carried out. Wide-scale fumigation with glyphosate causes a variety of conditions, including intoxification, chronic disease and in not a few cases death (Giarracca & Teubal, 2014).

In August 2010, molecular biologists, geneticists, epidemiologists and endo-crinologists, as well as professionals from other branches of medicine, pre-sented their studies during the Conference of Doctors of Crop-sprayed Villages at the National University of Córdoba, the first time that a public university had invited researchers and academics to discuss the use of agrochemicals as part of the current agricultural model. They concluded that 'there is scientific evidence that is sufficiently strong and consistent to confirm that pesticide exposure increases health risks'. Using national and international research results and records of patients, renowned specialists associated agrochemicals with different types of cancer, miscarriages, malformations and impaired fertility.

For many years, residents of San Jorge in the province of Santa Fe—in the middle of the soy production area—had reported the effects of agrochemicals that caused allergies, poisoning and respiratory problems. In March 2009, a court prohibited these fumigations. The decision was appealed, but in December a precedent-setting verdict was handed down: a civil and commer-cial court of appeal announced a firm ruling prohibiting fumigations within 800 meters (if by land) and within 1500 meters (by way of aerial fumigation) near residential areas. With an eye on campaigning by residents of the locali-ties of La Leonesa and Las Palmas against fumigations on a rice farm, and to prevent direct action, the judges invoked the precautionary principle that in view of the possible irremediable environmental damage, protective measures had to be taken. On the same day of the verdict, the Argentine government approved the launching of Monsanto's new soybean, RR2, which is 'more pro-ductive and resistant to agrochemicals'. The government plans to increase grain production by 60 per cent by 2020 (ibid.).

In conclusion, the technological package involved in soy production threatens food sovereignty, produces important health problems via fumiga-tions of all types, has negative effects on the quality of the soil, impacts on the biodiversity of flora and fauna in rural areas, and contributes to the dissemination of toxic residues throughout the environment. Furthermore, the massive use of fertilizers and agrochemicals in general affects lakes, rivers and oceans in vast regions of the world and also has a bearing on global climate change (drought and floods), as has recently been the case in Argentina.

The expulsion of populations from agriculture and from rural areas, mostly small and medium-scale peasant farmers and labourers, is not a minor 'exter-nal effect' of this activity. While labour is 'saved' and huge profits are made, the soyazation process entails the disappearance of farms and the reduction of food production oriented to local needs.

Class Struggle on the Global Commons: The Case of Argentina[36]

As noted earlier, the expansion of FDI into exploration for oil and gas and the mining of minerals and metals has resulted in increased economic concentration as well as landgrabbing (foreign investment in large-scale land acquisitions) and expansion of what we might term 'agro-extractivism'.[37] But yet another outcome of this territorial development has been the emergence of new forms of class struggle and forces of resistance on what we might view as the 'global commons' of land, water and associated natural resources on the expanding frontier of extractive capitalism.

Boaventura de Sousa Santos (2005), a professor of sociology at the School of Economics at the Portuguese University of Coimbra, points out that more than 80 percent of natural resources and the biodiversity that humanity requires for its subsistence in the future belong to indigenous and peasant communities, a significant number of which are found in Latin America. The indigenous people and peasants everywhere existed for millennia prior to colonialism and were capable of sustaining their livelihoods and communities on the basis of a traditional culture that respected both the integrity of mother earth or nature (known as *Pachamama* in the Andes) and the intimate symbiotic relationship of their agrarian societies with nature.

Indigenous Peoples in Argentina and Brazil: A Struggle for Survival

While the indigenous peoples of Argentina, according to Giarracca and Teubal were the first to resist having their communities cornered and harassed by old or new corporations, such as the old sugar mills or Benetton in the Patagonia, they were not the first to appear in the media or the public arena. In Argentina, they note—and there is nothing particular to Argentina here—there is a long practice of ignoring or 'invisibilizing' the pre-existing inhabitants of these territories, unlike in neighbouring Brazil, especially in Mato Grosso do Sul, where the indigenous population were ruthlessly expelled from the land by 'farmers' and ranchers anxious to expand into the rich farmland of the agribusiness frontier in both the Amazonian region and the southern Pampas. In two countries in which the old agro-export capitalist economy

---

36   The following discussion is based on Giarracca & Teubal (2014).

37   Borras et al. (2011) document this as a process of capitalist development across the globe. As for Latin America and the Caribbean, they write that 'there has been a significant increase in [foreign] investments in land and agriculture during the past decade. The level of these investments', it is noted, 'is high for nearly all seventeen countries' studied in the region (p. 10).

is entrenched and widely celebrated, the idea that there may be other uses for the national territory—better uses of landand other ways of producing food-is difficult to imagine.

The indigenous populations in these areas are widely viewed by large landowing farmers, ranchers and corporations as an anachronism, a nuisance and an obstacle to progress. In the long and continuing struggle of the indigenous groups and communities to resist the advance of the large soy and sugarcane plantations and agribusiness in their territories they have been either systematically pushed off the land, invisibilized or exterminated as dictated by circumstances.

An emblematic case study of these symptomatic conditions and the resulting struggle for land respect for territorial rights and survival is that of the Kolla in the north-western provinces of Argentina. The Kolla are organized and live in communities that extend from the Bolivian border into the Argentine province of Salta. These communities have a long history of intense and violent struggle to reclaim territories that were usurped by a sugar mill belonging to one of the main oligarchic families of the north. Among other actions they led a series of '*caravanas*' or large-scale displacements of indigenous populations to the cities, where they encamped and made their claims. In February 2009, the Supreme Court of Justice, in response to a claim presented in 2008 by the indigenous communities and peasants of the departments of San Martín, Orán, Rivadavia and Santa Victoria in Salta, ordered suspension of a deforestation project authorized the previous year. In ordering this suspension the court invoked the precautionary principle set out in Article 4 of the Ley General del Ambiente, No. 25,675.

At this time the Kolla communities of Salta organized the *Coordinadora de Organizaciones Kollas Autónomas*, which included virtually all the communities in the province of Qullamarka, thus strengthening the resistance and their protest actions for their territorial rights and autonomy. This permitted them to take action in defence of their livelihoods, including the deforestation of their territories. Once the Supreme Court presented its ruling the Qullamarka also denounced the advance of mining in their territory, repudiating the pillage of resources and contamination of the commons. The Qullamarka in this struggle defended a territory of more than a million hectares against diverse projects, including mining and tourism, that involve what Harvey has termed a process of 'accumulation by dispossession' as well as a plundering of the territory's wealth of natural resources. In fighting for its customary rights and communal title to the land the Qullamarka have also had to contend with the interventions of the state and NGOs (Giarracca & Teubal: 2014).

Giarracca and Teubal (2014) document similar struggles in Chaco and Formosa, where communities of the Qom, Wichí and Mocoví led important mobilizations for the purpose of instigating a public debate over the situation affecting the indigenous populations in these provinces, namely their displacement in a context of landgrabbing and deforestation. In a context in which important and profound transformations are taking place in social structures and productive systems access to land has become one of the main claims structuring the historical demands of these and other indigenous communities in the country.

The struggles of the Mapuche ('people of the land'), who straddle the border between Argentina and Chile in the south of both countries warrant special consideration. These indigenous communities have organized themselves in recent decades in order to recuperate their lands and defend their territorial and customary land rights. Thie border area is a region with a wide biodiversity, including minerals and petroleum, and consequently it has been the object of diverse confrontations with economic interest groups that are the main agents of plunder and dispossession in the territory. These groups act with the complicity of the provincial government, which are not disposed to protect the communities or to regulate the indiscriminate sale and concession of lands and goods.

As a result of the complicity of government officials with the landgrabbers and extractive capitalists, and because of the futility and delay involved in legal procedures for restitution of their territory, a number of communities have taken direct action, provoking class conflict over access to the commons. Giarracca and Teubal make reference to several noteworthy landmarks in this regard. In the mid-1990s, 42,000 hectares were recovered in the locality of Pulmarí in the province of Neuquén after a long process of land occupation and legal actions that lasted over a decade. The conflict concerned the continuing nonfulfillment of a statute, according to which the *Corporación Interestadual Pulmarí* (which included national and provincial authorities as well as representatives of the Mapuche) was to take charge of the combined administration of a parcel of land of 110,000 hectares. Also in Neuquén the Mapuche have opposed and continue to resist the activities of oil companies in their territory, both the Spanish-owned Repsol-YPF and now the nationalized YPF, mostly because of their use of new technologies that are even more contaminating and destructive than fracking.

Another paradigmatic case study documented by Giarracca and Teubal concerns the Pillán Mahuiza community in the province of Chubut in its confrontation with the Spanish corporation Santander. This corporation planned to construct a series of dams on the river Carrenleufu, which would flood 11,000 hectares of land in an area with much biodiversity and some communities.

The construction of these dams would have a decidedly negative impact on the population and communities that live there and work the land, and that would have to be relocated, resulting in material and cultural dispossession. To provoke these communities to abandon their territory and the struggle for their territorial rights the companies and the corrupt officials in their pay and service have used a variety of tactics, including intimidation with threats and abuses, bribes and assassination.[38]

Giarracca and Teubal (2014) have studied a number of cases of extractive capitalism, colonialism and imperialism—and the struggles engendered by the activities involved in the process of capitalist development. However, Brazil provides an even more advanced setting for a series of case studies into this process and associated struggles. One of these cases is set in the Brazilian state of Mato Grosso do Sul, home to a small number of tribal and farming communities with ancestral rights to a vast territory found on a new but rapidly expanding frontier for extractive capital and agribusiness. In their resistance against the incursions of extractive capital (big landowning 'farmers and agribusiness corporations') into their territory a number of tribal groups and communities have fought back by occupying farms and ranches set up by these agrarian capitalists (Glusing, 2014). In occupying the farms and ranches these groups are fighting for their land, protecting the borders of their reservations, resisting the construction of hydroelectric power plants in their regions and protesting against the advance of the agricultural industry, which is destroying their homeland.

What is particularly instructive about this case of resistance by the Terena tribal group is how that it illustrates so clearly the relation between capital and the state in the development process of extractive capital in Brazil, as well as (more concretely) the power of the big farmers lobby and the subrdination of the PT regime under Rousseff to the large landowning agrarian elite who constitute a decisive power bloc in the legislative assembly and have a virtual stranglehold over the regime's agricultural policy.[39]

---

38 No systematic studies have been conducted on the range of tactics used in this struggle on the global commons and indigenous territory but there is considerable anecdotal evidence that the tactics used in similar and related struggles between the mining companies of global capital and the local indigenous communities in Peru that are negatively impacted by their operations are also in play in Argentina. On these tactics of struggle, and the tactics that can be used by the indigenous communities in response, see Zorilla (2009).

39 The government, meanwhile, has capitulated to the farm lobby. When President Dilma Rousseff visited Mato Grosso do Sul in April 2013 the farmers booed her because of her

The occupations themselves are a reaction to the ruthless treatment of Brazil's indigenous peoples over the years of 'accumulation by dispossession'.[40] Thirteen years ago (the year 2000, in which the government reaffirmed its historic commitment to right the wrongs perpetrated against the country's indigenous peoples), the government promised to turn over a ranch's 145 square kilometers (56 square miles) of land to the indigenous tribes that had been expelled from its use.[41] But the 'farmer' affected used a series of legal manoeuvres to delay the transfer—until the indigenous people lost patience. With the help of social networking tool Facebook, they gathered together more than 1000 members of their tribe from the surrounding region and invaded the farm in the early morning of May 15, wielding homemade explosives, swinging wooden clubs and waving spears. Private security guards fired into the air, but they were vastly outnumbered. Together with the rancher's wife, family and members of the staff, they took refuge in the house. After tough negotiations, the owners were allowed to leave. The police moved in with live ammunition 15 days later. One of the occupiers was shot to death and another one was wounded, but the indigenous people are not giving up. Since then, the Terena have built a village on the grounds of Fazenda Buriti. They are now farming the fields, planting manioc and corn; some are driving around in the farmer's tractors but all of them have declared themselves ready to defend their hard-fought gains.

---

announced plans to expand the reservation system for indigenous populations whose reseves of land in many cases are to small even for subsistence. However soon Rousseff completed a radical shift on indigenous policy by freezing the planned reservation expansions, capitulating to the farm lobby. In contrast, she has never met with lawmakers who represent the indigenous peoples, who have no lobby.

40   This 'accumualtion by dispossession' process has been decades in the making but in the context of a growing world demand for energy and agro-food products, including beef, factory farms have expanded their cropland in Mato Grosso do Sul by more than 30 percent in the last four years alone. The state has some of the most fertile soil in the country, another reason for the virulence of the conflict. The resistance of the more numerous Guarini has not been as virulent in part because the land at issue in their struggle is not as fertile, and in part because they have been pushed into more marginal land that they have tried to farm or work productively.

41   The land used to belong to Paraguay, until Brazil annexed it in 1870. At the time, the government drew the new border straight through ethnic communities, and it had the indigenous people rounded up like cattle and locked away on reservations. Then it divided up the land among white settlers. Once the military dictatorship ended in the mid-1980s, Brazil received a new, democratic constitution, which awarded the indigenous peoples the rights to the regions from which they had been expelled. But the land, once covered by jungles, now consists of soybean and sugarcane plantations as well as grazing land for cattle.

The Peasantry

In their documentation of the land struggle in Argentina Giarracca and Teubal (2014) make particular reference to the work of several organizations involved in the *Mesa Nacional de Organizaciones de Productores Familiares*, and that currently form part of the *Movimiento Nacional Campesino Indígena* (MNCI). These organizations, they note, have employed tactics such as preventing evictions in diverse actions to reclaim the land and their territories, as well as direct confrontations with soy producers and land invaders. Within the movement it appears that several organizations are particularly active, including the *Movimiento Campesino de Santiago del Estero-Vía Campesina*, the *Movimiento Campesino de Córdoba, the Unión de Trabajadores Sin Tierra* (Mendoza), the *Red Puna (Jujuy) and the Encuentro Calchaquí*. Several urban organizations in Buenos Aires and Rosario that are close to regional peasant organizations and movements such as the *Coordinadora Latinoamericana de Organizaciones del Campo* (CLOC) and *Vía Campesina* are also incorporated into the movement and actively participate in the struggle, coordinating their actions and movilizations.

Their main propositions and demands of these organizations and movements are:

- an effective and comprehensive agrarian reform, to democratize the control over the means of production and redress the problem of poverty in the countryside and the city;
- food sovereignty, in opposition to agribusiness and defense of a productive culture that provides healthy food for the population, by means of adhenrecne to the principles of *comercio justo* (fair trade);
- the respect of peasant and indigenous territorial rights and terriories, recognizing community use and ownership of land as well as the commons;
- respect of the 'social function' of land, which implies respect for the biodiversity of the environment and the social rights of workers, and food production in the context of the right to a dignified life; and
- respect for the collective organizations of peasant famers and indigenous communities, such as the *Coordinadora de Comunidades Indígenas y Trabajadores Rurales de Argentina*.

The latter organization is the result of the amalgamation of different organizations with different collective identities but who all form part of CLOC, such as the *Consejo Asesor Indígena, the Unión de Campesinos Poriajhú* (in Chaco) and the *Campamento de Trabajo* (Córdoba). As with the organizations mentioned above the land struggle and confrontations with agribusiness are the main aspects of their protests and resistance.

As for the land struggle the main issue over the years has been land reform—redistribution of the land, which in most of Latin America is highly skewed in terms of ownership.[42] Over the past decades, especially in the 1960s and 1970s, this structure led to large waves of rural migrants, peasant farmers forced to abandon their communities and agriculture, and move to the cities in search for a better way of life. It also led to and fed a growing movement of rural landless workers in Argentina as well as Bolivia modelled on the Brazilian example. Another option exercised by these landless 'peasants' or 'rural landless workers', an alternative to both outmigration and the land struggle, has been to rebuild local food markets that have been decimated by decades of capitalist development and nefarious US trade and aid policies.

In this context mention can also be made of the resurgence of the *Ligas Agrarias* (Agrarian Leagues), which is intent on recapturing the experiences of the peasant movement in the 1970s, an experience shared with peasants in Brazil. This movement is promoted by the ex-leaders of the previous *Ligas Agrarias* in the provinces of Chaco, Santa Fe and Corrientes. The structure assumes a regional character and is inserted into national organizations that coordinate peasant action. This organization has established itself as a civic association and some of its members occupy public office.

Finally, worth mentioning—or at least Giarracca and Teubal do so—is the *Asamblea Campesina e Indígena del Norte Argentino* (ACINA), a coordinating body and assembly of diverse peasant and indigenous organization in Argentina's North formed in 2006. Some of the organizations brought together by ACINA, with extensive experience of land and class struggles dating back to the 1980s, also participate in the *Frente Nacional Campesino*, a national front of peasants formed in the class struggle for land. The presence of powerful groups such as the *Unión de Pequeños Productores del Chaco*, as well as the *Mesa de Organizaciones de Pequeños Productores del Chaco*, which integrates all the organizations of the province, is also significant. The importance of ACINA is in its creation of a regional organizational and political space that contributes to the generation of other organizations and relationships among

---

42   The structure of social inequality in regard to land ownership, in which a majority of landholdings are concentrated and owned by a small class of big landowners, while most have been rendered landless or near-landless, or forced to eke out a precarious existence in production for local food markets, is the subject of a voluminous literature. There is a similarly voluminous literature on the associated or resulting land struggle—the struggle for land reform (see Moyo & Yeros, 2005).

indigenous communities and peasant organizations at the provincial and national level.

Conclusion

Our analysis of the contemporary dynamics of agrarian extractivism—land-grabbing for energy, minerals, and metals, and agrofood—leads us to conclude that Henry Bernstein (2010: 82–84) was substantially correct in the propositions that he established regarding the impact of globalization on agriculture and the agrarian question today. These propositions are that:

1. the policy of trade liberalization, implemented within the framework of the Washington Consensus, has led to a shift in global trade patterns of agricultural commodities (increased south–north flows);
2. futures trading in agricultural commodities, i.e. 'speculation spurred by financialization', has resulted in an increase in the price of agrofood products on different markets;[43]
3. the removal of subsidies and other forms of support to small farmers in the south together with the promotion of 'export platforms' (especially of animal feeds and high-value commodities) and large-scale foreign investment in the acquisition of land for extractive purposes;
4. the increasing concentration of global corporations in both agri-input and agro-food industries, marked by mergers and acquisitions and the economic power of fewer corporations commanding larger market shares;
5. introduction of new organizational technologies deployed by these corporations along commodity chains from farming (harvesting and feeding) to retail distribution (the 'supermarket revolution');
6. the push by these corporations to patent intellectual property rights in genetic material, particularly as regards terminator seeds and other genetically modified products, with a devastating impact on the environment, the health of the population, biodiversity in agricultural production, rural livelihoods based on small-scale production and farming,

---

43   Speculative investments in financial derivatives in 1998 exceeded by a factor of 2.4 the nominal value of global production; by 2002 the ratio of these speculative investments to global production was 4.3: 1, and in 2006 it went up to 11.7:1 before falling slightly to 10.5:1 by the end of 2009. In 2012 this ratio was reduced to 8.9:1 de 2012 and by mid-2013 it was 8.6: 1 (Bank for International Settlements).

and access of small family farmers and peasants to seeds, and food security;

7.   a new technical frontier of engineering plant and animal genetic material (genetically modified organisms or GMOs), together with specialized monoculture, has contributed to a significant loss of biodiversity;

8.   a new profit frontier of agrofuel production, dominated by agribusiness corporations, with a consequent loss of food security and food sovereignty;

9.   the negative health consequences of the corporate agribusiness model of agriculture and the rising level of toxic chemicals in 'industrially grown and processed' foods—contributing to a trend toward nutritional diet deficiencies, obesity-related illness, and growing hunger and malnutrition; and

10. the environmental costs of the industrialization of food farming, including increased levels of fossil-fuel use and their carbon emissions.

Another conclusion we draw from our analysis of the dynamics of agricultural extractivism, a conclusion that Bernstein might have but did not reach, is that each twist and turn in the capitalist development process generates different forces of resistance, and that in the current context the dynamics of class struggle have shifted from the demand for land reform and higher wages/ improved working conditions, and resistance against the neoliberal policy agenda, towards a defence of the commons (of land, water and natural resources) and an organised resistance against the socioenvironmental impacts of extractive capitalism—including environmental degradation and forced abandonment. The class struggle, in short, has moved away from workplaces to the streets and in some contexts the sites of extractive operations and the communities that are directly and negatively affected by these operations.

CHAPTER 4

Trade and Development in an Era of Extractive Imperialism

Capitalism is a system in crisis. An oft-repeated truism, but what does it mean—beyond a succession of different phases of capitalist development in which the system is pushed to the limits of its capacity to expand the forces of production and then restructured by mobilizing the forces of change released by the crisis?[1] Take the post-World War II process of capitalist development, which has been periodised as an era of state-led development celebrated by historians as the 'golden age of capitalism' (two decades of unprecedented rapid economic growth that came to an end with a system-wide production crisis at the turn into the 1970s), followed by a decade of restructuring and transition to what has been described as a 'brief history of neoliberalism',[2] the beginnings of which can be traced back to the early 1980s in conditions of a fiscal crisis of the capitalist state attributed by conservatives to the excessive costs of the social and development programs of the liberal reformist development state; (ii) a matrix of forces released by actions taken to find a way out of the crisis and restructure the system; and (iii) a new world order based on market fundamentalism and the Washington Consensus[3] regarding the virtues of free market capitalism and the 'structural reforms' needed to bring it about.

1   There are a number of theories regarding the propensity of capitalism towards crisis, including the proposition of a built-in tendency for the average rate of profits to fall, which sets up
a cyclical pattern of development induced by the efforts of capitalists to offset this tendency,
and the associated ideas of a tendency towards overproduction (vis-à-vis the market) or
underconsumption (due to lack of purchasing power). The dominant idea, however, is that a
systemic crisis is normally not terminal, but is in fact functional for the system in bringing
about needed periodical 'restructuring' that weeds out inefficient operators. The one idea
that can be added is that crisis, whether systemic or merely financial, weakens the institutional structure of the system, generating forces of change that can be mobilised in different
directions, to the right or the left.
2   The neoliberal doctrine of the virtues of free market capitalism and the evils of government
intervention was elaborated by a group of intellectuals, mostly economists, associated with
the Mont Pelerin Society, a thought collective founded on the initiative of Friedrich Hayek, a
classical liberal and advocate of 'Austrian economics' back in the late 1940s. In 1947 Hayek
invited 39 scholars, mostly economists, with some historians and philosophers, were invited
to gather to discuss the dangers facing 'civilization' (i.e. capitalism and democracy).
3   This consensus was famously summed up by Williamson (1990) in the form of a 10-point
program of structural reforms in macroeconomic policy.

This chapter will delineate the forces of change associated with the new geoeconomics of capital in Latin America. The argument can be summed up in the proposition that capitalist development in this context resulted in the construction of three alternative economic models, each used to mobilize forces of change in one direction or the other, each associated with a particular type of polity and policy regime, and a particular system for arranging and managing trade and investments as well as relations with US power and the agencies of global capital.

The argument is constructed as follows. First we outline the contours of capitalist development within the institutional and policy framework of the neoliberal world order, with a focus on the economic model used by governments as a template and script for the structural reforms mandated by the Washington consensus.[4] Here it is argued that the structural reforms implemented in accordance with the neoliberal agenda (privatization, financial and trade liberalization, market deregulation, administrative decentralization) resulted in, inter alia, a massive inflow of global capital liberated from the regulatory constraints of the developmental state. This capital took the predominant form of FDI directed towards non-traditional or modern manufacturing, high-tech information-rich services, and natural resource extraction. Other outcomes included the project of a free trade regime designed to deepen and extend the financial and trade liberalization process, and a process of uneven capitalist development that was materialized in the construction of a model to promote development (inclusive growth: boosting economic growth while reducing extreme poverty) and conduct international relations of trade and investment within the policy framework of the new world order. This model is associated with projects for a North American Free Trade Area (NAFTA), which took effect in January 1994, and then, close to a decade on (2003), the project to establish a Free Trade Area for the Americas (FTAA), which was defeated by an anti-imperialist alliance, and more recently (in 2010) the Pacific Alliance (PA) that has brought together Chile, which hitherto had avoided joining any regional integration project, with Peru, Colombia and Mexico, in a regional alliance of neoliberal regimes on the Pacific coast aligned with the US in a series of bilateral trade arrangements. The PA, a nascent regional economic

---

4 As is well known the mechanism use to enforce this agenda was the external debt contracted by governments in the region, particularly Mexico, Argentina and Brazil, but also Chile. The first governments that came under this structural adjustment regime were Mexico and Jamaica but by the end of the decade, in a short space of only six years, all but four governments in the region were (Argentina, Brazil, Peru, and Venezuela). Venezuela to some extent was shielded from these pressures because of its abundant reserves of oil.

integration bloc formed less than three years ago but in which up to 92 per cent of trade has been liberalized (tariff free), is the world's seventh-largest recipient of FDI, receiving USD 71 billion in 2012, much of it attracted by the profit making opportunities provided by the most liberal regime for resource extraction in the mining sector (in the case of Mexico, zero royalties and an effective tax rate of 1.2 percent on the value of exported minerals).[5]

The second part of the chapter elaborates on the outcome of these developments in the 1990s, with a third cycle of neoliberal structural reforms and a broad popular movement of resistance against the neoliberal policy agenda.[6] Here it is argued that the neoliberal 'structural reform' process not only failed to deliver on the promise of economic growth but it generated unsustainable conditions of inequality and poverty and a level of social discontent that threatened to destabilise the political system of neoliberal regimes, leading to governability concerns[7] as well as the construction of a model for another more sustainable form of development and an alternative trade regime.

---

5   In his latest report, the Auditor General of Mexico, according to the investigative journalist Francisco Bárcenas (2012: 31), put his finger on the ulcer that has caused Mexico to bleed minerals profusely over the years. The auditor established that the fees paid by the mining companies, 70% of which are Canadian, for their concessions to mine minerals are below the costs of the administrative procedures. The auditor's report reads: 'The amount of the fees currently paid is symbolic and contrasts with the volumes extracted from the non-renewable mineral resources, since their value is well above the concession fees charged by the State over, as observed in the period 2005 to 2010, when the value of production amounted to [USD 46 billion] and the fees charged were only [USD 543.4 million], some 1.2 per cent of the first'.

6   Actually it was the third rather than second cycle of neoliberal reforms in that the first cycle, which many associate with Thatcher, Reagan and the neoconservative counterrevolution and the 'new world order' in the 1980s, was initiated under the military regimes installed in Chile, Argentina and Uruguay in the 1970s. In most accounts of this and subsequent cycles of neoliberal free market fundamentalist 'structural reform' the role of Washington and US imperialism is downplayed.

7   Expressions of this concern included Karl (2000) and Kapstein, both of whom were concerned that the excessive inequalities and growing poverty brought about by the 'forces of economic freedom' under the Washington Consensus would incubate new forms of resistance that would destabilise the fragile democracies and neoliberal policy regimes formed in the process. A more recent expression of the same concern, undoubtedly a factor in the thinking behind the post-Washington Consensus, is provided in a report commissioned by the US National Council on Intelligence (NCI). According to this report the main threat towards security in the region is posed by the failure of governments to alleviate extreme poverty in spite of 'the greater integration into the global economy in the past decade' (National Council on Intelligence (2004: 78.) This failure, the Report adds, could spark regime- and system-destabilising 'populism and radical indigenous action'.

The result was a new consensus on the need to bring the state back into the development process and move towards a more inclusive form of development—what would take shape and become known as the 'new developmentalism' (Bresser-Pereira, 2006, 2007, 2009).[8]

Development in these conditions also took form as a project taken on by some governments to realign their international relations of trade and investment, resulting in a rejection of the neoliberal model of free market capitalism and the construction of alternative trade schemes focused on expanding intraregional trade and regional integration, as well as diversifying trade relations in a global context, and breaking out of the orbit of US power. This project took a number of forms, including in particular, Mercosur, an alternative trade scheme that bound together Argentina and Brazil,[9] two of the region's largest economies, with Uruguay and Paraguay, two of the region's smallest, into what would become the world's fourth largest trading if not integrated economic bloc and what some regarded as 'the most progressive trade integration scheme in the developing world' (Paiva & Gazel, 2003: 117).

We then turn towards recent developments under changes in the world economy that included a reconfiguration of economic power and a realignment of international relations of trade, and a growing demand for unprocessed natural resources that provoked a 'primary commodities boom' and led a number of countries in South America to turn back towards an extractivist strategy of national development. Here it is argued that these and other changing conditions (such as widespread rejection of the neoliberal model) led to the formation of a post-neoliberal state and the search for a new economic model, as well as the construction of an alternative trade and investment regime (ALBA)[10] designed for 'another world' beyond capitalism as well as a neoliberalism.

---

8   Unlike the strategy and models associated with the developmental state from the 1950s to the 70s the post-Washington Consensus on the need to 'bring the state back in' was concerned not to re-establish the regulatory and interventionist developmental state but to secure 'a better balance between state and market'. The economic model and development paradigm associated with this school of thought promoted an extractivist strategy of national development (the extraction and development of natural resources) rather than industrial development strategy based on the exploitation of surplus agricultural labour.

9   Bolivia, Chile, Colombia, Ecuador, Guyana, Peru and Suriname currently have associate member status.

10   Alianza Bolivariana de los Pueblos de America. When the project was launched 'Alianza' (Alliance) was framed as 'Alternative'.

The concluding section of the argument points towards the uneasy coexistence in Latin America today of three different types of political regime, each associated with a distinct economic model and a particular system for organizing international relations of trade and investment. We conclude with an assessment of the correlation of forces engaged in the development process related to these three models and a brief discussion of the pitfalls and challenges presented by extractivism as a strategy of national development—a strategy common to each of the three models used to organise production and trade in Latin America today.

Capitalist Development in the New World Order: The Neoliberal Model

The neoliberal world order was constructed in the early 1980s under conditions of a fiscal crisis in the north and a debt crisis in the south[11] and within the framework of what has been described as the 'Washington Consensus' on the virtues of and need for free market capitalism. This new world order was designed with the aim of reactivating the accumulation (or economic growth) process and liberating the 'forces of economic freedom' (the market, private enterprise) from the regulatory constraints and excessive costs of the developmental state. The means of bringing about this new world order (rules to govern international relations of trade and investment) and globalization process was a program of 'structural reforms', which was designed to open up and adjust the economies in the region to the forces operating in the world economy, namely, privatization (and denationalization) of state enterprises, financial and trade liberalisation, and deregulation of capital and product (and labour) markets. These reforms also implied and entailed downsizing of the state in regard to its role in the economy and the responsibility for economic production and social development, and administrative decentralization—to

---

11   The response of different governments and international organisations in the 1970s was to restructure a way out of the systemic production crisis, but it was not until the 1980s that the conditions for a definitive restructuring of the system became available, and the context for this restructuring process (a restructuring of macroeconomic policy) was provided by the fiscal crisis and the external debt crisis. The first provided conditions of a conservative counterrevolution that would bring to power regimes committed to an entirely different institutional and policy framework based on the neoliberal model designed to free the market and other 'forces of economic freedom' from the regulatory constraints of the development state.

generate a more democratic form of governance, allowing for greater social participation, i.e. the engagement of civil society in the responsibility for governance and promoting social development.

The neoliberal reform agenda was designed as a means of integrating economies in the region into a global economic system governed by the same rules of free trade and marked by increasing interdependence, liberalization, and competition for investments. The purpose or stated aim of this 'globalization' agenda was to reactivate the capital accumulation process and to expand the forces of production to the mutual benefit of all countries participating in the process, presented by advocates as the only way forward. 'There is no alternative', Margaret Thatcher was notoriously quoted to have stated.

Needless to say, as with so many development processes the consequences of actions taken in pursuit of this idea diverged widely from the purported goal and stated objectives. In the case of Washington Consensus the process set in motion by means of the implicated 'structural reforms' (privatization, liberalisation, deregulation, decentralization) is clear as regards its dynamics and outcomes, having been subject to careful scrutiny and close study in diverse contexts (Petras & Veltmeyer, 2001, 2011; Veltmeyer & Petras, 2014). Outcomes include (i) new inflows of capital in the form of FDI directed towards a) nontraditional manufacturing, b) high-tech services, and natural resource extraction; (ii) construction of a free trade regime to deepen and extend the financial and trade liberalization process; (iii) wholesale destruction of the productive forces in both agriculture and industry, exacerbating a deep agricultural crisis and accelerating the resulting rural–urban migration process, which was constructed by theorists of development as a pathway out of rural poverty (labour, migration); (iv) formation of an 'informal sector' of the urban economy in which rural migrants are forced to work 'on their own account' in the streets rather than in factories and shops, industrial plants and offices for wages or a salary; (v) a 'decade lost to development' (i.e. productive investment), with increasing levels of inequality in the distribution of wealth and income, and (vi) the generation of new (urban) forms of poverty, which, according to ECLAC, increased the overall 'official' poverty rate from somewhere around 40 to 48 percent; and the generation of widespread protests against IMF-mandated austerity measures and neoliberal reforms, as well as new forces of resistance mobilized by a new generation of social movements.

The aim of the World Bank's 'structural adjustment program' and the associated neoliberal agenda was to pave the way for an expansion and increased operations of capital, particularly in the form of FDI, the bearers of which were the MNCs that dominate international trade in goods and services. Regarding this wave of investment and associated capital flows see the discussion below. There are four different types of FDI depending on the reasons for a firm to invest abroad, namely: (i) resource-seeking capital used to secure access to low-cost labour or natural resources; (ii) market-seeking capital used to open or penetrate new markets, or maintain already existing ones; (iii) efficiency-seeking capital to reconstruct existing production by taking advantage of a lower cost structure in the host economy or economies of scale; and (iv) strategic asset-seeking capital used to enable the MNCs to protect or develop their ownership specific advantage—to acquire the assets of existing firms.

The latter was reflected in the acquisition of state enterprises put up for sale by governments in the privatization agenda (to revert the nationalization policy of the 1960s and 1970s). It is estimated that at least 30 percent of the inflows of private capital in the 1990s—from 1990 to 1996 when the inflow of FDI increased sixfold and Latin America was converted into a major destination point for asset-seeking capital—was unproductive in that it did not entail the transfer of technology, simply the purchase of already existing assets, which led to the denationalization of key firms and entire sectors such as banking in Mexico, where all of the country's big banks except one were acquired by foreign firms.

The inflow of both productive and unproductive flows of investment capital, and the privatization and denationalization of firms and economic enterprises with the potential to expand market share or compete on the world market, were facilitated by policies pursued under the Washington Consensus within the framework of the new world order.

In addition to the destruction of significant forces of production in industry and agriculture, the consequences of an increased orientation of production towards the world market included a reduction in intra-regional trade as well as an expansion of 'unequal exchange' on a north–south axis. Other outcomes included an expansion of the market for US-produced goods and services, leading to an overall favourable trade surplus of the US with economies in the region, allowing the government to balance the growing deficit on its trading account with economies in other regions of the world economy.

To further expand this market, the US government promoted a policy of 'open regionalism' together with a scheme (NAFTA) designed to integrate the three North American economies (the US, Canada and Mexico), and then to further integrate them into a continental-scale free trade zone: the Free Trade Area of the Americas (FTAA), a project that in 2003 fell victim to diverse forces of anti-imperialist resistance as well as the opposition of governments such as Brazil concerned to counter the power of the US to impose an arrangement serving US economic interests and to advance the economic interests of the country's agro-export agri-business elite.[12] Thwarted in its efforts to impose a continental wide free trade zone[13] the US subsequently turned towards a strategy of a la carte bilateral agreements with different governments in the region, creating a kind of hub-and-spoke arrangement of trade agreements.

The New Developmentalism: Capitalism under the Post-Washington Consensus

Inspired by the ideas of Raúl Prebisch, first Secretary General, of the United Nations' Economic Commission for Latin America (ECLA), a number of regional integration initiatives were made in the 1960s within the framework of an industrial policy based on an 'import substitution' approach to industrialization. The creation of the Latin American Free Trade Association (LAFTA) was supposed to surmount the inherent scale limitations of the small domestic markets while allowing industries to become competitive on a regional level. But by 1980, on the LAFTA had been replaced by the less ambitious Latin American Integration Association (LAIA, *Span. ALADI*), which was largely structured around bilateral trade preferences.

Partly due to the limited progress on LAFTA's economic front six of LAFTA's eleven members (Bolivia, Colombia, Ecuador, Peru, Chile and later Venezuela)

---

12   US plans to impose a NAFTA-style free trade deal on the entirety of the Western hemisphere were defeated in Miami in November 2003 at a Ministerial meeting for the FTAA. Many observers attributed the defeat of US plans to Brazil having outmanoeuvered the US in negotiations over the terms of the proposed free trade agreement. However, as pointed out by Lori Wallach, director of Public Citizen's Global Trade Watch, 'powerful social movements in Latin America against the FTAA...made it impossible for those governments to agree to a full NAFTA expansion' (Weismann, 2003). Even so, the Latin American trade ministers were also unwilling to succumb to imperialist pressures to adhere to proposals designed to advance and protect the interests of American corporations in areas such as intellectual property rights, investment rules and US agriculture, while surrendering the capacity of Latin American governments to protect the public sector of their economies [On this see 'NAFTA's Investor Rights: A Corporate Dream, a Citizen's Nightmare', *Multinational Monitor*, April 2001]; and squash the ability of FTAA countries to protect public services from demands for privatization [see 'Serving Up the Commons', Multinational Monitor, April 2001].

13   A key sticking point for Brazil in the FTAA negotiations was the refusal of the US to negotiate agricultural issues of concern to Brazil and other countries in the region. US negotiators insisted that said these issues had to be handled at the WTO, where they could be negotiated as well with the EU and Japan. But Brazil argued that if agriculture is a WTO issue, then so is intellectual property and other controversial issues.

established an intra-regional trade bloc: the Andean Pact. Although very ambitious on the political front, including the institution of supra-national organizations, the backing out of Chile in 1976 signalled the beginning of an internal
crisis. Shortly afterwards, although it still continues to exist in some form
(headquartered in Peru), in condition of a deep recession the bloc virtually fell
apart—another casualty of the new world order. Further sub-regional arrangements were created in Central America but given the political and military
conflicts that cast a huge shadow over the CACM, with little success. At the
same time in the Caribbean a proposal to establish a common market was
advanced in the form of CARICOM, but it was hindered by the reluctance of
member states to reduce trade barriers. Finally, in conditions of the 'new world
order' these diverse regional integration schemes finally fell apart, a development that was reflected in a severe contraction of intra-regional trade. By the
end of the decade (the 1980s) less than 20 percent of trade in regionally produced goods and services took place among member states in the region.

The 1990s has been viewed both as the 'golden age of US imperialism'—in
regard to the advance of US capital and the hold of Washington over the policy
regime adopted by most governments in the region[14]—and a period in which
a popular movement of indigenous communities, landless rural workers and
peasant farmers, halted the advance of capital and the neoliberal agenda of
governments in the region. Both views are undoubtedly correct in pointing
towards forces evidently in play. However, neither view captures an essential
feature of the decade: the transition towards a new consensus on the need for
a different development strategy and a new economic model. It was evident
that the neoliberal 'structural reform' process had not only failed to deliver on
the promise of economic growth but it generated a destabilising level of social
discontent and widespread opposition to the neoliberal policy regime. The
result, or perceived solution, was the construction of a new consensus on the
need to bring the state back into the development process, and for a more
inclusive form of development—what would become known as the 'new

---

14   By the end of the 1980s all but four major countries in the region had succumbed to the
      Washington Consensus, but three of these countries—Argentina, Brazil and Peru—were
      integrated into the globalization process as well as the orbit of US power. At the same
      time, the neoliberal reform agenda was extended in the form of the agricultural modern-
      ization law adopted by governments in Mexico and elsewhere to promote a 'market-
      assisted' land reform process, legislation (abolition or reduction of royalties on the
      extraction of minerals and metals) designed to attract resource-seeking private invest-
      ment, and labour market reform (increased flexibility, removal of measures designed to
      protect public sector employment.

developmentalism'. However, this was only a part of the problem. Another part was an economy geared to US economic and geopolitical interests (increased market share, accessing and mobilizing the region's wealth of human and natural resources), dependence on the investments and operations of global capital, and subjection to the power of the multinational corporations that dominated the world market. A third problem faced by many governments at the time in their concern to advance economic and social development was the power of the imperial state behind these corporations. Imperialism is at issue in the concern and efforts of so many governments to restructure their international relations of trade and investment, and reduce their dependence on trade with the US.

Washington Consensus policies in the 1980s promoted inter-regional trade on a south–north axis rather than intra-regional trade. This was reflected in a reduction of intra-regional trade and the growth of trade along a north–south nexus. But the 1990s saw the emergence and a move towards what ECLAC economists in the context of a broader globalization process termed the 'new regionalism'—expanding intra-regional trade on the basis of existing intra-regional trade blocs but integrating these blocs into the global economy. In this context ECLAC, formerly an exponent of an industrialization policy based on state intervention in the form of subsidies, protectionism and regulated markets, declared itself a proponent of 'open regionalism' within a global economy marked by increasing interdependency, liberalization, and competition for investments. Accompanied by domestic market-oriented reforms in the form of privatization, deregulation and balanced budgets ('stabilization'), Open Regionalism implied the orientation of production towards both inter- and intra-regional forms of international rather than local markets—a reliance on international trade rather than the domestic market as the fundamental engine of economic growth, a strategy that profoundly reshaped the political-economic landscape in the region but led to less rather than more intra-regional trade.

The most important expression of this open regionalism is Mercosur, an arrangement that binds together four countries in the Southern cone of South America (Argentina, Brazil, Paraguay and Uruguay) into a regional trade scheme that encompasses 47 percent of Latin America's population, representing more than half of its GDP.[15] Although Mercosur has evolved as a

---

15   In 2004, intraregional commerce in Mercosur and the Andean Community constituted
      12.9 and 10.4 % of total trade, respectively. This is in contrast to what they export
      to other Latin American nations (15.4 and 16.8%), the US (18.3 and 46.6%), and the EU
      (23.0 and 11.0%).

predominantly commercial initiative, based on the successful implementation of a trade liberalization program, it has gradually incorporated a variety of non-trade issues to its agenda. Referring to the inherent 'trade and cooperation nexus', which distinguishes its integration scheme from a pure free trade agreement, the bloc from the beginning sought to enhance regional cooperation in matters of technology transfer and industrial policy as well as a range of socio-political and developmental concerns such as education, justice, environment, energy, technology, health and foreign policy.

Addressing these issues were considered to be crucial for the establishment of a sense of community and a regional identity based on shared values and principles. To face and mitigate the societal impact of greater economic integration, Mercosur's Labour ministers proposed, only two months after the signing of the Asunción Treaty (1991), the creation of a *Social Charter* for Mercosur. The charter addressed labour aspects and improved working conditions, as well as issues of development and poverty alleviation (Ruiz-Dana, Goldschagg, Claro & Blanco (2007: 20). The decision to establish a structural fund of USD 100 million per year, to address the problem of asymmetries and inequalities within the bloc, was momentous. The main objective of this *Fund for Structural Convergence* (FOCEM) was to develop competitiveness; to encourage social cohesion, particularly in the smaller economies of Paraguay and Uruguay; to support the functioning of the institutional structure; and to strengthen the integration process. Nonetheless, the fund was clearly under-capitalized in consideration of the large number of people living below the poverty level in the Southern Cone (approximately 95 million, according to ECLAC 2003). Seeing that poverty is the outcome of the structure of social inequality in regard to both income and land rather than the effect of overall underdevelopment, FOCEM evidently did not address the crucial problem of national income inequality. In this Mercosur reflected the limitations of the post-Washington consensus—in viewing neoliberalism and social exclusion (extreme poverty) rather than capitalism and structured social inequalities in the distribution of income and land as the essential problem.[16]

---

16   These limitations and the thinking behind the post-Washington Consensus were clearly manifest in the address to the General Assembly of the United Nations given in October 2013 by President Mujica of Uruguay. The address was received as rather radical in its call for a free and classless society, but it is was evident that for Mujica capitalism was not the problem, not even inequality or social exclusion; the problem rather was self-exclusion and poverty for which the poor themselves rather than the system were held responsible.

Changing Dynamics of Foreign Investment in Latin America

As noted earlier the neoliberal reforms implemented in the 1980s as the price of admission into the new world order not only released the 'forces of economic freedom' from the regulatory constraints of the developmental state but generated a massive inflow of capital in search for profit-making opportunities related to assets, resources and markets. This was in the 1990s, which saw a sixfold increase in the inflows of capital in the form of FDI in the first four years of the decade and then another sharp increase from 1996 to 2001, which tripled, in less than 10 years, the foreign capital accumulated in the region in the form of foreign-company subsidiaries (ECLAC, 2012: 71).[17] Another major inflow occurred in the first decade of the new millennium, in conditions of a primary commodities boom that worldwide affected (benefitted?) primarily South America. In 2009 Latin America received 26 percent of the capital invested globally in mineral exploration and extraction. And according to the Metals Economics Group (MEG), a 2010 bonanza in world market prices led to another increase of 40 percent in investments related to mineral exploration and mining, with governments in the region, both neoliberal and post-neoliberal, competing fiercely for this capital.

The main targets for FDI in Latin America over the past two decades have been services (particularly banking and finance) and the natural resources sector—the exploration, extraction and exploitation of fossil and biofuel sources of energy, precious metals and industrial minerals, and agrofood products.[18]

---

17   The 'real FDI boom in Latin America and the Caribbean', according to ECLAC took place in the second half of the 1990s when 'many State-owned assets were privatized and many sectors, which until then had received little FDI, were opened up and deregulated. It was during this period that transnational corporations began to expand their role in the region's economies. Their level of influence held steady in the years immediately after the boom (between 2002 and 2009) and has recently started to trend slightly up again (ECLAC, 2012: 72).

18   The share of the extractive industries in global inward FDI stocks declined throughout the 1990s until the start of the current commodity boom in 2003, after which it recovered to about 9% in 2005 (Figure 4.1). The decline of the primary sector's share in global FDI has been due to its slower growth compared with FDI in manufacturing and services. In absolute terms, however, FDI in the primary sector has continued to grow: it increased in nominal terms nearly five times in the 1970s, 3.5 times in the 1980s, and four times from 1990 to 2005 (WIR 2005; annex Table A.I.9). The stock of FDI in extractive industries was estimated at $755 billion in 2005 (UNCTAD, 2011: Annex Table A.I.9).

In the previous era of state-led development FDI had predominantly served as a means of financing the capitalist development of industry and a process of 'productive transformation' (technological conversion and modernisation), which was reflected in the geoeconomics of global capital and the dynamics of FDI flows at the time. However, the new world order and two generations of neoliberal reforms changed and dramatically improved conditions for capital, opening up in Latin America the market for goods manufactured in the North (the US, Canada and Europe) and providing greater opportunities for resource-seeking capital—consolidating the role of Latin America as a source and supplier of natural resources and exporter of primary commodities, a role that was reflected in the flows of productive investment away from manufacturing and services towards the extractive industries (see Table 4.1).

The noted sectoral shift in the distribution of FDI was particularly evident and very pronounced in the wake of what has been described as a 'global financial crisis', a crisis that had relatively minimal repercussions in Latin America, so much so that some analysts would ask 'What crisis? (Porzecanski, 2009). In the wake of this crisis, the inflow of resource-seeking investments in 2008 reached unprecedented levels, accentuating the trend towards primarization in the context of the growing demand for energy, minerals, and foodstuffs for the industries and expanding middle classes of the emerging markets of China and the other BRIC countries. The scope of this primarization process, and the reliance of neoliberal and post-neoliberal regimes in South America on the export of primary commodities for foreign exchange and fiscal revenues, is evident in the data presented in Table 4.2.

At the turn into the new millennium the service sector still accounted for almost half of FDI inflows, but Table 4.3 points towards a steady and increasing flow of capital towards the natural resources sector in South America, especially

TABLE 4.1   *Percentage distribution of FDI by sector in Latin America*

	'00	'01	'02	'03	'04	'05	'06	'07	'08
Resources	10	12	12	11	12	13	12	15	30
Manufacturing	25	26	38	35	38	37	36	35	22
Services	60	61	51	48	46	48	51	49	47

SOURCE: ARELLANO (2010).

TABLE 4.2   *Exports of primary products, per cent of total exports*

	1990	2000	2004	2006	2008	2011
Argentina	70.9	67.6	71.2	68.2	69.1	68.0
Bolivia	95.3	72.3	86.7	89.8	92.8	95.5
Brazil	48.1	42.0	47.0	49.5	55.4	66.2
Chile	89.1	84.0	86.8	89.0	88.0	89.2
Colombia	74.9	65.9	62.9	64.4	68.5	82.5
Ecuador	97.7	89.9	90.7	90.4	91.3	92.0
Mexico	56.7	16.5	20.2	24.3	27.1	29.3
Peru	81.6	83.1	83.1	88.0	86.6	89.3
Venezuela	89.1	90.9	86.9	89.6	92.3	95.5
LA	66.9	40.9	46.2	51.3	56.7	60.9

SOURCE: ECLAC, *STATISTICAL YEARBOOK FOR LAC*, 2004: 138; 2012.

mining, over the past decade.[19] In 2006 it grew by 49 percent to reach USD 59 billion, exceeding the total FDI inflows of any year since the inception of economic liberalization in the 1990s (UNCTAD, 2011: Figure II.18). Income on FDI (i.e. profits on capital invested in the resource sector) was particularly high in Brazil and Chile, $14 billion and $20 billion respectively, leading to a surge in the share of retained earnings in total FDI inflows.[20] In the South American

---

19   According to ECLAC (2010) Canadian FDI in Latin America and the Caribbean is a recent phenomenon, taking place mainly in the 2000–2008 period. Since 1995, from 42 to 56% of the Canadian stock of FDI in developing countries has been concentrated in Latin America (42% of CAD60 billion in 2008). And most of this FDI to Latin America on an annual flow basis was in the natural resources sector—ranging from 10 to 12% from 2000 to 2007, but rising to 30% in 2008; and most of this 'natural resources seeking' FDI went to the mining sector, which accounts for up to 50% of mining exploration in the region—up from 30% a decade ago.

20   In the context of this investment, the region remains the world's leading source of metals: iron ore (24%), copper (21%), gold (18%), nickel (17%), zinc (21%), bauxite (27%) as well as silver (*Journal of Developing Societies*, 2012). Oil made up 83.4 percent of Venezuela's total exports from 2000 to 2004, copper represented 45% of Chile's exports, nickel 33% of Cuba's exports, and gold, copper and zinc 33% of Peru's. In 2006, Peru occupied second place in Latin America in the production of copper (fifth in the world) and was first in the production of gold and zinc, occupying respectively the sixth and third place in the world (De Echave, 2008: 323). Together with agricultural production, the extraction of oil, gas

TABLE 4.3   *Net inflows of FDI, by leading country in Latin America (US$ billion)*

	2000	2001	2002	2003	2004	2005	2006	2007	2008	2009	2010	2011	2012
Argentina	10.4	2.2	2.2	1.7	4.1	5.3	5.5	6.5	9.7	4.0	7.9	9.9	12.6
Bolivia	0.7	0.7	0.7	0.2	0.1	−0.3	0.3	0.4	0.5	0.4	0.6	0.9	1.1
Brazil	32.8	22.5	16.6	10.1	18.2	15.1	18.8	34.6	45.1	25.9	48.5	66.7	65.3
Chile	4.9	4.2	2.6	4.3	7.2	7.0	7.4	14.5	16.8	12.9	15.4	22.9	30.3
Colombia	2.4	2.5	2.1	1.7	3.0	1.0	6.7	9.1	10.6	7.1	6.8	13.4	15.8
Mexico	18.0	29.8	23.7	16.5	23.7	21.9	19.3	27.3	22.0	16.6	21.4	21.5	13.4
Peru	0.8	1.1	2.2	1.3	1.6	2.6	3.5	5.3	4.1	6.4	8.5	8.2	12.2
Venezuela	4.7	3.7	0.8	2.0	1.5	2.6	−0.6	0.7	1.7	−2.2	1.9	3.8	3.2

SOURCE: ECLAC (2012: 50).

countries for which data are available, income on FDI soared from an average of ten percent in 2000–03 to 61 percent in 2006.[21] Despite the global financial and economic crisis at the time, FDI flows towards Latin America and the Caribbean reached a record high in 2008 (US$128.3 billion), an extraordinary development considering that FDI flows worldwide at the time had shrunk by at least 15 percent. This countercyclical trend signalled the continuation of the primary commodities boom and the steady expansion of resource-seeking capital in the region.

The rapid expansion in the flow of FDI towards Latin America in the 1990s reflected the increased opportunities for capital accumulation provided by the neoliberal policy regimes in the region. In the new millennium, however, conditions of capital accumulation and the context for capitalist development had radically changed. In this new context, which included a major

---

and metals remains central to the region's exports. From 2008 to 2009, the exports of primary commodities accounted for 38.8% of the total in Latin America (Campodónico, 2008; CEPAL, 2008, 2010; UNCTAD, 2009: 64).

21   ECLAC (2012: 71) attributes the extraordinary increase in the profits of transnational corporations in the region since 2003 to a combination of two factors: a substantial FDI stock and higher returns on that stock—'a sharp rise in the profitability of FDI in the region'. (ECLAC, 2012: 71). Data on FDI disaggregated by sector shows that investments in the mining and hydrocarbon sectors, particularly in Peru, Chile and Colombia with declared profit rates of 25%. By contrast, returns on investments in Mexico barely averaged 3%, reflecting the concentration of FDI in other sectors.

realignment of economic power and relations of trade in the world market, and the growth in both the demand for and the prices of primary commodities, the shift of FDI towards Latin America signified a major change in the geoeconomics and geopolitics of global capital. Flows of FDI into Latin America from 2000 to 2007 for the first time exceeded those went to America, only surpassed by Europe and Asia. And the global financial crisis brought about an even more radical change in the geoeconomics of global capital both in regard to its regional distribution (increased flows to Latin America) and sectoral distribution (concentration in the extractive sector). In 2010, in the throes of a financial and production crisis the advanced capitalist economies at the centre of the system and the epicentre of the crisis (the US and the EC) attracted and received less than 97 of global flows of investment capital—for the first time since UNCTAD has tracked and kept records of these flows, i.e. since 1970 (Zibechi, 2012). In 2005, the 'developing' and 'emerging' economies attracted only 12 percent of global flows of productive capital but in 2010, against a background of a sharp decline in these flows, these economies overcame the 50 percent barrier (CEPAL, 2010). In the same year FDI flows into Latin America increased by 34.6 percent, well above the growth rate in Asia, which was only 6.7 percent (UNC-TAD, 2012).

The increased flow of extractive capital into Latin America over the past two decades has been primarily in the mining sector of South America's economies. According to the World Bank (2005: 20), over the first of these decades (1990–1997) worldwide investment in mining exploration grew by 90 percent, but in Latin America the growth was 400 percent (and for Peru, one of the region's leading mining economies, an astounding 2000 percent). In 1997, Latin America concentrated 40 percent of total mining investments (De Echave, 2008: 21). Thirteen years later worldwide it was the fourth largest destination point for investments in mining exploration (Panfichi & Coronel, 2011: 395). And since 1994, Latin America has been the largest recipient of investments in mining exploration, attracting a yearly average of around 26 percent of the worldwide budget in exploration (Metals Economics Group, 2011: 4–5). At the beginning of 1990s the region received approximately 12 percent of global investment in mining; by 2009 it received approximately 30 percent (Bebbington, 2009a: 15; De Echave, 2009b: 105).

Whatever forces impelled the massive inflow of 'resource-seeking' investment capital in the 1990s over the past decade the flow of productive investment capital into Latin America was fuelled by two factors: commodity prices, which remained high through most of this period, attracting 'natural-resource-seeking investment',[22] and the solid economic growth of the South American sub-region, which encouraged market-seeking investment. This flow of FDI was concentrated in four South American countries—Argentina, Brazil, Chile and Colombia—which accounted for 89 percent of the sub-region's total inflows. The extractive industry in these countries, particularly mining, absorbed the greatest share of these inflows. For example, in 2009, Latin America received 26 percent of global investments in mineral exploration (Sena-Fobomade, 2011). And together with the expansion of oil and gas projects, mineral extraction constitutes the single most important source of export revenues for a majority of countries in the region.

   Although the flow of resource-seeking capital since the years of the global financial crisis has been concentrated in four South American countries Brazil accounted for the bulk of these flows as well as FDI flows in general. FDI flows to Brazil reached a new high in 2008 of USD 45 billion, 30 percent above the record level posted the year before. Mexico, the second largest recipient of FDI in the region, was hit hard by the financial crisis and consequently saw FDI inflows fall 20 percent over the same year. Much of this fall can be attributed to the decline of FDI in the services and manufacturing sectors, and reduced US imports. In contrast, 'natural resource seeking FDI' drove an expansion of capital flows into Argentina, Chile and Colombia, especially in the mining sector. Thus, while efficiency- and market-seeking FDI have more weight in private capital flows into Mexico and the Caribbean resource-seeking FDI accounts for the bulk and weight of FDI in the region (UNCTAD, 2007: 122–123). Thus, South America today is the centre of gravity for the new geoeconomics and geopolitics of global capital—the new extractivism and the postneoliberal state.

Progressive Extractivism: A New Model for Latin America?

The new millennium opened with a boom—a primary commodities boom stimulated by changes in the global economy, specifically, the ascent of China as an economic power and the associated demand by industry and the growing middle class for raw materials—industrial minerals and precious metals,

---

22   The largest originator of this 'resource-seeking; investment was China, which has surpassed the US as the primary source of FDI into Latin America (Glave & Kuramoto, 2007: 148; World Bank, 2011a: 8–9). According to the World Bank (2011b: 22) the robust growth in Latin America is an 'important measure of its connections to China, both directly (via trade and increasingly also FDI channels) and indirectly (mainly via China's impact on the international prices of commodities)'.

energy (bio- and fossil fuels), and agrofood products. The demand for these commodities, stimulated by security needs of some governments related to energy and food, as well as 'economic opportunities' for multinational corporations in the extractive sector, led to the growth of what the World Bank (2011) has described as 'large-scale foreign investment in the acquisition of land'—'landgrabbing', in the parlance of critical agrarian studies (Borras, Franco, Gomez, Kay and Spoor, 2012).

The volume of the capital deployed to this end (the extraction of non-renewable natural resources) and the profits made in the process are staggering. Higginbottom (2013:193) estimates that from 1997 to 2010 the multinationals that dominate the world economy extracted a total of US$477.6 billion in profit and direct investment income from Latin America, most of it derived from primary commodity exports. As for the financial returns to other foreign investors the *Financial Times* on April 18, 2013 published an article that documented the fact that traders in commodities have accumulated large reserves of capital and huge fortunes in the context of the primary commodities boom and the financialization of capitalist development. As the author of the article observed: 'The world's top commodities traders have pocketed nearly $250bn over the last decade, making the individuals and families that control the largely privately-owned sector big beneficiaries of the rise of China and other emerging countries'—and, we might add, beneficiaries of the turn towards extractivism and export primarization.

A wave of resource-seeking foreign direct investment was a major feature of the political economy of global capitalist development at the turn into the first decade of the new millennium. Another was the demise of neoliberalism as an economic doctrine and model—at least in Latin America, where powerful social movements successfully challenged this model. Over the past decade a number of governments in South America, in riding a wave of anti-neoliberal sentiment generated by these movements experienced a process of regime change—a tilt towards the left and what has been described as 'progressive extractivism'.[23] The political victories of these democratically elected 'progressive' regimes opened a new chapter in Latin American history,

---

23 From the post-neoliberal perspective of the centre-left regimes formed in South America over the last decade, a strategy of natural resource extraction is viewed as a means of bringing about a process of inclusive development—using resource rents and taxes on corporate profits as a means of reducing poverty and securing a more equitable distribution of the social product—'progressive extractivism', in the conception of Eduardo Gudynas (2010, 2011), a senior researcher at the Uruguay-based Latin American Centre of Social Ecology (CLAES).

notwithstanding the fact that the wide embrace of resource-seeking foreign direct investment, or extractive capital, has generated deep paradoxes for those progressive regimes in the region committed to addressing the inequality predicament and the crisis of nature.

Some leaders and social movements in this context speak of revolution—Venezuela's 'Bolivarian' revolution, Bolivia's 'democratic and cultural revolution', and Ecuador's 'citizens' revolution'—and, together with several governments that have embraced the new developmentalism (the search for a more inclusive form of development), these regimes have indeed taken some steps in the direction of poverty reduction and social inclusion, using the additional fiscal revenues derived from resource rents to this purpose. Yet, like their more conservative neighbours—regimes such as Mexico's and Colombia, committed to both neoliberalism and an alliance with 'imperialism'—the left-leaning progressive regimes in the region find themselves entangled in a maze of renewed dependence on natural resource extraction (the 'new extractivism') and primary commodity exports ('reprimarization'). Further, as argued by Gudynas (2010), this new 'progressive' extractivism is much like the old 'classical' extractivism in its destruction of both the environment and livelihoods, and its erosion of the territorial rights and sovereignty of indigenous communities most directly affected by the operations of extractive capital, which continues to generate relations of intense social conflict.

Despite the use by 'progressive' centre-left governments of resource rents as a mechanism of social inclusion and direct cash transfers to the poor it is not at all clear whether they are able or disposed to pursue revolutionary measures in their efforts to bring about a more inclusive and sustainable form of development, or a deepening of political and economic democratization, allowing the people to 'live well', while at the same time continuing to hoe the line of extractive capital and its global assault on nature and livelihoods. The problem here is twofold. One is a continuing reliance of these left-leaning post-neoliberal regimes (indeed, all but Venezuela) on neoliberalism ('structural reforms') at the level of macroeconomic public policy. The other relates to the so-called 'new extractivism' based on 'inclusionary state activism' and continued reliance on FDI—on striking a deal with global capital in regard to sharing the resource rents derived from the extraction process.

The problem here relates to the inherent contradictions of extractive capitalism and the machinations of the imperial state in support of extractive capital (= extractivist imperialism). These contradictions are reflected in a process of very uneven economic and social development—economic concentration tending towards the extremes of wealth and poverty—and what economists choose to call 'the resource curse' (the fact that so many resource-rich countries are developmentally poor, while many resource-poor countries have achieved a high level of economic and social development).[24] One expression of this resource curse is what economists term the 'Dutch disease', reflected in a the slowdown currently experienced by Brazil in its engine of economic growth—down from an average of over six per cent a year from 2003 to 2010 to 0.9 percent in 2012. Another is the boom-bust cycle characteristic of extractivism and natural resource development. The slowdown of the commodity super-cycle in the same year (Konold, 2013) suggests that extractive capitalism has not yet outgrown this propensity.[25]

Perhaps the most serious 'contradiction' of 'natural resource development'—development based on the extraction of natural resources (as opposed to human resource development based on the exploitation of labour)—is that a large part of the benefits of economic activity are externalised, i.e. appropriated by groups outside the country and region, while virtually all of the costs—economic, social and environmental—are internalized and disproportionately borne by the indigenous and farming communities contiguous to the open pit mines and other sites of extraction. These costs have given rise to a powerful forces of resistance—social and environmental movements that form the social base of the contemporary search in the region for 'another development', development that not only seeks to move beyond neoliberalism but that rejects capitalism as well ('the socialism of the 21st century', as conceived by Hugo Chávez).

ALBA: New Trade for New Times

The *Alternativa Bolivariana para los Pueblos de Nuestra América* (ALBA) was conceived in 2004 by Hugo Chávez and Fidel Castro as an alternative to the FTAA (ALCA), the neoliberal project defeated the year before by the mobilizations of the anti-imperialist movement and the opposition of Brazil and other governments in their concern to accelerate the process of regional integration and—in the words of Hugo Chávez—to 'counterbalance the global dominance of the US' (Wagner, 2006). Advanced as a new model of intra-regional trade,

---

24   On this resource curse see Acosta (2009) and Auty (1993, 2001).

25   Global commodity prices dropped by 6 % in 2012, a marked change from the dizzying growth during the 'commodities supercycle' of 2002–12, when prices surged an average of 9.5 % a year, or 150% over the 10-year period (Konold, 2013). On the other hand, while prices declined overall in 2012, some commodity categories—energy, food, and precious metals—continued their decade-long trend of price increases.

an alternative to schemes of regional integration within the neoliberal world order, ALBA now encompasses nine countries including in addition to Venezuela and Cuba, Bolivia, Ecuador, Nicaragua and several CARICOM countries.[26] Unlike the neoliberal or WTO model, which is based on a simple reciprocity of commercial exchange in which each party agrees to exactly the same rules of trade, ALBA involves a series of bilateral trade arrangements that are differentiated to take into account the development status and needs of each country. Thus, Venezuela in its agreement under ALBA with Bolivia or Cuba does not require reciprocity in the removal of all trade barriers. Nor do the regional agreements between governments seek trade liberalization or base trade on world market prices. Moreover, regional integration under ALBA is explicitly designed to advance the specific and different national development agenda of each country, and any bilateral or multilateral agreement is tailored to the development requirements of each country, recognizing the asymmetry of economic and social development (Girvan, 2011). Thus ALBA is based on an entirely new model of regional integration that reflects the socialist values and principles of the Bolivarian Revolution. However, in addition to a shared commitment to socialist principles the model also reflects the thinking and worldview of the indigenous communities in the region. This is evident in an emerging radical consensus engineered by a coalition of social movements in support of a *minga* of resistance and popular action.

On the 29th of February 2009, a regional alliance[27] of indigenous communities and peasant social movements convoked a 'Minga of Resistance' (collective action) in association with 'other peoples and processes' (Abya Yala, 2009).[28] And such collective action, in the search for an alternative to

---

26   With a total population of over 70 million people the member nations of ALBA are Antigua and Barbuda, Bolivia, Cuba, Dominica, Ecuador, Nicaragua, Saint Vincent and the Grenadines and Venezuela. Suriname and Saint Lucia were admitted to ALBA as guest countries and Haiti is pending full membership. On ALBA as aregional trading bloc see Girvan (2011).

27   This alliance includes the *Coordinadora Andina de Organizaciones Indígenas* (CAOI), the *Coordinadora de Organizaciones Indígenas de la Cuenca Amazónica* (COICA), the *Consejo Indígena de Centro América* (CICA), the *Movimiento Sin Tierra del Brasil* (MST), *Vía Campesina*; the organizations of the Unity Pact (*Pacto de Unidad*) of Bolivia; and diverse indigenous organizations of Colombia, Ecuador and Peru—meeting most recently on the 26th of February, 2009, in the locality of the Unity Pact in La Paz.

28   *Minga* is a Quechua word meaning 'collective action' having wide currency among the indigenous poor, both indigenous and mestizo, in the Andes. The call to collective action that is at once local and global has gained force subsequently from both its cultural and historical references to a shared experience of subjugation. By calling their movement a

capitalism as well as neoliberalism, is indeed underway in the popular sectors of different countries in the region, especially in the Andes. See for example the Convocation (January 20, 2009) of the Social Movements of America at the World Social Forum in Belém. Departing from a diagnosis of the 'profound crisis' of capitalism in the current conjuncture that the agents and agencies of capitalism and imperialism are seeking to 'unload' [*descargar*] on 'our people', the representation of a broad regional coalition of American social movements announced the need, and the intention ('un *proyecto de vida de los pueblos frente al proyecto del imperialismo*') to create a popular form of 'regional integration' (ALBA) 'from below'—'social solidarity in the face of imperialism'.

From this perspective the global crisis was, and remains, not a matter of dysfunctional financial institutions and unregulated capital markets but rather a systemic crisis, a crisis of the model used to formulate public support in relation to agricultural production as well as the rules used to govern international relations of trade and investment. Thus, at issue is not the regulation or freedom of capital flows and trade but the sustainability of the global food regime and local markets, rural livelihoods and food sovereignty, small-scale production for local markets, indigenous territorial rights regarding land and resources, protection of the environment and the ecosystem on which both livelihoods and local communities, and life itself, depend.[29]

For example, along the line of principles ratified in a succession of ALBA summits, and supportive of popular action against the neoliberal model and neoliberal policies, a coalition of organizations in Mexico's peasant movement proposed that the government's anti-crisis plan in 2009 include a policy of local production regarding corn and rice, milk, vegetable oil, pork products, etc., ending the policy of free agricultural imports under NAFTA, which, as the Zapatistas had predicted, has been the cause of a major production crisis in

---

Minga, the indigenous participants call attention to both the work that must go into politics and the need for collective action.

29   The principles of proposed action (*la minga*), ratified in subsequent ALBA summits include: (i) defence of the sovereignty of the people and their right of self-determination, supported with policies of autonomous development, equity, internationalism, and solidarity with the people in struggle; (ii) a united front against neoliberal policies, including in particular privatization and denationalization; iii) support for forms of agricultural production that guarantee food sovereignty, that respects life and mother earth; (iv) promoting solidarity among people and nations; (v) unity in support of the feminist struggle against patriarchy and sexism in all of its forms; (vi) support of an emancipatory [anticapitalist] culture; and (vii) political participation of the people in the construction of a new State committed to the consolidation of ALBA and its objectives.

agriculture, if not its 'death knell'. As for the local production and importing of vegetable oil, the President of the Senate's Rural Development Commission pointed out that in just one case (the elimination of import duties for vegetable oil) government policy put at risk many rural livelihoods and cost the economy up to 10,000 jobs in the sector plus an additional 30,000 indirect jobs (Pérez, 2009).

At issue in this and other such actions taken in the popular sector is whether the political and intellectual Left in the region are up to the challenge levelled by *Abya Yala*—willing to actively support, if not lead, the forces of resistance and revolutionary change that are being formed in the popular sector. As for the Mexican government—by no means progressive or leftist in orientation, indeed, explicitly neoliberal—it responded to this challenge in the same way as have other governments such as Brazil, which is self-defined as postneoliberal in the sense of the post-Washington Consensus on the need for 'inclusionary state activism', by implementing a 'new social policy' geared to poverty reduction and inclusion of the rural poor in programs of development assistance. In Mexico's case the basic mechanism of this anti-crisis response is 'Oportunidades' (Opportunities), a program designed to assist those with scarce resources and most directly negatively affected by the global crisis. With a negotiated World Bank loan of US500 million this program in 2009 was expected to pump USD 4 billion into the countryside and the local economy, continuing the time-honoured (albeit dishonourable) tradition of using rural development as a means of demobilizing the social movements and defusing revolutionary ferment in the countryside.

In opposition to this approach—to combine a policy of social inclusion and poverty reduction with a policy of regional integration and globalization—ALBA proposes an alternative model of regional integration based on socialist principles of social justice, fair trade and a more equitably shared development of the forces of production. In this regard ALBA has turned out to be a key centre of reference and organizing space in the formation and articulation of a region-wide social movement in support of a common program for diverse forces of resistance against neoliberalism, capitalism and imperialism.[30]

---

30   Among the 160 or so movements that constitute the Council of the Movements for ALBA (Consejo de Movimientos Sociales del ALBA) formed in May 20, 2007, at an ALBA summit meeting in Venezuela, are the Movimiento de Pobladoras y Pobladores, la Asociación Nacional de Medios Comunitarios Libres y Alternativos (ANMCLA), El Frente Nacional Campesino Ezequiel Zamora, el Frente Nacional de Campesinos y Pescadores 'Simón Bolívar', CONIVE, el Frente Bicentenario de Mujeres 200, La Red de Colectivos La Araña Feminista, la Red Nacional de Sistemas de Truke, el Frente Nacional Comunal 'Simón

Conclusion

The dynamics of capitalist development in Latin America over the past three decades have given rise to the construction of three alternative models of capitalist development, each giving rise to or associated with a particular policy regime and a particular way of organizing the forces of production and conducting international relations of trade and investment. The first model has crystalized around what used to be termed the Washington Consensus but now dubbed (by *The Economist*) the Davos Consensus. It takes the form of a proposal to bring about a process of sustainable resource development, or 'inclusive growth', with 'the private sector' (= the multinational corporations) as the 'driver' or motor of this growth (Canada, House of Commons, 2012). The model is associated with various neoliberal regimes on the Pacific coast (Chile, Colombia, Peru, Mexico) aligned with US imperialism, and various projects to construct a free trade area based on the rules of the neoliberal world order—NAFTA, FTAA, the Pacific Alliance.[31] The second model is based on the post-Washington Consensus on the need for inclusionary state activism and a more inclusive form of national development. It is associated with the left-leaning postneoliberal regimes formed in South America in conditions of a wave of anti-neoliberal resistance at the turn into the 21st century. The trade regime that best reflects the organizing principles of this model—open regionalism within a system of global capitalism—is Mercosur. The third model has taken shape in the form of an emerging radical consensus on the need to not only move beyond neoliberalism but to reject capitalism. The intra-regional trade scheme that embodies the principles of this radical consensus is ALBA, an anti-imperialist alliance of post-neoliberal regimes oriented towards 'the socialism of the 21st century'.

Despite the project of expanding intra-regional trade neither Mercosur or ALBA has managed to substantially increase intra-regional trade or reduce the regional differences in the level of development, and this is not only because of the concept of open regionalism within a global economy, but the continuing

---

Bolívar', Red Nacional de Comuneros, la Red de Organizaciones Afrovenezolanas, el Movimiento Nacional de Televisoras Comunitarias-ALBA TV, Movimiento de Mujeres Ana Soto, el Movimiento Gayones, OPR Bravo Sur, la Compañía Nacional de Circo, Colectivo Nuevo Nuevo Circo, Jóvenes por el ALBA, la Alianza Sexo—Genero Diversa Revolucionaria.

31   The Pacific Alliance is also connected to the proposal of a Trans-Pacific Partnership between member states, the US and Canada, and six Asian economies, creating the world's biggest free trade zone.

commitment of both neoliberal and post-neoliberal regimes to extractivism, as well as conflicts internal to Mercosur related to what might be termed 'Brazilian sub-imperialism.'[32] The new extractivism, like the old extractivism, dictates a north–south rather than an intra-regional axis of international trade in that the market for extracted natural resources are predominantly in the global north or the emerging markets of the BRIC countries, not in the region. Nor does extractivism promote or create conditions for a more inclusive and sustainable form of national development. This is because extractivism and natural resource development, like the 'new industrialism',[33] is both destructive of the environment and technology-intensive with relatively fewer development implications than human resource and industrial development based on the exploitation of labour. Indeed, it is estimated, in the case of the mining sector, that the participation of labour in the fruits of natural resource development—in the profits and resource rents generated from exporting the products—is from six to nine per cent, and the share of the governments in these rents is even less.

Thus, the issue is not inclusionary state activism or the socialism of the 21st century, but a continuing reliance on resource-seeking foreign investments. As for ALBA, despite its promise as a model of alternative development as well as trade (and its success in challenging the imperialist free trade agenda) it is not likely to serve as a catalyst of a more inclusive and sustainable form of socialist development, or systemic social transformation. This would require the nationalization and socialisation of the commanding heights of the regional economy, as well as abandonment of extractivism as a development strategy. And this is because the social and environmental costs of production far outweigh any benefits, and these benefits are limited and highly concentrated (and externalised—received outside the country) while the costs are exceedingly high and widespread. However, extractivist socialism or socialist industrialization is not likely to be any more sustainable in terms of the environment and livelihoods, small-scale production

---

32   Different analysts as well as Brazil's partners, especially Uruguay and Paraguay, whose economies are dwarfed by Brazil's, have long accused Brazil of imperialist designs and actions (the quest for regional hegemony). These claims are to some extent reinforced by the huge surplus on its agricultural trade account that Brazil has generated with its neighbours, as well as its large-scale acquisition of land for soya production in Paraguay and Uruguay.

33   The term 'the new industrialism' refers to the industries that are currently being set up in Argentina and elsewhere in the region that are not only highly contaminating and destructive of the environment but employ ultra-modern labour-saving technologies such as robotics.

for local markets, and communities, than extractivist capitalism, even in its 'progressive' form. The problem is fundamental. Extractivism has undermined ALBA as an alternate development and trade model, limiting its use as an instrument of substantive social change and genuine development. Thus it is that extractivism has been rejected not only in the streets but by the social movements that are otherwise united in their active support of ALBA.

To conclude, Latin America's problem is not neoliberalism but capitalism. Neither extractivism nor industrialism, post-neoliberal policy reforms or diversified and fair trade, provide a way out of the fundamental problems caused by capitalism. For one thing, industrialism vs. extractivism is a false dichotomy or choice arising out of a misplaced commitment to 'economic growth' under capitalism: both today are more of a problem than a solution. For another, the fundamental problem is a system geared to private profit rather than human needs, a problem that neither globalization, regionalization or alternate forms of trade can solve. In addition to the nationalization and socialization of production what is needed is another world and a different model concerned with and focused on small-scale cooperative production and medium-sized business enterprises that are geared to and designed to strengthen food sovereignty and both local and regional markets; socialism and self-reliance rather than capitalism and imperialist exploitation, protection of regional producers and regional integration rather than neoliberal globalization; expansion of ALBA as an economic and political organization with a regional development agenda; the expansion and consolidation of a regional development bank to counter the impact of the IDB and to replace the current reliance on FDI and the World Bank/IMF for capital and development finance;[34] strengthening and creating other regional political organizations

---

34   Currently there are two models of such a regional development bank: BancoSur and
       ALBA Bank. The former is a monetary fund and lending organization established in
       2009 by Argentina, Brazil, Paraguay, Uruguay, Ecuador, Bolivia and Venezuela with an ini-
       tial capital of US$20 billion. Argentina, Venezuela, and Brazil were to have each pledged
       $4 billion, while Uruguay, Ecuador, Paraguay and Bolivia were to have contributed smaller
       amounts. The aim of the bank is to lend money to nations in the Americas for the
       construction of social programs and infrastructure. In 2012 member states of ALBA
       agreed to deposit 1% of their international reserves into a jointly administered
       development bank as a way of deepening regional economic cooperation and
       development.

such as Unisur[35] as a counterweight to imperialism. In short, get rid of both capitalism and imperialism.

---

35   UNISUR, formerly the South American Community of Nations, is a union of South American nations created in 2008 to propel regional integration on issues including democracy, education, energy, environment, infrastructure, and security and to eliminate social inequality and exclusion. It was inspired by and modeled after the European Union. Its members are Argentina, Bolivia, Brazil, Chile, Colombia, Ecuador, Guyana, Paraguay, Peru, Suriname, Uruguay, and Venezuela. Panama and Mexico hold observer status.

CHAPTER 5

Class Struggle on the New Frontier of Extractive Capitalism

This book is concerned with the economic, social and political dynamics of capitalism and imperialism in the current era of neoliberal globalization. These dynamics are rooted in an economic and social structure formed by the relationship of individuals in diverse societies to the capitalist system of global production, and the state sanctioned rights and perquisites of private property in the means of social production, i.e. the power of the capitalist class to make decisions in their own class interest. Because the workings of this system at both national and international levels is predicated on capital accumulation, i.e. exploitation and profit-making (the extraction of surplus value from labour), we need to have a good understanding of the nature of the structure of social and international economic relations that underlies the dynamics of capitalist development. This is because capitalist relations of production are inherently conflictual, pitting one class against another in a struggle to bring about change in one direction or the other. Marx, among others, viewed this struggle as a major driving force of social change—revolutionary transformation of one system into another.

To provide a conceptual and theoretical foundation for our analysis of the dynamics of capitalist development and imperialist exploitation we introduce our discussion of class struggle in the current context of neoliberal globalization and extractive imperialism with some brief notes on class and class struggle. These notes are designed as an introduction to a reflection on some critical dimensions of class and class struggle today, as a kind of scaffolding for the construction of our ideas on capitalism and imperialism in subsequent chapters (Part II). While the first part of Chapter 6 focuses on the class struggle in Latin America, the second concerns the form taken by the class struggle and resistance on the new frontiers of extractive capitalism and imperialism.

Class Analysis: Social Class and Class Struggle

The political economy of capitalist development is predicated on class analysis—analysis of the social and economic structure formed in the process of development and the forces of political change generated in the process. This 'development' is accompanied by a process of productive and social transformation based on the concentration of capital[1] and the proletarianization of the direct producers, i.e. the conversion of small-landholding agricultural producers (the 'peasantry' in the discourse of critical agrarian studies) into a working class, a class compelled to sell its labour power to capital for a wage.[2]

In Chapter 4 we outline anddiscuss this process of productive and social transformation, with reference to a classic and on-going debate regarding the 'agrarian question'. At issue in this question is the proletarianization of agricultural producers including peasants and farmers, a process set in motion under conditions of what Marx described as 'primitive [original] accumulation', or, as David Harvey (2003) would have it, 'accumulation by dispossession'. The complex dynamics of this development process have been debated in different contexts and the debate has by no means been settled. But on one issue there is no debate—that the social structure of capitalist societies is based on the capital-labour relation, which defines two basic classes: the capitalist class, or the bourgeoisie, owners of the fundamental means of production; and the working class, or proletariat, that class which by virtue of having been dispossessed of their means of production is compelled to exchange labour-power for a living wage.

On this issue there is little to dispute. But what remains unclear after three decades of capitalist development within the neoliberal world order are the contours of the social structure of societies in Latin America. There is no question that the capital-labour relation forms the base or nucleus of the social structure. However, it is evident that a large part of the economically active population in these societies is not directly tied into the capital-labour relation, i.e. they are not in a position to accumulate capital on the basis of their ownership claims or property in the means of production; nor are they forced to exchange their labour for a living wage. At least half of the working class in the urban areas of the economic structure work not for wages in industrial plants, or factories and offices, but work on their own account on the streets in what has been described as the 'informal sector' without a labour contract, in

---

1   Capital, in this context, is theoretically defined as wealth used to expand production (or, money invested to the purpose of generating a higher return.

2   The theory of this 'development' is formulated by Marx as the 'General Law of Accumulation', which specifies a twofold tendency for, on the one hand, capital in its expansion to concentrate into fewer and larger units of production, and, on the other, for the 'multiplication of the proletariat' (the class which, dispossessed of the land and their means of production, own nothing except their capacity to labour, which they are therefore compelled to exchange for a wage. This theory also conceptualized the formation of an 'industrial reserve army' of workers whose labour was surplus to the requirements of capital and thus held in reserve.

conditions of low income and poverty. In the rural areas a large part of the dispossessed peasantry exist as a semiproletariat—landless or near landless, with one foot in the countryside, and the other in labour, working for wages off-farm or sporadically or seasonally in the urban centres, perhaps returning to the rural communities on weekends.

Until the mid-1990s these disposed and impoverished rural proletarians, viewed by development theorists and practitioners as the 'rural poor', and by many Marxists as an industrial reserve army, were encouraged to take one of the development pathways out of rural poverty, namely agriculture, labour, and migration. But with the evident lack of opportunities or the absorptive capacity of the labour market, the rural proletariat was encouraged instead to stay in the rural areas, subsisting by diversifying their source of household income. These indigenous and farming communities have borne the brunt of capitalism in its latest offensive—landgrabbing, 'natural resource extraction' and extractive imperialism.

In this context it is not an easy matter to define the relationship of each and all individuals to production, that is, their class position. As noted the capital-labour relation still is the basis of the social structure, but at least one half of the urban population and an even larger part of the rural population, while proletarianized to varying degrees, do not directly exchange their labour-power for a wage. Thus, in order to establish the position of these individuals and groups in the social structure the authors betimes have resorted to other conceptions of class such as: *social class*, defined by the relationship of individuals to consumption or the market rather than production (with categories of analysis such as lower, lower middle, upper middle, upper); *occupational class*, defined by the relationship of individuals to work, to the work they do within the social and technical division of labour;[3] *income class*, a statistical grouping of the population according to the level or the share of national income;[4] and *political class*, regarding the relationship of individuals to power, particularly in regard to the state.[5]

---

3   This conception of class can be traced back to Emile Durkheim in the structural-functionalist tradition of sociological analysis. It assumes that work is the basic social institution of modern society, determining an individual's status and that to each status within the hierarchy of occupational groups there corresponds a 'certain coefficient of well-being' (level of income, etc.), viewed as a just reward for the contribution made to economic production.

4   This conception of class is used by most economists in viewing individuals or households as 'income earners' and grouping the population in statistical rather than social terms of percentiles (deciles or quintiles of income earners in a hierarchy of national income).

5   In this conception of political class individuals are viewed in terms of their form of political participation or membership in a political party (organizations formed to pursue power), a

However, when it comes to understanding the dynamics of class struggle the authors and contributors to this book necessarily turn towards and rely on a Marxist conception of class, defined by the relationship of individuals to production, as well as Marx's theory regarding the dynamics of class conflict and struggle. Here it is assumed that the dispossessed, i.e., the proletariat in one form or the other, is the fundamental agency of revolutionary change, and that the demands in the class struggle, the driving force behind the resistance, is the struggle for land, higher wages and improved working conditions—the two classic forms of the class struggle. In the conditions of capitalism and imperialism today these struggles persist but they have merged with, and in some contexts have been overshadowed by the struggle to resist the closure of the commons—to divest communities from access to the global commons of land, water and resources, over which the indigenous population in different contexts retain or claim territorial rights. As for the dynamics of the resistance the forces of resistance in the current context have been mobilized against either or both (i) the neoliberal policies that generate or release the forces of capitalist development destructive of their communities and livelihoods; and/ or (ii) the negative socioenvironmental impacts of extractive capitalism on what might be termed the 'new proletariat'—the indigenous and farming communities that bear the brunt of the latest onslaught.

Our analysis of the dynamics of capitalist development is based on the Marxist concept of social class, but we make reference to these other conceptions of class as the occasion demands. Within this conception of class we can identify the capitalist class as those who own the major means of production and are in a position to exploit labour, extracting surplus value from their labour power by means of the wage; the working class, by the same token, includes all those who, dispossessed or bereft from owning any means of production are compelled to exchange their labour power for a wage or work for a living. Of course the working class so defined takes diverse forms and is both stratified and politically divided. Then there are those who own means of production but are not in a position to exploit labour. These small property owners can be defined in Marxist terms as the petit bourgeoisie.

As for the broader social structure—since it is estimated that less than one half of the economically active population in Latin American social formations has a direct relationship to the dominant capitalist mode of production—at times we turn to one or the other of these alternative notions

---

social movement (organizations used to contest power or bring about revolutionary change or political reform), or the state (in which individuals can be viewed as representing the interests of one class or the other).

of class. Thus, for example, in conceptualizing the structure of social inequality in the distribution of income it is useful to categorize or group individuals
according to their relationship to income or the market (their capacity for
material consumption) rather than production. In these terms the poor are
those whose income level is so low as to deprive them of the capacity to meet
their basic needs let alone participate in the market. The 'middle class' by the
same token refers to those individuals, households or groups whose relation to
the market, or 'life chances' (access to productive resources, a job and income),
allow them to purchase the goods and services that provide for them a decent
standard of living, a package of consumption goods that typically includes
adequate housing (afford a mortgage or rent) at less than 40 percent of income,
transportation in the form of ownership of an automobile, access to education
and healthcare and abundant food and the ability to eat out at a decent restau-
rant at least once a week, afford regular recreation and an annual vacation, and
have a savings account.

Most of the debate that has surrounded this form of class analysis has to do
with establishing the income line between poverty and the middle class: for
some it is established by definition at just over the poverty line ($2.50 a day,
according to the World Bank), allowing policymakers and analysts to point
towards a measure of success in reducing the rate of poverty in the country—
in lifting millions out of poverty into the ranks of the middle class—by virtue
of a policy of social inclusion and direct transfers of income to the poor
(Veltmeyer & Tetreault, 2013). Other analysts are careful to use a more meaningful definition of the middle class by establishing its lower limit (level of
income and consumption) at a more realistic level (for example, earnings of at
least $10 a day, measured in purchasing power parity terms). By this measure
(used to identify the lower ranks of the so-called middle class, i.e. the lower
middle class) there is a stratum of low-income earners within the middle class
and between middle class and poverty status. By the same definition the middle class, defined in terms of their consumption capacity, can be clearly distinguished from the working class defined in Marxist terms in that there is a clear
demarcation between these two classes in terms of their capacity to consume
or relation to the market. The 'middle class' in this analysis, including its upper
ranks (the upper middle class) also corresponds closely to certain occupational group or labourforce categories, especially to those classified in terms of
their 'function' as professional-management-business 'services', what some
sociologists have categorized as the 'professional management class'. By the
same token or definition, the labourforce category of 'retail sales, office work
and personal service correspond to the 'lower middle class' category or, in
Marxist terms, is part of the working class.

An advantage and the superiority of Marxist class analysis is that unlike other forms of class analysis it includes both a structural and a political dimension. In structural terms it is assumed, for the sake of analysis, that in the production process people enter into relations that are independent of their will, i.e. subjecting them to conditions that are objective in ther effects according to their location in the class structure. In political terms Marx argued—and many sociological studies have confirmed—that a fundamental contradiction of capitalist systems, between the forces of production that tend to expand, and the relations of production that over time end up as a fetter, that the capital-labour relation is based on the exploitation of labour (extraction of surplus value), and when workers become aware of this, as they will do in the course of the class struggle, class consciousness translates into class conflict.

And the capital-labour relation is not the only contradiction of capitalist development. Another operates at the level of international relations, when these are structured so as to allow capitalists at the centre of the system to exploit labour and extract surplus value from the direct producers. Another fundamental contradiction is that capitalism is predicated on primitive accumulation, or accumulation by dispossession, i.e. the separation of the direct producers from the land and their means of production. This is an absolute requirement of capitalist development, but it pits the direct producer and their communities against capital in a struggle to resist proletarianization and the exploitation of their labour power, and to retain access to the land as a means of production. In the current context of capitalist development and extractive imperialism it means resisting the forces working to dispossess them in order to gain access to the resources to which they lay claim or to gain access to a source of cheap surplus labour.

The Changing Contours of Class Struggle in Latin America

The concept of class struggle is central for understanding the economic and political dynamics of capitalist development in the context of what we have described as the new geopolitics of capital and extractive imperialism, the actions taken by the imperial state at the centre of the system in support of capital and to advance its economic interests in both the global arena and on the new frontiers of capital accumulation. It is always so, but particularly in the era of imperialist globalization, that the class struggle has an international as well as national dimension, inasmuch as the agencies of capital development and imperial power—the multinational corporations, international financial organizations and imperial states—directly intervene, or act through proxy

collaborator states, in the class struggle between labour and capital at the centre and heartland of the system. This is especially evident in Latin America
today with the ascendancy of extractive capital: giant agro-mineral capitalist
enterprises and multinational corporations play a major role in shaping public
policy, to the detriment of labour as well as the communities of rural landless
workers, semiproletarianized peasant farmers and indigenous peoples directly
affected by the operations of extractive capital. As we argue elsewhere this is
true not only in regard to regimes such as Columbia and Mexico that are
aligned with US imperialism and continue to pursue a neoliberal policy agenda
('structural reform') but also to those regimes in South America seeking to
establish a more inclusive form of national development.

The dynamics of class struggle vary over time and place, depending on the
socioeconomic and political conditions, organization, past trajectory, the source
and distribution of income, and the conditions of capitalist development—
dispossession, proletarianization and economic exploitation. The capital-
labour relation necessarily remains the economic base of the social structure,
but under conditions of peripheral capitalist development a large part of
the 'economically active population' do not exchange their labour-power for a
living wage, generating in the process new forms of accumulation, exploitation
and struggle.

The nature and dynamics of the class struggle, and the conflicting demands
of labour and capital, vary in terms of comprehensiveness, intensity, geographic location and class interests mobilized in the capitalist development
process. The issues range from demands over wage and working conditions,
and the land struggle, to broader struggles ranging from public policies affecting budget allocations, investment decisions and issues of property ownership,
to issues of dispossession, environmental contamination, and the destructive
impact of extractive operations on local communities.

Class struggles involve two basic antagonists. Ruling class struggle 'from
above', in which various sectors of capital use their social power, economic
control and state penetration to maximize present and future profits to
monopolize state budgetary allocations to limit the income share of labour
and to dispossess and displace petty commodity producers and local inhabitants from resource-rich regions. Popular class struggle 'from below' involves a
panoply of classes ranging from employed and unemployed industrial workers, unionized public and private salaried employees, petty commodity producers, an urban proletariat of self-employed street workers and a rural
semi-proletariat of landless or near-landless workers, as well as peasant farmers and indigenous communities. The demands of these classes and groups
range from a greater share of national income and repossession of land and

resources usurped by the state on behalf of agro-mineral corporations, to a change in government policy (abandonment of the neoliberal policy agenda) and systemic change in property ownership and class relations.

A key determinant of the scope and depth of class struggle is the point at which a particular 'economic model' is in a phase of ascendancy in its capacity to expand the forces of production or that it has reached its limits, pushing the system into a situation of economic crisis. Thus, in recent years we witnessed the rise of 'neoliberalism', roughly between the mid-1970s to the end of the 1990s, a period in which capital was on the offensive, waging class war and succeeding in halting and reversing the advances made by workers and peasant in the previous period of state-led development, privatizing the economy, deregulating markets, liberalizing trade and the flows of capital, and pillaging the public treasury. In the late 1990s to the early 21st century, however, neoliberalism as an economic doctrine and model experienced a legitimation crisis, precipitating intense class struggle from below ranging from unemployed workers movements in Argentina, to mass indigenous movements in Bolivia and Ecuador, resulting in the overthrow of incumbent regimes and the emergence of a number of post-neoliberal regimes in South America. On these dynamics see, inter alia, Petras & Veltmeyer (2001, 2005b, 2009, 2011).

Likewise the decline of a decade-long boom of primary commodity exports, which seems to have gone bust in 2012 (with the rate of economic growth in Brazil falling from a average of six percent as of 2003 to 0.9% in 2012), has spawned the rise of mass urban movements protesting the policies of the postneoliberal regime in Brazil and Argentina, and even in Chile in regard to university and high school students protesting the government's neoliberal policies in the area of education.

Changes in the economic configurations of Latin America, especially the expansion of the agro-mineral, financial and commercial sectors and the decline of the manufacturing sector, has had a profound impact in shaping the class structure, trade union organization and class conflict. Trade union membership, for example, has fallen precipitously. In Brazil trade union membership has declined from 32.1 percent in the early 1990s (prior to the election to the presidency of the past-Marxist then-neoliberal Cardoso in 1994) to 17 percent in the middle of the decade under Luis Inácio [Lula] da Silva's Workers Party (PT) regime (2005). In Argentina from 1986 to 2005 trade union membership declined from 48.7 to 25.4 percent. In Mexico membership declined from 14 to 10 percent between 1985 and 2005. Chile is the exception: starting from a low of 11.6 percent in 1986 union membership rose to 16 percent in 2005. Moreover, the decline in trade union membership has been accompanied by the decline of industrial workers, especially in labour-intensive light consumer industries, negatively impacted by imports of cheap textiles, shoes, toys and so on, from Asia as part of the trade off between exports of agro-minerals and imports of manufactured goods.

The decline in trade unions has been accompanied by a decline of the political influence or organized labour in state policies and a turn from political issues (the government's neoliberal policy agenda) towards narrow 'corporate' wage and workplace issues. As a result strikes have declined and are increasingly focused on immediate issues.

The political and social space in the class struggle, vacated by the industrial workers, has been occupied by mass social movements in the countryside led by peasants, indigenous groups and landless workers during the neoliberal era and by urban struggles led by low-paid service workers and lower middle class employees in the 'late' post-neoliberal period. This is evident in the million-member mass urban struggles in Brazil in May–June 2013.

The change in the economy and social struggles has led to major shifts in the locus of class struggles and socioeconomic demands. Prior to the 1990s major strikes, protests and other class actions were organized at the workplace by employed, unionized industrial workers. During the 1990s the axis of struggle shifted to the streets, countryside, and neighbourhoods as the class struggle was spearheaded by rural landless workers, unemployed workers and the downwardly mobile middle class. In the first decade and a half in the 2000s, the locus of class struggle is focused in the Indian and provincial communities adjoining sites of agro-mining corporate exploitation. The struggles focus on resisting dispossession, uprooting and destruction of habitat. The urban mass movements in the major Brazilian cities combine the lower middle class, informal workers and students. They are organized in the streets: the centre of organization and confrontation is located in the neighbourhoods and communities. The target is the post-neoliberal state. The trade union power of convocation has been dwarfed by a ratio of 20 to 1: two million working people joined marches protesting massive corruption, misallocation of budgetary resources and declining living standards and the quality of basic services in health, education and transport.

The new class struggle is basically made up of the younger generation of non-unionized workers, many in the informal sector and low-paid service workers who are highly dependent on public services and lack the social protection of the state.

The complex and changing physiognomy of the 'class struggle from below' is matched by the continuities and changes in the 'class struggle from above'. The ruling classes have shifted from a position embracing brute force, via military dictatorships and ultra-authoritarian rule in launching the neoliberal counterrevolution during the early 1970s and mid-1980s, to support for a nego-tiated transition to electoral politics as a means to consolidate the model and to rapidly implement the neoliberal agenda during the 1990s.

In the face of the anti-neoliberal popular uprisings at the end of the 1990s the agro-mineral elite embraced the post neoliberal centre-left regimes and secured privileged places in the new model, accepting increased taxes and roy-alty payments in exchange for vast state subsidies and large-scale land grants ('land grabs').

With the decline of the mega-boom (post-2012) different sectors of the rul-ing class have adopted different strategies: some (mostly agro-mineral sectors in Brazil) have pressured for a return to neoliberalism within the centre-left regimes; others, especially agro-business association in Argentina, have orga-nized 'mass actions' to undermine the post neoliberal regimes and foreign financial and investment houses have shifted capital to more lucrative sites in other regions.

While the class struggle in its multiple expressions is a 'constant' and mov-ing force in determining economic strategies and the direction of social policy, the organizational form that it takes has changed dramatically over the past half century. Even what appear to be similar organizations such as 'move-ments', 'trade unions' and 'community-based mobilization' have great varia-tions in their internal make-up and mode of operation. Adding to the complexity, organizations change over time in their structure and relationship to the state, depending on the politics of the regime in power.

To illustrate this point, during the 1970s, trade unions in Chile, Argentina, Peru, and Uruguay were highly political, playing a major role in mobilizing and uniting with parties and neighbourhood movements in promoting the social-ization of the economy and resisting the military takeovers. Likewise, during the later phases of the military dictatorships in Brazil and Peru militant trade unions engaged in massive strikes to hasten the advent of democratic electoral politics. Subsequently, with the rise of post-neoliberal regimes, most of the trade unions engaged in tripartite collective bargaining over narrow corporate' demands, eschewing any community-based struggles over broader social issues and, in many cases, supporting regime policies through co-opted lead-ers. In other words 'trade unions', have at different times served as 'social van-guards' and allies of mass movements, mediators in social compromises and active collaborators and transmission belts of the state. The same is true of 'social movements'. During the onset and onslaught of the neoliberal regimes, social movements played a leading role in challenging the ascendant regimes and overthrowing them during the economic crises. The 'movements' varied from neighbourhood-based unemployed urban workers in Argentina, to community-based indigenous movements in Ecuador and Bolivia, to central-ized rural workers movements in Brazil. With the rise of the post-neoliberal regimes and the upswing of the mega-cycle, the unemployed workers move-ments virtually disappeared in Argentina, important sectors of the Indian movement, especially the 'cocaleros' in Bolivia lost their autonomy and became a political prop for the Evo Morales regime, and the MST (or Landless Rural Workers Movement), diminished their land take-over activity in pursuit of economic subsidies from the Lula-Dilma regimes in Brazil.

What is striking about the notion of 'social movements' is that when the class struggle by older, more established and/or co-opted movements declines, new vibrant movements burst onto the scene. In Bolivia the TIPNIS movement led the struggle against the extractive strategies of the Morales regime. In Brazil, the million-strong urban mass movements challenged the policies, priorities and corrupt politicians of the Lula-Dilma regime. Eco-indigenous movements bypassed the co-opted trade union and social movements in Ecuador, Argentina, Mexico, Paraguay and elsewhere. New dynamic community-based civic and class organizations engage in mass con-frontations with extractive-mineral multinationals and the state in Colombia, Peru, Ecuador and elsewhere.

The dynamic of extractive capitalism, with its radical policies of uprooting, displacing and dispossessing entire communities, provokes comprehensive, cross-class alliances, which challenge the power and prerogatives of the state to dictate development policy, at least with regard to regional exploitation of resources. With the decline of the extractive mega-cycle and the drop in demand for commodities and subsequent decline in prices, as growth in China, India and the rest of Asia slows, a new comprehensive 'national' (as opposed to regional) class struggle shows signs of returning. The elite debate class strate-gies. The extractive capital sectors demand intensified production to compen-sate for declining prices; others secure cut-backs in taxes and social costs; still others, in post-neoliberal regimes, call for a 'new development model' in the face of mass unrest (Lula-Rousseff in Brazil). The centre-left is squeezed by both ends of the class structure, in the post-mega-cycle class conflict. Post neo-liberal regimes, fearful of the flight of capital, are pressured to make greater tax concessions to capital on the one hand, and fearful of the rising mass urban movements demanding positive and effective increases in public services and employment, vacillate between social concessions and police repression.

Given the high degree of dependency built into the extractive model, extricating the regime from its links to commodity trade and building a new balanced model will involve a broader and deeper commitment to the popular classes and a return to class struggle from below.

To conclude, class struggle has clearly been internationalized under conditions of what in Latin America is described as the 'new extractivism'—a policy of 'inclusionary state activism' in the use of resource rents extracted from extractive capital to bring about a more socially inclusive form of development (poverty reduction) as per the post-Washington Consensus. Imperial intervention is a central part of class struggle from above and is endemic, whether in the form of multinational corporations, investing and disinvesting, or via imperial state-promoted military coups and destabilization policies or by direct or proxy military invasions. Anti-imperialist class struggle from below is less prominent, yet manifests itself in international aid and solidarity policies from Venezuela via ALBA, international strategy meetings of peasants, indigenous people and solidarity movements. Yet the bulk of the class struggle against exploitation finds expression in movements by oppressed and dispossessed peoples who rely mainly on their own resource base in contrast to the ruling classes, which depend on strategic imperial allies.

Class Struggle on the New Frontier of Extractive Imperialism

There are two ways of understanding the dynamics of resistance in current conditions of the new extractivism. One is in terms of the response to the negative socioeconomic and environmental impacts of extractivism and the agency of social and environmental movements formed from the social base of indigenous and farming communities contiguous to the mines and extractive operations (Svampa, 2012). See Leff (1996), Toledo (2000) and Tetreault in this volume with regard to the dynamics of this resistance in Mexico, and Lust (2014) and Bebbington (2011) in regard to Peru and elsewhere in the Andes. Through the political ecology lens used by these authors, the resistance movement today is, as Tetreault (2014:242) phrases it:

> on the cutting edge of a search for an alternative modernity...impl[ying] greater participation in decision making, local control over local natural resources...and a rationale that draws attention to and emphasizes the importance of the matrix of environmental, social and cultural factors.

Exponents of this political ecology approach emphasize the negative impacts of extractive capital and mega-mining projects such as open-pit mining—one of the world's most polluting, devastating and dangerous industrial activities—on the environment and the habitat of indigenous and farming communities, particularly as they relate to access to clean or potable water. Examples of these impacts and associated struggles abound.

Another way of understanding these resistance movements and explaining their dynamics is in terms of their connection to the class struggle. Jan Lust, in the case of Peru, and Kyla Sankey in regard to Colombia, take this approach to conclude that the forces engaged in the struggle, and the social base of the social movements formed in this resistance, constitute in effect a new proletariat composed of waged workers and miners, communities of peasant farmers and semiproletarianized rural landless workers surplus to the requirements of extractive capital, and, most significantly, indigenous communities concerned with retaining access to their share of the global commons, securing their livelihoods and protecting their territorial rights and way of living. As Sankey (2014) argues in the case of Colombia, the social and political struggles that surround resource extraction, and the associated upsurge in the forces of resistance, have 'been accompanied by the entrance of new actors onto the scene'. While waged workers continued to play an important role in the class struggle and the broader resistance movement—accounting for close to one-half of the collective acts of protest since 2005—at least 25 per cent of collective actions involved the communities negatively affected by the operations of extractive capital, and these communities were the major driving force of a growing resistance movement, as they clearly are in Mexico. Looking more closely at the forces engaged in the class struggle, it is possible to identify the contours of a new class system or social structure. First, we have the social groupings that share what Svampa (2012) terms 'the commodity consensus' ('consenso de los commodities'). This includes elements of the middle class, including those that take the form of an associational-type social organization or non-governmental organization, which for the most part have been formed within the urban middle classes.

Notwithstanding the environmental concerns of many of its members and its organizations—the middle class can best be defined in terms of the relationship of individuals to consumption rather than to production—this social class is complicit in the operations of extractive capital to a significant degree, with a rather mild or muted opposition and resistance to the environmental implications of unregulated resource extraction and to the social justice considerations regarding issues of class and excessive social inequality in the distribution of wealth and income. These forces constitute the centre-left of the ideological and political spectrum and are readily accommodated to both capitalism and extractivism via a reformist program that combines extractivism with the new developmentalism.

Another major actor in the resistance to extractive capitalism is the community: that is, the indigenous and other communities located close to (and negatively impacted by) the operations of extractive capital and associated megaprojects. These forces tend to be anti-imperialist and anti-capitalist as well as anti- or post-neoliberal in their political orientation. They (correctly) distinguish between corporate capitalism, which they oppose, and small-scale production in the private sector, which they support. They include certain sectors of organized labour but are predominantly made up of proletarianized and semi-proletarianized rural landless or near-landless workers, or small landholding family farmers and peasants whose concerns for their livelihoods are based on access to land, and indigenous communities concerned about protecting their territorial rights to water and land, securing their freedom from both exploitation and the degradation of the environment, and maintaining their relationship to nature. On this broad social base, the forces of resistance predominantly take the form of social movements opposed not so much to extractivism as to extractive capitalism, or the neoliberal model of public policy as well as the underlying system.

For many in this social and political sector, 'socialism' is not understood as an economic system but as a matter of principle (equality and social justice) that can be actualized in different ways. It can even be accommodated to capitalism in the form of local development in the local spaces of the power structure formed within and on the basis of the broader capitalist system. In this context, some elements of the resistance movement are simply looking for a bigger piece of the pie, on both the local level (greater monetary compensation and investment in community development) and the national level (higher taxes and royalties from the mining companies for social redistribution). Furthermore, the fact that these movements are anti-capitalist does not necessarily imply that they seek to conserve anachronistic social and production relations; nor does it mean that they intend to overthrow the dominant capitalist system. It simply means that theirs is a project to distribute more equitably and share the wealth.

In addition to these two forces of resistance, one located in the urban middle class and taking form as an environmental movement and a 'civil society' of social organizations, the other located in the indigenous communities of proletarianized peasant farmers—the resistance to corporate capital and extractive capital, and to government policy in the service of capital (capitalism) and the empire (imperialism), is once again taking the form of organized labour. An example of this is the recent formation in Bolivia of an anti-capitalist coalition of diverse social forces, including groups of organized public sector workers and miners, that have come together to engage the class struggle against extractive capital, agribusiness and the agrarian elite.

Several conclusions can be drawn from this brief sketch of the class struggle in Latin America and the Caribbean today. One is that the struggle under current conditions assumes multiple forms, including a struggle over land, ownership of natural resources and improved access to the global commons, as well as the model used to organize agricultural production. One such model is based on the corporate exemplar of large-scale capitalist production (with inputs of imported capital and advanced modern technology) and oriented towards the world market; the other is based on small-scale production and geared to the domestic market. The corporate model is geared to a development strategy based on large-scale foreign investment in land, natural resource extraction, and the formation of joint venture partnerships between the private sector (multinational corporations that provide both capital and technology) and the state in a new association with capital. In opposition to this corporate model, the resistance movement, which includes Vía Campesina (a global movement of small-scale peasant and family farmers) and a coalition of indigenous communities negatively impacted by extractivism in its diverse forms, is oriented towards small-scale local production and alternative non-capitalist forms of development and trade (Abya Yala, 2009).

Another conclusion is that a large part of the resistance movement is anti-neoliberal and anti-imperialist but not necessarily anti-capitalist. The characterization of the resistance movements discussed in this book as anti-capitalist and anti-imperialist (as well as anti-neoliberal) is shared by the network ('articulation') of social movements that over the past decade has converged around Hugo Chávez's proposed model of an alternative (non-neoliberal) system of international trade—ALBA. From the 16th to the 20th of May 2013, over 200 social movement delegates from twenty-two countries met to debate a continent-wide plan of action constructed around the principles of this alliance, which include the need 'to do battle against the transnational corporations and the processes of privatization' and 'to defend the rights of mother earth and to live well' (in harmony with nature and social solidarity) as well as 'international solidarity' (*Minga Informativa de Movimientos Sociales*). At this 'founding assembly' of a continental social movement network (Social Movements for ALBA), the anti-systemic nature of the network was articulated in the declaration of the need to mobilize and unify the diverse sectors of the popular movement—indigenous communities, peasant farmers' organizations, the organized working class, rural landless workers, the proletarianized rural poor, the semi-proletariat of informal sector street workers, the middle classes (intellectuals and professionals, university students and the youth, small business operators) and a civil society of nongovernmental organizations—around a program of opposition to capitalism, imperialism and patriarchy (the '*voracidad capitalista, imperialista y patriarcal*') in a struggle for 'authentic emancipation with socialism on its horizon'.

But as Tetreault (2014) notes in his analysis of the resistance to extractivism in Mexico, and as Lust (2014) and Sankey (2014) in their studies on extractive capitalism and the resistance in Peru and Colombia emphasize, neither the founding of this continental network of social movements nor the formation of a resistance movement in each country where extractive capital has made major inroads means the end of capitalism. For one thing, while the resistance movement is generally opposed to the dominant extractivist development model and its destructive effects on the environment and livelihoods, very few are yet prepared to abandon the operative capitalist system.

PART 2

Extractive Capitalism and Popular Resistance

∵

CHAPTER 6

Extractive Capitalism and the Resistance in Guyana

Dennis Canterbury

The purpose of this chapter is twofold: to highlight some of the key issues concerning the extractive industries in Guyana and to examine the modus operandi of the post-neoliberal extractive capitalist model in the country. In Guyana the new extractive model is characterized by an increase in capital from the 'emerging economies', state repression of working people, collusion between the state elites and foreign capital from emerging economies to deny the working people their lawful rights, the cheating of the Guyanese people of their wealth, environmental destruction, the disturbance of the livelihood and communities of indigenous peoples, abuse of women, a plethora of illegal activities including corruption, money laundering, smuggling and a land grab.

We begin with an analysis of mining and investment in Guyana's economy and the increasing role of capital from emerging economies. The mining industry has attracted the bulk of the FDI in Guyana in recent years. We then turn towards the struggle of working people in the bauxite industry, and assess the challenges concerning indigenous peoples, and small-scale miners. The third Part concerns the landgrabbing phenomenon, which in the Guyana context includes the search for rare earth minerals and uranium exploration.

Mining Operations and Investment in Guyana

In 2011 agriculture, forestry and fishing contributed 20 percent of the GDP, while services contributed 65.3 percent and mining (69.4 percent for gold and 17.7 percent for bauxite) contributed 11 percent (Bank of Guyana, 2012). Small and medium-scale gold and diamond mining in percentage terms contributed the highest value to Guyana's mineral production between 2005 and 2010 (Mining Journal, 2011). They contributed more that two-thirds of mineral production value between 2008 and 2010, over 60 percent in 2006 and 2007 and almost 50 percent in 2005. Since the closure of Omai Gold Mines in 2005, large-scale mining only takes place in the bauxite subsector. The contribution of bauxite to mineral production value fluctuated but overall declined between 2005 and 2010. Quarrying, stone and sand took third place in the country's mineral production value in the same period.

The size of the mining sector increased significantly over this period—by 19.2 percent in real terms—on account of positive growth in bauxite, gold and diamond output / declaration (Bank of Guyana, 2011). Bauxite output increased by 68 percent. Largely as the result of the increased demand for calcined (RASC) and metal grade (MAZ) bauxite, the mineral from which alumina is derived, by the alumina refineries of China (Aluminum International Today, 2009). At present China imports 45Mt of bauxite, although the export duty in Indonesia forced the Aluminum Corporation of China (CHALCO), China's largest aluminum producer, to declare that it will cutback alumina production, and other producers in China have announced plans to restrict production by 10 percent (ibid.).

As for gold production increased by 17.7 percent between 2010 and 2011. The medium- and small-scale gold mining subsector, the largest employer of labour in the mining industry, led this increase as they sought to capitalize on high gold prices on the international market. The subsector employs more than nine times the number of workers employed in bauxite mining, while stone and sand quarrying employs the least number of workers in the mining industry (Mining Journal, 2011). This disjuncture in employment between small- and medium-scale mining and large-scale bauxite mining was consistent between 2005 and 2010.

The Guyana Mining Act (1989) allows for four scales of mining operations: small (1500 ft x 800 ft whilst a river claim consists of one mile of a navigable river); medium-scale prospecting and mining permits, which cover between 150 and 1200 acres each; and prospecting licenses for areas between 500 and 12,800 acres, with 'permission for geological and geophysical surveys for reconnaissance surveys over large acreages with the objective of applying for prospecting licenses over favourable ground selected on the basis of results obtained from the reconnaissance aerial and field surveys'.[1]

There was a 28 percent decrease in both large- and medium-scale prospecting licenses issued between 2009 and 2010, while mining permits for medium-scale mining increased by 9.4 percent for medium-scale mining operations and 6.3 percent for small-scale operations. By contrast, there were only seven Petroleum exploration licenses issued in both 2009 and 2010 (Guyana Geological Survey and Mines).

The sheer volume of activity in medium and small-scale mining attests to the fact that they are leading the employment of mine and gold workers in officially declared production activities. Furthermore, although there was an increase in permits for medium-scale mining and small-scale claims between 2009 and 2010, there was an increase in the number of persons employed in medium and small-scale gold and diamond mining, and a decline in the

---

1   The Guyana Geological and Mines Commission, http://www.ggmc.gov.gy.

percentage contribution of medium and small-scale mining to Guyana's mineral production over the same period.

Foreign Direct Investment, 1999–2010

From 1999 to 2010 the value of total investment in Guyana increased by over 100 percent, and it increased by 20.4 percent just in 2010. Most of this increase was in the transport and telecommunication sectors, followed by mining and quarrying, agriculture, forestry and fishing. The government sector led on the value of total investment in 2010 with US$303 million compared with US$281.5 million in the private sector, although total investment in the public sector in the period under consideration (1999–2010) was less than that in the private sector—US$1.9 billion compared with US$2.4 billion (Table 6.1).

The Increasing Role of Capital from the 'Emerging Economies'

One feature of the extractive industries in Guyana is the increasing role of capital from the emerging economies. Basically US, Canadian, and Australian capital is engaged in prospecting activities, while capital from non-traditional

TABLE 6.1   *Total investment, 1999-2010*

Years	Private (Local & FDI)	Public (Government)	Total investment
	Value in US$ Million		
1999	157.0	81.0	238.0
2000	152.0	98.5	250.5
2001	166.0	91.0	257.0
2002	162.0	101.5	263.5
2003	155.5	97.0	252.5
2004	152.5	98.0	250.5
2005	157.0	109.5	266.5
2006	205.0	209.0	414.0
2007	222.5	211.5	434.0
2008	259.5	209.0	468.5
2009	285.5	265.0	550.5
2010	281.5	303.0	584.5

SOURCE: US STATE DEPARTMENT, 2012 INVESTMENT CLIMATE STATEMENT—GUYANA.

sources such as Malaysia, China, Russia, and India are engaged in actual production, while Brazilian capital is engaged in landgrabbing for rice production.

The extractive industries in Guyana are characterized by mining (diamonds, gold, copper, bauxite, manganese, rare earth minerals) and forestry products (timber, plywood, fuel wood, and wildlife). However, small-scale local operators are engaged in lumber extraction, fuel wood production, and the export of wildlife. Extractive operations in these industries involve actual production—bauxite, gold, diamonds, forestry products; exploration—bauxite, gold, rare earth minerals, diamonds, manganese; and the resuscitation of the manganese mine. Whereas in the colonial period European, US and Canadian capital dominated the extractive industries currently the so-called 'emerging economies' are playing a greater role in active production while foreign transnationals are engaged primarily in exploration.

The transnationals operating in Guyana's mining sector include eight Canadian, one Australian, and two American companies. Those engaged in exploring for gold include the Azimuth Resources, an Australian company; the US company Sandspring Resources (gold and copper); and the Canadian transnationals Guyana Goldfields, Sacre-Coeur Minerals, GMV Minerals, Guyana Frontier Mining Corp, and Takara Resources. At the present time there is no transnational company engaged in large-scale gold production in Guyana, an industry that is dominated by small- and medium-scale miners, including some joint ventures. However, Canadian Guyana Goldfields is soon to begin production, which will make it the number one gold producer in the country, surpassing the combined gold output/declaration of all small- and medium-miners.

The Canadian company U3O8 Corp. is exploring for uranium, and Reunion Manganese, the wholly owned subsidiary of Reunion Gold Corporation of Canada, is exploring for manganese. And Reunion is soon to begin manganese production at Matthews Ridge while the American company Rare Earth Elements International (REEI), is engaged in exploration for rare earth minerals.

The Chinese and Russian transnationals Bosai Minerals Group, and the Bauxite Company of Guyana, (BCGI), a subsidiary of the Russian Aluminum Company (RUSAL), are currently the principal bauxite producers in Guyana. The Chinese are mining the McKenzie (now Linden) property formerly owned by the Aluminum Company of Canada (ALCAN), and the Russians are mining the bauxite property at Kwakwani, formerly owned by the US mineral company, Reynolds. Both of these (US and Canadian) companies were nationalized in the 1970s and were subsequently sold to the Chinese and Russians. The Canadians, nonetheless, still have a strong presence in the bauxite industry in

Guyana. The Canadian transnational First Bauxite controls large holdings in Guyana's key coastal bauxite belt. The company's properties include Bonasika in the Essequibo, previously drilled by ALCAN in the 1940-60s.[2]

The Malaysian transnational Samling Strategic Corporation Sdn. Bhd,[3] which operates as a subsidiary of Yaw Holding Sdn Bhd, is the principal producer in the forestry sector through the Barama Company. Barama is the leading forest resource and wood products company in Guyana, employing about 1000 workers. The company engages in sale of hardwood logs and sawn timber, and the manufacturing of plywood, decking and flooring products.

Land grabbing for the purposes of food production, forestry products and rare earth materials involves Brazilian, Indian and US capital. Paulo Cesar Quartiero, a large-scale Brazilian rice producer, is interested in acquiring land in Guyana to grow rice for export to Brazil. Under suspicious circumstances Café Coffee Day an Indian company has acquired Guyanese land reportedly for agricultural purposes but is engaged in the export of lumber to India to produce high-end furniture. Rare Earth Elements International, has grabbed large tracts of land in Guyana to explore for rare earth minerals.

The Bauxite Industry and Struggle of the Working People

The bauxite industry is a major source of social unrest against extractive capital currently operating in Guyana. The union busting tactics of RUSAL has led to a prolonged three-year fight with the Guyana Bauxite and General Workers' Union, with the government and RUSAL on one side and the union and working people on the other. The actions of the Bosai Minerals Group and the Guyana government against the bauxite community at Linden, with the government and Bosai on the same side against the working people is the most serious of the unrest.

The social disturbance at Linden sparked by the actions of Bosai Minerals Group, and the decision of the Guyana government to increase electricity tariff in the area has been the most serious and brutally repressed in recent memory of the country. The conflict has evoked the most extreme form of state violence, when on July 18, 2012, the police opened fire on a crowd of peaceful demonstrators killing three of them—24-year-old Shemroy Bouyea, 46-year-old Allan Lewis, and 17-year-old Ron Somerset—and wounding several others. This

---

2 First Bauxite Corporation News Release—First Bauxite Corporation Announces Appointment of New Director and Option Grant, August 17, 2012.

3 Sendirian Berhad—equivalent to incorporated in Malay.

was the first time since Guyana gained its political independence from the UK that the country experienced such levels of state violence against demonstrators. The shootings at Linden are reminiscent of the Ruimveldt Riots in 1905 and the Enmore Riots in 1948 when the colonial police on those separate occasions opened fire on innocent working people, killing and wounding several of them.

Here we consider the events and processes in the bauxite industry in Guyana concerning the Bosai's acquisition of the Linden operations, the social unrest spawned by the increase in electricity tariff at Linden, and the union busting tactics of RUSAL at Kwakwani.

From Omai Bauxite Mining to Bosai Minerals Group

The nationalist government in Guyana undertook a 'mortgage-financed' take over of the bauxite industry during 1970s, and the country fell out of favour with the international financial institutions. The Canadian government then led the way to restore Guyana into the favour of the international financial institutions (Black & McKenna, 1995) and the government-implemented structural adjustment program in the 1980s initiated a process for the privatization of the bauxite industry. The price that Guyana paid for the Canadian services in this connection was to re-open its natural resources sector to exploitation by Canadian extractive capital. Canadian extractive capital quickly became involved in Guyana's gold industry, and then back into the country's bauxite industry at Linden buying it for almost next to nothing and then selling it off for more than 300 percent profit, cheating the Guyanese people.

The privatization program did not work out the way it was scheduled between the IMF/World Bank Group and the Guyana government. The nationalized bauxite company at Linden was scheduled for privatization by the end of 1999. Failing to secure a buyer by that time the government solicited Cambior the parent company of Omai Gold Mines to become involved in the country's bauxite industry. In order to test the feasibility of the company taking over the bauxite operations Cambior became engaged in contract mining at Linden between 1999 and 2004. In December 2004, Cambior and the Guyana-government entered into a partnership to co-create the Omai Bauxite Mining at Linden. Cambior owned 70 percent and the Guyana government 30 percent of Omai Bauxite Mining (Government of Guyana. 2006).

Cambior purchased its 70 percent shares for US$10 million—US$5 million in cash and US$5 million in mining equipment transferred from its Omai Gold Mines, which were closed in 2005. The purchase included the power plant a separate company called Omai Services Incorporated which supplied the bauxite company and community with electricity. Cambior then projected that it would invest US$40 million in the Omai Bauxite Mining operations. But two years after Cambior purchased the bauxite operations at Linden it temporarily ceased production, claiming that bauxite sales had dropped. The company pointed out that it was experiencing difficulties due to operations of Chinese bauxite producers who used coal as a cheap energy source in their production process, compared with oil used by the Omai Bauxite Mining. The Chinese bauxite producers were also accused of being in receipt of state subsidies, which enables them to sell at a lower price. The Guyana government is reported to have threatened to bring the matter to the attention of the World Trade Organization for redress. Cambior assured the Linden community that the temporary closure of its bauxite operations would not affect the supply of electricity because its Omai Services, which controls the power plant, was a separate entity to the mining company, Omai Bauxite Mining.

Meanwhile, in the same year (2006) Cambior sold out to IAMGOLD Corporation, a Canadian gold mining company, for more than C$1.2 billion. In the same year as well, IAMGOLD sold Omai Bauxite Mining and Omai Services for US$46 million to Bosai Minerals Group, a privately owned Chinese business. The Guyana-government that owned 30 percent in the Omai Bauxite Mining and Bosai signed an agreement to allow Bosai to buy the 70 percent shares of OMBI in February 2007.

The first point to note here is that Omai Gold Mines was winding down its operations that were set to close in 2005. Thus, Cambior sold its own mining equipment to itself therefore in essence purchasing the bauxite company for only US$5 million. Second, when the Bauxite Mining and Omai Services Incorporated were sold there was no evidence that Cambior had made any further investment in them. Third, undoubtedly, Cambior was making secrete arrangements for its purchase by IAMGOLD Corporation, at the same time that it was claiming its Linden bauxite operation had to be closed temporarily due to high production cost, and falsely promising the people to continue supplying them with electricity. And fourth, the Guyanese people were cheated out of US$41 million because Cambior really purchased the bauxite company for US$5 million and then, with no new investment it was sold by IAMGOLD Corporation to Bosai Mineral Group for US$46 million.

Bosai Minerals Group was established in 2004 and comprises more than 12 plants, subsidiary companies and branch entities located across China and in Guyana and Ghana. The company engages in industrial minerals mining, fusion manufacturing, international trade and real estate, and had a total asset of RMB5.0 billion at the end of 2009. Its principal products are aluminum metal, metallurgical grade alumina, brown fused alumina, calcined bauxite, coke fuel and coal. Bosai Minerals Group Inc. is ranked among China's top 500 privately owned companies, the top 500 Chinese manufacturers, China's top 50 non-ferrous metal enterprises, and number one in the production of calcined bauxite and brown fused alumina.[4]

Electricity Tariff and Social Unrest in Linden

The extraction of natural resources from Guyana has generated different forms of conflict in the mining and forestry sectors. Historically there has been conflict between the workers and the mining companies that led to unionization, the introduction of worker and community non-wage benefits, improvement in working conditions, and better wages. The working people's struggles have also brought about state repression in support of foreign-owned mining companies and the state-owned mining enterprises. The police massacre of working people in Linden who were protesting against the government-proposed increase in electricity rates in 2012, has taken the working class struggle and state-repression to another level.

The government announced through its minister of finance in his annual budget that it was going to increase electricity rates in the bauxite mining community at Linden as of July 1, 2012. The budget stated that 'electricity costs between $5 and $15 per kWh' at Linden 'while on the GPL (Guyana Power and Light) grid consumers pay an average of $64 per kWh'. The government claimed that the 'total cost of this electricity subsidy' to Linden 'was $2.9 billion' in 2011, which was 'the equivalent of 10 percent of GPL's total revenues'. According to the government, the purpose of the reforms of the electricity tariff subsidy is to give 'effect to a progressive alignment of the subsidized rates with the national rates that are applicable on the GPL grid' (Government of Guyana, 2012). The government sought to increase electricity tariffs in Linden in 2008 but backed down due to a threat of social unrest.

The President of Guyana provided a number of other reasons why the government planned to increase the electricity tariff at Linden. First, the size of the population at Linden, said to be growing rapidly, was identified as one of the reasons for the high electricity subsidy. The Government Statistical Bureau estimated the population in Region 10–Linden, at 41,112 and increasing. Second, the government argues that its predecessor—the PNC administration—also wanted to increase electricity rates at Linden, and to merge them with those of the national grid. However, the opposition countered that at the time that the PNC wanted the merger Linden had produced electricity at a far cheaper rate than the national grid and that the PNC's intention was to have Linden supply the national grid with cheaper electricity. The merger was not to increase the rates at Linden but to lower the rate charged in the rest of the country.

---

4   http://www.cqbosai.com/en/m_aboutus/content.asp?id=16&pid=17.

Third, while it was searching for a buyer, the government subsidized electricity at Linden to make the bauxite company more attractive to foreign investors. Fourth, the electricity subsidy discourages energy conservation at Linden, whereas higher rates will force the residents to conserve on energy.

Data on the consumption (kilowatt per month), the old charges, the proposed new charges as of July 1, 2012, and the percentage change in charges show the extent of the problem facing workers. The percentage change in price paid for consumption (kilowatt per month) ranges from negative 33.3 percent to 810 percent. The consumption of 50 kWh per month sees a lowering of the rates by 33.3 percent. But, consumers will not benefit from this lower rate because the average rate of consumption kilowatt per month is 157 kWh.[5] This means that the average person in Ram's study would have to pay an increase of over 600 percent. From the outset, therefore, the government is really introducing a more than 600 percent increase in electricity charges at Linden while claiming that the increase will be 'progressive'. Furthermore, according to regional officials there is now a 50 KWh ceiling that actually puts the proposed increase at about 400 percent when tied to consumption.[6] In the new arrangement bauxite pensioners would no longer receive 300 kWh free, but only 50 KWh and will have to pay at existing rates for any kWh electricity in excess of that amount.

The working people of Linden took to the streets against the government proposals to increase their electricity rates. The government has since backed down from implementing the reforms but only at a high cost to working people, the Linden community, the bauxite company and the government itself. The *Observer* predicted the social unrest in a letter titled 'Lindeners are on their own, and the Administration knows it', to the editor of the GuyMine published on June 16, 2012. According to the *Observer*:

> [t]here must be an expectation that Lindeners will take to the streets to vent their frustration at the increase. For a government that is struggling under the burden of daily revelations of egregious corruption, the calculation must be that such a development will distract the rest of the populace, and help sap the energy of the opposition.[7]

The residents at Linden called a public meeting at the Old Palm Tree Cinema at Wismar on July 17. The purpose of the meeting was to set the stage for

---

5 This average rate was determined by a study conducted by Christopher Ram (2012).

6 GuyMine News, 'Linden asks President Ramotar for talks on electricity hike', July 19, 2012.

7 GuyMine News, Lindeners are on their own, and the Administration knows it.

protest against the increase in electricity rates. The organizers planned for the protest to take place from the Christianburg Community Center to the Toucan Call Centre at Kara Kara. Their idea was to shut down the Linden community—involving all businesses, including the public transportation system (privately owned boats, mini buses and taxis), for five days beginning on Wednesday, July 18.

Most businesses, the post office, public transport, and power and water supply, were closed on the first day of the protest with the exception of commercial banks. While on the Mackenzie-Wismar Bridge, which crosses the Demerara River, several of the elderly demonstrators decided to sit to take a rest. The demonstrators occupied the bridge for a lengthy period of time. The Mackenzie-Wismar Bridge is the gateway into Guyana's hinterland by road, where the mining and forestry industries are located. The alternative rout to the hinterland through the Bartica-Potaro road is much longer and more expensive. The demonstrators blocked Mackenzie-Wismar Bridge with debris, which the police attempted to clear with little success.

Then in cold-blooded fashion that afternoon, the police opened fire on the demonstrators murdering three of them and wounding several others. The Trinidad-based pathologist revealed that two of the three slain protesters were shot in the region of their hearts with 'bronze-tipped metal fragment' rounds, and that the third was shot in the back. Giles (2012) provides a list of the names of the murdered and injured and their types of injuries.[8]

The police shootings and teargasing of peaceful protesters comprising women, children and men escalated the social unrest at Linden. Several buildings at Linden were burnt to the ground and roads were blocked with debris, timber, burning tires, and dug out ditches. Fire destroyed a building that housed several government entities including the Guyana Revenue Services, the Linden Care Foundation, and the Institute of Distance and Continuing Education. The One Mile Primary School, the largest one of its type in Region 10 that housed 830 students, the Linden Electricity Company, the Ministry of Agriculture offices, the Guyana Energy Agency, and Linmine Secretariat were set ablaze. Fire razed two other buildings as well as the toll, security and Guyana Energy Agency booths at the Mackenzie-Wismar Bridge, and an attempt was made to burn the bridge.

Support for the protesters poured in from across the country, the Caribbean region and internationally. Anti-government public rallies and vigils in

---

8 Source: 'Linden massacre list of victims shot by Guyana Govt Killers'. http://propaganda press.wordpress.com/2012/07/20/linden-massacre-list-of-victims.

support of the protesters were held in Georgetown the capital city of Guyana and at Buxton village. Protest activities were organized in the Guyanese Diaspora in Toronto, London, and New York. The Washington-based Inter-American Commission on Human Rights (IACHR) condemned the killings and called on 'the State of Guyana to use force in strict conformity with its international obligations and the applicable international principle'.[9] The Caribbean Community (Caricom) Secretariat was silent on the issue almost a full month after the shootings. The United Workers Party of St Lucia called on Caricom to 'immediately investigate the proposed electricity tariffs' that fuelled the initial protest.[10]

The demands of the protesters were initially for the government to rescind its decision to increase the electricity rates. But, after the shootings and tear-gasing the demands were expanded to include justice for the murdered and wounded. The working people of Linden gained an important victory from their open confrontation with the Guyana-state that lasted for more than a month. The government acceded to their demands not to increase the electricity rate, and for justice over the police action. The protesters represented by a delegation comprising representatives from A Party for National Unity (APNU) a coalition of political parties including the People's National Congress (PNC), the Working People's Alliance (WPA), Guyana Action Party (GAP), National Front Alliance (NFA); the Alliance for Change (AFC); and the Chairman of Region 10 signed an agreement with the government to end the protests on August 21.

The agreement secured was widely hailed by the workers and their representatives as a significant victory to address broad-ranging issues that affected the Linden community and Region 10 as a whole. But, they were unprepared for the tactics employed by the government to stall the process. The government has not been acting in good faith to allow the agreement to be implemented properly. For example, the chairman of the electricity technical review committee resigned in a one-sentence correspondence to the members of the committee in October without giving any reason for his resignation. The problem however is that the chairman could not resign through the committee because it did not appointment him to the position. The committee was plagued by problems from its inception and found it difficult to obtain the appropriate documents—including the power purchase agreement between

9   Organization of American States Press release: IACHR condemns deadly repression of
     public protest in Guyana, August 3, 2012
10   Caribbean Journal. 2012. 'St Lucia's Stephenson King Condemns CARICOM "Silence" on
     Guyana Unrest', August 16.

the government and the producer of electricity in Linden—to carry out its mandate (Scott Chabrol, 2012).

The commission of inquiry held hearings from September to November 2012, to find out what happened and the causes. It too had its problems with the resignation of its administrator who cited prior commitments (Isles, 2013a). The commission restarted its hearings on compensation claims for the wounded and those who suffered losses in income and property as a result of the disturbances in January 2013.

The Commission restarted its hearings on compensation claims in January 2013, and completed its report in late February 2013 (Isles, 2013b). It found that the police were responsible for the shooting death of the three persons and that although the discharge of rounds was 'somewhat reckless', the action was 'justified' because the crowd was 'hostile' (Chabrol. 2013). The Commission provided compensation for the deceased persons, injured persons, and loss of property. The relatives of the deceased objected to the small amount paid as compensation but the government claims that it is unlikely that the compensation will be increased (Isles, 2013).

The Commission blamed the political opposition for the escalation of the social unrest after the police shooting. It claimed that there was no direct evidence given at the hearing that the police unit at the bridge shot the three deceased, and that the Home Affairs Minister had given instructions to the Guyana Police Force in relation to the incident on July 18, other than testimony from the Minister that he gave a general direction on July 17th, 2012 to the Commissioner of Police that he should take all lawful steps to maintain law and order in Linden (Chabrol, 2013).

Class Dimensions of the Social Unrest at Linden

The class dimension of the working people's struggle against the increase in electricity rates was quite evident in the responses by the money moguls in the gold mining industry. The blocking of the Mackenzie-Wismar Bridge had a negative effect on gold mining communities that could not obtain foodstuffs, fuel and other necessities because of the cut-off of vehicular traffic into the hinterland. Some gold moguls took a stance against the demonstrators demanding the police clear the bridge to allow cargo to pass through into the hinterland. The Regional Chairman for Region 10 even reported at a meeting that some of these individuals threatened to shoot demonstrators in order to clear the bridge to get stuff through to the gold mines. Now, these are considered small-scale miners, many who came from the ranks of the working class but whose class interests now coincided with those of the ruling elites in Guyana.

The Linden Chamber of Commerce and Development representing business interests at Linden had a different position that was more closely related to that of the workers. Its members too were going to be negatively affected by the increase in electricity rates, so it was in their interest to close their businesses if that action would lead eventually to lower rates. Also, the Chamber wanted to know the price at which Bosai sells electricity to the Linden Electricity Company in order to help to determine what the increase in rates should be. The Chamber called for an increase in electricity tariffs 'over a three to five year period' to allow Linden residents the 'time to adjust their electricity consumption patterns'. It presented that argument in the light of the fact that the majority of Linden residents 'use electrical stoves and hot plates rather than gas stoves'.

Linden was once an economically vibrant town in the heyday of the bauxite company. The town then boasted enviable social and public utility services comparable to the rest of the Caribbean. But, with the advent of structural adjustment the town was virtually brought to a standstill with massive layoffs of bauxite workers. The bauxite company that once employed thousands of workers now employs only a few hundred. Linden is now a severely depressed area. Why would the government want to increase the economic burden on such a community by increasing its electricity rates? Undoubtedly, the ruling elites in Guyana have decided to punish the people at Linden because they voted against the government in the 2011 national elections. Guyana's politics in based on racial voting—the government is considered to be an East Indian government and Linden is predominated by Guyanese of African decent. To buy votes at Linden the government recently outlaid a substantial amount of money through the Linden Economic Advancement Program (LEAP) to further the economic development of the area. However, the program was a failure due to corruption and other negative factors, as the LEAP money ended up in the hands of East Indian contractors who reside elsewhere and had no real positive impact on the Linden community.

The Behind-the-Scene Role of Bosai

The Chinese transnational Bosai Minerals Group produces electricity through Bosai Minerals Services, which it sells to the Linden community. The Guyana government pays Bosai for the electricity it supplies to Linden. Without doubt, Bosai had a role in stirring up the social unrest in Linden, as can be gleaned from an examination of some facts concerning the company's operations in Guyana. First, Bosai Minerals Services Inc. supplies electricity to both the Bosai

Minerals Group bauxite operations at Linden and the Linden community. But, there is a disparity between what Bosai Minerals Services claims to be its profit in 2012 and what the public record shows. Bosai claims that it made a profit of US$233,000 in 2010, while the public records 'show that the company made a profit (before tax) of G$76,342,000, the US Dollar equivalent of $380,000' (Ram, 2012).

Second, Bosai Minerals Services is making a profit from the government's electricity subsidy. Guyanese taxpayers are therefore subsidizing a Chinese transnational company to supply electricity to Linden for a handsome profit. Thus, the size of the government's subsidy is not determined purely by the consumption of electricity by Linden residents. Two other factors that influence the size of the government's subsidy are Bosai's bauxite production, which also uses electricity supplied by Bosai Minerals Services, and the profit margin of Bosai Minerals Services. The increase in tariffs would mean that the working people of Linden would be subsidizing both Bosai' bauxite production and Bosai Minerals Services profit margin. The government can reduce its subsidy without increasing electricity rates. All this would mean is that Bosai would earn less profit from the government's subsidy. But, the ruling elites are prepared to side with the interests of foreign extractive capital against those of the working people at Linden.

Third, the financial data suggest that Bosai Minerals Group buys fuel from the State Oil Company of Suriname at a lower price than what Bosai Minerals Services Inc. pays for fuel from the same supplier (ibid.). This disparity in fuel cost is highly questionable. It is possible that Bosai Minerals Services Inc. is inflating the price of its fuel to cheat the working people at Linden who buy electricity from the company. And, if the Guyana government subsides that electricity, then Bosai is cheating the Guyanese taxpayers the source of the subsidy.

Fourth, the Public Utilities Commission (PUC) regulates electricity services in Guyana but Bosai does not fall under the PUC. Thus, Bosai can charge the Linden community whatever it wants for electricity. Bosai is therefore operating outside of the laws of Guyana, and the government seems powerless to reign in the company, due to its apparent private threat to pull out of the country if it is regulated. Bosai was exempted from paying property tax and royalty for five years to December 8, 2009, but the company sought a five-year extension and paid no royalty or property tax in 2010. The royalty rate the company must pay when it does is a meagre 1.5 percent.

Although the Guyana government paints a picture that the electricity subsidy at Linden is a drain on the country's economy the national earnings from Bosai's operations show otherwise. The reality is that the bauxite operations at

Linden contribute millions to the country's coffers. The Guyana government owns 30 percent of the shares in bauxite operations at Linden. The government was paid $440 million in revenues for the bauxite operations, in 2010 and on top of that it received $708 million 'from corporate taxation.' Linden is not a drag on the Guyana-economy the government needs to reinvest the money it makes from the bauxite operations to stimulate the economic development of the community.

The Russian Aluminum Company (RUSAL) Union-Busting Tactics

RUSAL and the Guyana government founded the Guyana Bauxite Company Inc. (BCGI), in 2004. RUSAL owns 90 percent of the company and the Guyana government 10 percent (Government of Guyana. 2006). RASUL acquired the Aroiama Mining Company from the Guyana government in 2006, which was transferred to the Bauxite Company of Guyana in the same year. Based in Kwakwani in the Berbice River and employing about 1000 workers directly or indirectly, RUSAL also has bauxite mines at Kurubuka and Korite, which have a combined deposit of close to 80 million tonnes. RUSAL plans to commence work on new deposits and increase bauxite production by 1.9 billion tonnes in 2013. The BCGI faced a major industrial dispute in 2009, which is on going and is in conflict with the Berbice River community where it is located.

The workers at RUSAL the fourth largest supplier of bauxite to the US resorted to industrial action when the company proposed to lay off 75 workers in 2009, in return for a 10 percent wage increase for those who remained in the company's employ.[11] In the ensuing struggle, the company terminated the labour agreement with the Guyana Bauxite and General Workers Union (GB & GWU). BCGI moved to derecognize the union by threatening workers to sign a petition it prepared to that effect as a condition for employment. The company issued suspension letters to a number of workers involved in the strike, but the union and BCGI agreed that letters of suspension issued to workers would be withdrawn. Instead, the company issued dismissal letters to workers at the same time that it was negotiating terms of resumption with the union to bring an end to the strike. The dismissal letter, which was sent to a selected group of workers, was signed by BCGI's Russian General Manager Sergey Kostyuk and dated November 25. The letter read in part:

> ...you engaged in unlawful industrial action against [BCGI] at Aroiama, Berbice. Your unlawful actions have adversely affected BCGI's operations resulting in severe economic losses. In addition to the above you have

---

11   'Strike stops output at RUSAL bauxite mine in Guyana', Reuters, November 24, 2009.

> engaged in disruptive activities at BCGI's premises at Aroiama. Accordingly, BCGI hereby exercises its lawful right to terminate your employment with immediate effect.[12]

On receiving word of the termination letter, the union promptly walked out of the negotiations. Thereafter, the company announced that it had ceased its operations in Guyana indefinitely, and refused to transport workers to the mines at Kwakwani and Aroiama.

The workers erected a road bloc at Maple Town Aroiama preventing ingress and egress to the mining site. They blocked the Kwakwani Airstrip disrupting flights to the area. The police were brought out in force to clear the roads and airstrip blocked by the protesters. The Guyana government was slow to intervene to help to settle the dispute in favour of workers. Comparatively, it intervenes with much speed to settle industrial disputes in the sugar industry, which it owns. Most likely the slowness to intervene in labour dispute at BCGI is probable due to the ownership structure of the company. BCGI is essentially a foreign-owned enterprise and the government is faced with a dilemma because of its sweetheart deal with the company. The government is usually reluctant to intervene in foreign companies that clearly violate the laws of Guyana. Indeed, the government became apologetic for BCGI stating that whereas in other countries, bauxite companies closed their doors and left, in Guyana RUSAL and Bosai Minerals Group, have not done so but are trying to minimize the impact of the global downturn on jobs.

The two-week industrial action that commenced on November 22 for a wage increase and against the company's plans to lay off 75 workers cost the company US$350 millions. Solidarity for the bauxite workers came from different sources outside of the country including the London-based African Socialist International and the Oilfield Workers Trade Union of Trinidad and Tobago.

The management of the BCGI on the advice of its labour consultant Mohamed Akeel, who was once the Chief Labour Officer in Guyana for more than a decade, formed a Workers Committee as an illegal substitute for the GB & GWU. The company resorted to the Workers Committee after its failed attempt to have workers sign up to bring in the National Association of Agricultural, Commercial and Industrial Employees (NAACIE) as their bargaining agent. It must be noted that the Minister of Labour Nanda Kishore Gopaul is one of the big wigs in the NAACIE. The actions of the BCGI were in

---

12   Quoted in Cathy Richards. 2009. 'Bauxite strike talk collapse', Stabroek News, November 27.

violation of the Trade Union Recognition and Certification Act Chapter 98:07, Section 23 (1), which states

> [w]here a trade union obtains a certificate of recognition for workers comprised in a bargaining unit in accordance with this Part, the employer shall recognize the union, and the union and the employer shall bargain in good faith and enter into negotiations with each other for the purpose of collective bargaining.[13]

The GB&GWU prepared a presentation that was made to the Trade Union Recognition and Certification Board in Guyana in which it outlined the nature of its grievance with RUSAL. The document states that:

> on the matter of the Guyana Bauxite & General Workers Union (GB & GWU) and the Bauxite Company Guyana. (BCGI)...the Union charges that BCGI and the Minister of Labour are involved in acts inimical to the best interest of Bauxite workers, the communities of which they are a part and the peace and stability of the industrial sector. These are manifest in the following: The refusal of the BCGI to meet with the Union to discuss matters pertaining to workers' welfare in as much as there exists a legal Certificate of Recognition between the parties; The company's actions of coercing members of the Union to sign a company prepared petition to request a poll with a view of de-recognizing the Union under Section 31 of the Trade Union Recognition Act, Chapter 98:07, and; In light of public statements reported in the Stabroek News, January 2, 2010 where the Minister of Labour said the Ministry has not conducted an investigation to determine whether the signatures were taken fairly and not under duress yet opined that it may indicate that those signatures were gotten of free will.[14]

The fallout from the strike is ongoing and the GB & GWU has been pushing back against the company's union-busting tactics since March 12, 2010. The union is not alone in its struggle, as solidarity has been pouring in from across the world. In a press release the union stated that within 24 hours of the launching of its petition against BCGI's union busting tactics in

13   See Presentation made to the Trade Union Recognition & Certification Board by the Guyana Bauxite & General Workers Union, January 12, 2009.
14   See the presentation made to the Trade Union Recognition & Certification Board by the Guyana Bauxite & General Workers Union, January 12, 2009.

collusion with the Guyana government, over 800 letters were sent to the Minister of Labour,

> from as far as Australia, Pakistan, India, USA, Japan, United Kingdom, Turkey, Sweden, Oman, Papua New Guinea, Caribbean and Ukraine, by organizations such as the America Federation of Labour-Congress of Industrial Organization (AFL-CIO), British Trade Union Congress, Federación Trabajadores Pasteleros, Industrial Workers of the World, unions, rights organization, universities, students bodies, interest groups and individuals. The petition is now in English, French and Dutch and translation into other languages is currently in process in order to widen the campaign.
>
> GUYANA BAUXITE and GENERAL WORKERS UNION, 2010

The matter between the GB & GWU and the BCGI-RUSAL was only sent to arbitration in March 2012, more than three years after it began. The arbitration will determine whether both sides 'have indulged in prudent industrial/labour relations practices, and whether or not they have complied with known labour and industrial relations laws and conventions on a number of critical issues'. (Kaieteur News, 2012). Specifically the arbitration will look into 'the wages dispute between the Company and the Union with respect to the period January 1, 2009 to December 31, 2010 which resulted from the application of Term # 7 of the terms of Resumption signed between the Company and the Union on August 25, 2009'. Also, the arbitrator will investigate 'the dispute which led to the suspension of 67 workers who protested unsafe working condition at the Company's operation during the period May 2009'.

In addition, the arbitration tribunal will look into 'the dispute between the Company and the Union with respect to the dismissal of fifty-seven employees from the Company during the period December 1–10, 2009'. Further, it will investigate 'the dispute between the Company and the Union with respect to the dismissal of five employees namely; Winsworth Blair, Elmiton McAlmont, Laurel George, Marcel Odonoghu and Lennox Daw, who protested conditions of storage of food material in areas allegedly infested with rodents and roaches, and the use of the said food materials in the kitchen to prepare meals for staff at the Aroaima Location'. Finally, the tribunal will investigate 'the allegedly threatening of workers by the General Manager of BCGI, Ruslan Volokhov on May 8, 2011 who were protesting the non-availability of potable water at the camp site in Aroaima'.

BCGI-RUSAL however, did not send any representative to the first hearing of the tribunal but moved to the High Court of Guyana and secured a temporary stay of the arbitration proceedings (Scott Chabrol, 2012). Meanwhile, the union is still awaiting the Minister of Labour to reissue letters for the arbitration proceedings to begin.

It is quite clear that extractive capital from emerging economies behave in the same anti-working class manner as their counterparts from the Euro-American imperial world. Although it might be associated with the development of infrastructure in mineral rich developing economies the primary interest of such capital is profit generation. Based on the Guyana-experience, extractive capital from emerging economies in the post-neoliberal period will not reverse the resource curse, but will perpetuate it.

Indigenous Peoples, Small-Scale Artisanal Miners and Women Issues

Undoubtedly, natural resource extraction is having a debilitating impact on indigenous peoples around the globe and Guyana is no exception. The United Nations Special Rapporteur on the rights of indigenous peoples in an analysis of the impact of extractive industries operating within or near indigenous communities reported that these industries 'are becoming the greatest challenges to the exercise of the rights of indigenous peoples' (United Nations, 2011). According to the report '[t]his situation is further evidenced by the lack of understanding of basic minimum standards on the effects of extractive industries affecting indigenous peoples and about the role and responsibility of the State to ensure protection of their rights' (ibid.). In this section we examine some of the issues pertaining to the challenges posed by mining to indigenous communities in Guyana, small scale and women miners.

Indigenous Peoples and Mining in Guyana
The indigenous peoples in Guyana have historically engaged in traditional artisanal mining techniques—bucket, sifter and panning without chemicals. In some cases such as in Region 7 there are community-owned land dredges operated by indigenous peoples. Also, they work on land dredges and in pit mining ventures owned by non-indigenous people interests. However, indigenous peoples' communities face a number of problems caused by the mining industry located in their homesteads.

The indigenous peoples' communities are faced with a number of problems and challenges caused by the mining industry. These challenges include:

[l]imited environmental regulation and ongoing violation of Amerindian rights, mining concessions are issued to third parties by the Guyana Geology and Mines Commission (GGMC) on traditional Amerindian lands without the knowledge of or free, prior and informed consent (FPIC) of affected communities, as required under the Amerindian Act (though FPIC only applies to small- and medium-scale mining on or near to titled lands), corruption of community leaders by mining interests, piecemeal support for training in low-impact mining, weak/unaccountable management of community dredges, no local or national standards yet agreed for low-impact community mining, [and] low-impact mining standards such as those developed by the Association for Responsible Mining (ARM) require revision in order to fit current mining practices in Guyana....

GRIFFITHS & ANSELMO, 2010

Large- and medium-scale gold mining with dredges, and open pit mining are the cause of major destruction to the environment and local communities. Indigenous youths and women are subjected to sexual exploitation and low paying jobs in mining camps using toxic chemicals and dredges. Living and working under such conditions have a negative impact on the health of the indigenous peoples and others. The health problems in the gold and diamond mining sector include mercury poisoning, malaria, typhoid, dengue, diabetes, etc. Also, hygiene is a major problem, due to inadequate facilities for disposal of human and other waste. The poor hygiene situation is one of the causes of the high incidence of malaria and typhoid in gold mining communities. Undoubtedly, the health, environmental, social and cultural costs to the indigenous communities are far greater than the cash benefits that accrue to them from mining. Also, the monopolistic and oligopolistic conditions under which businesses operate in gold mining communities are the cause of inflation in those areas.

Besides the challenges that indigenous communities face due to gold mining and logging there are other problem areas that must be considered. The pollution of water used by indigenous villages is a major source of conflict these communities have with the mining entities. Nowadays, residents in indigenous communities like the Chi Chi District in western Guyana near Venezuela cannot drink or bathe in water from the river nearest to their community. They have to resort to digging their own pits or trenches to collect rainwater for domestic use, or to travel long distances to find creeks that are not polluted. The river water is polluted with chemicals and sedimentation from river and land dredges that the local and Brazilian miners operate in the area

(Wilkinson, 2012). Also, miners in the Potaro region near Brazil 'twice excavated the main road and uprooted underground state water main pipes while looking for gold, stranding residents on both sides of large craters and cutting off water supplies' (Griffiths & Anselmo, 2010).

The government indicated that it would soon increase the fees and fines for environmental degradation. The negative social and environmental effects of mining also include damage to the river banks, which take several years to be mitigated, the widening of river channels and weakening of soil at river banks, which result in toppling of trees into rivers, blockages, and changes to main river channels resulting in un-navigable channels. In addition, the increase turbidity of 'rivers and creeks result [in]... from reduced visibility and light penetration in water [causes] a reduction of the photosynthetic ability of aquatic plants, and the inhibition of respiration of some species of fishes resulting in their death' (Wilkinson, 2012). The government indicated that 'the death of a few susceptible species causes significant impacts on the food web and can result in a reduction of freshwater fish species which are a primary source of food for riverain communities' (ibid.). Furthermore, river mining pollutes drinking water, and creates 'huge sand and gravel islands that are restricting water flow and flooding upstream and devaluing of Guyana's tourism product including sports fishing' (ibid.). Indigenous communities downstream of active dredging operations complain that they are unable to undertake subsistence fishing and hunting, washing and bathing, and to access potable water close to settlements.

The Amerindian People's Association (APA), an umbrella organisation representing the indigenous community, identified a number of negative effects of mining on their communities. These include an 'increase in prostitution, drug and human trafficking, pollution, the inability of Amerindians to consume fish and other marine life and even river mouths being blocked by heavy sedimentation' (ibid.). Wildlife is also disappearing because of equipment noise, dirty water and the increase in human activity in the hinterland. The indigenous peoples also depend on wildlife to feed themselves.

Government officials estimate that nearly 15,000 Brazilians including illegal miners now reside in Guyana's hinterland. Many of the Brazilians who now settle in Guyana were pushed out of Venezuela and Suriname. The high gold price on the world market is attracting investors in the Guyana gold industry from Australia, South Africa, the US, Brazil and Canada. The industry has attracted investment of more than one billion dollars in recent years. A number of foreign companies now prospecting for gold in Guyana are expected to begin producing in the near future. It is projected that when Guyana Goldfields begin production it will more than double the output of gold produced by the Omai Gold Mines, which operated in Guyana for 12 years ending in 2005.

There is an increase in murders, suspected murders, disappearances, armed robberies, rape and abuse in the gold fields. The police investigated nearly 50 murders in 2011, about 40 more than normal, as well as fights over gold and women or from drunken rum sprees by miners on time off. There are recent reports of ranks of the Guyana Defense Force had beaten and robbed several miners of raw gold.

Small-Scale Miners versus the Minister

Conflict in the mineral extraction sector in Guyana takes on different forms including between large and small-scale miners in the gold sector, and over government measures. For example, the mining industry opposed new conditions and regulations for 'preserving the Amazon jungle as a part of Guyana's contribution to mitigating climate change' (Wilkinson, 2010). The Guyanese government signed a forestry preservation deal in 2009 with Norway to receive up to 250 million dollars over a five-year period. This has resulted in efforts by the government to increase regulations in the extractive sector—gold, diamonds and forestry products. Some of the new and controversial measures include a six-month waiting period for approval of mining permits. The government's position is that this measure is to permit the Guyana Forestry Commission 'to allow commercial but controlled harvesting of areas before small and medium scale miners armed with shovels, power hoses and land dredges, move in and commence operations' (ibid.). Miners argue that they have no commercial interest in trees and that the six-month rule is unenforceable due to the fact that the forest is so vast and some mining areas are so far away from administrative control.

The conflict has led to the resignation of the president of the Guyana Gold and Diamond Miners Association who was forced out by miners on the grounds that he was taking sides with the government in the dispute. Also, the approximately 4000 miners resorted to blocking access to the mining town of Bartica in protest against the regulation. It is estimated that Guyana has 25,000 miners with about one-third of them coming from Brazil. Statements from the Guyana-president indicated that the government was prepared to repress small and medium miners in an effort to appease Norway and the World Bank concerning the protection of Guyana's forest (Wilkinson. 2010).

The Guyana-president is reportedly to have said his administration 'will have to go it alone if we cannot do it together' with the miners. The president also threatened to banish the use of mercury in the recovery of gold and diamonds. Undoubtedly, the government has exercised a preference to please the World Bank and Norway over the small and medium-scale miners who are the first to feel the squeeze of tighter controls and tougher new rules in the gold and diamond mining industry. Besides pleasing foreign forces, the miners believe that the government really wants to prevent them from felling trees that are of commercial value for the timber industry. The miners argue that what is really needed is not new regulations but for 'the geological commission to enforce in an organized way the existing systems for reforestation and cooperation between timber harvesters and miners'. The small and medium-scale miners are becoming a powerful force in Guyana in the light of the fact that in the absence of any large-scale gold mining operation, the industry was second in foreign exchange importance after sugar (Wilkinson, 2010). Also, the Guyana-government halted granting mining permits in the New River 'until further notice' in the light of widespread concerns by the indigenous communities in the area, as stated above (Demerara Waves, 2012).

The Guyana government introduced a moratorium on new licenses in an effort to address the problem of illegal mining in the interior. The moratorium produced a conflict situation as enraged miners accused the government of abusing its powers. The miners resorted to their organization the Guyana Gold and Diamond Association (GGDMA), which organized an emergency meeting at which it passed a motion of no confidence in the government minister responsible for mining, and raised money to bring a court challenge to the moratorium. The GGDMA threatened street protests if a compromise was not reached, and the government announced that the ban would only last for one month. The miners argued that they were aware of the environmental and other problems in the mining industry. They observed that miners who were caught violating the country's laws and destroying the environment should be prosecuted, but that the entire industry should not have to suffer for the violations of errant miners. The GGDMA stated that 'the mining act is clear on how an errant miner should be punished' and that it sees 'no reason for all applications to be turned away'. In its view, the government should just 'deal with those who create problems' (Caribbean 360, 2012).

Women Miners at Issue

Women are becoming increasingly involved in the natural resource extractive sector in Guyana, as miners, cooks, sex workers, etc. Human trafficking involving women and girls in forced prostitution in the gold industry to generate profit for traffickers and pleasure for miners is a major issue of concern. According to the U.S. Department of State's Trafficking in Persons Report, 'The limited government control of Guyana's vast interior regions, combined with profits from gold mining and the prostitution that accompanies the industry provide conditions conducive for trafficking' (U.S. Department of State, 2012b). The report stated that 'Guyanese from rural, economically depressed areas are particularly vulnerable to trafficking in mining areas and urban centres'.

Also, exploitive child labour practices within the mining industry and forestry sector, which helps to line the pockets of miners and forestry companies, are other concerns. For example, Bert Wilkinson reported in the Associated Press that a young child who appeared no older than eight years old was found panning for gold in a mining camp in Guyana (Wilkinson, 2012a). The mother of the boy was believed to be working in another gold mining camp. The Guyana Gold and Diamond Miners Association has no statistics on children working in the mining sector, but crude estimates place the numbers in the hundreds.

The problems that women miners face in Guyana have forced them to form the Guyana Women's Miners Association (GWMA). Over 70 women have joined the GWMA and indication of the growing number of women who participate in gold and diamond mining. Some of the women miners have their own dredges, while others work as cooks. The women miners argue that working in the minefields is far more problematic for them than it is for men. The physical aspect of mining is a major challenge in itself that women miners have to contend with on a daily basis. The added problems such as the daily abuse, exploitation, and stigmatization as prostitutes, discrimination, and bullying are major trials with which they must contend. But, the draw of women into the goldfields is driven by the harsh economic conditions in Guyana along with the high price for gold, despite the hazards including an increase in murders, disappearances, armed robberies, and rape. Many of these crimes go unreported and remain unsolved.

The leader of the GWMA Simona Brooms in an interview with the Stabroek News papers is reported to have pointed out that she personally got involved and helped a woman, who was not a gold miner, escape from her captor (Stabroek News, 2012.). Brooms 'also referred to instances where women are forced into sex work by their male partners or by other women who exploit them. Women are also forced to become partners of men they do not want because the option would be rape with total impunity' (ibid.). According to Brooms other miners 'turn a blind eye' to these conditions of women 'there is no condemnation, no support for the victim, no ostracizing of the rapist/ abuser. There are no police stations or outposts close to many of the mining sites and no one bothers to call the police unless the crime involves the loss of life, gold or money'. Brooms noted that '[o]ther crimes are met by a wall of silence from men and women who do not want to get involved, but are nevertheless condoning the obscenities by their inaction'(ibid.). Business and dredge owners operating in the mining sector recruit women to work as cooks and shopkeepers in the industry but they make no accommodation for perquisites such as bathroom facilities for them.

In a land dispute between a female gold miner Joan Chang and the Guyana Geological and Mines Commission (GGMC) and the Isseneru Village Council, the High Court ruled in favour of Chang. The Village Council claimed that Chang was working its titled lands. But, it was the GGMC who issued her with two cease work orders on complaints from the village. Chang took legal action to stop the Council from interfering with her operation. The GGMC and the Isseneru Village Council planned to appeal the court ruling on the grounds that the Amerindian Act to protect the rights of the Amerindians was bypassed (Isles, 2013c). This case shows the complexities facing women miners. Although Ms. Chang had the official documents to mine the property the very authorities that assigned her the claim turned around and took her to court for it.

Landgrabbing, Rare Earth and Uranium Exploration

The Land Grab

The global landgrabbing phenomenon where governments and corporations buy up lands in foreign countries has arrived in Guyana with detrimental effects to the indigenous peoples. Typically the land grab allows foreign companies to grow food for export to the investing countries, or to secure water resources, rare earth, etc., and for speculation purposes. The land grab is driven among other things by high food prices, and the growing global demand for biofuels. The global demand for minerals is identified as another major cause of the land grab spearheaded by the extractive industries (Sibaud, 2012). The global demand for natural resources is real as the production of iron ore is up by 180 percent, cobalt 165 percent, lithium 125 percent, and coal 44 percent (ibid.). According to Sibaud (2012):

> The extractive industries have grown significantly in the last 10 years, due to changes in consumption patterns, and a throwaway culture where regular technology upgrades are considered the norm. In the last 10 years, exploration budgets have increased nine-fold, from two billion to 18 billion dollars. The period between 2005–2010 saw China's mining sector grow by nearly a third, while Peru's mining exports grew by one third in 2011 alone. Meanwhile, the region of Puno in the South of the country has seen mineral concessions almost triple between 2002 and 2010.

The land grab in Guyana is more so for the extraction of natural resources given the gold rush in the country, rather than for agricultural and biofuels production. This is not because the Guyana government did not want to sell-off the country to land grabbers involved in agricultural production. Indeed, in the light of the global food crisis, the Guyana-government sought to sell-off the country's lands to Libyan and US investors for the cultivation of mega-agricultural farm projects (The Tripoli Post, 2009). A delegation from Libya visited the country in 2009 to have talks on a mega-agricultural project in Guyana. However, the government is still waiting for the large investment dollars in agriculture to turn the country into a key producer in the Caribbean's multi-billion dollar food industry[15]—the region imports almost US$4 billion in food, annually.

Also, Paulo Cesar Quartiero a large-scale Brazilian rice producer expressed interest in buying-up lands in Guyana for agricultural purposes. Brazilians are ever present in Guyana with their government 'financing the construction of roads, bridges and other infrastructure' in the country. This is to open up the interior of Guyana among other things to 'large-scale agricultural projects that will export crops to Brazil' (GRAIN, 2010). Quartiero was reportedly negotiating with the Guyananese government for a 99-year lease to large areas of indigenous lands in the Rupununi savannah to grow food. The Brazilian Supreme Court had forced Quartiero and other rice farmers to abandon lands they illegally took from indigenous communities in Raposa Serra do Sol in Brazil (*Stabroek News*, 2009). The Brazilian farmers planned to produce rice in Guyana, not for sale in Guyana but for export to the Brazilian market.

Also, the Texan based RiceTec, a 'multinational seed company' approached the government 'for about 2000 ha of land in the same' Rupununi savannah 'region—a diverse and fragile ecosystem that is home to several indigenous peoples' (GRAIN, 2010). The Guyana government was also working with several investors interested in large projects including soybean, livestock, cattle and rice at Pirara in the country's Region 9.

Café Coffee Day a coffee-making company in India was awarded some 1.8 million acres of forestland in Guyana in 2011. News of the deal was broken by the Times of India, which reported that 'V.G. Siddhartha, best known for his Café Coffee Day (CCD) chain, has taken 1.85 million acres of Amazonian forestland on a 30-year lease from Guyana in South America, to start a furniture business in India' (Kaieteur News, 2012). The Times of India reported that the company had already started operations in Guyana. There were reports that in two months CCD shipped almost 50 containers of log from Guyana. The main

---

15   'Yet to see huge regional investment in agricultural sector', Farmland.org, June 22, 2009.

logs shipped were washiba, a hardwood to make top-end furniture, purple-heart greenheart, and snakewood (Kaieteur News, 2012a).

The Guyanese political opposition described the Café Coffee Day deal as 'shady'. The government insists that the company was not registered in large-scale exploration in the country. Indeed, the Guyana government made the land deal, with Vaitarna Holdings Private Inc. (VHPI) that is a subsidiary of CCD, which was issued a State Forest Exploratory Permit (SFEP) previously issued to Simon and Shock Intl. (SSI), a US company, and a Timber Sales Agreement (TSA) previously issued to Caribbean Resources Limited (CRL).

Rare Earth Elements (REE)
In the mad scramble for minerals globally rare earth elements in Guyana have become a center of attraction for extractive capital. Rare Earth Elements International, (REEI) a US-based mineral exploration company acquired a rare earth property at Port Kaituma in 2012.[16] The property comprises 44 square miles with over 200 concessions. The Guyana Geological and Mines Commission estimated in 2009 that the initial deposit of Colimbite-Tantalite in the ground is in excess of US$10 million at current market price.

'Rare earth elements are a group of seventeen chemical elements that occur together in the periodic table' consisting of 'yttrium and the 15 lanthanide elements'. These elements "are all metals and the group is often referred to as the 'rare earth metals'".[17] In the last twenty years the explosion in demand for products that require rare earth metals has been driving extractive capital to the furthest reaches of the planet. Rare earth elements are used in many devices such as computer memory, DVD's, rechargeable batteries, cell phones, car catalytic converters, magnets, fluorescent lighting, and many more products. For example, rare earth elements provide the US military superiority because of their use in the production of 'night-vision goggles, precision-guided weapons and other defence technology such as armoured vehicles and projectiles that shatter upon impact in thousands of sharp fragments'.[18]

---

16   'REE International Acquires Rare Earth Property With Estimated Value of $10 Million', Marketwire—Mining and Metals, March 20, 2012.

17   REE—Rare Earth Elements and their Uses: The demand for rare earth elements is rising rapidly but their occurrence in minable deposits is very limited. http://geology.com/articles/rare-earth-elements/

18   'REE International Acquires Rare Earth Property With Estimated Value of $10 Million', Marketwire—Mining and Metals, March 20, 2012.

Uranium Exploration in Guyana

The long-term demand for uranium is on the increase driven by China and
India that are expanding their nuclear generation capacities. Guyana has a role
in the expanding exploration for uranium as two Canadian mining companies
are exploring for the mineral in the country. U308 Corporation–a Canadian
mining company based in Toronto–is exploring for uranium in Guyana's
Roraima Basin. U308 Corporation has uranium exploration rights to approximately 1.3 million ha in the Roraima Basin. Also, Argus Metals of Vancouver,
British Columbia in Canada, recently acquired a license to explore for the mineral at Port Kaituma—the area where the notorious Jim Jones' Peoples Temple
was located.

The president of Argus Metal observed that the 'Kaituma project is one of
the few undrilled global uranium exploration targets with the potential size to
have a significant impact on uranium markets and is located one-half kilometers from a deep water shipping port, an active paved airstrip and is traversed
by all-weather roads and rail grade'.[19] Argus Metal purchased the Kaituma
Project from StrataGold Corporation (a subsidiary of Victoria Gold Corp.) and
Newmont Overseas Exploration.

Conclusions

The conclusions drawn from the foregoing analyses of the dynamics of extractive capitalism in Guyana are instructive.

First, the state is being relied on to play an increasing role in the economic
development process through joint ventures. The Chinese model of mineral
resource extraction in the Democratic Republic of Congo, and in Guyana
where the state has an increasing percentage ownership in the foreign owned
bauxite companies in the country are cases in point. In Guyana, the bauxite
companies were at first privately owned, then they were nationalized and
became wholly state-owned, but when they were resold to private interests the
state retained a hold in their capital stocks.

Second, mining is playing an increasing role in the Guyana economy in
terms of its contribution to the GDP. Also, the mining industry attracts a significant share of foreign direct investment inflows.

Third, capital from the emerging economies is currently playing an increasing role in production in the extractive industries, while capital from the

---

19   Argus Receives Title and Uranium License for the Large-scale, Drill-ready Kaituma
      Uranium/Gold Project Marketwire—Mining and Metals | January 31, 2012.

advanced capitalist countries is engaged more in exploration, and financial speculation, but is poised to step in at any time to resume its hegemony.

Fourth, the state is in collaboration with capital from the 'emerging economies', which are dominant in the bauxite industry in Guyana in anti-working class activities such as union-busting. Indeed, the state has resorted to severe repression of bauxite workers demonstrations that led to the police murdering three peaceful protesters.

Fifth, mining has a particularly negative impact on the livelihoods of indigenous peoples and their communities in Guyana, and several conflict situations are ever present in the gold fields with the natives, including women miners.

Sixth, the prevalence of criminal activities, including money laundering, gold smuggling, foreigners illegal mining for gold, corruption, murders, rape, etc., is another dimension of the dynamics of the extractive industries in the current period.

Seventh, the current phase of extractive capitalism is characterized by the phenomenon described as landgrabbing in which foreign companies are acquiring large stretches of lands to explore for uranium and rare earth minerals.

Finally, the labour movement once more is beginning to play a very important part in the growing movement of resistance to extractive capitalism.

CHAPTER 7

Extractive Capitalism and Brazil's Great Leap Backward

Brazil has witnessed one of the world's most striking reversals in modern history: from a dynamic nationalist industrializing to a primary export economy. From the mid-1930s to the mid-1980s Brazil averaged nearly ten percent growth in its manufacturing sector largely based on state interventionist policies, subsidizing, protecting and regulating the growth of national public and private enterprises. Changes in the 'balance' between national and foreign (imperial) capital began to take place following the military coup of 1964 and accelerated after the return of electoral politics in the mid-1980s. The election of neoliberal politicians, especially with the election of the Cardoso regime in the mid-1990s, had a devastating impact on strategic sectors of the national economy: wholesale privatization was accompanied by the denationalization of the commanding heights of the economy and the deregulation of capital markets (Petras & Veltmeyer, 2003). Cardoso's regime set the stage for the massive flow of foreign capital into the agro-mineral, finance, insurance and real estate sectors. The rise in interest rates as demanded by the IMF and World Bank and the speculative market in real estate raised the costs of industrial production. Cardoso's lowered tariffs ended industrial subsidies and opened the door to industrial imports. These neoliberal policies led to the relative and absolute decline of industrial production.

The Presidential victory of the self-styled 'Workers Party' in 2002 deepened and expanded the 'great reversal' promoted by its neoliberal predecessors. Brazil reverted to becoming a primary commodity exporter, as soya, cattle, iron and metals exports multiplied and textile, transport and manufacturing exports declined (Petras, 2005). Brazil became one of the leading extractive commodity exporters in the world. Brazil's dependence on commodity exports was aided and abated by the massive entry and penetration of imperial multi-national corporations and financial flows by overseas banks. Overseas markets and foreign banks became the driving force of extractive growth and industrial demise.

To gain a better understanding of Brazil's 'great reversion' from a dynamic nationalist-industrializing to a vulnerable imperial driven agro-mineral extractive dependency, we need to briefly review the political economy of Brazil over the past fifty years to identify the decisive 'turning points' and the centrality of political and class struggle.

The Military Model: Modernization from Above

Under the military dictatorships (1964–1984) economic policy was based on a hybrid strategy emphasizing a triple alliance of state, foreign and national private capital (Evans, 1979) focused primarily on industrial exports and secondarily on agriculture commodities (especially traditional products such as coffee).

The military discarded the nationalist-populist model based on state industries and peasant cooperatives of the ousted leftist President Goulart and put in place an alliance of industrial capitalists and agribusiness. Riding a wave of expanding global markets and benefiting from the repression of labour, the compression of wages and salaries, comprehensive subsidies and protectionist policies, the economy grew by double digits from the late 1960s to the mid-1970s, the so-called 'Brazilian Miracle' (Serra, 1973: 100–140). The military while ending any threats of nationalizations, put in place a number of 'national content' rules on the foreign multi-nationals which expanded Brazil's industrial base and enlarged the size and scope of the urban working class, especially in the automotive industry. This led to the growth of the metal workers union and later the Workers' Party. The 'export model' based on light and heavy industry, foreign and domestic producers, was regionally based (southeast). The military modernization strategy heightened inequalities and integrated the local 'national' capitalists to imperial MNCs. This laid the groundwork for the onset of the anti-dictatorial struggles and the return of democracy. Neoliberal parties gained hegemony with the turn to electoral politics.

Cardoso: Neoliberalism and the Ascendancy of Extractive Capital

The electoral opposition which succeeded the military regimes was initially polarized between a liberal, free market, agro-mineral elite allied with imperial MNC and on the other hand a worker, peasant, rural worker and lower middle class nationalist bloc, intent on promoting public ownership, social welfare, the redistribution of income and agrarian reform. Militant labour formed the CUT; landless peasants formed the MST and both joined the middle class to form the PT.

The first decade of electoral politics 1984–94, was characterized by the tug and pull between the residual statist capitalism inherited from the previous military regime and the emerging liberal 'free market' bourgeoisie. The debt crises, hyper-inflation, massive systemic corruption, the impeachment of President Collor and economic stagnation severely weakened the statist capitalist sectors and led to ascendancy of an alliance of agro-mineral and finance capital, both foreign and local capitalists, linked to overseas markets. This retrograde coalition found their political leader and road to power with the election of Fernando Henrique Cardoso, a former leftist academic turned free market zealot.

The election of Cardoso led to a decisive break with the national statist policies of the previous sixty years. Cardoso's policies gave a decisive push toward the denationalization and privatization of the economy, essential elements in the reconfiguration of Brazil's economy and the ascendancy of extractive capital. By almost all indicators Cardoso's neoliberal policies led to a precipitous great leap backward, concentrating income and land, and increasing foreign ownership of strategic sectors. Cardoso's 'reform' of the economy at the expense of industrial labour, public ownership and the country's mass of organized landless rural workers provoked widespread strikes and land occupations. Expanding the extractive economy in response to the growing world demand for agrofood products, energy and industrial minerals, and opening up the Amazon to extractive capital on the frontier of biofuel production, was at the expense not only of the ecology and inhabitants of the region but of both manufacturing and high-end services where both production and labour earnings overall declined as a percentage of GNP and relative to output and exports of primary commodities. Although Dilma Rousseff, Lula da Silva's handpicked successor as President of The country, sought or professed to continue his policy emphasis on substituting the production of high-value manufactured goods for low-value commodities, the record shows that this has not happened. The structure of Brazilian exports since 2004 has shifted in the opposite direction. Since Lula's second term in office and over Rousseff's tenure Brazil's export earnings from manufactured goods continue to fall while those from primary goods continue to rise and in 2012 have taken over as the main source of export earnings for the first time.

The reason for this change in the structure of production and exports in the direction of a trend towards primary commodity exports without a doubt is the growing demand for foodstuffs and minerals, especially iron ore, now Brazil's biggest commodity export by far (over 17 percent of total exports), in the other BRICs, especially China, where soaring demand for both soft and hard commodities has turned the country into Brazil's biggest trading partner, overtaking the US. And the Chinese appetite for Brazilian resources is not limited to iron ore. The country recently replaced the US as the main export destination for Brazilian crude oil, and China is also a leading destination for chemical wood pulp, Brazilian soybeans and biofuel.

In response to the dynamic forces of the global market the average growth rate of Brazilian industry over the past two years declined to a dismal

0.3 percent, after posting a negative growth rate of 5.5 in 2009 (www
.indexmundi.com). At the same time employment in the industrial sector fell
by 26 percent, unemployment rose to over 18.4 percent and the 'informal sector' grew from around 40 percent in 1980 to around 54 percent in 2009.[1]

Privatization of public enterprises such as the giant and lucrative telecommunication firm Telebras led to the massive firing of workers and subcontract-
ing of labour at lower wages and without social benefits. Under Cardoso, Brazil
had the highest rates of social inequality (as measured by the Gini coefficient)
in the world—bar Sierra Leone, one of the poorest countries of the world. Over
the course of his eight-year administration Lula implemented a new social
policy (NSP) targeted at the poor, which managed to not only reduce the rate
of poverty (some 40 percent over the course of his regime) but also reduce the
structure of social inequality in regard to income distribution.[2] However, the
beneficiaries of this social policy were limited to the masses of the urban and
rural poor who had been the primary victims of the previous two decades of
neoliberal 'structural reform'. The NSP allowed Lula to claim success in achieving a more social inclusive form of development, but it was based almost
entirely on a policy of 'conditional cash transfers' (CCT) to poor households.
However, although this policy de facto reduced the incidence of extreme poverty by transferring directly to poor households cash to the amount deemed by

---

1   The informal sector of the urban economy is difficult to measure, depending as it does on the
    definition used. In the case of Brazil, for example, the World Bank has the informal economy
    as 31–34%, when measured in terms of a legal definition of employment, to 54 percent in
    terms of a productive definition of employment. The World Bank has it at 42 percent in 2009,
    but some analysts see this definition as restrictive, i.e. based purely on 'structural' criteria and
    excluding 'conditional' criteria such as the lack of social security/pensions, which would
    bring Brazil's informal sector, according to World Bank statistics, up to 62 percent.

2   The UNDP (2010) in its most recent report on human development in Latin America and the
    Caribbean argued that there is a direct correlation between structured social inequalities (in
    power and production relations) and the persistence of poverty. As for the source of the
    problem (the inequality-poverty nexus) the UNDP Report is clear. It is located and can be
    found in the institutionalized practices and 'structures' brought about by powerful economic
    interests that have advanced with the policies instituted under the Washington Consensus.
    In the words of the Report, there exists a 'direct correspondence between the advance of
    globalization, neoliberalism, and the advance of poverty social inequality, social inequity'
    (UNDP, 2010: xv). 'The most explosive contradictions', the Report adds, 'are given because the
    advance of [neoliberal] globalization marches hand in hand with the advance of poverty and
    social polarization'. It is undeniable, the Report continues, 'that the 1980s and 1990s [were]
    the creation of an abysmal gap between wealth and poverty', and that this gap is the most
    formidable obstacle to achieving human development (UNDP, 2010: xv).

the World Bank sufficient to lift them out of a state of extreme poverty, it had no effect on the structure of social inequality based on landholding, which indeed was increasingly concentrated. By the same token, most workers, both in the private and the public sector, did not benefit or only marginally shared in the proceeds of the extractive process and primary commodity exports.

The reason for this is that the operations of extractive capital are notoriously technology-intensive and thus labour-saving or displacing Thus labour in most cases, whether it is mining or agriculture, receives but a small part of the surplus value generated, even though the remuneration of their labour might be at a higher level than the labour displaced. As we argue elsewhere, workers also receive but a small part of the ground rent extracted by the state from capital for the right to access and extract the resource, and to profit from its sale An example of this issue is the displacement of dairy farms and their workers with the introduction of biofuels production (the conversion of sugarcane from the production of sugar to the production of ethanol) in Sao Paulo.

It is difficult to assess the competition for labour between the dairy sector and the expanding sugarcane sector due to lack of data, although some data suggest that the sugarcane sector may be 'more competitive [in the labour market]' by paying higher wages. In the period between 2000 and 2005 the sugarcane sector in SP state used to pay better wages (around 30 percent more) when compared to other sugarcane regions, and this undoubtedly because labour unions in this region were strong and well organized (Moraes, 2007; Ricci et al., 1994). In this period, Novo et al. (2010) note, there was a clear reduction (–23 per cent) of total workers in the sector despite an increase of sugarcane production due to the mechanization of the harvesting process. However, these sugarcane workers were paid well relative to workers holding other agricultural jobs (Macedo, 2005 in Smeets, 2006).

Several comments and caveats are in order here. First, available data on the average wage paid in other agricultural work do not include non-wage benefits, as housing, transport or goods (milk, electricity, vegetables, etc.) offered by employers when workers live in the farm. The latter does not happen in the case of the sugarcane harvesters, usually migrants, who used to live in outskirts of the cities and have no complementary wage. Secondly, available data do not take fully into account the high variability on the type of job considered in calculating the average wage. There is a clear separation between seasonal jobs (harvesting workers, the vast majority) and permanent employees (semi- or highly-skilled agricultural workers, lorry drivers and machines operators) (Smeets, 2006). The former received almost the same as the minimum national wage, while the latter category earns much higher wages. The competition with dairy activity could be placed in this group of permanent jobs since it requires more highly qualified labour.

To turn from Cardoso's relation to labour to his relation with capital, Cardoso used state subsidies to promote foreign capital, especially in the agrarian export and mining sectors, while the small and medium-size farmers were starved of credit. His program of financial deregulation led to currency speculation and massive windfall profits for Wall Street banks as the regime raised interest rates by over 50 percent. Widespread indebtedness and bankruptcies in the agricultural sector led to the dispossession of thousands of small and medium-sized family farmers in addition to the masses of poor peasant farmers who continued their land struggle against the agro-export capitalists in the sector. Although the government implemented a widely touted agrarian reform program designed to resettle on the land hundreds of thousands of landless families the program had no impact on the overriding trend towards concentration in landownership. The concentration of land under the presidencies of Lula and Rousseff took a decisive turn as 0.7 percent of large landowners owning farms over 2000 hectares increased their acreage from 39.5 to 43 percent of Brazilian farmland (IBGE, 2009).

During Cardoso's eight years in office (1994–2002) there was a tsunami of foreign investment: over $50 billion flowed in just the first five years—ten times the total of the previous 15 years. Foreign-owned agro-mineral companies among the top foreign owned companies (as of 1997) numbered over one-third and growing. Between 1996 and 1998 foreign MNCs acquired eight major food, mining and metal production firms. The MNCs include Bunge, which operates the full spectrum of its business interests (agribusiness, sugar and biofuels, oil seeds, food products and fertilizer) in both Brazil and Argentina, and today has emerged as Brazil's largest agricultural exporter.

Cardoso's neoliberal policies opened the door wide open for foreign capital takeover of critical industrial and banking sectors. Nevertheless, it was the subsequent Workers Party presidents Lula and Rousseff who completed the Brazilian economy's Great Leap Backward by decisively turning to extractive capital as the driving force of the economy.

Lula and Rousseff: From Neoliberalism to Extractive Capitalism

Cardoso's privatizations were sustained and deepened by the Lula regime. First, Cardoso's outrageous privatization of the Vale do Doce iron mine at a fraction of its value was defended by Lula; the same was the case with Cardoso's de facto privatization of the state oil company Petrobras. Lula embraced the restrictive monetary policies, budget surplus agreements with the IMF and followed the budgetary prescriptions of the IMF directors (Petras, 2005: Chap. 1).

The Lula regime (2003–2011) took Cardoso's neoliberal policies as a model to further reconfigure Brazil's economy to the benefit of foreign and domestic capital located now in the primary, raw material export sector. In 2005 Brazil exported $55.3 billion dollars in raw materials and $44.2 billion in manufacturing goods; in 2011 Brazil tripled its raw material exports to $162.2 billion while its manufacturing exports increased to a mere $60.3 billion.[3] In other words, the difference between the value of raw material and manufacturing exports increased from $13 billion to over $100 billion in the last five years of Lula's regime. The relative deindustrialization of the economy, the growing imbalance between the dominant extractive and manufacturing sector illustrates the reversion of Brazil to a colonial style of development.

Agro-Mining Capitalism, the State and the People

Brazil's export sector benefited enormously from the rise in commodity prices. The prime beneficiary was its primary agro-mineral sector. But the cost to industry, public transport, living conditions, research and development and education was enormous. Agro-mineral exports provided great revenues to the state but also extracted great subsidies, tax benefits and profits.

Brazil's industrial economy was adversely affected by the commodity boom because of the rise in the value of its currency, the *Real* by 40 percent between 2010 and 2012 that increased the price of manufacturing exports and decreased the global competitiveness of the country's manufacturing (Kingstone, 2010). Under these conditions the share of primary commodities in total exports increased from 47 percent in 2004 to 66.2 percent in 2011, while the share of manufactures declined from 53 to 39 percent (UNDATA, 2012: 102). The PT regime's 'free market' policies also facilitated the entry of lower priced manufactured goods from Asia, particularly from China. While primary exports to China boomed, Brazil's manufacturing sector, particularly consumer goods such as textiles and footwear, from 2005 to 2010 declined by over 10 percent (Brazil Exports, op cit.). The combination of global competition from lower labour cost producers, the growing shift of both foreign investment and exports towards primary commodities, and the 'Dutch disease' effect of these exports

---

3 Brazil Exports by Product Section (USD) http://www.INDEXMUNDI.com/trade/exports/Brazil.

on the competiveness of the country's industrial producers, led to a decline in the growth of production in recent years. As for industrial production the recovery in the growth rate (−5.4 per cent in 2009, 11 percent in 2011) was short-lived (0 percent in 2011). If it were not for the expansion of exports of vegetable and mineral products, up by 30 percent from 2010 to 2011 (and 42 percent of total exports), Brazil's paltry economic growth rate in 2012 (0.9 per cent) would have been fallen to the negative side of the ledger.[4]

Under the Lula-Rousseff regime, the extreme dependence of the economy on the export of a limited number of commodities led to a sharp decline in the productive forces, as measured by investments in technological innovations, especially those related to industry. Moreover, Brazil became more dependent than ever on a single market. From 2000 to 2010 Chinese imports of soy—the major agroexport—represented 40 percent of Brazil's exports; Chinese imports of iron—the key mining export—constitute over a third of the total exports of that sector. China also imports about 10 percent of Brazil's exports of petrol, meat, pulp and paper. Under the Lula and Rousseff regimes, Brazil has reverted to a quasi-mono-cultural economy dependent on a very limited market. As a result the slowdown of China's economy has predictably led to a decline in Brazil's growth to fewer than two percent from 2011 to 2013 (*Financial Times*, 3/26/13, p. 7).

Finance Capital's Economic Paradise

Under the Workers Party free market policies, finance capital flooded into Brazil, as never before. Foreign direct investment jumped from about $16 billion in 2002 during the last year of the Cardoso regime to over $48 billion in the last year of Lula's rule.[5] Portfolio investment—the most speculative sort—rose from a negative $5 billion in 2002 to $67 billion in 2010. Net inflows of FDI and portfolio investments totalled $400 billion during 2007–2011 compared to $79 billion during the previous five- year period. Portfolio investments in high interest bonds, securities returned between 8 and 15 percent, triple and quadruple the rates in North America and Europe. Lula and Rousseff are poster presidents of Wall Street. By most important economic indicators the policies

---

4 Industry contributes more or less 26 percent to the GDP, while agriculture contributes around 5.2 percent (and 20 percent of employment) and services 68.5 percent (CIA World Factbook, 2013).
5 Brazil's Surging Foreign Investment: A Blessing or Curse? VSITC Executive Briefing on Trade Oct. 2012.

of the PT regime have been the most lucrative for overseas financial capital and the investors in the primary agro-mineral sectors in the recent history of Brazil.

The Agro-Mineral Model and the Environment

Despite their political rhetoric in favour of family farming, the Lula-Rousseff regimes have been among the biggest promoters of agribusiness in recent Brazilian political history. The largest share of state resources allocated to agriculture, finances agribusiness and large landowners. According to one study, in 2008/2009 small holders received about us$6.35 billion, while agribusiness and large landholders received $31.9 billion (us) in funding and credit.[6] Less than four percent of government resources and research was directed to family farming and agro-ecological farms.

Under Lula the destruction of the rain forests occurred at a rapid pace. Between 2002 and 2008 the Cerrado region's vegetation was reduced by 7.5 percent or over 8.5 million hectares, mostly by agro-business corporations. The Brazilian Cerrado is one of the world's most biologically rich savannah regions concentrated in the center-east region of the country. According to one study 69 percent of all the land owned by foreign corporations is concentrated in Brazil's Cerrado (Fernandes & Clements, 2013). Between 1995 and 2005 the share of foreign capital in Brazil's agro-industrial grain sector jumped from 16 to 57 percent. Foreign capital has capitalized on the neoliberal policies under Cardoso, Lula and Rousseff to move into agro-fuel (ethanol) sector, controlling about 22 percent of Brazilian sugar cane and ethanol companies (Rainforests, op cit.)—and rapidly encroaching on the Amazon forest.

Between May 2000 and August 2005, thanks to the expansion of the export sector, Brazil lost 132,000 square kilometers of forest due to the expansion of large landowners and multinationals engaged in cattle raising, soya and forestry (Rainforests, op cit.) Between 2003 and 2012 over 137 square kilometers have been deforested, aided and abetted by multi-billion dollar government infrastructure investments, tax incentives and subsidies.

Brazil has the largest cattle-herd in the world (over 50 percent larger than the us) but the expansion of production of the country's livestock and crops has led to land clearing and cattle ranching is the leading cause of deforestation in the Brazilian Amazon and a major source of greenhouse gas (GHG)

---

6 http://rainforests:mongabay.com/amazon_destruction.

emissions, contributing up to 75 percent of Brazil's total emissions. Estimates attribute over 40 percent of this deforestation and these emissions to big capital and MNC meat processing corporations. The Lula-Rousseff regimes' major infrastructure investments, especially roads, opened previously inaccessible forestlands to corporate cattle firms. Under Lula and Dilma, commercial agriculture, especially soya beans, became the second biggest contributor to deforestation of the Amazon.

In 2008 damage to the Amazon rainforest surged 67 percent. Under pressure from indigenous, peasant and landless rural workers' and ecology movements the government took action to curtail deforestation. It declined from a peak of 27,772 square kilometers in 2004 (second only to the highest ever under Cardoso in 1995, 29,059 square kilometers) to 4656 sq. km. in 2012 (Rainforests, op cit.).

Accompanying the degradation of the natural environment, the expansion of agro-business has been accompanied by dispossession, assassination and enslavement of indigenous peoples. The Christian, Pastoral Land Commission reported that landlord violence reached its highest level in at least 20 years in 2004 Lula's second year in office. Conflicts rose to 1801 in 2004 from 1690 in 2003 and 925 in 2002 (Rambla, 2013).

According to the government, cattle and soy corporations exploit at least 25,000 Brazilians (mostly dispossessed Indians and peasants) under 'conditions analogous to slavery'. Leading NGOs claim the true figure could be ten times that number. Over 183 farms were raided in 2005 freeing 4133 slaves (Rainforests, op cit., p. 8).

Mining: The Vale Rip-Off as Privatization and the Number One Polluter

Nearly 25 percent of Brazil's exports are composed of mineral products—highlighting the growing centrality of extractive capital in the economy. Iron ore is the mineral of greatest importance, representing 78 percent of total mining exports. In 2008, iron ore accounted for $16.5 of a $22.5 billion of the industry's earnings (Ericsson & Larsson, 2013). The vast majority of iron exports are dependent on a single market: China. As China's growth slows, demand declines and increases Brazil's economic vulnerability.

One firm, Vale, privatized during the Cardoso presidency through acquisitions and mergers controls almost 100 percent of Brazil's productive iron mines. In 1997 Vale was sold by the neoliberal state for $3.14 billion, a small fraction of its value. Over the following decade it concentrated its investments in mining, establishing a global network of mines in over a dozen countries in

North and South America, Australia, Africa and Asia. The Lula–Dilma regime played a major role in facilitating Vale's dominance of the mining sector and the exponential growth of its value: Vale's net worth today is over $100 billion but it pays one of the lowest tax rates in the world, despite being the second largest mining company in the world, the largest producer of iron ore and the second largest of nickel. Maximum royalties on mineral wealth rose from two to four percent in 2013 (*The Economist*, June 2, 2013); in other words during the decade of the 'progressive' government of Lula and Dilma, the tax rate was one-sixth that of conservative Australia with a rate of 12 percent.

Vale has used its enormous profits to diversify its mining operations and related activities. It sold off businesses such as steel and wood pulp, for $2.9 billion—nearly the price paid for the entire mineral complex. Instead it concentrated on buying up the iron mines of competitors and literally monopolizing production. Vale expanded into manganese, nickel, copper, coal, potash, kaolin, bauxite; it has bought out railroads, ports, container terminals, ships and at least eight hydroelectric plants; two-thirds of its hydro-electrical plants were built during the Lula regime (http://en.wikipedia.org/wiki/Vale_(mining _company)). In short, monopoly capitalism flourished during the Lula regime with record profits in the extractive sector, extreme damage to the environment and massive displacement of indigenous peoples and small-scale producers. The Vale mining experience underlines the powerful structural continuities between the neoliberal Cardoso and Lula regimes: the former privatized Vale at a 'fire-sale' price; the latter promoted Vale as the dominant monopoly producer and exporter of iron, totally ignoring the concentration of wealth, profits and powers of extractive capital.

In comparison to the exponential growth of monopoly profits in the extractive sector, Lula and Dilma's paltry two dollars a day subsidy to reduce poverty hardly warrants calling the regime 'progressive' or 'centre-left'.

While Lula and Dilma were enraptured with the growth of Brazil's 'mining champion' (Vale), others were not. Into 2002 Public Eye a leading human rights and environmental group gave Vale an 'award' as the worst corporation in the world: 'The Vale Corporation acts with the most contempt for the environment and human rights in the world' (*Guardian*, January 27, 2012). The critics cited Vale's construction of the Belo Monte dam in the middle of the Amazon rain forest as having 'devastating consequences for the regions unique biodiversity and indigenous tribes' (ibid.).

The mining sector is capital intensive, generates few jobs and adds little value to its exports. It has degraded water, land and air; adversely affected local communities, dispossessed Indian communities and created a boom and bust economy.

With the marked slowdown of the Chinese economy, especially its manufacturing sector in 2012–2014, iron, copper prices have fallen. Brazil's export revenues have declined, undermining overall growth. What is specially important is that channelling resources into infrastructures for the agro-mineral sectors has resulted in the depletion of funds for hospitals, schools and urban transport—which are run down and provide poor service to millions of urban workers.

The End of the Extractive Mega-Cycle and the Rise of Mass Protests

Brazil's extractive led model entered a period of decline and stagnation in 2012–2013 as world market demand—especially Asia—declined especially in China (*Financial Times*, July 13, 2013: 9). Growth hovered around two percent, barely keeping up with population growth. The class-based growth model, especially the narrow stratum of foreign portfolio investors, monopoly mining and big agro-business corporations that controls and reaped most of the revenues and profits, limited the 'trickle down effects' which the Lula-Dilma regimes promoted as their 'social transformation'. While some innovative programs were initiated, the follow-up and quality of services actually deteriorated.

In-patient hospital beds declined from 3.3 beds per 1000 Brazilians in 1993, to 1.9 in 2009, the second lowest in the OECD (*Financial Times*, July 1, 2013). Hospital admissions financed by the public sector have fallen and long waits and low quality is endemic.

Federal spending on the health system has fallen since 2003, when adjusted for inflation according to the OECD study. Public spending on health is low: 41 percent compared to the UK at 82 percent and the US, 45.5 percent. The class polarization embedded in the agro-mineral extractive model extends to government spending, taxes, transport and infrastructure: massive financing for highways, dams, hydro-electric power stations for extractive capital versus inadequate public transport and declining spending for public health education and transport.

The deeper roots of the mass upheavals of 2013 are located in the class politics of a corporate state. The Cardoso and Lula-Dilma regimes over the past two decades have pursued a conservative elitist agenda, cushioned by clientelistic and paternalistic politics which neutralized mass opposition for an extended period of time, before the mass rebellion and nationwide protests unmasked the progressive facade.

Leftist publicists and conservative pundits who claimed Lula as a 'pragmatic progressive' overlooked the fact that during his first term, state support for the agro-business elite was seven times that offered to the family farmers who represented nearly 90 percent of the rural labourforce and provide the bulk of food for local consumption. During Lula's second term, the Ministry of Agriculture's financial support for agro-business during the 2008–2009 harvest was six times larger than the funds allocated for Lula's poverty reduction program, the highly publicized 'Bolsa Familia' program. Economic orthodoxy and populist demagogy is no substitute for substantive structural changes, involving a comprehensive agrarian reform embracing four million landless rural workers, and a re-nationalization of strategic extractive enterprises like Vale in order to finance sustainable agriculture and preserve the rainforest.

Instead Lula and Dilma jumped full force into the ethanol boom: 'sugar, sugar everywhere'—but never asking 'whose pocket does it fill?' Brazil's growing structural rigidity, its transformation into an extractive capitalist economy, has enhanced and enlarged the scope for corruption. Competition for mining contracts, land grants and giant infrastructure projects encourages agro-mineral business elites to pay-off the 'party in power' to secure competitive advantages. This was particularly the case for the 'Workers Party' whose executive and party leadership (devoid of workers) was composed of upwardly mobile professionals, aspiring to elite class positions who looked toward business payoffs for their 'initial capital', a kind of 'initial accumulation through corruption'.

The commodity boom, for almost a decade, papered over the class contradictions and the extreme vulnerability of an extractive economy dependent on primary goods exports to limited markets. The neoliberal policies adapted to further commodity exports led to the influx of manufactured goods and weakened the position of the industrial sector. As a result the efforts of Dilma to revive the productive economy to compensate for the decline of commodity revenues have not worked: stagflation, declining budget surpluses and weakening trade balances plague her administration precisely when the mass of workers and the middle class are demanding a large-scale reallocation of resources from subsidies to the private sector to investments in public services.

Rousseff's entire political fortune and that of her mentor Lula were built on the fragile foundations of the extractive model. They have failed to recognize the limits of their model, let alone formulated an alternative strategy. Patchwork proposals, political reforms, anti-corruption rhetoric in the face of million person protests spanning all the major and minor cities of the country do not address the basic problem of challenging the concentration of wealth, property and class power of the agro-mineral and financial elite. Their MNC allies control the levers of political power, with and without corruption and block any meaningful reforms.

Lula's era of Wall Street Populism is over. The idea that additional revenues from extractive industries can buy popular loyalties via consumerism, funded by easy credit, has passed. Wall Street investors are no longer praising the BRICS as a new dynamic market. As is predictable they are shifting their investments to more lucrative activity in new regions. As portfolio investments decline, and the economy stagnates, extractive capital intensifies its push into the Amazon and with it the terrible toll on the indigenous population and the rain forest.

The year 2012 was one of the worst years for indigenous peoples. According to the Indigenous Missionary Council, affiliated with the Catholic Church, the number of violent incidents against the Indian communities increased 237 percent (Rainforest, op cit.). The Rousseff regime has given Indians the least number of legal title (homologado) to land of any president since the return of democracy (seven titles). At this rate the Brazilian state will take a century to title land requests of the Indian communities. At the same time in 2012, 62 indigenous territories were invaded by landowners, miners and loggers, 47 percent more than in 2011. The biggest threat of dispossession is from mega dam projects in Belo Monte and giant hydroelectric projects being promoted by the Rousseff regime. As the agro-mineral economy falters the Indian communities are being squeezed ('silent genocide') to intensify agro-mineral growth.

The biggest beneficiaries of Brazil's extractive economy are the world's top commodity traders who worldwide pocketed $250 billion over the 2003–2013 period, surpassing the profits of the biggest Wall Street firms and five of the biggest auto companies. During the mid-2000s, some traders enjoyed returns of 50–60 percent. Even as late as 2013 they were averaging 20–30 percent (*Financial Times*, 4/15/13: 1). Commodity speculators earned more than 10 times what was spent on the poor. These speculators profit from price fluctuations between locations, from the arbitrage opportunities offered by an abundance of price discrepancies between regions. Monopoly traders eliminated competitors and low taxes (5–15 percent) have added to their mega wealth. The biggest beneficiaries of the Lula-Dilma extractive model, surpassing even the agro-mineral giants are the twenty biggest commodity traders-speculators.

Extractive Capital, Internal Colonialism and the Decline of the Class Struggle

The class struggle, especially its expression via strikes led by trade unions and by rural workers located in campsites (*campamentos*) to launch land occupations has declined precipitously over the past quarter of a century. Brazil during the period following the military dictatorship (1989) was a world leader in strikes with 4000 in 1989. With the return of electoral politics and the incorporation and legalization of the trade unions especially in tripartite collective bargaining framework, strikes declined to an average of 500 during the 1990s. With the advent of the Lula regime (2003–2010) strikes declined further from 300–400 a year (Zibechi, 2013). The two major trade unions, CUT and Forca Sindical, allied with the Lula regime became virtual adjuncts of the Ministry of Labour: trade unionists secured positions in government and the organizations received major subsidies from the state, ostensibly for job training and worker education. With the commodity boom and the rise in state revenues and export earnings, the governments formulated a trickle down strategy, increasing the minimum wage and launching new anti-poverty programs. In the countryside, the MST continued to demand an agrarian reform and engaged in land occupations but its position of critically supporting the Workers Party in exchange for social subsidies led to a sharp decline in campsites (*campamentos*) from which to launch land occupations.

At the start of Lula's presidency (2003) the MST had 285 *campamentos*; in 2012 it had only 13. The decline of class struggle and the co-optation of the established mass movements coincided with the intensification of extractive capitalist exploitation of the interior of the country and the violent dispossession of the indigenous communities. In other words, the heightened exploitation of the 'interior' by agro-mineral capital facilitated the concentration of wealth in the large urban centers and the established rural areas, leading to co-optation of trade unions and rural movements. Hence, despite some declaratory statements and symbolic protests, agro-mineral capital encountered little organized solidarity between urban labour and the dispossessed Indians and enslaved rural workers in the 'cleared' Amazon. Lula and Dilma played a key role in neutralizing any national united front against the depredations of agro-mineral capital.

The degeneration of the major labour confederations is visible not only in their presence in government and in the absence of strikes but also in the organization of the annual May 1 workers meetings. The recent events have included virtually no political content. There are music spectacles, spiced with lotteries offering automobiles and other forms of consumerist entertainment, financed and sponsored by major private banks and multinationals. In effect this relation between city and Amazon resembles a kind of internal colonialism, in which extractive capital has bought off a labour aristocracy as a complicit ally to its plunder of the interior communities in the interior and on the frontier of extractive capitalism.

Mass Movements: The Extractive Model under Siege

If the CUT and Forca Sindical are co-opted, the MST is weakened and the low-income classes received monetary raises, how and why did unprecedented mass movements emerge in close to a hundred major and minor cities throughout the country?

The difference between the new mass movements and the trade unions was evident in their capacity to mobilize support during the June/July (2013) days of protest: the former mobilized two million, the latter 100,000. What needs to be clarified is the difference between the small student and local groups (*Movemiento Passe Livre-MPL*), which detonated the mass movements over a raise in bus fares and the pharaonic state expenditure on the World Cup (soccer championship) and Olympics and the spontaneous mass movements which questioned the state's budgetary policies and priorities in their entirety.

Many publicists for the Lula-Dilma regime accept at face value the budgetary allocations destined for social and infrastructure projects, when in fact only a fraction is actually spent as much is stolen by corrupt officials. For example, between 2008 and 2012 R$6.5 billion was designated for public transport in the principal cities but only 17 percent was actually spent (*Veja ano* 46, No.29, August 17,/2013). According to the NGO Contas Abertas (Open Accounts) over a ten-year period Brazil spent over R$160 billion in public works that are unfinished, never left the drawing board or were stolen by corrupt officials. One of the most egregious cases of corruption and mismanagement is the construction of a 12-kilometer subway in Salvador, with the provision that it would be completed in 40 months at the cost of R$307 million. Thirteen years later (2000–2013) expenditures increased to nearly one billion *reales* and barely six kilometers have been completed. Six locomotors and 24 wagons purchased for 100 million *reales* have broken down and the manufacturers warranty has expired (Veja ano 46. no 29 7/17/13). The project has been paralyzed by claims of corrupt overcharging (*sobrefacturación*) involving federal, state and municipal officials. Meanwhile 200,000 passengers are forced daily to travel on dilapidated buses.

The corruption infecting the Lula-Dilma administration has driven a wedge between the achievements claimed by the regime and the deteriorating everyday experience of the great majority of the Brazilian people. The same gap exists regarding expenditures to preserve the Amazon rain forest, indigenous lands and territories, and to fund the anti-poverty programs: corrupt PT officials siphon funds to finance their election campaigns rather than reduce environmental destruction and reduce poverty.

If the wealth from the boom in the agro-mineral extractive model percolated into the rest of the economy and raised wages, it did so in a very uneven and distorted fashion. The great wealth concentrated at the top found expression in a kind of new caste-class system in which private transport—helicopters and heliports—private clinics, private schools, private recreation areas, private security armies for the rich and affluent was funded by state promoted subsidies. In contrast the masses experienced a sharp relative and absolute decline in public services in the same essential life experiences. The raise in the minimum wage did not compensate for 10-hour waits in crowded public emergency rooms, irregular and crowded public transport, daily personal threats and insecurity (50,000 homicides). Parents, receiving the anti-poverty dole sent their children to decaying schools where poorly paid teachers rushed from one school to another barely meeting their classes and providing meagre learning experiences. The greatest indignity to those receiving subsistence handouts was to be told that in this class divided society they were 'middle class'—that they were part of an immense social transformation that lifted 40 million out of poverty as they crawled home from hours in traffic, back from jobs whose monthly salary paid for one tennis match at an upscale country club. The agro-mineral extractive economy, accentuated all Brazil's socioeconomic inequalities and the Lula-Dilma regime accentuated these difference by raising expectations, claiming their fulfillment and then ignoring the real social impacts on everyday life. The government's large-scale budgetary allocations for public transport and promises of projects for new subway and train lines have been delayed for decades because of widespread corruption. Billions of dollars spent over the years have yielded minimum results—a few kilometers completed. The result is that the gap between the regime's optimistic projections and mass frustration has vastly increased. The gap between the populist promise and the deepening cleavage between classes could not be papered over by trade union lotteries and VIP lunches. This is especially so for an entire generation of young workers who are not attached to the memories of Lula the 'metal worker' from a quarter century earlier. The CUT, the FS, the Workers' Party, are irrelevant or are perceived to be part of the system of corruption, social stagnation and privilege. The most striking feature of the new wave of class protest is the generational and organizational split: older metal workers are absent, young unorganized service workers are present. Local spontaneous organizations have replaced the co-opted trade unions.

The main point of political confrontation in Brazil today can be found not in the workplace but in the streets as well as in Amazonia and other places on the new frontier of capitalist development—extractivism. The demands transcend monetary wages and salaries—the issues are the social wage, living standards, national budgets. Ultimately the new social movements raise the issue of national class priorities. The regime is in the process of dispossessing hundreds of thousands of residents of favelas—a social purge—to build sports complexes and luxury accommodations. Social issues inform the mass movements. Their organizational independence and autonomy underline the deeper challenge to the entire neoliberal extractive model. Even though no national organizations or leadership of these mass movements has emerged to elaborate an alternative the struggle continues. The traditional mechanisms of co-optation are failing because there are no identifiable leaders to buy off. The regime, facing the decline of export markets and commodity prices, and deeply committed to multi-billion dollar non-productive investments in the Games, has few options. For one thing, the PT long ago lost its anti-systemic cutting edge. Its politicos are linked with and funded by the banks and agro-mining elites. The trade union leaders protect their fiefdoms, automatic dues deductions and stipends. The mass movements of the cities like the indigenous communities of the Amazon will have to construct or find new political instruments. But having taken the path of direct action they have taken a big first step.

CHAPTER 8

Resistance and Reform in Mexico's Mining Sector

Darcy Tetreault

Mexico has become the number one recipient of investment in mining exploration in Latin America. In the context of booming metal prices during the
first decade of the 21st century, foreign and national-based mining companies
have extracted almost twice as much gold and half as much silver as was
extracted from the country during the entire 300-year period of conquest and
colonialism. Today Mexico is the world's leading silver producer, tenth in gold
and copper, and among the top ten in lead, fluorite, bismuth and various other
minerals.

This frenzy of activity has translated, not just into high rates of profit for
mining companies, but also into multiple environmental problems and social
conflicts, which can be classified into two groups: labour conflicts and eco-
territorial conflicts. The former have important antecedents in the years
leading up to the Mexican Revolution that broke out in 1910; they are part of a
long and ongoing battle between capital and organized labour. The national
context of this struggle began to change in the 1980s, during the transition to
neoliberalism, with the privatization of state-owned mining companies, the
deregulation of collective labour contracts and the decomposition of the corporatist political system that had regulated the demands of unionized miners
since the late 1930s. In recent years, the federal government—under the control of the right-wing National Action Party (*Partido de Acción Nacional*, PAN)
and in alliance with big Mexican capital—launched direct attacks against
unionized miners.

In parallel fashion, since the 1990s foreign mining companies, mostly
Canadian, have expanded the mining frontier to the isolated and marginalized regions of the country, where small-scale farming and ranching activities take place. After almost 500 years of capitalist mining in Mexico, with
evolving technology to get after the increasingly dispersed remaining mineral deposits, this territorial expansion has implied the use of extensive
open-pit mining, with industrially efficient ore-leaching techniques that uti-
lize large quantities of cyanide and other highly toxic substances. From a
North-South perspective, the environmental consequences of this can be
seen as a form of eco-imperialism (Foster, 2003). Moreover, since mining-
induced environmental degradation most directly affects rural populations

where small-scale (infra-)subsistence farming activities persist, it gives new impetus to the ongoing process of (semi-) proletarianization.

The expansion of mega-mining projects in Mexico and elsewhere has met with resistance. The reformist current of resistance movements call for mining companies to share a greater portion of their wealth with the local population and to mitigate the worst environmental impacts of their activities; while the radical current articulates an emphatic 'no' to large-scale mining projects, advocating development alternatives that are more harmonious with Mother Earth.

How has imperialism manifested itself in Mexico's mining sector during the neoliberal era? In what ways do the country's resistance movements constitute anti-imperialist and anti-capitalist struggles? And, to what degree have these movements influenced the formulation of national public policy regarding mining? With these questions in mind, this chapter begins with a review of the neoliberal reforms applied to the country's mining sector during the last two decades of the 20th century. From there, it goes on to analyse ensuing labour and eco-territorial conflicts.

As will be shown, some of the demands of unionized miners and those of the reformist current of social environmental movements have found sympathetic ears in the federal government since Enrique Peña Nieto (EPN) became president in December of 2012, in the context of a legitimacy crisis. In particular, the new federal administration has proposed changes to the country's mining law in order to impose a five percent royalty on mining profits and to create mechanisms to channel this new source of public revenue toward financing social development projects in mining regions. In addition, during its first year in office, EPN's team has tried to recuperate the state's role in mediating conflicts between capital and labour in the mining sector.

The arguments developed in this chapter can be summarized as follows: First, while the neoliberal agenda can be seen as an imperialist project promoted by the US government and Washington-based international financial institutions, it was adopted and implemented by the Mexican government in such a way as to privilege the accumulation of nationally-based mining capital, particularly with regards to the privatization process. Subsequently, the liberalization of Mexico's mining sector has provided profit-making opportunities with high rates of return, not just for mining capital based in Mexico, but rather for all capital with a transnational orientation, irrespective of its national origin. Canadian mining companies in particular have been able to take advantage of this imperial-centred development strategy, largely because of the various forms of support they receive from their home government. Second, most struggles against imperialism in Mexico's mining sector have taken the form of eco-territorial movements, which can be seen as a form of resistance to 'accumulation by dispossession' inasmuch as they seek to maintain mineral resources, land, water, livelihoods, cultural landscapes and sacred sites outside of the sphere of the profit-maximizing logic of capitalist accumulation. Finally, it is argued that the reform initiative promoted by EPN's government constitutes an attempt to legitimize and consolidate the mega-mining development model and thereby undermine support for anti-mining and anti-imperialist movements. The current federal government, like previous ones, evades the deeper social and ecological questions regarding the desirability of pursuing environmentally destructive extractivism.

Neoliberal Reforms in Mexico's Mining Sector

After the Revolution 1910 to 1917, Mexico's mining policies were gradually reoriented so as to give the state greater control over mineral extraction and processing. Article 27 of the 1917 Constitution established that mineral resources belonged to the nation and that they could only be exploited by Mexicans (individuals or companies) through concessions granted by the federal government. Notwithstanding the anti-imperialist spirit of this provision, it was not until the 'Mexicanization of the mining law' was promulgated in 1961 that decisive measures were taken to exercise more national control over mining activities, by declaring that all mining companies operating in the country had to be comprised of at least 51 percent Mexican capital. In 1976, additional modifications were made to the Mining Law in order to strengthen state participation, especially in the production of iron, copper, coal and sulphur. In this way, by the late 1970s, the state owned 15.1 percent of country's mining property; private Mexican capital controlled 48.2 percent and the participation of foreign capital—mostly US at that time—was reduced to 36.7 percent (Urías, 1980: 957).

This was the culmination of the 'mexicanization' project. The results were mixed. On one hand, between 1961 and 1977, proven mineral reserves increased by a factor of almost seven; the mining workforce grew from 60,000 to 150,000 workers, and average annual investments tripled (Urías, 1980: 955). On the other hand, productive growth was mediocre and heterogeneous. While there were significant increases in the production of iron, copper and coal; the production of silver, zinc and lead stagnated (Delgado Wise & Del Pozo Mendoza, 2002: 23). More generally, even though the state managed to gain more control over the sector, partially reorienting it toward internal markets in order to feed the process of input-substituting industrialization; new forms of financial, commercial and technological dependence emerged (Sariego et al., 1988). Likewise, even though the mexicanization of mining resulted in the redistribution of foreign property, concentration and centralization persisted. In 1980, there were 104 big mining companies in the country that controlled approximately 85 percent of the production; the remaining 15 percent was divided between 63 medium-sized and 850 small mining firms (SHCP cited in Urías, 1980: 959), which could barely survive with the assistance of the state-run Mining Promotion Commission (Comisión de Fomento Minero—CFM).

The transition towards a development model based on neoliberal precepts began in August of 1982, when the federal government announced a 90-day moratorium on interest payments to service the country's external debt, which had accumulated during the previous decade, precipitating what would later be called 'the debt crisis'. The underlying structural causes had to do with over-accumulation on the global level, manifest in low economic growth rates since the late 1960s (Harvey, 2003). This situation put the strategy of import-substituting industrialization (ISI) in check and opened the door to the neoliberal agenda promoted by the International Monetary Fund (IMF), the World Bank, and the US government. The same agenda (deregulation, privatization and free trade) was embraced by the most influential blocs of the Institucional Revolucionary Party (Partido Revolucionario Institucional, PRI) and by the most powerful factions of Mexico's bourgeoisie (Cypher & Delgado Wise, 2012).

As in other Latin American countries, the first round of structural adjustments included draconian cuts to social spending, the closing and sale of unprofitable state-run enterprises, the dismantling of protectionist barriers that restricted commercial trade and the free movement of transnational capital, the suppression of salaries, the weakening of unions and a series of constitutional and legal changes designed to create an attractive climate for private investment. The mining sector was not exempt from this restructuring process.

During the worst years of the crisis (1982–1987) the demand for metals and minerals dropped, with devastating consequences for small- and medium-sized mining companies. Five thousand of them were shut down during the first semester of 1982, leaving more than 60 thousand miners out of work (Burnes, 2006: 234). The parastatal iron and steel industry also incurred losses, resulting in the slowing down of production and the closing of plants. By 1987, the CFM had divested itself of nine of its 42 companies, six were in the process of being liquidated, two were for sale, and another one was in the process of being transferred (Sariego et al., 1988: 261). On the whole, Mexico's mining sector registered a negative average annual growth rate (-2.6%) between 1980 and 1987 (Morales, 2002: 52).

On December 29th, 1982, the Ministry of Patrimony and Industrial Promotion (*Secretaría de Patrimonio y Fomento Industrial*) was converted into the Ministry of Energy, Mines and Parastatal Industry (*Secretaría de Energía, Minas e Industria Paraestatal,* SEMIP) in order to carry out 'restructuring', 'modernization' and 'reconversion' programs. During Miguel de la Madrid's presidential term (1982–1988), the government eliminated export taxes on metals and minerals, and reduced tariffs on the importation of machinery and equipment. Other measures introduced during this period include differential discount rates for production taxes, fiscal promotion certificates, and higher discount rates for the depreciation of fixed assets. It also warrants mentioning that, in 1988, the government established the General Law of Ecological Equilibrium and Environmental Protection (*Ley General de Equilibrio Ecológico y la Protección al Ambiente,* LGEEPA), which obliged mining companies to undertake environmental impact assessments (EIA) before initiating new mining or mineral-processing activities.

The bulk of the neoliberal reforms was applied to the mining sector during Carlos Salinas de Gortari's presidency (1988–1996). Besides maintaining the aforementioned fiscal measures, Salinas privatized mineral reserves, mining companies and processing plants. This was mostly done between 1989 and 1992, when the government sold off the public shares of 22 of the country's 24 parastatal mining companies (Morales, 2002: 56). In some cases, these assets were sold with little transparency and at prices far below their market value. Two examples serve to illustrate: (1) Compañía Minera de Cananea, with the largest copper reserves in the country, was awarded to Grupo Mexico for 475 million dollars, only half of the amount offered by Protexa two years earlier and less than a quarter of its value, according to Nacional Financiera's estimates (Ibarra, cited in Delgado Wise & Del Pozo Mendoza, 2002: 34); and (2) *Altos Hornos de México and Siderúrgica Lázaro Cárdenas-Las Truchas* were sold in parts (to Grupo Alfa, Grupo Acerero de Norte, Grupo Villacero and Grupo Ispat) for a total of 755 million dollars, compared to an estimated value of at least six billion dollars (Sancristán Roy, 2006: 56).

Parallel to the process of privatizing state-run mining companies, 6.6 million hectares of national mineral reserves were put on the market, the majority of which were then transferred to three giant consortia: Grupo Mexico, property of Jorge Larrea, who is now the third richest man in Mexico; Industrias Peñoles, whose largest stock holder is Alberto Bailleres, the second richest man in the country; and Grupo Frisco, which belongs to Carlos Slim, the richest man in the world. In this way, the Salinas administration helped large Mexican firms establish monopoly control over the country's mining infrastructure and the most important mineral deposits, before completely opening the sector to FDI.

In 1990, modifications were made to the Mining Law in order to facilitate the divestment of national mineral reserves and to allow for greater foreign participation, especially in exploration activities. In addition, the new law introduced mechanisms to simplify the bureaucratic procedures associated with the granting of mining concessions, to stimulate investment in exploration activities and to foster the adoption of advanced technologies.

Two years later, in June of 1992, the government ushered in a new Mining Law, the same one that is still in effect today. Among its most important provisions, this law: (1) allows for the participation of companies that are 100 percent foreign owned, under the condition that they establish a legal address in the country; (2) eliminates the pre-existing limits on the area of concessions and extends concession periods from 25 to 50 years, making them renewable thereafter; (3) extinguishes the CFM; and (4) establishes in Article 6 that '[t]he exploration, exploitation and processing of minerals [...] will take precedence over whatever other use or productive utilization of the land'. It goes without saying that this last provision has important ramifications for smallholder farmers and indigenous groups, since it introduces the possibility of expropriating their land and handing it over to mining companies. In the same spirit, modifications were made to Article 27 of the Constitution and to the Agrarian Law in 1992 in order to permit the renting and selling of *ejidal* and indigenous land. And finally (5), it is important to point to the second part of Article 6 of the Mining Law, which stipulates that only the federal government can tax mining activities. Leaving aside the anti-constitutionality of this provision (since the faculties of distinct levels of government can only be determined by the Constitution), the intention is clear: sub-national governments (state, municipal, ejidal/community) are not allowed to exercise fiscal controls over mining activities.

All of this formed part of a broader process of liberalization, privatization and deregulation that culminated in 1994, when the North American Free Trade Agreement (NAFTA) came into effect. NAFTA's Chapter 11 gives foreign companies the right to sue host governments for any public policy or action that denies them investment or profit opportunities. In this fashion it seeks to provide legal certainty for transnational capital, something that was reinforced in the mining sector by the modifications made to the Mining Law and to the Foreign Investment Law in 1996.

According to Burnes (2006), 1994 marked a turning point for mining in Mexico. After several years of crisis, metal and mineral prices rose and FDI began to arrive in growing quantities, especially from Canada. Morales

(2002: 52–53) estimates that between 1993 and 1999 the average annual growth rate of mining production was 3.2 percent. Ernesto Zedillo's government (1994–2000) doled out 11,800 mining concessions, covering an area of 35.9 million hectares, that is, more than four times the surface area that was under concession during the previous six-year presidential term (Morales: 2002: 61). As the 20th century came to a close, practically all of the country's mineral reserves had been divested; the most important mines and processing facilities were in the hands of large Mexican companies, strategically associated with foreign capital, with a high level of vertical integration, diversification and transnationalization.

The Consolidation of Neoliberal Policies and the Mining Boom

The 21st Century began with a boom. The demand for metals and minerals—as well as other primary commodities—increased dramatically, largely due to the rapid process of industrialization in China and, to lesser degree, India. At the same time, it is important to keep in mind that the mining bonanza of the first decade of the new millennium goes hand in hand with the financialization of the global economy, the predominance of speculative investments and the oligopolistic conditions that characterize the sector worldwide. The financial and economic crisis that unfurled in the centre of the global economy during the second half of the first decade of the 21st century brought with it a rise in the price of precious metals, as investors sought a safe haven for their speculative capital.

Under these structural conditions, the PAN took over Mexico's federal government, first in the year 2000 under the leadership of Vicente Fox, and then again in 2006, when Felipe Calderón became president, through elections stained by accusations of fraud, and with the support of the most powerful business associations in the country. Vicente Fox—who was the president of Coca-Cola's Latin American division before entering the arena of electoral politics—stated in a candid moment that the PAN was a political party 'of businessmen, [created] by businessmen and for businessmen'. This translated into almost unconditional support for the interests of (trans-)national capital in the mining sector, even more so during Felipe Calderón's presidential term, when the government launched a direct attack on mining unions, as we shall see in the next section.

The two PAN administrations did not make significant changes to the country's mining laws and institutions. Rather, they consolidated the orthodox neoliberal policies inherited from the PRI. The Mining Law was slightly modified on two occasions near the end of Fox's presidency: the first time, in April of 2005, to further simplify the administrative procedures for granting concessions, by amalgamating exploration concessions and exploitation concessions into one; and also to make institutional adjustments, for example: the Ministry of Commerce and Industrial Promotion (Secretaría de Comercio y Fomento Industrial) was converted into the Ministry of Economy (Secretaría de Economía) and the Council for Mineral Resources (Consejo de Recursos Minerales) was replaced by Mexican Geological Service (Servicio Geológico Mexicano), giving shape to the current institutional configuration. The second time that the Mining Law was modified, in July of 2006, was to permit the use of gases that emanate from coal mines as a source of energy, with an eye on the explosion that killed 65 miners in Pasta de Conchos, on February 19 of the same year.

Beyond these minor adjustments to the formal dimension of mining policy, the two PAN administrations stand out for their eagerness to grant concessions. Between 2000 and 2010 they granted 26,559 mining concessions, covering an area of 56 million hectares, equal to 28.6 percent of the country's territory (López Bárcenas & Eslava Galicia, 2011: 29). It is important to point out that, in general, these concessions were granted without the knowledge of the local population, thereby violating the right of indigenous communities to 'free, prior and informed consent', consecrated in Convention 169 of the International Labour Organization, which Mexico ratified on the September 5, 1990, as well as the United Nations' Declaration on the Rights of Indigenous Peoples, adopted by the General Assembly on September 13, 2007, with Mexico voting in favour.

The two PAN presidencies were also characterized by the administrative disorder that reigned in the mining sector between 2000 and 2012, as observed and documented by the Auditor General (Auditoría Superior de la Federación) in a report that came out in early 2012 (ASF, 2012). Among other things, the Auditor General observed a series of irregularities in the list of 20,958 active mining concessions managed by the General Directorate of Mines (*Dirección General de Minas,* DGM), for example, duplications, errors in the names of mining companies, errors in surface areas, unpaid fees, and most seriously, almost half of the concessions on said list correspond to mining companies that are not even registered before the Finance Ministry. Furthermore, only 31.9 percent of obligatory annual reports were submitted by mining companies in 2010, and the DGM did not sanction those that did not submit them by applying the fines stipulated by law.

In addition, the Auditor General observed that the cost of a mining concession in Mexico is 'symbolic' and does not even cover related administrative costs. According to the Report, between 2005 and 2010, the federal government collected 6.54 billion pesos from mining companies (equal to approximately 503 million US$ in 2010, at an exchange rate of 13 pesos to the dollar), which only represents 1.2 percent of the value of mining production during the same period: 552.4 billion pesos (USD 42.5 billion). In fact, unlike other Latin American countries that oblige mining companies to pay the state a percentage of their earnings in royalties, in Mexico these companies only have to pay a small fee for the right to explore and extract minerals: starting at 5.70 pesos per hectare (44 cents) during the first two years, and increasing to 124.74 pesos per hectare (about USD 9.60) after 10 years.

With regards to Mexico's environmental policy, while it has been strengthened during the neoliberal era through the specification of norms and the construction of a complex framework of agencies on all three levels of government, in practice environmental considerations continue to be subordinated to the interests of big capital. This is illustrated by the notorious case of the San Xavier mine in the state of San Luis Potosí. With the help of the Ministry of the Environment and Natural Resources (*Secretaría de Medio Ambiente y Recursos Naturales*, SEMARNAT), the Canadian company New Gold has been able to continue exploiting this open-pit gold and silver mine, located in a Protected Natural Area, in spite of court orders to shut it down, emitted by the Ninth Collegiate Court on Administrative Matters (*Noveno Tribunal Colegiado en Materia Administrativa*) in June of 2004 (Silva, 2010).

Another example to illustrate the collusion that exists between environmental authorities and transnational mining capital is the case of Peñasquito, in the municipality of Mazapil, in the state of Zacatecas. In this arid region, Canadian-based Goldcorp exploits the largest open-pit gold mine in Mexico, consuming around 40 million cubic meters of water per year (m^3/year), especially in the cyanide leaching process that it employs to extract gold from ore. According to a study published by the National Water Commission (Comisión Nacional de Agua, CONAGUA) in 2007, the aquifer exploited by Goldcorp— called 'Cerdos'—has an annual recharge capacity of 10.1 million m^3/year. By federal decree, CONAGUA is not allowed to grant concessions for greater volumes of water extraction. However, as observed by Claudio Garibay and his collaborators (2011), in order to help Goldcorp get around this law, CONAGUA simply announced in August of 209 that the annual recharge rate of said aquifer and suddenly increased to 54.4 million m^3/year.

Beyond this anecdotal evidence, the fact that Mexico permits the development of huge open-pit mines and the use of large quantities of highly toxic substances in mineral processing is the most patent manifestation that environmental considerations are relegated to a second order when they conflict with the interests of powerful business groups. In fact, the disaccord between the importance attributed to the environment in the official discourse and the lax environmental standards in practice is reflected in SEMARNAT's budget, equivalent to just 1.91 percent of the government's projected expenditure in 2012 and approximately 0.36 percent of the Gross Domestic Product (GDP) in the same year.[1] Likewise, based on data published by the Ministry of the Economy (SE, 2012: 22), it can be estimated that the mining companies operating in Mexico between 2005 and 2010 only channelled on average two percent of their investments toward protecting the environment.

In the final analysis, the government counts on the self-regulation of mining companies, in accordance with voluntary certification schemes like the Clean Industry Certificate awarded by the Federal Attorney's Office for Environmental Protection (*Procuraduría Federal de Protección al Ambiente*, PROFEPA) or ISO 14000, which establishes international standards for the generation of documents regarding environmental management. It bears mentioning that these schemes form part of a broader campaign to promote corporate social responsibility (CSR), endorsed on the international level by the largest mining companies in the world, under the auspices of the Global Mining Initiative.

All things considered, the mining sector in Mexico has growth spectacularly since the beginning of the new millennium. The real value of annual mining production quadrupled between 2000 and 2011,[2] reaching 23.12 billion dollars in 2012. In this way, mining has become the country's fourth largest foreign currency earner, after the automotive industry, electronics and petroleum (CAMIMEX, 2013). In addition, as mentioned above, Mexico has become the number one destination in exploration investments in Latin America and the fourth in the world, after Canada, Australia and the United States (Metals Economics Group, 2013). Taking into consideration not only investments in exploration, but rather the totality of foreign investments in the country's mining and metallurgy sector, Mexico attracted on average 568.7 million dollars annually in FDI between 2005 and 2011.

While this may sound impressive, FDI continues to be overshadowed by investments made by nationally based mining capital. In fact, FDI only represented one fifth of the total investments in the sector between 2005 and 2011, underlying the persistent domination of Mexican firms. See Figure 8.1.

---

1 SEMARNAT's budget was 54,717,658,406 pesos in 2012 (http://www.apartados.hacienda.gob .mx/presupuesto/temas/pef/2012/temas/tomos/16/r16_apurog.pdf).

2 Author's calculation, based on data obtained from the Ministry of Economy (SE, 2012:14; 2005:11).

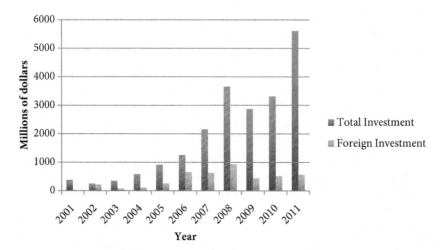

FIGURE 8.1   *Total investment and foreign investment in Mexico's mining and metallurgy sector 2001–2011*
SOURCE: AUTHOR'S ELABORATION WITH DATA FROM CAMIMEX (2012) AND SE (2005; 2012).
NOTE: THE ANNUAL INVESTMENTS PUBLISHED BY CAMIMEX (2012) DO NOT COINCIDE EXACTLY
WITH THOSE PUBLISHED BY SE (2012) FOR THE YEARS 2005, 2006 AND 2011.

To be sure, there is a handful of giant nationally based mining companies that continue to exercise oligopolistic control over mining production in Mexico. In the production of non-ferrous metals, two companies stand out: Grupo Mexico and Industrias Peñoles. The former accounts for more than two thirds of the copper produced in Mexico in 2012, one fifth of the lead, one sixth of the zinc and various other metals in lesser proportions. As for Industrias Peñoles, in the same year it produced—either directly or through its subsidiary Minera Fresnillo, in association with the US company Newmont—approximately one-third of the national production in silver, zinc and lead, and one-fifth of the gold.[3] Carlos Slim's mining company, Frisco, also produces large quantities of these metals, but it occupies a distant third place. These three firms are vertically integrated insofar as they control processing plants, railroads and marketing channels; and they are transnationally oriented, with diverse investments in various Latin American countries, and in strategic alliance with other multinational corporations.

The iron and steel sector also exhibits monopolistic characteristics. Grupo Acerero del Norte (GAN)—owned by Mexican businessmen Xavier Autrey

---

3   Author's calculations, based on data published by CAMIMEX (2013).

Maza and Alonso Ancira Elizondo—control more than 90 percent of the national coal production, three quarters of the coke, and 30 percent of the iron.[4] The rest of the iron extracted from Mexico is produced by two transnational giants: Ternium and ArcelorMittal, of Argentinian/Italian and Indian origin, respectively.

Canadian mining capital goes after precious metals. Mining companies from north of the 49th parallel produced almost two thirds of the gold and half of the silver in Mexico in 2012. Goldcorp is by far the most powerful Canadian mining company operating in Mexico. By itself it controls around one quarter of the country's gold and silver production.[5]

The relative success that Canadian mining companies have had in penetrating Mexico's mining sector has much to do with the various forms of support that they receive from the Canadian government. The 'mechanisms of Canadian imperialism in Latin America's mining sector' include: pushing for neoliberal reforms, under-regulating the Toronto Stock Exchange (TSX), providing tax benefits, direct subsidies and diplomatic support to Canadian mining companies operating abroad, and refusing to regulate them outside of the country (Tetreault, 2013). While these mechanisms do not in and of themselves constitute imperialism, they reflect the imperialist strategies of a middle power that has helped to shape the evolution of the global capitalist system towards the principles of free trade, privatization and deregulation; thereby giving Canadian-based capital access to Mexico's mineral resources and cheap labourforce.

During the first five years of Felipe Calderón's term in office, the number of concessions granted to foreign mining companies more than doubled, from 390 in 2006 to 803 in 2011. More than three quarters of these concessions were given to Canadian companies. In fact, of the 288 foreign mining companies registered in Mexico, 208 are Canadian. To be sure, 62 percent of the projects managed by foreign capital are associated with precious metals, specifically gold and silver (SE, 2012: 21), with limited industrial applications. It is also important to point out that 79.4 percent of the concessions granted to foreign companies are still in the exploration phase (SE, 2012: 20), which suggests that the majority of the environmental destruction and social upheaval is yet to come.

Foreign mining companies are the ones that are investing most of the 'venture capital' in exploration.[6] In some cases, they are combing over zones where

---

4   Author's calculations, based on data published by CAMIMEX (2013).
5   Author's calculations, based on data published by CAMIMEX (2013).
6   In 2010, foreign capital made 70 percent of the investments in mining exploration in Mexico (González Rodríguez, 2011: 7).

mining activities took place in the past; in others, they are looking for precious metals in isolated regions previously unexplored, populated by marginalized peasants and indigenous groups. These are the 'regions of refuge' referred to by the famous Mexican anthropologist Gonzalo Aguirre Beltran (1991), where cultural diversity intersects with biological diversity (Toledo, 2002). The arrival of large mining projects to these regions imply the displacement of small-scale agricultural activities, the deterioration of fragile ecosystems, the destruction of cultural landscapes and the generation of internal conflicts. As Garibay (2010: 134) observes: 'In contrast to the subterranean mining of the past, which was integrated in the local social space as another activity, the new mining, because of its technological nature, its economic imperative and political power, points toward social exclusion and the radical destruction of pre-existing cultural landscape'.

The Labour Movement in Mexico's Mining Sector

In June of 1906, Mexican miners employed by the Cananea Consolidated Copper Company in the state of Sonora went on strike to demand a reduction of the working day to eight hours and wages equivalent to those paid to their US counterparts working in the same mine. They were violently repressed, leaving seven dead and many others injured. Considered to be one of the most important precursors to the Mexican Revolution, the strike in Cananea was by no means an isolated event; during the first decade of the 20th century, miners organized themselves to articulate collective demands in San Luis Potosí, Real de Catorce, Santa Rosalía and elsewhere. As Guerra (1983) explains, the mining regions in the north of the country served as a cradle for the Revolution. Mexican miners were influenced by the anarcho-syndicalist ideas espoused by the Flores Magón brothers and, once the armed conflict began, they swelled the ranks of the revolutionary troops.

After the armed phase of the Revolution, the state tried to extinguish anarcho-syndicalism with a two-pronged approach: the execution of leaders and the undermining of support through the institutionalization of labour rights (Sariego et al., 1988). Article 123 of the 1917 Constitution set the groundwork by establishing a maximum workday of eight hours, a minimum wage to satisfy the basic needs of workers and their families, access to housing, the legality of unions and strikes, and the right to decent health and safety standards in the workplace. However, it was not until the 1930s that lasting political pacts began to be constructed between the state and organized labour. The first milestone was the promulgation of the federal Labour Law of

1931, which sought to recuperate the rights establish in Article 123 of the Constitution.

The second milestone in the strengthening of the labour movement in the mining sector and in the eventual construction of a corporatist political system was the creation in April of 1934 of the National Union for Mine, Metallurgical and Similar Workers of the Mexican Republic (*Sindicato Nacional de Trabajadores Mineros, Metalúrgicos y Similares de la República Mexicana,* SNTMMSRM).[7] With the support of populist president Lázaro Cárdenas, the SNTMMSRM carried out a wave of strikes between 1934 and 1936, obliging (mostly foreign) mining companies to substantially increase wages and concede to a series of demands, including: collective contracts that prohibited the hiring of workers not affiliated with the union, a seniority system to regulate the promotion of workers, better safety standards, social security, health services, the creation of consumer cooperatives in mining districts, and the provision of housing in isolated areas (Bernstein, 1964; Sariego et al., 1988).

There is no doubt that these conquests improved the working conditions and contributed to the wellbeing of miners and their families during Cárdenas' presidency and beyond. In this way, a material base was established for a social pact that was eventually institutionalized around the PRI during the ISI period, as part of a complex framework of unions and confederations that sought to represent labour in all sectors of the economy. During the following decades, until the arrival of neoliberalism, this corporatist system served to reconcile the interests of the working class and those of capital, in a development project oriented toward fostering industrialization and high economic growth rates, based on a Fordist model that included the construction of 'universal' social policies for workers in the formal sector.

In the middle of the 20th century, federal authorities intervened in the election of the SNTMMSRM's leaders in order to subordinate the mining union to the imperatives of import-substituting industrialization. In 1949, the General Executive Committee of the SNTMMSRM followed Vicente Lombardo Toledano when he left the Confederation of Mexican Workers (Confederación de Trabajadores Mexicanos, CTM) to form a rival national-level labour confederation with a socialist bent: the General Union of Mexican Workers and Peasants (*Unión General de Obreros y Campesinos de México,* UGOCM). One year later, the federal government provoked and took advantage of a rupture in the

---

7 The original denomination was: Sindicato Industrial de Trabajadores Mineros, Metalúrgicos, Siderúrgicos y Similares de la República Mexicana (SITMMSSRM). It has also been called Sindicato Nacional de Trabajadores Mineros, Metalúrgicos, Siderúrgicos y Similares de la República Mexicana (SITMMSSRM).

leadership of the SNTMMSRM in order to support a moderate faction led by Jesus Carrasco. From that moment onward, the union would be controlled by relatively docile leaders, in the context of an authoritarian political system built on clientelistic relations, beginning with the President of the Republic, passing through the General Executive Committee of the SNTMMSRM, and following a chain of command right down to the union's commissions on the local level (Zapata, 2008).

In 1960, one year before the 'Mexicanization of the mining law' came into effect, Napoleón Gómez Sada became the Secretary General of the SNT-MMSRM, a position that he would occupy for four decades. In Mexico, union leaders that maintain strict control over their bases during long periods, developing clientelistic relations that imply individual and collective rewards for loyalty and sanctions for insubordination, are called *charros*. There is no doubt that Napoleón Gómez Sada approached this 'ideal type', in Weberian terms. Under his leadership, the faculties of the General Executive Committee were extended and consolidated, engendering the centralization of decision making regarding collective contracts, strikes and the selection of executive committee members on the local level.

During the third quarter of the 20th century, Mexico's corporatist system served to contain and mitigate labour conflicts in the mining sector. Clientelistic relations were articulated with redistributive social policies associated with the universal welfare state in such as was as to maintain a certain material standard of living for miners and their families, above the national average. In the 1970s, miners were incorporated into the Mexican Social Security Institute (Instituto Mexicano de Seguridad Social, IMSS). Another factor was the state's increased participation in the extraction and processing of metals and minerals. As Sariego et al. (1988: 338) observe, by converting itself into one of the principal employers in the sector, the state acquired the function of regulating labour markets, establishing parameters with respect to salaries and benefits. In addition, by incorporating social criteria into a long-term development vision, the state-run sector helped to stabilize jobs in the mining sector vis-à-vis oscillations on the world market. Between 1952 and 1976, there were few strikes and those that did take place were isolated and short-lived (ibid.).

Cracks began to appear in this political system during the second half of the 1970s, heralded by a series of strikes, some of which did not have the support of the General Executive Committee of the SNTMMSRM, in defence of salaries and benefits. In the iron and steel industry alone, there were 18 major strikes between 1975 and 1985 (Gaitán, 1986). At the same time, struggles emerged on the local and national levels to democratize the miners' union, resulting in sanctions for dissident currents that challenged the authority of the General Executive Committee.

In spite of this resistance, living conditions deteriorated considerably for miners and their families in the context of the debt crisis (1982–1985), when the federal government imposed austerity measures that included the suppression of salaries and drastic cuts to social spending. As mentioned above, the closing of mines and of processing plants during the debt crisis translated into the loss of tens of thousands of jobs. What is more, the 'modernization' programs implied the adoption of labour-saving technologies and the emergence of a new class of workers in the mining sector, with technical skills to operate more sophisticated machinery and to monitor automated processes.

These tendencies were consolidated with a second round of neoliberal policies, applied during Carlos Salinas' presidential term (1988–1994). During this phase, salary caps were established and, with the cooperation of union leaders on the national level, the federal government began to promote the deregulation of collective contracts, increasing the prerogatives of capital in all facets of the employee-employer relation (Zapata, 2008). In this fashion, Mexico's labour policy was subjected to the neoliberal and imperialist logic of offering a cheap and flexible labourforce to transnational capital, in an effort to attract FDI.

There was resistance to the privatization process. For example, in 1989 miners in Cananea carried out a strike to protest the sale of the Compañía Minera Cananea to Grupo Mexico. The Salinas administration responded with two lines of action: first it declared that the company was bankrupt; and then, in August of the same year, it sent in the armed forces to break the strike. Another strike during the same year, at one of the country's largest iron-ore mines and processing facilities, Siderúrgica Lázaro Cárdenas-Las Truchas (SICARTSA), could not resist the federal government's insistence in applying neoliberal policies. In the end, 1775 employees were let go and the contracts of those who survived were made more flexible, before privatizing the mine and its processing facilities in 1991 (Zapata, 2008: 131). On the national level, the number of jobs in the mining sector dropped from 242 thousand in 1989, to 165 thousand in 1993 (SEMIP, 1993: 21).

In spite of massive layoffs—not only in mining but in all sectors of the economy—there were relatively few strikes in Mexico during the 1990s, while the number of strikers decreased substantially (Zapata, 2008: 125). Somehow, the corporatist political system managed to contain the labour movement during the painful process of neoliberal restructuring around privatization, flexibilization and wage suppression. The SNTMMSRM, still under the leadership of Napoleón Gómez, could not resist this current.

The year 2000 presaged changes in the corporative relations between union-ized miners and the state; in the first place because, after 71 years of PRI governments, the PAN won the federal elections with the presidential candidacy of Vicente Fox; and second, because Napoleón Gómez Sada became deathly ill and, after serving for 40 years as Secretary General of the SNTMMSRM, he was replaced by his son, Napoleón Gómez Urrutia. This succession was questioned, *inter alia*, because Napoleón Gómez junior had never worked as a miner; instead, he had earned a doctorate in economics from Oxford University. In spite of this anomaly, the Fox administration recognized his nomination as the new Secretary General as part of a broader attempt to conserve the corporatist system inherited from the PRI and to mould it around the political projects of the PAN.

During the first years of the new millennium, in the context of the mining boom, Gómez Urrutia proved to be a dynamic and ambitious leader. He applied his academic abilities to demonstrate that mining companies in Mexico were extracting extraordinary profits and he encouraged the bases to pressure for higher wages and better working conditions in general. Between 2000 and 2005, there were 39 strikes in the mining sector; ten were declared illegal and four 'non-existent' (Zapata, 2006). With this militancy, various local sections of the SNTMMSRM managed to acquire higher salaries and monetary perks, without improving security conditions in the mines.

In spite of the limited nature of these gains, Gómez Urrutia's successful negotiations did not sit well with the neoliberal policy of supressing wages, and his militancy irritated Mexican mining magnates, especially Germán Larrea, owner of Grupo Mexico. At the same time, Gómez Urrutia clashed with high-ranking government officials in Fox's administration—in particular, Carlos Abascal, who was then head of the Ministry of Labour and Social Welfare (Secretaría del Trabajo y Previsión Social STPS)—because he criticized and resisted Abascal's proposal to reform the federal Labour Law in the direction of greater flexibility.

For such insolence, Napoleón Gómez Urrutia became the target of a political attack, coordinated between the PAN and big nationally based mining capital, provoking a rupture in the corporatist relations between the state and unionized labour. On the 17th of February, 2006, the new Minister of STPS, Francisco Javier Salazar, announced that the government would no longer recognize Gómez Urrutia as leader of the SNTMMSRM, arbitrarily assigning the position to another labour leader: Elías Morales. This manoeuvre detonated a political bomb in Mexico, which found an eco two days later in the literal explosion that occurred in the Pasta de Conchos coal mine in the state of Coahuila, killing 65 miners.

Gómez Urrutia suggested that the explosion amounted to 'industrial homicide', blaming not only the owner of the mine, Germán Larréa, but also the STPS for its lack of supervision and negligence in ensuring decent safety standards. Shortly thereafter, he was accused of embezzling part of a 55-million-dollar trust fund that was created for the union to help lubricate the sale of the country's largest copper mine to Grupo Mexico. In March of 2006, Gómez Urrutia fled to Canada and has remained there since, directing loyal sections of the SNTMMSRM through virtual channels. Since 2006, he has been re-elected three times as Secretary General.

The government's attempt to dismiss Urrutia Gómez put the rest of the country's unions on alert. En 2006, they formed the Solidarity Front in Defense of National Unionism (Frente de Solidaridad en Defensa del Sindicalismo Nacional). This agglomeration denounced the STPS's intervention insofar as it put the autonomy of unions at risk, particularly with regards to electing leaders. For its part, the SNTMMSRM's General Executive Committee called for a general strike in early March, 2006, in order to protest the dismissal of Gómez Urrutia, affecting mines, refineries and smelting plants in eight states of the Republic. On the 20th of April, strikers at SICARTSA, in the state of Michoacán, were violently evicted by police forces from all three levels of government, leaving two miners dead and around 40 injured.

In short, the events of 2006 translated into an unprecedented crisis in the relation between the state and labour unions organized on the national level (Pérez & Sánchez, 2006; Zapata, 2006). The federal elections that same year reflected this crisis. Fox's attempts to eliminate left-of-centre candidate Andres Manual López Obredor (AMLO) from the presidential race and his illegal use of public revenue to promote the continuation of the PAN; the smear campaign orchestrated by big business against AMLO and the evidence of fraud put the autonomy of the Federal Electoral Institute (Instituto Federal Electoral) in question, as well as the legitimacy of the second PAN administration.

In an effort to confront this legitimacy crisis and to project the image of a strong president, Felipe Calderón started a war against drug traffickers, with tragic consequences that can only be quantified in brute form by the headcount of 83 thousand executions between 2006 and 2012. The Calderón administration also took the offensive against unions. For example, the parastatal company responsible for distributing electrical energy in the central region of Mexico, Light and Force (*Luz y Fuerza del Centro*), was closed and liquidated, leaving 44 thousand members of the combative Mexican Electricians Union (*Sindicato Mexicano de Eletricistas*) out of work. The same government launched an initiative to reform the federal Labour Law in order to increase the flexibility of collective contracts, proposing mechanisms designed to intervene in the internal life of unions, specifically to make union elections more transparent.

During Calderón's six-year term (2006–2012), the federal government and Mexican mining capital sought to weaken and divide the labour movement through repression, co-optation and a campaign of defamation directed against the SNTMMSRM's leaders. In the words of Juan Luis Sariego, a veteran researcher in the area:

> The government and business groups are trying to wipe out all traces of mining unionism that openly questions the flexibilization of mining labour [...] in this confrontation there is no doubt that the large nationally based companies are the ones that have taken the lead, to the point of making the government's decisions regarding conflicts and labour negotiations depend on them.
>
> 2011: 157

Along these lines, between 2006 and 2012, the STPS refused to recognize Gómez Urrutia as Secretary General of the SNTMMSRM. It was not until May of 2012, after receiving orders from the Nation's Supreme Court of Justice (Suprema Corte de Justicia de la Nación), that the STPS reluctantly granted this recognition. Consequently, Gómez Urrutia was disqualified as a legitimate negotiator during most of Calderón's term, including with regards to the long and drawn out strikes that took place in Cananea, Sombrerete, Taxco and El Cubo.

At the same time, arrest warrants were issued for Gómez Urrutia and other members of the General Executive Committee of the SNTMMSRM, including Carlos Pavón, the union's Secretariat of Political Matters. Pavón was jailed for eight days in December of 2008 for his alleged involvement in an attempt to defraud Altos Hornos de México (AHMSA, which belongs to GAN). When he was released, he changed political course, pointing the finger of accusation towards Gómez Urrutia. In 2009, he founded a rival national-level mining union, appropriating his ex-comrade's father's name: The Napoleón Gómez Sada Mining and Metallurgy Union (Sindicato Minero Metalúrgico don Napoleón Gómez Sada, SMMNGS). Suffice to say that this union seeks to establish 'a respectful pact' with large Mexican mining companies, asking them to 'respect the autonomy of the union in exchange for not carrying out unjustified strikes' (Martínez, 2010). At the same time, a dissident current emerged within the SNTMMSRM, led by Héctor Jiménez Coronado: The National Mining Alliance (Alianza Minera Nacional), which also seeks to be more cooperative with federal authorities and with the main employers in the sector (i.e. Grupo

Mexico, GAN, Industrias Peñoles and Grupo Frisco). The multiple media outlets controlled by the Mexican bourgeoisie have shed a positive light on these
dissident leaders, while vilifying Gómez Urrutia.

In these ways, during Calderón's presidential term, the government-
business alliance successfully divided mining labour. At the same time, the
federal government accelerated the granting of concessions to foreign companies, mostly Canadian, who do everything possible to keep their employees
from affiliating themselves with the SNTMMSRM (Sariego, 2011). In fact, some
of these foreign companies have been accused of violating the country's official labour laws, by firing miners that attempt to create local chapters of the
SNTMMSRM (Muñoz Ríos, 2013a). Canadian mining companies tend to create
sham unions—'sindicatos blancos', controlled by the employers—in order to
circumvent the demands of organized labour. Nevertheless, in recent years the
labour struggle has penetrated some Canadian-owned mines. For example, in
2010 the miners working at Goldcorp's Peñasquito mine in the state of Zacatecas
created Section 305 of the SNTMMSRM, with links to the Executive Committee
led by Gómez Urrutia, who took advantage of his exile in Vancouver to negotiate face-to-face with the directors of Goldcorp over the terms of the miners'
collective contract.

Union conflicts have also affected Excellon Resources' La Platosa mine in
the sate of Durango. In this case the labour struggle overlaps with an eco-
territorial conflict that involves the *ejido* La Sierrita, an agrarian community
that owns the land affected by the company's subterranean mining of silver,
zinc and lead. With regards to the labour dimension of this conflict, an inter-
union dispute has emerged involving three organizations: the faction of the
SNTMMSRM loyal to Gómez Urrutia; the SMMNGS, led by Carlos Pavón, and a
so-called 'white union' called Adolfo López Mateo, in which the miners were
registered by Excellon, without their knowledge. In this scenario, Excellon has
been accused of violating the human and labour rights of its Mexican employees, among other reasons, for firing the miners who organized the creation of
Section 309 of the SNTMMSRM, and also because it has created a local political
climate characterized by acts of hostility and physical aggression towards the
miners that support the SNTMMSRM.

Eco-Territorial Conflicts

The other dimension of the social struggle around mineral extraction in
La Platosa has ecological content insofar as the *ejidatarios* from La Sierrita
demand indemnification for the use and deterioration of their collective

landholdings and natural resources. In fact, these smallholder farmers have had to fight for agreed-upon monetary payments for renting land, social development projects and promises to give the local population the opportunity to provide services to the mine. In this sense, the struggle in La Platosa is representative of the reformist current in the social environmental movements that have arisen to confront the rapid territorial expansion of mining activities in Mexico during the last two decades. This current seeks the redistribution of the costs and benefits derived from mining, the mitigation of the most pernicious environmental impacts, as well as more significant contributions to the economic and social development of the communities affected by mining.

There are innumerable local-level struggles with this orientation in Mexico and in other parts of Latin America. They converge with reformist proposals on the national and international levels that range from voluntary corporate social responsibility to the regulation and tributary regimes associated with the 'new extractivism' practiced by 'progressive' governments in South America, in particular Venezuela, Bolivia and Ecuador, and to a lesser degree Argentina, Brazil and Uruguay (Gudynas, 2010). Moreover, as we will see in the following section, the current proposal to make changes to the Mexican Mining Law responds to some of the demands from this reformist current.

The counterpart to these reformist struggles are the movements that express a categorical 'no' to mining. These movements are not prepared to accept mega-mining projects under any circumstances, promoting alternative development paths that seek to be more sustainable in ecological and social terms, for example: eco-tourism, community-based forestry, agroecology, etc. With this posture, smallholder farmers and indigenous groups threatened by mega-mining projects are not willing to put a price tag on their health, livelihoods, natural patrimony and sacred sites. In accordance with one of the slogans associated with this radical current, 'life is worth more than gold', with reference to cultural valuations that are incommensurable with those derived from the cost-benefit calculations associated with neoclassical economics (Martínez-Alier, 1997). Perhaps the Mexican conflict most emblematic of this radical current is the one that revolves around the San Xavier open-pit gold mine in San Luis Potosí, mentioned above.

How many eco-territorial mining conflicts are there in Mexico? Through a systematic (but not exhaustive) review of newspapers, Internet sites and academic publications, 29 high-profile conflicts around mega-mining in Mexico have been identified (see Table 8.1). There are surely more that, for one reason or another, have not been documented or were not detected in this research. Likewise, there are latent conflicts where the local population knows little or nothing about the plans to develop mega-mines. Even so, taking into

TABLE 8.1 *Mining projects in Mexico that have provoked high-profile eco-territorial conflicts*

Name of project	Project's stage	Company (and subsidiary)	Country of origin	State	Municipal	% of municipal pop. In poverty	Indigenous groups affected	Community-based & civil society organizations	Types of demands	Partial successes
Caballo Blanco	Seeking authorization of EIA	Goldcorp	Canada	Veracruz	Actopan/Alto Lucero	54.1%/67.2%	No	Asamblea Veracruzana de Iniciativas y Defensa Ambiental LAVIDA	No to mining	Postponement of approval process of EIA
Chicomuselo	Suspension	Blackfire	Canada	Chiapas	Chicomuselo	89.80%	No	Frente Cívico de Chicomuselo	Compliance with agreements	Suspension of exploitation
Cinco de Mayo	Suspension	MAG Silver (El Cascabel)	Canada	Chihuahua	Buenaventura	58.60%	No	El Barzón	No to mining	Suspension of exploration
Concordia	Development	Vista Gold	United States	Baja California Sur	La Paz/Los Cabos	24.7%/28.5%	No	Medio Amb. y Sociedad, y En Defensa del Medio Amb. y Desarrollo Rural Sust.	No to mining	None

TABLE 8.1   *Mining projects in Mexico that have provoked high-profile eco-territorial conflicts* (cont.)

Name of project	Project's stage	Company (and subsidiary)	Country of origin	State	Municipal	% of municipal pop. In poverty	Indigenous groups affected	Community-based & civil society organizations	Types of demands	Partial successes
Dolores	Production	Minefinders (Minera Dolores)	Canada	Chihuahua	Madera	58.50%	No	La Asamblea Permanente de Huizopa	Mitigation of env. impacts and more benefits	None
El Arco	Development	Grupo México	Mexico	Baja California	Ensenada	36.10%	No	Ejido Villa Jesús de María	No to mining	None
El Doctor	Suspension	Linear Gold (Plata Real)	Canada	Oaxaca	Magdalena Teitipac	94.00%	Yes	Comisión por la Defensa de la Integridad Territorial y Cultural	No to mining	Suspension of development
El Limón	Exploration	Torex Gold (Media Luna)	Canada	Guerrero	Cocula	69.70%	Yes	Ejidos de Real de Limón y Nuevo Balsas	No to mining	Suspension of exploration
La Colomera	Exploration	Ternium	Argentina / Italy	Michoacán	Coahuayana	65.30%	No	Guardianes de la Selva	Mitigation of env. impacts and more benefits	More Indemnification
La Lupe	Closed	JDC Minerals	China	Puebla	Zautla	79.30%	Yes	Unidad Indígena Totonaca Nahua	No to mining	Closing of mine

Project	Status	Company	Country	State	Municipality	%		Organization		
La Platosa	Suspension	Excellon Resources (Minera Excellon)	Canada	Durango	Tlahualilo	50.80%	No	Ejido La Sierrita, Sección 309 del SNTMMSRM	Compliance with agreement	Court order to give land back
Las Encinas	Production	Ternium	Argentina/Italy	Michoacán	Aquila	78.80%	Yes	Comunidad indígena San Miguel de Aquila	Compliance with agreement	Partial compliance with agreement
Los Filos-Nukay	Production	Goldcorp (Minera Nukay)	Canada	Guerrero	Eduardo Neri	71.90%	Yes	Comité de Defensa de la Tierra de Carrizalillo	More Indemnification	More Indemnification
Mina Esperanza	Seeking approval of EIA	Esperanza Resource	Canada	Morelos	Temixco	56.80%	Yes	Movimiento de Pueblos y Ciudadanía Unida Contra la Minera Esperanza Silver	No to mining	SEMERNAT did not approve EIA
Mina Tayahua	Production	Frisco-Tayahua	México	Zacatecas	Mazapil	72.70%	No	Ejido Salaverna, El Barzón	Mitigation of env. impacts and more benefits	None
Minera Espejeras	Suspension	Frisco	México	Puebla	Tetela de Ocampo	78.20%	Sí	Tetela Hacia el Futuro	No to mining	Suspension of exploration

TABLE 8.1 *Mining projects in Mexico that have provoked high-profile eco-territorial conflicts* (cont.)

Name of project	Project's stage	Company (and subsidiary)	Country of origin	State	Municipal	% of municipal pop. In poverty	Indigenous groups affected	Community-based & civil society organizations	Types of demands	Partial successes
Motozintla	Suspension	Linear Gold Corp	Canada	Chiapas	Motozintla	81.30%	Yes	Ejidos Carrizal y Buenos Aires	No a la minería	Suspension of exploration
Mulatos	Production	Alamos Gold (Mina de Oro Nacional)	Canada	Sonora	Sahuaripa	54.70%	No	Ninguno	Mitigation of env. impacts	None
Natividad	Closed	Sundance	Canada	Oaxaca	Capulálpam	39.60%	Yes	Comunidad indígena Capulálpam	No to mining	Closing of mine
Palmarejo / Trogan	Production	Coeur d'Alene Mines	United States	Chihuahua	Chínipas	87.20%	No	Ejidos Palmarejo, Guazarapes y Agua Salada	Mitigation of env. impacts and more benefits	None
Peña Colorada	Production	Consorcio Benito Juárez Peña Colorada	Argentina / India	Colima / Jalisco	Minatitlán / Cuautitlán	50.1%/85.7%	Yes	Consejo de Mayores, Frente Regional pro-Manantlán y Cuenca del Marabasco	No to expansion and more indemnification	Limited expansion and more indemnification

Project	Status	Company	Country	State	Municipality	%		Organization	Demand	Outcome
Peñasquito	Production	Goldcorp (Ser Minero Zacatecas)	Canada	Zacatecas	Mazapil	72.70%	No	Ejidos Cedros y Vergel, Frente Popular de Lucha de Zacatecas	More indemnification	More indemnification
Real de Catorce	Suspension	First Majestic Silver	Canada	San Luis Potosí	Catorce	64.30%	Yes	Frente por la Defensa de Wirikuta	No to mining	Postponement of project
San Antonio	Seeking approval of EIA	Argonaut Gold (La Pitalla)	Canada	Baja California Sur	La Paz	24.70%	Yes	Agua Vale más del Oro, Medio Ambiente y Sociedad	No to mining	SEMERNAT did not approve EIA
San José del Progreso	Production	Fortuna Silver y Continuum Resources (Minera Cuzcatlán)	Canada	Oaxaca	San José del Progreso	89.90%	Yes	Coordinadora en Defensa de los Recursos Naturales y Nuestra Madre Tierra del Valle de Ocotlán	No to mining	None
San Xavier	Production	New Gold	Canada	San Luis Potosí	Cerro de San Pedro	32.50%	No	Frente Amplio Opositor a la Minera San Xavier	No to mining	None

TABLE 8.1   *Mining projects in Mexico that have provoked high-profile eco-territorial conflicts* (cont.)

Name of project	Project's stage	Company (and subsidiary)	Country of origin	State	Municipal	% of municipal pop. In poverty	Indigenous groups affected	Community-based & civil society organizations	Types of demands	Partial successes
Tehuantepec	Preparing applications for approvals	AHMSA	Mexico	Oaxaca	Santa María Zaniza	95.20%	Yes	Comunidades Indígenas de la Sierra Sur, Barca-DH	No to mining	Postponement of project
Tequesquitlán	Production	GanBo	China	Jalisco	Cuautitlán	85.70%	No	Ejido Teques-quitlán, Frente Regional pro-Manantlán y Cuenca del Marabasco	No to mining	None
Tuligtic	Exploration	Almaden Minerals Ltd (Minera Gavilán)	Canada	Puebla	Ixtacamaxtitlán	81.30%	Yes	Serranos Unidos, Tetela hacia el Futuro	No to mining	None

SOURCE: AUTHOR'S ELABORATION, BASED ON A SYSTEMATIC REVIEW OF INTERNET SITES, NEWSPAPER ARTICLES AND ACADEMIC PUBLICATIONS. THE STATISTICS REGARDING THE INCIDENCE OF POVERTY ON THE MUNICIPAL LEVEL COMES FROM THE NATIONAL COUNCIL FOR THE EVALUATION OF SOCIAL DEVELOPMENT POLICY (CONSEJO NACIONAL DE EVALUACIÓN DE LA POLÍTICA DE DESARROLLO SOCIAL, CONEVAL), HTTP://WWW.CONEVAL.GOB.MX, *ANEXO ESTADÍSTICO DE LA MEDICIÓN MUNICIPAL 2010.*

consideration that there are currently over 800 mining projects associated with foreign capital and that these only represent around 20 percent of the investments in the Mexico's mining sector in recent years, the low number of high-profile conflicts suggests that in the vast majority of cases mining companies have managed to penetrate rural communities without having to face organized resistance.

As can be observed in Table 8.1, 25 of the high-profile cases have to do with projects carried out by foreign companies (86%); 18 by Canadian companies. Again, these are the companies that are expanding the mining frontier to the isolated regions of the country, where it meets resistance from smallholder farmers and indigenous groups struggling to protect traditional livelihoods and cultural landscapes. The imperialist nature of this expansion has provoked widespread indignation, which gives impetus to resistance movements. In fact, anti-mining movements, critical media and social-activist circles have focused most of their attention on denouncing the pillage of foreign mining companies, even though Mexican companies continue to take the lion's share of the booty.

From a different angle it can be confirmed that eco-territorial conflicts tend to take place in municipalities with high rates of poverty. Twenty-four of the conflicts occur in municipalities with an incidence of poverty of over 50 percent of the population and in 14 cases, the poverty rate is over 70 percent, according to official statistics. Of course, this is just an approximation, among other reasons because mining sites are frequently located in the more marginalized parts of the same municipalities, close to localities with even more poverty. It is also important to point out that its not only the local population that is affected by mining, for example: Huichol Indians are affected by First Majestic Silver's plans to reopen silver mines in Wirikuta, the sacred territory that forms part of their annual spiritual pilgrimage, even though they do not live there.

Another observation regarding Table 8.1: sixteen of the high-profile conflicts affect indigenous groups, that is, more than half. There is no doubt that indigenous groups have been disproportionately affected by mega-mining projects and that these have played a leadership role in resistance movements. However, one should avoid falling into the trap of thinking that the indigenous factor always translates into the defence of Mother Earth. In the state of Morelos, for example, where the Canadian company Esperanza Resource seeks to develop an open-pit gold and silver mine less than one kilometer from the archaeological site Xochicalco and just 16 kilometers from the city of Cuernavaca, the majority of the Nahua farmers from Tetlama, the indigenous community whose territory contains the coveted minerals, insists on

supporting the project and on renting their land in exchange for monetary payments, gifts and promises of employment (Enciso, 2013). In this case, environmental organizations from Cuernavaca and other nearby communities are the
ones that are leading the resistance movement.

Finally, in the last three columns of Table 8.1, an effort has been made to
distil the essence of the local resistance movements' demands and their partial
successes. Once again, these are just approximations, among other reasons
because reformist and anti-mining currents can coincide in the same local
space. Having said this, we can observe that 18 of the 29 high-profile cases deal
with movements that are predominantly oriented towards rejecting mega-
mining projects; while eleven seek greater indemnification, mitigation of environmental impacts and/or the company's compliance with previously
established agreements. It is interesting to note that more than 70 percent of
the movements that say 'no' to mining revolve around projects that have still
not entered the production phase. Evidently, there is a greater chance of successfully blocking a project before permission is obtained for changes in land-
use rights and before mining companies invest large sums of money in getting
the project underway.

With regards to partial successes, in 12 of the cases included in Table 8.1, the
resistance movements have managed to get the project suspended or closed; in
five the local population has received greater indemnification; in two the
judicial branch of the federal government has ordered the respective mining
companies to give rented land back to the affected agrarian communities; and
in the remaining ten cases no tangible results have been registered. At the
same time, it is important to keep in mind that some of the partial successes
of these movements transcend the local ambit, especially with regard to
consciousness raising.

Where there is resistance, it has been strengthened in recent years by the
construction of strategic alliances with progressive elements of civil society.
On the regional level, there are two organizational efforts that stand out, both
in indigenous zones: the Sierra Norte in the state of Puebla, with the leadership
of organizations such as the Unión Indígena Totonaco Náhuatl, Tetetla Hacia
el Futuro and Consejo Tiyat Tlali; and Costa Chica in the state of Guerrero,
where the support of organizations such as the Tlachinollan Mountain Centre
for Human Rights (*Centro de Derechos Humanos de la Montaña Tlachinollan*)
and the Regional Coordination of Community Police and Authorities
(*Coordinadora Regional de Autoridades Comunitarias-Policía Comunitaria*)
have become formidable obstacles for mining capital.

In 2008, two national-level networks were created: the Mexican Network for
People Affected by Mining (*Red Mexicana de Afectados por la Minería*, REMA)

and the National Assembly of Environmentally Affected People (Asamblea Nacional de Afectados Ambientales, ANAA). The latter brings together, not just the victims of mining destruction, but people affected by diverse forms of environmental degradation and natural resource dispossession. These networks provide a space for participants to exchange information, share experiences, strengthen alliances, coordinate strategies and articulate demands. REMA's demands, for example, include a moratorium on open-pit mining and a series of constitutional and legal reforms in order to put an end to rapacious mining practices that privatize profits and socialize costs (REMA, 2009).

Resistance movements in Mexico are articulated with those of other Latin American countries, *inter alia*, through the Meso-American Movement against the Extractive Mining Model (*Movimiento Mesoamericano contra el Modelo Extractivo Minero*, M4). The M4 was created at the beginning of 2012 and brings together more than 60 organizations from Panama, Costa Rica, Mexico, El Salvador, Honduras and Guatemala. Like the umbrella organizations on the national level, the M4 coordinates meetings that bring together representatives of multiple resistance movements. In contrast to the political expressions that seek to mitigate the most nefarious effects of mega-mining and to extract more benefits for the local population, the M4's slogan is 'from Panama to Canada, mining is a no-go'.[8]

Reformist Initiatives Proposed by EPN's Team

Since the PRI regained control of the federal government in December of 2012, with Enrique Peña Nieto (EPN) in the presidential seat, the executive branch has responded to some of the demands coming from the reformist currents of the eco-territorial and labour movements sketched out above. Before looking at the current government's reform proposals, it is important to mention that the legitimacy of EPN's government was strongly questioned because of the irregularities surrounding the federal elections that took place in July of 2012. Televisa, the country's largest television network, owned by one of the richest men in Mexico, Emilio Azcárraga, unabashedly favoured EPN by shining positive media attention on him for years, grooming his image in soap-opera fashion. Then, in the weeks leading up to the election, the PRI bought votes with pre-paid cards—issued by Soriana (a large Mexican supermarket chain), Monex and other financial-service groups—which were to be activated the

---

8   In Spanish it rhythms: '¡De Panamá a Canada, la minería no va!'.

day after the election, on the condition that the EPN won. Student demonstrations, before and after the election, underlined the magnitude of this legitimacy crisis.

With this in mind, the 'Pact for Mexico', signed on the 23rd of January of 2013 by the recently inaugurated president and by the national leaders of the country's three main political parties, can be seen as part of a strategy to gain legitimacy and to mark the difference between the PRI and the PAN. In one of the five main sections of this pact, EPN's government promised to come up with 'a new law for mining exploitation that reviews the scheme for concessions and payments for federal rights linked to production', with the objective of collecting taxes to be used 'primarily for, and in direct benefit of, the municipalities and communities where mining exploitation is established' (Promise number 61, Pacto de México). Furthermore, the federal government promised to prohibit coal mining via rudimentary vertical shafts, known as *pocitos*, which have been responsible for multiple fatalities in the north of the country.

Three months later the Parliamentary Newspaper published a proposal—put together by a commission composed of representatives from the Ministry of Finance and Public Credit (Secretaría de Hacienda y Crédito Público) and from the Ministry of Economy (Secretaría de Economía)—to make changes to the country's Mining Law and to the Fiscal Coordination Law. This proposal was approved on April 23, 2013, by Mexico's Chamber of Deputies, with 359 votes in favour and 77 against, and then turned over to the Senate, without any further progress for the rest of the year. It bears mentioning that the PAN does not support this proposal, nor do business groups in the industry, for example: the Mexican Chamber of Mining (Cámara Minera de México).

The gist of the proposal is to collect a five percent royalty on the profits derived from mining in Mexico and then use this revenue to finance social development and environmental projects in the municipalities and states where mining activities take place. In this scheme, 30 percent of the revenue from this royalty will be channelled to the General Participation Fund (*Fondo General de Participaciones*), whose resources are divvied up between all states according to a complex formula; while the other 70 percent is to be used to create a new fund: the Fund for Contributing to the Sustainable Regional Development of Mining States and Municipalities (*Fondo de Aportaciones para el Desarrollo Regional Sustentable de Estados y Municipios Mineros*, FADRSEMM).

According to this scheme, the FADRSEMM's resources will be divided equally between the municipal- and state-level governments, where mining activities take place. To administer this fund, each state will create a Committee for the Regional Development of Mining Zones (*Comité de Desarrollo Regional para las Zonas Mineras*, CDRZM), headed by the minister of Agrarian, Territorial and Urban Development (*Secretaría de Desarrollo Agrario, Territorial y Urbano*); and including one representative of the state government, one representative of the municipal government, two representatives of the mining companies operating in the area, and one representative of the indigenous communities or *ejidos* affected by mining.

From a reformist perspective, this proposal represents a timid step forward in economic distributive terms. If the law comes into being, it will recuperate part of the taxes that mining companies used to pay during the period of import-substituting industrialization (1940–1982) and it will create mechanisms for channelling the new source of revenue towards the country's mining regions. On the other hand, the proposal is very limited in the extent that it seeks to foster the participation of the population adversely affected by mining activities in decisions regarding the use of the FADRSEMM's resources. In fact, mining companies are meant to have twice as much say as affected communities in the CDRSM, assuring that the former's interests take precedence over the latter's. Likewise, state and municipal governments will only be allowed to participate in decision making regarding *how* to spend the new source of revenue; otherwise, the status quo will be maintained by not permitting these levels of government to apply taxes or any significant regulatory measures to mining activities.

From a broader perspective, the reform proposed by EPN's government does not broach the question of whether or not the local population has the right to reject mega-mining projects. According to the Constitution and the existing laws, the federal government is the custodian of the nation's subterranean resources; it can hand them over to capital of any national origin for 50-year periods; and mining activities take precedence over all other productive activities. This political orientation, however, clashes with the United Nations' Declaration on the Rights of Indigenous Peoples wherever the government and mining companies do not obtain 'free and informed consent prior to the approval of any project affecting their lands or territories and other resources, particularly in connection with the development, utilization or exploitation of their mineral, water or other resources'. Ultimately, the anti-mining movement seeks to extend the right to 'free, prior and informed consent' to all rural communities, irrespective of their ethnic identity.

Another important omission in the reform proposal endorsed by the current government of Mexico is that it does not address the question of workplace security. The concerns over the dangers of vertical-shaft coal mining included in the Pact for Mexico, were not included in the proposal approved by the Chamber of Deputies in April of 2013. Likewise, the deregulation of the miners' collective labour contracts remains intact and the current government has not taken any initiative to eliminate the 'flexibility' reflected in the existing laws.

On another level, we can observe that EPN's administration has made an effort, during its first year in office, to repair the old corporatist system and reclaim the role the state had during the 71 years of PRI rule during the 20th century, as mediator between capital and labour in the resolution of conflicts. Along these lines, the current head of the STPS, Alfonso Navarrete Prida, publically declared in June of 2013 that his government recognized Napoleón Gómez Urrutia as the legitimate leader of the SNTMMSRM (Muñoz Ríos, 2013b), even though the Sixth Unitary Tribunal of the First Circuit in Penal Matters (*Sexto Tribunal Unitario en Materia Penal del Primer Circuito*) issued new arrest orders against this union leader in March of the same year.

In this way, the STPS managed to successfully mediate the resolution of two labour conflicts in the summer of 2013 between sections of the SNTMMSRM and Grupo Frisco: one in the San Francisco del Oro mine in the state of Chihuahua, and the other in a mine called 'María', in Sonora. In a third conflict involving Grupo Frisco, at the El Coronel mine in the state of Zacatecas, the STPS managed to arbitrate an agreement between labour and management, in spite of an inter-union struggle that divides these miners between the SMMNGS and the SNTMMSRM. In contrast to these 'successful' negotiations, the STPS has not been able to mediate the resolution of conflicts that involve sections of the SNTMMSRM and Grupo Mexico, in particular three strikes that began during Calderon's presidency in Taxco (Guerrero), Cananea (Sonora) and Sombrerete (Zacatecas).

There are two other aspects of the current conjuncture that merit mention: first, in 2013 we saw two unprecedented court decisions that favoured smallholder farmers, ordering Excellon Resources and Goldcorp to return rented *ejidal* land to La Sierrita (in the state of Durango) and Cerro Gordo (in Zacatecas), respectively; and second, Alfonso Navarrete Prida announced in October of 2013 that the Attorney General's Office (Procuraduría General de la República) was looking into the technical viability of recovering the 63 cadavers that remain trapped in the Pasta de Conchos mine since 2006 (Muñoz Ríos, 2013c). Incidentally, this responds to one of the principal demands of Familia de Pasta de Conchos, a non-governmental organization representing the family members of the dead miners, which has collaborated with other civil-society actors to expose the deplorable and dangerous working conditions in the coal-mining region located in the north of the country. At the same time, representatives of Grupo Mexico, which has been accused of causing the explosion in Pasta de Conchos through negligence, have interjected with a legal petition to prevent the rescue operation, arguing that it would create a high risk of hurting people and nearby communities, as well as plants and animals in the region.

Final Reflections

It is not hard to see the imperialist elements of the neoliberal project at work in Mexico's mining sector. Neoliberalism is in itself an imperialist project insofar as it gives capital from the core of the global economy easy access to the abundant natural resources and cheap labour available in the global South. Canadian mining companies derive surplus value from exploiting Mexico's mineral reserves through their control of privileged natural deposits (what Marx called 'ground rent'), through the high rates of labour exploitation implied by low wages, and through their ability to 'externalize' the environmental and social costs of mega-mining in small-scale farming and indigenous communities. This surplus value circulates on the TSX and is transferred to the metropolitan centers of Canada, where companies invest in office space, employ qualified personnel, sponsor events, and so on; and where major stockholders reside and spend money on private property, schools and diverse forms of luxury consumption. All of this speaks to the continued relevance of North-South analysis.

At the same time, it is important to keep in mind that the neoliberal agenda was not only pushed in imperialist fashion onto Mexico from the outside by the IMF, the World Bank and the US and Canadian governments, but it was also enthusiastically embraced and shaped by the Mexican bourgeoisie and its technocratic accomplices in government. In fact, the degree to which the Mexican state has bent over backwards to accommodate foreign mining capital, after having generously transferred public mineral reserves and infrastructure to nationally based big business, is a function of the degree to which the federal government has been captured by the faction of the Mexican capitalist class whose interests are aligned with the neoliberal agenda.

Along these lines, Schneider (2002) observes that Mexican big business is extraordinarily well organized on the national level, more so than in any other major Latin American country. This helps to explain why it has been so successful in imposing its interests on the Mexican state. Four national level business organizations stand out: the Mexican Council for Businessmen (*Consejo Mexicano para Hombres de Negocios*, CMHN), an elite group of 36 businessmen, including the mining magnates mentioned in this chapter; the Business Coordinating Council (*Consejo Coordinador Empresarial*, CCE), an economy-wide peak association that draws most of its funding and leadership from the CMHN; the Coordinator for

Foreign-Trade Business Associations (*Coordinadora de Organismos Empresariales de Comercio Exterior*, COECE), a spin-off from the CCE that helped to promote the interests of Mexican big business during the NAFTA negotiations; and the Employers' Confederation of the Republic of Mexico (*Confederacion Patronal de la República Mexicana*, COPARMEX), formed in 1929 by a powerful group of bourgeois dynasties based in Monterrey. The membership of all of four these organizations saw opportunities in the neoliberal agenda for acquiring public assets and forming strategic alliances with foreign capital.

The point to emphasis here is that national-level governments on both sides of the imperialist relation mobilize public resources and implement neoliberal policies in such a way as *to favour the accumulation of their own nationally-based capital*. On the Mexican side, the notoriously corrupt Salinas administration privatized the country's mineral resources and mining infrastructure in a way that allowed a handful of Mexican businessmen to gain oligopolistic control over the sector before opening it up to imperialist exploitation; while on the Canadian side, the federal government helped its nationally-based mining companies to gain access to Mexico's extensive, relatively unexplored and recently privatized mineral resources, and to its cheap, repressed and flexible labour, by doing its part in pushing and shaping the neoliberal agenda on the regional stage (Gordon, 2010) and by subsidizing and under-regulating mining companies that trade on the Toronto Stock Exchange (Denault and Sacher, 2012). Moreover, on both ends of the North American continent, nationally based mining capital is linked to its home country in important ways, including with regard to the location of main headquarters, the nationality of CEOs and major stockholders, location of the companies' stock market exchanges and, in the case of Canada, the large number of mining-company shares held by governmental agencies that manage pension funds.

One of the theoretical implications of this is that, contrary to the image of amorphous capital that is everywhere and nowhere at that same time, without any identifiable national base (Hardt and Negri, 2000; Robinson, 2010); state-centered analysis is still relevant in explaining the dynamics of imperialism in our day (Petras & Veltmeyer, 2011; Wood, 2003). Furthermore, it is not just the United States that is imperialist; middle powers like Canada also exhibit imperialist tendencies that go well beyond riding on the coattail of the sole superpower (Gordon, 2010). In the case of Mexico's mining sector, after centuries of Spanish plunder during the era of conquest and colonialism, followed by growing US dominance after Independence (1810) that culminated during the dictatorship of Porfírio Diaz (1876–1910) and lasted until the 1960s, it is now Canada that has taken the imperialist offensive by helping its national-based mining capital penetrate Mexican territory and exploit its cheap labour.

This is not to say that the global economy has not been 'transnationalized' in many important ways as part of the neoliberal restructuring project. There is no denying that capital is more internationally mobile; transnational companies have properties and satellite headquarters all over the world. The industrial processes of individual corporations have been spread out across the globe, with the labour intensive and heavily contaminating activities relocated to the global South; transnational corporations form strategic alliances among themselves; and gigantic 'trans-Latina' consortiums have emerged, including the ones mentioned above. Furthermore, as Robinson (2010: 68) suggests 'the transnationalization of capital transnationalizes the basis upon which state mangers and political elites achieve their production'. All of this is present in our case study of Mexico's mining sector. The point is not to exaggerate these tendencies to the extent of losing sight of the contemporary relevance of state-centred and North-South analysis, what Katz (2011) calls the 'association model' for explaining the relationship between national bourgeoisies and imperial bureaucracies, and the 'structuralist vision' for analysing the asymmetrical power relations between core and peripheral nations.

From a class perspective, the power of imperialism in Mexico's mining sector consists in the flexibilization of labour, the suppression of wages and its ability to keep the combative SNTMMSRM out of foreign-owned mines. It is only in the last few years that the miners at Goldcorp's two most important gold mines in Mexico (Peñasquito and Los Filos-Nukay) have been able to form sections of the union led by Gómez Urrutia. In these cases the company was easily able to come to terms with the wage increases that were demanded. In most Canadian-owned mines, the miners have not been allowed or able to form independent unions; they are represented by company-controlled 'white unions'.

As outlined above, neoliberal policies were applied to the sector beginning in the 1980s, in spite of the resistance of combative sections of the SNT-MMSRM. Since then, the state has frequently resorted to diverse forms of repression to break strikes and weaken unions. Even though some labour conflicts have been peacefully resolved in recent years by granting salary increases and other concessions to miners, working conditions in Mexico's mining sector continue to be very poor by various measures, including wages: in 2012, the average daily wage for Mexican miners was 356.50 pesos (SE, 2013), equal to 27.40 dollars. While this rate is 37.1 percent higher than the national average, it only represents less than ten percent of the average salary of miners in Canada.[9]

---

9 The Mining Association of Canada reports that the average weekly wage for Canadian miners in 2011 was 1436 dollars (Mining Association of Canada, 2012: 6).

It is also important not to lose sight of how dangerous it is to work in Mexico's mines. Between 2006 and the beginning of 2013, there were 159 fatalities in the mining sector, half of them in the *pocitos* used for mining coal in the state of Coahuila (Rodríguez García, 2013). The government simply does not have sufficient personnel to meet its responsibility of inspecting all of the mines in the country and obliging mining companies to implement the security measures necessary to guarantee the safety of workers (CNDH, 2011); even less so in the case of informal and illegal mining, which is increasingly controlled by organized crime (Rodríguez García, 2013).

Moreover, modern mining operations are highly mechanized and automated, which translates into relatively few formal jobs; only 309,722 in Mexico in 2011, and of these, only one third are in extractive and processing activities (99,805 jobs). The other two thirds are derived from 'the fabrication of non-metallic mineral products' (127,425 jobs) and from 'basic metal industries' (82,492 jobs) (SE, 2012: 25). Even if we include these last two categories as jobs 'directly created by mining', as Mexico's Ministry of Economy does, the total number of jobs in the sector only represents two percent of formal employment on the national level and 0.62 percent of the economically active population in the country in the same year.

All things considered, unionism in Mexico's mining sector has been greatly debilitated in the neoliberal context. Mining unions are divided and collective contracts have been made more 'flexible'. But this is just the tip of the iceberg, since it only refers to formal-sector employment. There is also an informal sector, especially in the coal-mining region, where working conditions are similar in many respects to those that existed for the slaves that toiled in the mines of New Spain centuries ago (Familia Pasta de Conchos, 2011). What is more, even in the mega-mining projects carried out by transnational capital, labour segmentation divides workers with 'permanent' contracts from those with 'temporary' ones, with the latter typically being offered to the local population to construct infrastructure and provide services (Petras, 2013). This segmentation reduces the collective bargaining power of labour in negotiations with management, even more so because the federal government permits the hiring of 'scabs' and the formation of sham unions controlled by management, as in the case of Cananea. In this scenario, the traditional demands of the labour movement—for decent wages, workplace security, union autonomy and collective contracts that prohibit the hiring of non-unionized workers—are still extant.

The eco-territorial movements that have emerged since the 1990s can be seen as anti-imperialist struggles to the large extent that they are focussed on foreign mining projects. In fact, anti-imperialist sentiments are salient in the radical movements' discursive 'framing'. Once again, in this terrain it is convenient to distinguish between reformist currents that demand a fairer distribution of the costs and benefits derived from mining activities, and radical currents that reject these activities outright. The reformist currents overlap with the labour movement in the mining sector insofar as miners and the affected rural population are prepared to accept mega-mining projects, under the condition that they can participate equitably in obtaining economic and social benefits.

To a certain extent, the proposal of EPN's government to make changes to the Mining Law and to the Fiscal Coordination Law is an attempt to respond to the redistributive demands associated with reform-oriented social environmental movements. In essence, this proposal seeks to oblige mining companies to be 'socially responsible' by contributing to the social and economic development of mining regions. Whether or not it becomes law, has yet to be determined.

For its part, the radical currents that predominate in most of Mexico's eco-territorial resistance movements (86%) are not only anti-imperialist, they are also anti-capitalist insofar as they seek to prevent subsistence farmers from being separated from their means of production. It bears repeating that large open-pit mines destroy land, hoard water resources and contaminate the ecosystems that sustain the traditional livelihoods of smallholder farmers and of indigenous groups, impelling a process of proletarianization. In this way, the contemporary land grabbing associated with mega-mining is akin to Marx's model of 'original accumulation', described in the first volume of *Capital*. Furthermore, as Luxemburg (2003 [1913]) argued, similar processes can be observed, not just during the birth of capitalism, but throughout its long history, since capitalism must feed on elements outside of itself in the search for high rates of return and in order to at least temporarily resolve the realization-of-surplus-value dilemma. Building on this, with the important twist of emphasizing over-accumulation and not the lack of effective demand within the capitalist economy as the driving force behind imperialism, David Harvey has popularized the much broader concept of 'accumulation by dispossession' to explain the privatization of the commons during the neoliberal era. In this formulation, accumulation by dispossession includes '[the] privatization of land and the forceful expulsion of peasant populations; the conversion of various forms of property rights (common, collective, state, etc.) into exclusive private property rights; [...] and the suppression of alternative (indigenous) forms of production and consumption; colonial, neo-colonial, and imperial processes of appropriation of assets (including natural resources)' (Harvey, 2003: 145).

Based on this definition—much too broad for Brenner's (2006) liking—we can observe another level of 'accumulation by dispossession' in Mexico's mining sector: the transfer of publically owned mineral reserves and parastatal mining companies to the Mexican private sector (Tetreault, 2014), which took place two decades ago, even though this did not directly drive a process of proletarianization.

In any case, the anti-mining movements in Mexico (and elsewhere) are in essence anti-capitalist movements. They reflect what Martínez-Alier calls 'the environmentalism of the poor', not just because they are spearheaded by the rural poor affected or threatened by mega-mining projects, but also and more importantly because they are struggles that seek to 'remove natural resources from the economic sphere, from the generalized market system, from the mercantile rational, from the chrematistic valuation (the reduction of value to monetary costs and benefits), in order to keep or return them to the *oikonomia* (in the way that Aristotle used the word, similar to human ecology, opposite to chrematistic)' (Martínez Alier, 2009).

To be sure, in Mexico there have been few concessions made to anti-mining movements. In recent years, SEMARNAT has not approved the EIAs of a few highly controversial projects where strong resistance movements have emerged, for example: Caballo Blanco in the state of Veracruz, just three kilometers from a nuclear energy plant called Laguna Verde; Esperanza, right beside Xochicalco, an archaeological site in the state of Morelos; and Concordia, in a Protected Natural Area in state of Baja California Sur; all three promoted by Canadian capital. However, as this last case illustrates, SEMARNAT's rejection of the EIA does not necessarily kill a project; it can be revived, like a zombie, by changing its name and reformulating the EIA (Trasviña Aguilar, 2013).

In conclusion, since the late 1990s, toxic open-pit mega-mining has expanded throughout the country, in spite of the organized resistance mobilized by smallholder farmers, indigenous groups and civil society organizations. While Mexico's environmental policy has been strengthened since the 1980s by constructing an edifice of laws and institutions on all three levels of government, empirical evidence demonstrates that these laws are frequently circumvented in order to accommodate the interests of mining capital. In fact, the federal government invites the private sector to development large open-pit mines, facilitating access to the country's mineral, water and land resources; and it permits the use of millions of litres of highly toxic and poisonous substances, including in zones previously designated as protected areas. All of this suggests that anti-mining movements have had no significant impact on designing public policy.

On the other hand, these movements have been very successful in raising the consciousness of large sectors of the Mexican population regarding the risks and costs associated with mega-mining, and regarding the meagre benefits that these projects bring to affected communities and to the country in general. This higher level of consciousness is a first step in building the broad-based coalitions necessary to wrest the state apparatus from the dictates of neoliberal technocrats and ideologues. In the current conjuncture, this implies seeing EPN's proposal to reform the country's mining law for what it is: an attempt to co-opt dissidents and undermine the radical current of resistance to mega-mining.

CHAPTER 9

Canadian Resistance to the Northern Gateway Oil Pipeline

Henry Veltmeyer and Paul Bowles

The global commodities boom of the first decade of the twenty-first century has focussed attention back to extractivism as a development path. While this debate has specific local characteristics—for example, 're-primarization' in some Latin American countries, 'land grabbing' in parts of Africa, and a quest for 'energy superpower' status in Canada—they can all be seen as part of a wider concern over, and resistance to, the global dynamics of extractivist capitalism.

This paper has two purposes. The first is to provide a theoretical framework in which extractivism can be understood globally and within which specific country and regional debates can be situated. The second is to analyse resistance to a specific form of extractivism—re oil pipeline construction—in Northern British Columbia and to illustrate how it can be understood within the context of the turn of many countries towards natural resource extraction as a model of national development. While resistance to extractivism has been the subject of much analysis in the Latin American context, less is available on resistance in the global north (in fact, the global south in the northern hemisphere) and less still on a comparative analysis. This paper seeks to fill this void and, in doing so, demonstrates the similarities in extractivist resistance in both north and south.

Canada, we argue, provides a good case study for exploring such similarities as it engages in 'extractivist imperialism' abroad at the same time as the natural resource development on the unceded territory of indigenous groups in Canada represents a form of neocolonialism. As an entry point into the analysis, we provide a brief overview of Canada's extractivist push before turning to the general framework and the dynamics of resistance to the construction of pipelines to transport oil from the tarsands of Alberta to Asian markets.

The Problem

For decades after the signing of the automobile pact between the US and Canada the engine of economic growth was automobile manufacturing in the country's industrial heartland. But in a context of an economic downturn and a declining manufacturing sector Canada has turned back towards what has always been a major force of production in the country: the extractivist industry and manufacturing related to natural resource and staples production. With a growing demand in the world economy for fossil fuels and industrial minerals, as well as agro-food products, the current government has staked Canada's future on natural resource development, including the production for the exportation of Alberta tarsands oil. The tarsands have been at the centre of debate since the 1980s but it was not until the price of oil rose during the mid-2000s that it became economic to extract oil from the tarsands. Over the past decade, the extraction of oil from the tarsands has been ramped up, resulting in a number of megaprojects to build pipelines to take the tarsands oil to market—to the refineries of the Gulf Coast of the US via the Keystone pipeline the expansion of which is currently the focus of intense debate in the US and to markets in Asia via the proposed Enbridge pipeline from the tarsands in Northern Alberta to the port terminal of Kitimat in Northern British Columbia (NBC), another major pipeline that has also generated political opposition and resistance.

This provides the context for our analysis of the political dynamics of the resistance to Enbridge's 'Northern Gateway' project, particularly in regard to the indigenous communities on the route of the proposed gateway. Not only do these communities bear the brunt of the capitalist development process but they contain the major forces of resistance to it—to capitalism in its latest phase of development.

Apart from the unparalleled opportunities for Enbridge and other capitalist enterprises in the oil and gas sector to take advantage of arbitrage opportunities to make superprofits by bringing tarsands oil and natural gas to new markets in Asia, at issue in the Enbridge project is the federal government's strategy and plans for the country's economic development. As for Alberta, the provincial government naturally enough sees the Enbridge project as an opportunity for additional fiscal revenues and to solve its budgetary deficit situation. And British Columbia? It is not likely to make much from the pipeline, not even in terms of short-term construction jobs, and it would have to assume responsibility and account to British Columbians for the enormous risk and potential threat posed by the Enbridge project to the environment and the sustainability of key provincial industries such as the salmon fishery, as well as important watersheds and waterways and large tracts of land inhabited by First Nations groups and indigenous communities with territorial rights, if not sovereignty, over much of this land and these waterways.

In this controversial and conflictual situation the current BC provincial Liberal government has rejected the Enbridge proposal 'as it stands' but has left the door open for further negotiations, presumably including a greater share of the oil rent. In any case, the provincial government is staking the economic development of the province on another network of pipelines designed to transport liquefied natural gas to Asian markets, a project that is anticipated to have much greater economic spinoffs without near the same level of risk and the negative socioenvironmental impacts associated with the transportation of oil, and thus without the same level of unified resistance—at least not to date—of the First Nations communities and of environmentalists across the country as well in British Columbia.

The resistance to the transportation of tarsands oil engages diverse groups, grassroots organisations and communities as well as a broad coalition of citizens that has joined a civil society movement concerned for the implications of the tarsands for the environment and global climate change. But it draws its power from the mobilizing capacity of the indigenous communities in the direct path of the pipeline project. From the perspective of the First Nations, which includes both the tribal reserves (bands) under the ultimate authority of the Department of Aboriginal Affairs and Northern Development Canada and communities that can claim and have retained territorial rights as sovereign nations, the Enbridge project is a matter of life and death, raising questions about their very existence as a people and their territorial rights as sovereign nations.

As Hereditary Chief Na'mox of the Wetsu'wet'en explained to us, his starting point for opposition to pipelines is the elders' great saying, 'if we don't speak for the animals, the fish and the birds, who will?' Simply, very simply, very to the point and how could we give up something that our great great grandchildren will ask us one day 'why don't we have this anymore? Why didn't you stop this then? We don't have a right to let that happen.'[1] From this indigenous perspective the stakes could not be higher. As Jasmine Thomas, an Aboriginal leader explained, her resistance was based on 'our role as stewards of the water, doing what we can to make sure that the veins, you know, of our Mother Earth are healthy, so that we can continue to be healthy and we can continue to live how we have always lived'.[2] Hence the leading role of the First Nations and their communities as a protagonist in the struggle and growing resistance against not just against the Enbridge project and the neoliberal policies of the

---

1   Personal interview, June 10, 2013.
2   Personal interview, June 8, 2013.

federal government but of the operative capitalist system, which not only threatens their way of life and traditional culture but challenges their very right to exist as a modern society and sovereign nation with territorial rights.

The existence of the First Nations as a people and a culture is predicated on a symbiotic relationship of harmony with 'mother earth' and unrestricted access to the global commons of land, water and society's natural resources as illustrated in the quotation above. Given the fundamental impulse of capitalism to enclose the commons, privatise and commodify the social forces of economic production, and separate the direct producers on the land from their means of social production, capitalism stands in a relation of fundamental contradiction to the ability of First Nations communities to protect their traditional and modern culture, determine their own future, and to exist as a people and as a society.[3] Thus the resistance of the First Nations to Enbridge's Northern Gateway project reaches well beyond the limits of the global environmental movement (to protect the environment and the ecosystem via a regime of sustainable resource development and management). Unlike the environmental movement, with which it is aligned in opposition to the Northern Gateway project, it is fundamentally an anti-capitalist struggle, which distinguishes the indigenous movement, rooted in the community-based organizations of First Nations society and culture, from the class-based labour movement and the civil society-based environmental movement, both of which take capitalism as a given, seeking only to regulate it in the public interest (through, for example, inclusive and sustainable development).[4]

---

3   In the words of Roy Henry Vickers, a leading Aboriginal artist and public figure, 'Our ancestors are the land. So, when we allow some corporation to run a pipeline through this country because of the promise of money, what we are doing is endangering what was given to us, and we do not have the right'. Personal interview, June 11, 2013.

4   As an example of the anti-capitalist nature of indigenous resistance, consider the following critique of modern society offered by Vickers: 'When money becomes your addiction, that's all you think of. The only thing that you think is going to make you better is to get more money. Well that's the way people are thinking. What they don't understand is when you get old like me, you can't buy back your youth. There's no fountain of youth. When you lose a loved one, all the money, all the millions that you have cannot change that. You know? When we lose that river, all the trillions cannot bring it back. Cannot fix it. And so, there are things that if we think with a mind that is chained, thinking there is some other way to be better and money is at the root of it all, that will lead us to destruction because money can't. It's just a fallacy. It rises and falls with the whim of whoever is buying stocks and it's BS. What's real is the seasons and how much rain falls and how is the soil and are you looking after it properly or are you killing the soil because you are not taking care of it the way you should. Those are the real things'. Personal interview June 11, 2013.

To understand why this resistance has arisen at this particular historical juncture, in the next section we outline the two major debates that have followed the turn of so many governments in recent years towards an extractivist mega-project strategy of national development. This is because the Enbridge pipeline project raises issues that can best if not only be understood in the context of this debate. We then draw attention to the broader global context of capitalist development—the economics and politics of natural resource extraction in the global economy—before addressing several questions about the role of the Canadian state in advancing extractive capitalism both in Canada and elsewhere in the world. We conceptualise this role as extractivist imperialism—the form that imperialism seems to be taking at the dawn of a new era of capitalist development. The paper concludes with a brief analysis of the resistance to the Enbridge pipeline project, viewing the dynamics of this resistance through the lens of a theory constructed with reference to the resistance against extractivist capitalism and imperialism in Latin America. These struggles and this resistance movement are instructive for understanding the dynamics of the pipeline resistance in northern British Colombia. A brief analysis of these dynamics leads us to several conclusions regarding the economics and politics of natural resource extraction.

Framing the Debate

The economics and politics of natural resource extraction / development can be understood with reference to and in terms of two debates. One of these debates relates to the policy dynamics of the 'new extractivism' in Latin America. The other concerns the nature and political dynamics of the resistance.

The Economics and Politics of Natural Resource Extraction
The literature on the economic and politics of natural resource extraction in the current context of globalizing capitalism takes three distinct approaches towards natural resource development. The first has to do with an argument advanced inter alia by economists at the World Bank, who have presented the demand for raw materials and primary commodities—minerals and metals, sources of energy and agro-food products—as an unparalleled 'economic opportunity' of which resource-rich countries should avail themselves (World Bank, 2005, 2011). From this perspective, the resource-rich countries of Latin America and Africa should take advantage of the large-scale movements of 'resource-seeking' investors seeking to maximise the return on their capital in

the context of large-scale acquisition of land for the purpose of energy and food security. In the literature on these issues the agency and motor of natural resource development is the private sector in the form of transnational capitalist enterprises, the transnational corporations that have the requisite capital and the technology to exploit and develop the natural resources of these countries.

Another approach is to take a society's wealth of natural resources not as a blessing or an economic opportunity but as a 'curse', with reference here to the finding that, on average, developing countries highly endowed with natural resources were growing less rapidly than those that were less endowed, or that so many resource-rich countries failed to develop at all while many resource-poor countries are among the most advanced developed countries in the world today (Auty, 2001). Explanations of this resource curse (Auty, 1993; Haber & Menaldo, 2012; Sachs & Warner 2001) have made reference to or specified at least eight factors, any one of which sufficient to bring on this supposed curse, but in combination a recipe for underdevelopment rather than development.

One factor relates to the exploitation of labour—the 'unlimited supplies of surplus labour' generated by the capitalist development process. According to a line of development thought that prevailed from the 1950s to the 1970s the exploitation of labour and human resource development have much broader multiplier effects and far greater linkages into other economic and social sectors than an extractivist approach towards development.

Other factors include the Dutch disease, with reference to the negative exchange rate effect of primary commodity exports on other production sectors; the notion that what goes up (prices of primary commodities) must and often does come down, resulting in a boom-bust cycle if not a trend towards deteriorating terms of terms of trade for primary commodities; the use of foreign direct investment (FDI) as a mechanism for the extraction and transfer of surplus value; and the propensity of extractivism and natural resource development towards economic concentration, the use of relatively little labour relative to technology and capital, and excessive inequalities in the distribution of the social product and the benefits of economic growth—the 'inequality predicament' as conceived by the economists associated with UNDESA (2005); and, the incentive and means for political elites to form a (typically comprador) rent seeking coalition which is more interested in personal accumulation than national development.

A third approach has focused on the primary commodities boom in Latin America in the context of the turn of many governments in the region towards a post-Washington consensus regarding the need to bring the state back into the development process—to bring about a more inclusive form of development (Infante & Sunkel, 2009). In this context, government after government in the region turned towards extractivism—a strategic reliance on foreign direct investment in the exploration for, and the extraction of, minerals, fossil and bio-fuels, and agro-food products in high demand—and the exportation of these products, or 'reprimarization' as it is referred to in this context (Cypher, 2010).

The intention has been to pursue a post-neoliberal strategy of combining an extractivist development strategy with a new social policy of poverty reduction designed for a more inclusive form of development than had been the norm for the previous two decades. From this post-neoliberal perspective, a strategy of natural resource extraction was viewed as a means of bringing about a process of inclusive development—using resource rents and taxes on corporate profits as a means of reducing poverty and securing a more equitable distribution of the social product—'progressive extractivism', in the conception of Eduardo Gudynas (2010, 2011), a senior researcher at the Uruguay-based Latin American Centre of Social Ecology (CLAES).

Another variation of this political ecological approach is much less sanguine about the prospects of successful natural resource development. Reflecting a deep concern about the environmental and social costs of extractivism, the issue from this perspective is that is the costs extractive operations, many of them externalised and unaccounted for, far exceed the benefits of economic growth; moreover the benefits are highly concentrated, appropriated by very few (with even the government taking but a marginal share of the proceeds), while the costs are disproportionately borne by the poor and the most vulnerable segments of society that received few or none of the benefits.

The Resistance to Extractive Capitalism

The literature on the politics of natural resource development and the resistance can be placed into four categories. The first relates to what we might term the political economy of the resistance, an approach based on a class analysis of the objective and subjective conditions of the capitalist development process. From this perspective, the process and project of capitalist development generates both forces of change and forces of resistance to this change, forces that are rooted in the class structure of society and that take the form of a social movement in opposition to the economic model used by the state to make policy as well as the operating system (capitalism).

In Latin America these class-based social movements have assumed different forms. From the 1950s to the 1970s they took the predominant form of a labour movement in the resistance of workers to the exploitation of their labour and their struggle for higher wages and improved working conditions. In the countryside the class struggle took form as a land struggle based on the resistance of direct producers against forces that threatened to separate them from the land and to dispossess them from their means of production. In the 1990s, in the vortex of a second cycle and generation of neoliberal policies, the resistance was directed against the economic model used by the governments of the day to make policy. With the destruction of major forces of production in both agriculture and industry, and thus the decimation of the labour movement and its forces of resistance, the popular movement engaged in the resistance to the forces of capitalist development and neoliberal globalization found its social base in the indigenous communities and peasant organizations most directly affected by the incursions and operations of capital and the policies designed to facilitate these operations (Petras & Veltmeyer, 2001, 2005b, 2009, 2011).

Another approach to understanding the dynamics of resistance is grounded not in the political economy of capitalist development but rather a historical analysis of the impact of imperialism and colonialism on the social structure of indigenous nations and aboriginal societies, and the symbiotic relationship of these societies to the land and more broadly to mother earth or nature. An example of this approach is found in a number of studies made into the impact of the European (Spanish) 'conquest' and subsequent colonial rule on the societies constructed by the indigenous nations that inhabited the highlands and lowland of the Andes in South America, and also in the forces of resistance generated in the process—500 years of anti-colonial anti-imperialist struggle (Tellez, 1993)

There is a fundamental continuity between the studies of the resistance movement formed in the context of the conquest and colonial rule and a number of more recent studies into the social movements and the resistance to the forces of capitalist development associated with the neoliberal state— forces that eventually (December 2005) allowed Bolivia's indigenous movement to eventually capture state power (Webber, 2010, 2011). The common feature of these studies (see, for example, Farah and Vasapollo, 2011) is an emphasis on the fundamental role of the idea of a society existing in a relation of harmony with the land and mother earth and social solidarity as a belief system and an ideology serving to mobilize the forces of resistance. Evidently (see our discussion below) the same cosmovision and associated system of beliefs now serves to mobilize the resistance of an alliance of indigenous communities in Northern British Columbia to the transportation of Alberta tarsands oil across their territory and in particular the Northern Gateway pipeline.

A third approach towards in an analysis of the social movement dynamics of resistance emerged in the 1980s in the context of a critique of forms of structuralism, including Marxist class analysis. The focus of this post-modernist approach was on the formation of what appeared to the theorists of this approach as 'new social movements' (NSMS) that were forming and taking shape in Latin America's urban centres (Veltmeyer, 1997). Unlike the class-based labour movement and the rural land struggle, these movements did not turn against the economic model used by governments to make policy or target the underlying system. Rather, they were issue-oriented advocacy groups that protested a broad range of single issues from violence against women and the lack of democracy to environmental degradation. In the 1990s these 'new social movements' were reconceptualised as expressions of an emerging 'civil society', associations of individuals or citizens that shared a concern and mobilized action around a particular social issue.

In the 1990s these nongovernmental organisations NGOs were enlisted by the World Bank and other Overseas Development Associations as a strategic partner in the project of international cooperation in the development process—to mediate between the donors (aid-giving international organizations and governments) and the communities of the rural poor. In the broader context in the global north this 'global civil society' (Albrow et al., 2008) constituted the social base of both a global environmental movement and what took form as the 'anti-globalization movement', which was directed against the ideology of neoliberal globalization and associated economic and political practice. And they also formed the basis of a global scattering and movement of international nongovernmental organizations and advocacy groups in support of those communities negatively impacted by the operations of extractive capital in the south.

A characteristic and defining feature of the resistance politics of these civil society organizations is a concern for fairness, equity (equal opportunity) and social justice in the distribution of the social product and public goods, as well as the authentic identity of subaltern groups and peoples that are excluded from the system operative in contemporary mainstream society.

A fourth approach to an analysis of the forces of resistance to extractive capitalism, one that we favour and have used as a partial framework for our analysis of the pipeline resistance dynamics, is based on a class analysis in conditions of capitalist development—conditions generated by forces generated in the capitalist development process. From this class analysis perspective, sustainable resource development—which presupposes a regulatory regime that allows for corporate social and environmental responsibility, and for the mitigation of any negative impacts or environmental damage caused by the operations of extractive capital—is not at issue. Nor are the politics of identity at issue. At issue, rather, are the dynamics of capitalist development of the forces of production and the corresponding relations of production, as well as the forces of resistance that ensue from these relations. Capitalist development is predicated on separating the direct producers from the land and their means of production—'accumulation by dispossession' Harvey (2003) has it. Under conditions generated by the forces of capitalist development the direct producers on the land—peasant farmers in the Latin American context, indigenous communities in the Canadian context—are denied access to their share of the global commons (land, water, sub-soil resources and the forest) and subjected to a process of social and productive transformation, converting them into a proletariat, dispossessed from any means of social production except for their capacity to labour, that many are compelled to exchange for a living wage or a job at any cost.

In the Latin American context of the 'new extractivism' these forces of change and those of the resistance are very much in evidence, reflected as they clearly are in the formation of a powerful socioenvironmental resistance movement and the growing number—and increasing virulence—of the conflict and resource wars that have surrounded and continue to surround this movement (Bannon & Collier, 2003).

Unlike sporadic acts of collective protest that can be triggered and fuelled by any number of issues this resistance movement, as with any organized sociopolitical movement, needs to be analysed in terms of its social base, its organization and leadership, its relation to the state and the other forces of resistance, and an ideology that serves to mobilize collective action towards a desired goal, as well as the strategy and tactics of collective action. We take a few tentative steps in the direction of such an analysis towards the end of this paper.

Political Economy of Natural Resource Extraction

The new millennium opened with a boom—a primary commodities boom stimulated by changes in the global economy, specifically the ascent of china as an economic power and the associated demand by industry and the growing middle class for raw materials—industrial minerals and precious metals, energy (bio- and fossil fuels), and agrofood products. The demand for these commodities, stimulated by security needs of some governments related to energy and food, as well as the 'economic opportunities'

244 VELTMEYER AND BOWLES

for multinational corporations in the extractive sector, led to the growth of large-scale foreign investment in the acquisition of land (FAO, 2011; World Bank, 2011).

The volume of the capital so deployed and the profits made is staggering. Higginbottom (2013: 193) estimates that from 1997 to 2010 US- and EU-based multinationals extracted a total of US$477.6 billion in direct investment income out of Latin America, most of it derived from the primary commodity exports. As for profitable returns to other investors, the *Financial Times* in an article published on April 18, 2013 documented the fact that traders in commodities have accumulated large reserves of capital and huge fortunes in the context of the primary commodities boom. As the author of the article observed: 'The world's top commodities traders have pocketed nearly $250bn over the last decade, making the individuals and families that control the largely privately-owned sector big beneficiaries of the rise of China and other emerging countries'—and, we might add, beneficiaries of the turn towards or return to extractivism and export primarization.

The wave of resource-seeking foreign direct investment was a major feature of the political economy of global capitalist development at the turn into and the first decade of the new millennium. Another was the demise of neoliberalism as an economic doctrine and model—at least in Latin America, where powerful social movements successfully challenged this model. Over the past decade (since 2002 to be precise) a number of governments in Latin America in riding a wave of anti-neoliberal sentiment generated by powerful social movement with their social base in indigenous communities and peasant organisations, underwent a process of regime change. The political victories of anti-neoliberal movements and these post-neoliberal regimes have opened a new chapter in Latin American history, yet the embrace by these left-leaning regimes of resource-seeking foreign direct investment, or extractive capital, has generated deep paradoxes for those progressive regimes in the region committed to addressing the inequality predicament and the crisis of nature. Some leaders and social movements in this context speak of revolution—Venezuela's 'Bolivarian' revolution, Bolivia's 'democratic and cultural revolution', and Ecuador's 'citizens' revolution'—and, together with several governments that have embraced the new developmentalism (the search for a more inclusive form of development), these regimes have indeed taken steps in the direction of equality and poverty reduction, using the additional fiscal revenues derived from resource rents to this purpose. Yet, like their more conservative neighbours—regimes such as Mexico's and Colombia's committed to both neoliberalism and an alliance with

'imperialism'—the left-leaning progressive regimes in the region find themselves entangled in a maze of renewed dependence on natural resource extraction (the 'new extractivism') and primary commodity exports ('reprimarization').
Further, as argued by Gudynas (2010), this new 'progressive' extractivism is
much like the old 'classical' extractivism in its destruction of both the
environment and livelihoods, and its erosion of the territorial rights and sovereignty of indigenous communities most directly affected by the operations
of extractive capital, which continues to generate relations of intense social
conflict.

Despite the use by progressive governments of resource rents for certain
redistributive policies it is not at all clear whether they are able or disposed to
pursue revolutionary measures in their efforts to bring about a more inclusive
and sustainable form of development, or a deepening of political and economic democratization, allowing the people to 'live well' (*vivir bien*), while at
the same time continuing to hoe the line of extractive capital and its global
assault on nature and livelihoods.

The advance of extractive capital throughout Latin America and the
Caribbean, promoted by governments that despite all its evident contradictions and pitfalls, continue to view natural resource development as a pathway
towards both economic and social development, have stirred up a flurry of protest actions—and forces of resistance against both the destructive operations
of extractive capital and government policies that disregard indigenous territorial rights, advancing instead the rights of private property vis-à-vis the concessions given to foreign investors in the extractive industry to explore for and
exploit for profit.

The evident albeit surprising tendency of even the most 'progressive'
extractivist regimes to side with capital (foreign investors) against the local
communities in their relation of conflict with the mining companies in their
extractive operations can be explained as a coincidence of economic
interest—extraordinary profits for the companies, additional fiscal revenues
for the governments. However, this coincidence of economic interest is hidden
rather than manifest by the government's extractivist discourse, which
highlights the potential and anticipated contribution of natural resource
development to the country's future. Here the extractivist discourse of Rafael
Correa, President of a country (Ecuador), which, like Bolivia, has committed
itself to an indigenous development path of 'living well' as well as a 'citizens'
revolution', is particularly revealing. Opponents of mining and the government's extractivist strategy and associated policies, which include the most
powerful indigenous movement in the country (CONAIE), are branded by
Correa as 'childish' and 'environmental extremists'—in effect, as in the case of

Andrew Frank, Senior Officer of ForestEthics in his relation to the Canadian government, as 'enemies of the state'.[5]

In his support of the mining and oil companies with which he has negotiated a deal conducive to economic development and inclusive growth Correa has gone as far as to elicit the support of his neoliberal neighbours in combatting environmental extremism. In this stance, i.e. in viewing and presenting extractivism as a tool for advancing the revolution, Correa is aligned with Bolivia, another post-neoliberal 'revolutionary' regime seeking to reconcile the contradictory and conflicting demands of extractive capital and the communities most directly affected by the operations of this capital.

Notwithstanding the revolutionary pretensions of Correa and Morales, and their shared ideological commitment to a policy of inclusive development (poverty reduction) and 'living well', both regimes have been branded by opponents in the popular movement against extractivism as 'the most anti-indigenous government in recent years'—a servant of global capitalism rather than a custodian of mother earth. In effect, extractivism in this context has been rebranded as progressive, allowing the regime in the process to undermine the opposition, criminalize protest and "buy off" leaders and divide the social movement.

Canadian Mining Capital and Extractivist Imperialism

In recent years significant mining activity has moved from the developed to the developing world, with the latter's share of global trade in minerals and metals rising from less than a third to over one half. A landmark 2012 publication by the International Council on Mining and Metals points towards a huge wave of investments in recent years in Africa, parts of Asia and in Latin America (Interpress Service, June 23, 2013). One of the largest players in this process has been and remains Canada, itself heavily dependent on mineral exports but now home to close to 60 per cent of the capital invested worldwide in the mining of precious metals and industrial minerals (Keenan, 2010). ECLAC and UNCTAD data show that the biggest recipients of this mining capital are found in the booming economies of Latin America, with the overall effect of

5 On January 5, 2012 Andrew Frank, and other Vancouver-based staff of ForestEthics were called into an office of Tides, an environmental NGO funded by the Canadian government and sub-contracted ForestEthics, to be informed that the Canadian government considered them and ForestEthics to be an 'enemy of the state' (interview by authors, June 8, 2013).

consolidating the extractivist orientation of these economies, increasing the weight of primary commodities (minerals and metals, fossil and bio-fuels, and agro-food products) in exports and dramatically increasing the weight of the Canadian state in its interventions on behalf of Canadian mining companies in their deal-making with local governments and in their conflicts with the communities most directly and negatively impacted by the extractivist operations of Canadian mining companies.[6]

These operations have proven to be both destructive of the environment and livelihoods, providing the latest twist in a century-long process of capitalist development, a process in which the direct producers are separated from the land and their means of production, in this case because of the damage done to the ecosystem and the forces of privatization and commodification. This process of accumulation by dispossession has also proven to be highly controversial and conflictual, bringing Canadian mining companies into conflict with the communities most directly affected by the destructive operations of extractive capital and on the firing line of the mounting resistance. It is here where the intervention of the Canadian state on behalf and in support of Canadian extractive capital has been most useful and consequential. The Canadian government from the beginning was fully supportive of, if not an active participant in, setting up the rules of the new world order, which paved the way for the current wave of large-scale 'resource seeking' foreign direct investment into Latin America and the developing countries. However, the recent surge of anti-neoliberal sentiment in Latin America and the process of regime change in the direction of inclusive development forced the government to take a more active role in representing the interests of Canadian mining companies abroad and big oil at home thereby linking, conceptually and sometimes in practice, the economic development strategies and resistance movements pursued in the south and domestically.

The key strategy of the government in advancing the operations of extractive capital and an extractivist approach towards economic development— in the Latin American context, 'inclusive growth'—has been to promote a regime of Corporate Social Responsibility' (CSR) to counter the pronounced tilt of the post-neoliberal progressive extractivist regimes in South America towards 'resource nationalism'—to nationalize ownership of their society's wealth of natural resources and the economic enterprises used to exploit and

6   The Observatory of Latin American Mining Conflicts (OCMAL) has registered 155 major socio-environmental conflicts in Latin America's mining sector recent years, most of them in Argentina, Brazil, Chile, Colombia, Mexico and Peru. See the Observatory's website [www .olca.cl/ocmal] for details about these conflicts.

develop these resources. The government has advanced its CSR agenda in regard to the Latin American operations of Canadian mining companies—as a means of ensuring mining concessions and a license to operate with minimal regulatory intervention of the state—as well as its operations within Canada. However, the CSR strategy by no means limits the extent of the Canadian state's intervention in the field of natural resource development—what, in terms of the power relation involved (the projection of state power in support of capital and the subordination of the Latin American state and the local forces of resistance to this power) we very well might term 'extractivist imperialism' (Veltmeyer & Petras, 2014).

Other imperialist interventions include active participation in the ideological struggle to subordinate the developing country state to a global strategy of sustainable resource development—to opt in its economic development strategy for its model of private sector led 'inclusive growth' rather than the alternative model of 'inclusive development predicated on inclusionary state activism' (Arbix & Scott, 2010). Beyond this global strategy the Canadian government has experimented with and implemented a variety of policies and institutional mechanisms designed to impose its will against resistance—to paraphrase the sociologist Max Weber in his conception of power. They include the writing the environmental legislation for some governments, diplomatic pressure on these and other governments, and various forms of financial support provided to Canadian mining companies both directly and indirectly via CIDA (and now External Affairs and Trade), converting Canada's program of international cooperation for development, and its foreign aid program, into a mechanism of promoting the 'private sector' (i.e. Canadian-based multinational corporations) as an 'engine of inclusive growth' (Canada, House of Commons, 2012).

The Canadian government's actions and policies regarding these and other such mechanisms of extractivist imperialism have been well documented in regards to Latin America, leading to an on-going albeit fruitless academic and political debate. However, these imperialist actions and policies are by no means restricted to Latin America and developing countries where Canada (Canadian capital, that is) has a vested interest in the global process of natural resource extraction under way. The government's imperialist designs are equally evident in its relations and dealings with the First Nations and the way that it has proceeded to implement its national development plan and lay the groundwork for a green light to Enbridge's Northern Gateway pipeline project, changing and fast-tracking the regulatory approval process. As we briefly discuss below these relations, and the federal government's policy of internal colonialism (assuming the right of decision-making, reserving certain delimited areas for aboriginal communities and extending the authority of the Canadian state over indigenous peoples) have been conducted not on the basis of a relation of equality between sovereign nations, but as an imperial state and colonial power.

Extractive Capital and the Canadian State: The Enbridge Project

Amid the challenges faced by provincial governments as well as the federal government politicians of different ideological stripes have tried to imagine what an attractive picture of the future might look like. For many Canadians it would include a resumption of higher levels of economic growth that provides an equitable share of the social product to all Canadians in terms of the income needed to improve the standard of living and the quality of life. This, of course, requires a vibrant and growing economy, able to generate jobs and conditions of decent work and income. Although there has been no public debate on how best to generate the conditions of 'inclusive growth' it is evident that for the current Harper regime of the federal government it is a matter of 'sustainable resource development'—the extraction of natural resources and their exploration in primary commodity form, taking advantage of the growing demand and high prices in the global market for these resources. Of course there is nothing new about this in Canadian politics. Canada has always relied on the extraction of natural resources, and for a number of provinces—currently Alberta, British Colombia, Saskatchewan and Newfoundland—the pathway towards economic growth, employment and income generation, as well as fiscal revenues, has been natural resource extraction. For example, Alberta's take from the production of oil and gas in 2013, although down almost 40 per cent from two years earlier, will still be $7 billion, while Saskatchewan and Newfoundland will each take in about $2 billion, enough to lower the average tax rate. As for British Colombia the government currently in power is staking the province's economic development and pursuit of 'debt-free' status on natural gas—transporting provincial supplies to the emerging markets of Asia.

As for the federal government its stated commitment to natural resource extraction as a pathway towards sustainable development makes increased exports of oil to Asian markets a 'strategic imperative' (*The Prince George Citizen*, June 20, 2013). At issue in the construction of the pipeline and the permit to transport and export Albertan tarsands oil, is the government's goal of 'diversifying export markets to create jobs and economic growth for Canadians', as well as its strategy of sustainable and socially responsible resource development (ibid).

In line with the government's commitment to, or official line of, social and environmental responsibility regarding sustainable resource development and management it has established a process of public hearings held by a Joint Review Panel (JRP) of the National Energy Board (NEB) and Canadian Environmental Review Agency to provide opportunities for stakeholder groups to present as well meet its responsibility to consult with Aboriginal groups and the First Nations communities directly in the path of the proposed pipelines and whose land and livelihoods would be at risk in the event of any break in the pipeline and subsequent oil spill. Unlike Enbridge, the government has in fact conceded the possibility if not likelihood of any such spill, but according to a lawyer representing the government in its final argument in support of the proposed Northern Gateway pipeline at the JRP hearings 'Canada is well prepared for and ready to respond to oil spills' (ibid).

In response to criticism levelled against the federal government by many First Nations groups and communities that the government has failed to live up to its duty to consult with the Aboriginal people and communities potentially affected by the pipeline, or worse, failed to respect the territorial rights and sovereignty of the First Nations, which, in the case of the First Nations groups in Northern British Columbia were never signed away in any treaty, the federal government repeatedly trots out the argument that the natural resource sector is a large and important employer of aboriginal people, and that the Northern Gateway pipeline constitutes a 'huge economic opportunity' and development pathway for the First Nations facing chronic unemployment and social problems.

The Canadian government, in the context of the JRP process as well as its efforts to ensure 'corporate social responsibility' continues to stress that it 'takes its consultation responsibility seriously and will meet its obligations' (*The Prince George Citizen*, June 20, 2013).

Dynamics of Extractive Capital in Canada: The Alberta Tarsands

To sum up our argument thus far, one of the major conclusions drawn from studies of extractive capitalism is that it is a regressive form of capitalism with inherent contradictions and pitfalls and development implications. Another is that the operations and megaprojects of extractive capital are destructive of livelihoods and the environment, the ecological system on which economic activity and welfare of so many communities in the pathway of these operations and projects. A third is that the negative impacts and economic, environmental and social costs of extractive capitalism typically far exceed the benefits, and cannot be weighed and balanced in a policy of inclusive growth and corporate social responsibility. A fourth conclusion is that the operations and megaprojects of extractive capitalism are the major source of an emerging resistance movement that might very well end up not only opposing these operations and projects but the entire system.

So as to understand and appreciate the significance of the resistance to extractive capitalism and the opposition to Enbridge's Northern Gateway pipeline project consider the following facts provided by Council of Canadians, a citizen's advocacy organization with chapters across the country. First, the tarsands in Northern Alberta covers an area larger than Scotland, resulting in the province having the highest per capita carbon footprint of anywhere in the world. The production of toxic, tarsands bitumen is currently two million barrels per day, but fossil fuel producers want to boost that four or five times. The toxic ponds of wastewater from tarsands production currently cover 170 square kilometers, and eleven million liters leak from them every day. Over 14,000 kilometers of new tarsands pipelines are planned. And in Alberta alone, there have been 1500 pipeline spills over the last 20 years.

Notwithstanding the well-documented facts regarding the negative impacts and heavy environmental and social costs of Canadian mining and the extractive industry, and the potential negative impact of continuing to develop the tarsands, not a single one of Canada's political parties have taken a clear stand against or phasing out tarsands operations, not even the Green Party (Fidler, 2012).

Dynamics of the Pipeline Resistance

A popular movement against tarsands oil production and pipeline as well as tanker transportation of oil is on the rise and gathering steam in Canada. One of the biggest expressions of this movement to date was in Victoria, BC, on October 22, 2012, when 4000 to 5000 people rallied in front of the British Columbia Legislature to send a forceful message to the tarsands industry and its political representatives. 'No tarsands pipelines across BC! No oil tankers in coastal waters!' read the lead banners. Two days later, thousands of activists staged rallies at the offices across the province of more than 60 elected members of the Legislature. Both actions were organized by the recently formed Defend Our Coast coalition and the Council of Canadians, a broad coalition of nongovernmental organizations concerned with issues of social justice and the environment. Some eight months on (June 17 2013), after the last public JRP hearing another rally was held—this time in Terrace, a town on the proposed pipeline route. The rally might not have been as large, but representation from both First Nations groups and the environmental movement groups that organized the rally was extraordinarily inclusive in terms of both First Nations communities and organizations in the environmental movement. As in the case of the earlier rally in Vancouver the rally was overwhelmingly indigenous in appearance, but there was no question about the broader social base of support, which not only brought together virtually all indigenous communities and First Nations organizations on the proposed pipeline route, but the organizing coalition for the rally evidently crossed the well-established social divide between indigenous and non-indigenous communities, as well as the divisions among environmental organizations, indigenous groups and labour.

The depth and breadth of support among diverse communities, both indigenous and non-indigenous—and the unity in the struggle and opposition to Enbridge in particular was evident to the authors in their trek across the proposed pipeline trail in Northern British Columbia. The aim of this trek was to gather voices of protest and resistance to the pipeline and to gauge the strength of this resistance—to determine whether it had the makings of a broader social movement that could possibly scuttle the plans made by industry and the government. Although not conclusive, the diverse voices of resistance to the Enbridge pipeline project, coming from and representing all sectors of protestors and the resistance movement, were so united on the fundamental issues as to allow us nevertheless to formulate a number of theses regarding the resistance to extractive capitalism in Canada.

The protest actions taken in BC over the past year against various projects to build a pipeline to transport tarsands oil to a port terminal on the coast, and related proposals to transship oil and liquefied gas from port terminals in BC to Asian markets via mega-tankers, are part of a growing global socioenvironmental resistance movement against the destructive operations of extractive capitalism in conditions of the 21st century. This resistance brings together environmentalists and activists from across the country concerned with the negative impacts of these operations on the global environment and the ecology of local communities; citizens groups concerned with issues of social justice, sustainable development and democracy regarding public policy, environmental degradation and community development; elements of the labour movement concerned with issues of class exploitation and capitalist development; and, above all, diverse First Nations groups and indigenous communities concerned with the protection of their culture and the livelihoods and welfare of community members, their territorial rights and ways of living that are predicated on a relation of harmony with nature (mother earth) in all of its diverse forms, and their very existence as a people. At issue in this resistance are not only the destructive operations of extractive capitalism on both nature and society, but the dynamics of an economic system that places profits before people and the private interests over the public interest.

Conclusion

Extractive capitalism in its contemporary form is a blight on humanity, a predatory and relatively backward economic and social system based on the enclosure of the global commons and the unsustainable development of non-renewable and commodified natural resources, with profoundly negative implications for both human welfare and development, both national and local, as well as democracy. More generally, an extractivist strategy of economic development is fraught with contradictions, more of a curse than a blessing or economic opportunity.

In this context, the resistance to the Enbridge pipeline has a double signifi-cance. First, it cuts across and can be used to build a bridge over various social divides—between the indigenous and non-indigenous communities across the country, between the environmental movement based on an emerging global civil society and an indigenous movement formed in the protracted and epic struggle to preserve nature and society from the depredations of class exploitation and colonial rule. Second, it is at the extractivist frontier of a sys-tem that is not only putting at jeopardy the livelihoods of billions and the wel-fare of humankind but that threatens life both as given to us and as constructed over the centuries in diverse cultural and historical contexts. At issue on this frontier is a complex set of interactions between diverse systems, such as those that determine the carrying capacity of the earth's ecosystem or global climate patterns, in which a precarious balance can be disrupted by human activities that are driven by a mindless process of extended capital accumulation in the quest for private profit. One such issue is global climate change induced by the emission of carbon into the atmosphere, carbon released in the capital-ist development of fossil fuels used to drive modern industry and the capital-ist system. In this context, the Northern Gateway pipeline has been likened to the bloodline of the Alberta tarsands, and, as activists have argued, the first step to eventually closing down the tarsands—in the interest of preserving nature and society from the destructive dynamics of extractive capitalism—is to stop the pipeline. Hence the importance of the pipeline resistance led, not just as it happens but out of necessity, by Canada's First Nations. It is too early to tell how the fight against the pipeline will end and where the forces of resistance can take us. But there is hope in the position taken by the indigenous and other communities against Enbridge: '*The Answer is Still No!*' In this they join the rising chorus of protest in Latin America and elsewhere to form part of a global resistance to the machinations and depredations of global extractivism.

CHAPTER 10

Imperialist Dynamics of US-Venezuela Relations

US relations with Venezuela illustrate the specific mechanisms with which an imperial power seeks to sustain client states and overthrow independent nationalist governments. By examining US strategic goals and its tactical measures, we can set forth several propositions regarding (i) the nature and instruments of imperial politics in Venezuela; (ii) the shifting context and contingencies influencing the successes and failures of specific policies; and (iii) the importance of regional and global political alignments and priorities (Petras & Veltmeyer, 2013a).

A Historical-Comparative Approach

A comparative historical approach highlights the different policies, contexts and outcomes of imperial policies during two distinct Presidential periods: the ascendancy of neoliberal client regimes (Perez and Caldera) of the late 1980s to 1998; and the rise and consolidation of a nationalist populist government under President Chávez (Ellner, 2009).

During the 1980s and 1990s, US successes in securing policies favourable to US economic and foreign policy interests under client rulers, in the mind of Washington fixed the optimal and only acceptable model and criteria for responding (negatively) to the subsequent Chávez nationalist government (Petras, 2006).

US policy toward Venezuela in the 1990s and its successes were part and parcel of a general embrace of neoliberal electoral regimes in Latin America. Washington and its allies in the International Monetary Fund (IMF), the World Bank (WB) and the Inter-American Development Bank (IDB) promoted and supported regimes throughout Latin America, which privatized and de-nationalized over five thousand public enterprises in the most lucrative economic sectors (IMF, 1998; World Bank, 1991–2001). These quasi-public monopolies included natural resources, energy, finance, trade, transport and telecommunications. Neoliberal client regimes reversed 50 years of economic and social policy, concentrated wealth, deregulated the economy, and laid the basis for a profound crisis, which ultimately discredited neoliberalism. This led to continent-wide popular uprisings resulting in regime changes and the ruse if nationalist populist governments.

A historical-comparative approach allows us to analyze Washington's response to the rise and demise of its neoliberal clients and the subsequent ascendency of populist-nationalism and how regional patterns and changes influence the capacity of an imperial power to intervene and attempt to re-establish its dominance.

A Conceptual Framework

The key to understanding the mode and means of imposing and sustaining imperial dominance is to recognize that Washington combines multiple forms of struggle, depending on resources, available collaborators and opportunities and contingencies (Petras, 2010a).

In approaching client regimes, Washington combines military and economic aid to repress opposition and buttress economic allies by cushioning crises. Imperial propaganda, via the mass media, provides political legitimacy and diplomatic backing, especially when client regimes engage in gross human rights violations and high level corruption.

Conversely when attempting to weaken or overthrow a nationalist-populist regime, the empire will resort to multiple forms of attack including (Gollinger, 2006; Petras, 2010b): (i) corruption (buying off government supporters); (ii) funding and organizing opposition media, parties, business and trade union organizations; (iii) organizing and backing disloyal military officials to violently overthrow the elected government; (iv) supporting employers' lockouts to paralyze strategic sectors of the economy such as oil production; (v) financing referendums and other 'legal mechanisms' to revoke democratic mandates; (vi) promoting paramilitary groups to destabilize civil society, sow public insecurity and undermine agrarian reforms; (vii) financing electoral parties and NGOs to compete in and to delegitimize elections; (viii) engaging diplomatic warfare and efforts to prejudice regional relations; and (ix) establishing military bases in neighbouring countries, as a platform for future joint military invasions.

This multi-track strategy with its multi-prong tactics is implemented in sequence or combined depending on the opportunities and results of earlier tactical operations. For example, while financing Capriles Radonski's electoral campaign in April 2013 Washington also backed violent post-election assaults by rightist thugs attempting to destabilize the government in Caracas (Petras, 2012b, 2013). And while pursuing an apparent effort to re-open diplomatic relations via negotiations Secretary of State John Kerry simultaneously backed the inflammatory declarations of Samantha Power, a United Nations representative, which promised aggressive US intrusion in Venezuela's domestic politics.

US-Venezuelan relations provide us with a case study that illustrates how efforts to restore hegemonic politics can become an obstacle to the development of normal relations, with an independent country. In particular, the ascendancy of Washington during the 'Golden Age of Neoliberalism' in the 1990s, established a fixed 'mind set' incapable of adapting to the changed circumstances of the 2000s, a period when the demise and discredit of 'free market' client politics called for a change in US tactics. The rigidity, derived from past success, led Washington to pursue 'restoration politics' under very unfavourable circumstances, involving military, clandestine and other illicit tactics with little chance of success—given the new situation.

The failure of the US to destabilize a democratically elected nationalist popular regime in Venezuela occurred when Washington was already heavily engaged in multiple, prolonged wars and conflicts in several countries (Iraq, Afghanistan, Pakistan, Somalia, and Libya). This validates the hypothesis that even a global power is incapable of waging warfare in multiple locations at the same time.

Given the shift in world market conditions, including the increase in commodity prices, (especially energy), the relative economic decline of the US and the rise of Asia, Washington lost a strategic economic lever—market power—in the 2000s, a resource which it had possessed during the previous decade (*Financial Times*, 4/26/2011; Petras, 2011b). Furthermore, with the shift in political power in the region and the rise of popular-nationalist governments in most of Latin America, Washington lost regional leverage to 'encircle', 'boycott' and intervene in Venezuela. Even among its remaining clients, like Colombia, Washington could do no more than create 'border tensions' rather than mount a joint military attack.

Comparative historical analysis of the strategic changes in international and regional politics, economies, markets and alignments provides a useful framework for interpreting US-Venezuelan relations, especially the successes of the 1990s and the failures of the 2000s.

US-Venezuela Patron-Client Relations, 1960s–1998

During the 40-year period following the overthrow of the Dictator Perez Jimenez (1958) and prior to the election of President Hugo Chávez (1998), Venezuela's politics were marked with rigid conformity to US political and economic interests on all strategic issues (Gott, 2005; Wilpert, 2007). Venezuelan regimes followed Washington's lead in ousting Cuba from the Organization of American States, breaking relations with Havana and promoting a hemispheric blockade. Caracas followed Washington's lead during the cold War and backed its counter-insurgency policies in Latin America. It opposed the democratic leftist regime in Chile under President Salvador Allende, the nationalist governments of Brazil (1961–64), Peru (1967–73), Bolivia (1968–71) and Ecuador (in the 1970's). It supported the US invasions of the Dominican Republic, Panama and Grenada. Venezuela's nationalization of oil (1976) provided lucrative compensation and generous service contracts with US oil companies, a settlement far more generous than any comparable arrangement in the Middle East or elsewhere in Latin America.

During the decade from the late-1980s to 1998, Venezuela signed off on draconic International Monetary Fund programs, including privatizations of natural resources, devaluations and austerity programs, which enriched the MNCs, emptied the Treasury and impoverished the majority of wage and salary earners (IMF, 1998). In foreign policy, Venezuela aligned with the US, ignored new trade opportunities in Latin America and Asia and moved to re-privatize its oil, bauxite and other primary resource sectors. President Perez was indicted in a massive corruption scandal. When implementation of the brutal US-IMF austerity program led to a mass popular uprising (the 'Caracazo') in February 1989, the government responded with the massacre of over a thousand protestors. The subsequent Caldera regime presided over the triple scourge of triple digit inflation, 50 percent poverty rates and double-digit unemployment (World Bank, 2001).

Social and political conditions in Venezuela touched bottom at the peak of US hegemony in the region, the 'Golden Age of Neoliberalism' for Wall Street. The inverse relation was not casual: Venezuela, under President Caldera, endured austerity programs and adopted 'open' market and US-centred policies, which undermined any public policies designed to revive the economy. Moreover, world market conditions were unfavourable for Venezuela, as oil prices were low and China had not yet become a world market power and alternative trade partner.

US and the Rise of Chávez: 1998–2001

The US viewed the Venezuelan elections of 1998 as a continuation of the previous decade, despite significant political signs of changes. The two parties, which dominated and alternated in power, the Christian democratic COPEI, and the social democratic 'Democratic Action Party', were soundly defeated by a new political formation headed by a former military officer, Hugo Chávez, who had led an armed uprising six years earlier and had mounted a massive grass-roots campaign, attracting radicals and revolutionaries, as well as opportunists and defectors from the two major parties (Ellner, 2009; Wilpert, 2007).

Washington's successes over the previous decade, the entrenched ascendancy of neoliberalism and the advance of a regional US 'free trade agreement' blinded the Clinton regime from seeing: (i) the economic crisis and discredit of the neoliberal model; (ii) the deepening social and economic polarization and hostility to the IMF-US among broad sectors of the class structure; and (iii) the decay and discredit of its client political parties and regimes. Washington tended to write-off Chávez's promises of a new constitutional order and new 'Bolivarian' foreign and domestic policies, including nationalist-populist reforms, as typical Latin American campaign rhetoric. The general thinking at the U.S. Department of State was that Chávez was engaging in electoral demagogy and that he would 'come to his senses' after taking office.[1] Moreover Washington's Latin Americanists believed that the mix of traditional politicians and technocrats in his motley coalition would undermine any consequential push for leftist radical changes.[2]

Hence Washington, under Clinton, did not adopt a hostile position during the first months of the Chávez government. The watchword among the Clintonites was 'wait and see' counting on long-standing ties to the major business associations, friendly military officials, and corrupt trade union bosses and oil executives to check or block any new radical initiatives emanating from Venezuelan Congress or President Chávez. In other words, Washington counted on using the permanent state apparatus in Caracas to counter the new electoral regime.

Early on, President Chávez recognized the institutional obstacles to his nationalist socioeconomic reforms and immediately called for constitutional changes, convoking elections for a constituent assembly, which he won handily. Washington's growing concerns over the possible consequences of new elections were tempered by two factors: (i) the mixed composition of the elected assembly (old line politicians, moderate leftists, radicals and 'unknowns') and (ii) the appointment of 'moderates' to the Central Bank as well as the orthodox economic policies pursued by the finance and economic ministries. Prudent budgets, fiscal deficits and balance of payments were at the top of their agendas.

---

1 Interviews, U.S. Department of State, November 2009.
2 Interviews, U.S. Department of State, November 2009.

The new constitution included clauses that favour a radical social and nationalist agenda. This led to the early defection of some of the more conservative Chávez supporters who then aligned with Washington, signalling the first overt signs of US opposition. Veteran State Department officials debated whether the new radical constitution would form the basis of a leftist government or whether it was standard 'symbolic' fare, i.e. rhetorical flourishes, to be heavily discounted, from a populist president addressing a restive 'Latin' populace suffering hard times but not likely to be followed by substantive reforms.[3] The hard liners in Caracas, linked to the Cuban exile community and lobby argued that Chávez was a 'closet' radical preparing the way for more radical 'communist' measures.[4] In fact, Chávez policies were both moderate and radical: His political 'zigzags' reflected his efforts to navigate a moderate reform agenda, without alienating the US and the business community on the one hand, and while responding to his mass base among the impoverished slum dwellers (rancheros') who had elected him.

Strategically, Chávez succeeded in creating a strong political institutional base in the legislature, civil administration and military, which could (or would) approve and implement his national-populist agenda. Unlike Chilean Socialist President Salvador Allende, Hugo Chávez first consolidated his political and military base of support and then proceeded to introduce socioeconomic changes.

By the end of the year 2000, Washington moved to regroup its internal client political forces into a formidable political opposition. Chávez was too independent, not easily controlled, and most important moving in the 'wrong direction'—away from a blind embrace of neoliberalism and US-centred regional integration. In other words, while Chávez was still well within the parameters of US hegemony, the direction he was taking portended a possible break.

The Turning Point: Chávez Defies the 'War on Terror', 2000–2001

The first decade of the new millennium was a tumultuous period that played a major role in defining US-Venezuelan relations. Several inter-related events polarized the hemisphere, weakened Washington's influence, undermined collaborator-client regimes and led to a major confrontation with Venezuela.

---

3 Interviews at the U.S. Department of State, January 2001.
4 Interviews at the U.S. Department of State, January 2001.

First, the neoliberal model fell into deep crisis throughout the region, discrediting the US-backed clients in Bolivia, Argentina, Ecuador, Brazil and elsewhere. Secondly, repeated major popular uprisings occurred during the crisis and populist-nationalist politicians came to power, rejecting US-IMF tutelage and US-centred regional trade agreements (Petras & Veltmeyer, 2013b). Thirdly, Washington launched a global 'war on terror', essentially an offensive military strategy designed to overthrow adversaries to US domination and establish Israeli regional supremacy in the Middle East. In Latin American, Washington's launch of the 'war on terror' occurred precisely at the high point of crisis and popular rebellion, undermining the US hope for region-wide support. Fourthly, beginning in 2003, commodity prices skyrocketed, as China's economy took off, creating lucrative markets and stimulating high growth for the new left-of-centre regimes.

In this vortex of change, President Chávez rejected Washington's 'War on Terror', rejecting the logic of *'fighting terror with terror'*. By the end of 2001, Washington dispatched a top State Department official and regional 'enforcer' to Caracas where he bluntly threatened dire reprisals—destabilization plans— if Caracas failed to line up with Washington's campaign to reimpose global hegemony.[5] Chávez dismissed the official's threats and re-aligned his nation with the emerging Latin American nationalist-populist consensus. In other words, Washington's aggressive militarist posture backfired, polarizing relations, increasing tensions and, to a degree, radicalizing Venezuela's foreign policy.

Washington's intervention machine (the 'coup-makers') went into high gear: Ambassador Charles Shapiro held several meetings with the FEDECAMARAS (the Venezuelan business association) and the trade union bosses of the CTV, the Venezuelan Trade Union Confederation (Golinger, 2007). The Pentagon and the US Southern Command met with their clients in the Venezuelan military. The State Department increased contacts and funding for opposition NGOs and right-wing street gangs. The date of the coup had been set for April 11, 2002. With the build-up of pressure, preparatory for the threatened coup, the Chávez government began to assess its own resources, contacting loyal military units, especially among the armoured battalions and paratroopers.

In this heated and dangerous atmosphere, local neighbourhood committees sprang up and mobilized the poor around a more radical social agenda defending their government while the US-backed opposition unleashed violent

---

5   Interview by Petras with President Chávez, January 20, 2002.

street clashes (Ciccariello Maher, 2013). The coup was warmly welcomed by Washington and its semi-official mouthpiece, the *New York Times* (April 12, 2002, p.1), as well as by the right-wing Spanish Prime Minister Jose Maria Aznar (*El Mundo*, April 12, 2002, p.1). The illicit coup regime seized President Chávez, dismissed Congress, dissolved political parties and declared a state of emergency. The masses and leading sectors of the military quickly responded in mass. Millions of poor Venezuelans descended from the 'ranchos' (slums surrounding Caracas) and gathered before Miraflores, the Presidential Palace, demanding the return of their elected President—repudiating the coup. The constitutionalist military, led by an elite paratroop battalion, threatened a full-scale assault against the palace. The coup-makers, realized they were politically isolated and outgunned; they surrendered. Chávez returned to power in triumph. The traditional US policy of violent regime change to restore its hegemony had been defeated; important collaborator assets were forced into exile and purged from the military.

Washington had played a risky card in its haste and lost on several fronts. First of all, US support for the coup strengthened the anti-imperialist sectors of Chávez's Bolivarian movement. Chávez discarded any residual illusions of 'reaching an accommodation' with Washington. Secondly, the loss of key military assets weakened Washington's hope for a future military coup. Thirdly, the complicity of the business groups weakened their ability to influence Chávez's economic policies and nudged him toward a more statist economic strategy. Fourthly, the mass mobilization of the poor to restore democracy moved the government to increase spending on social welfare programs. Anti-imperialism, the demand for social welfare and the threat to Venezuelan national security led Chávez to establish strategic ties with Cuba, as a natural ally.

Washington's escalation of aggression and overt commitment to regime change altered the bilateral relationship into one of permanent, unbridled hostility. Spurred on by its having supported a failed coup, Washington resorted once again to 'direct action' by backing a 'boss's lockout' of the strategic oil industry. This was led by 'client assets' among the executives and corrupt sectors of the petroleum workers union.

Washington implemented its 'global militarization' of US foreign policy. Under the subterfuge 'War on Terror'—a formula for global intervention, which included the invasion of Afghanistan in 2001 and, the war against Iraq in 2003, imperial policymakers have plunged ahead with new aggressive policies against Venezuela.

The pretext for aggression against Venezuela was not directly linked to oil or Chávez's appeal for Latin American integration. The trigger was Chávez direct and forthright refusal to submit to a militarist global US empire as demanded by President Bush—one that conquered opponents by force and maintained a network of collaborator vassal states. The oil conflicts—Chávez' nationalization of US oil concessions and his appeal for regional integration, excluding the US and Canada, were a result of and in response to US overt aggression. Prior to the US-backed April 2002 failed coup and the oil-bosses' lockout of December 2002—February 2003, there were no major conflicts between Chávez and US oil companies. Chávez's conception of the Bolivarian unity of all Latin American states was still a 'vision' and not a concrete program for action. Chávez's takeover of US oil concessions was a defensive political move to eliminate a powerful political adversary that controlled Venezuela's strategic export and revenue sectors. He did not intervene in European oil companies. Likewise, Chávez's move to promote regional organizations flowed from his perception that Venezuela required closer ties and supportive relations in Latin America in order to counter US imperial aggression.

In other words, US empire builders used (and sacrificed) their economic assets in their attempt to restore hegemony via military means. The military and strategic dimensions of the US Empire took precedence over 'Big Oil'. This formed a template clearly evident in all of its subsequent imperial actions against Iraq, Libya and Syria and its severe economic sanctions against Iran. The same hegemonic priorities played out in Washington's intervention in Venezuela—but failed.

Contrary to some theorists of imperialism, who have argued that imperialism expands via economic 'dispossession' (Harvey, 2005), recent history of US-Venezuela relations demonstrate that 21st US imperialism grows via political intervention, military coups and by converting economic collaborators into political agents willing to sacrifice US corporate wealth to secure imperial military-political domination.

The imperial policymakers decided to overthrow Chávez because he had defied Washington and opposed Bush's global military strategy. The White House thought it had powerful assets in Venezuela: the mass media, the two major opposition parties, the principle business federation (FEDECAMARAS), the official trade union bureaucracy, sectors of the military and the church hierarchy...Washington did not count on the loyalty and affection that the unorganized masses and the popular movements has for President Chávez. Nor did imperial strategists understand that strategic military units, like the paratroops, retained nationalist, personal and political ties with their democratically-elected President.

Within 48 hours of the coup, Chávez was restored to power, striking the first blow to Washington's ambitions for 'regime change' in Venezuela. The second blow came with the defeat of the US-backed oil bosses' lockout. Washington had counted on its close ties with the senior executives of the state oil company (PDVS) and the heads of the oil workers union (Ellner, 2009; Wilpert, 2007). Washington did not realize that about half of the oil workers and a number of company and union bosses would staunchly opposed the lockout while other Latin American oil producers would supply Venezuela and break the 'bosses' strike.

These twin defeats, the military-business coup and the bosses' lockout, had a profound impact on US-Venezuelan relations. The US lost its strategic internal assets: business and trade union elites who then fled to 'exile' in Miami or resigned. Pro-US oil executives were replaced by nationalists. Washington's direct imperial intervention pushed the Chávez government in a new, radical direction as it moved decisively from conciliation to confrontation and opposition. The government of Venezuela launched a radical, nationalist, populist agenda and actively promoted Latin American integration. Venezuela inaugurated UNASUR, ALBA and PetroCaribe, undermining the US-centred free trade treaty (ALCA).

Washington's military-interventionist strategy was undermined by the loss of their key collaborators. The White House switched to its clients in the opposition parties and, especially, to so-called non-governmental organizations (NGOs) channelling funds via the 'National Endowment for Democracy' and other 'front groups'. They bankrolled a 'recall referendum', which was decisively defeated, further demoralizing the right-wing electorate and weakening remaining US clients (Golinger, 2006).

Having lost on the military, economic and electoral fronts, Washington backed a boycott of Congressional elections by the opposition parties- leading to the final debacle in its program to de-legitimize and destabilize the Chávez government. Pro-Chávez candidates and parties swept the election gaining an overwhelming majority. They went on to approve all of the government's nationalist-social reform agenda. The US-backed opposition lost all institutional leverage.

The US imperial failures from 2002–2005 did not merely 'reflect' mistaken policies; these signalled a more profound problem for the empire—its inability to make an accurate estimate of the correlation of forces. This strategic failure led it to continue throwing its marginalized domestic assets into conflict with less resources and support. Despite repeated defeats, Washington couldn't grasp that popular power and nationalist allegiances within the military had successfully countered the US business-military intervention. Political hubris underpinning a military-driven imperialist ideology had blinded Washington to the realities in Venezuela, i.e. Hugo Chávez possessed massive popular support and was backed by nationalist military officers. Desperate for some political 'victory' in its conflict with the government of Hugo Chávez, Washington staggered from one adventure to another without reflecting on its lost assets or disappearing opportunities. Washington did not understand the decisive political shifts occurring in Latin America and favourable global economic conditions for petroleum exporters. Organizing a 'recall referendum' in the face of Venezuela's double-digit growth, its radicalized population and the booming world prices for oil, was the height of imperial imbecility (Ellner, 2009).

Imperial Policy during the Commodity Boom 2004–2008

With virtually no collaborators of consequence, Washington turned toward the 'outside' destabilization strategy using its only loyal regional client, the death squad narco-President Alvaro Uribe of Colombia. Bogota granted Washington the use of seven military bases, numerous airfields and the establishment of Special Forces missions preparatory for cross border intrusions. The strategy would be to launch a joint intervention under the pretext that Venezuela supplied and sheltered the FARC guerrillas.

World events intervened to thwart Washington's plans: the invasion of Iraq and the bloody occupation of Afghanistan, looming conflicts with Iran and low intensity warfare in Somalia, Yemen and Pakistan, had weakened the empire's capacity to intervene militarily in Venezuela. Every country in the region would have opposed any direct US intervention and Colombia was not willing to go it alone, especially with its own full-scale guerrilla war against the FARC.

Venezuela's trade surplus and high export revenues rendered the traditional Washington financial levers like the IMF and World Bank impotent.[6] Likewise, Venezuela had signed multi-billion dollar arms trade agreements with Russia, undermining any US boycott. Trade agreements with Brazil and Argentina reduced Venezuela's need for US food imports.

All the oil multinationals continued normal operations in Venezuela, except US companies. The government's selective nationalization program and gradual increases in taxes and royalty payments undercut EU support for the US, given the high world price of oil (exceeding $100 dollars a barrel). Chávez's left-turn was well-funded. The oil revenues funded a wide-range of social programs,

---

6   In 2008 the Chávez government broke ties with the IMF and World Bank. Interview of an official, Venezuelan Foreign Office, November 2008.

including subsidized food, housing and social welfare, healthcare and educational programs led to a sharp drop in poverty and unemployment. This secured a strong electoral base for Chávez. The 'pivot to the Middle East', following Bush's declaration of the 'Global War on Terror, bogged the US down in a series of prolonged wars, undermining its quest to regain regional power (Weisbrot & Sandoval, 2008).[7]

More significantly, the 'Latin Americanists' in the State Department and Pentagon were stuck in the 1990s paradigm of 'free markets and vassal states' just when the most important countries in the region had moved toward greater independence in terms of trade, greater intra-regional integration and social inclusion. Unable to adapt to these new regional realities, Washington witnessed the region's rejection of US-centred free trade accords. Meanwhile China was displacing the US as the region's main trading partner (*Financial Times*, 2011; Petras, 2011b). Without its collaborator elites among the military to act as 'coup-makers for empire', the US-imperial reach shrunk. Coups failed in Bolivia and Ecuador further radicalizing political relations against the US.

Washington did not lack partners: New bilateral trade agreements were signed with Chile, Panama, Colombia and Mexico. The Pentagon engineered a bloody coup in Honduras against a democratically elected President. The National Security Agency engaged in major cyber-spying operations in Brazil, Argentina, Mexico and the rest of the continent (*La Jornada*, September 30, 2013). The White House poured over six-billion dollars into Colombia's armed forces to serve as a proxy for the US military. These 'gains' had little impact. US support for the coup-makers in Honduras may have overthrown an ally for Chávez in ALBA but it led to even greater diplomatic isolation and discredit for Washington throughout Latin America. Even Colombia denounced the US coup against the Honduran president. While US military support for Colombia contributed to some border tensions with Venezuela, the election of President Santos in Bogota brought significant movement toward peaceful reconciliation with Venezuela. Whereas trade between Colombia and Venezuela had fallen to less than $2 billion dollar a year, with Santos' conciliatory policy it rose sharply to nearly $10 billion (Petras, 2011a).

Washington's external strategy was in shambles. The program of NSA cyber-spying against regional leaders, revealed by Edward Snowden, resulted in outrage and greater animosity toward Washington. The President of Brazil was especially incensed and cancelled a scheduled major state White House visit

---

7   National Institute of Statistics cites the reduction of extreme poverty of over 50%, a decline from 5.4 million Venezuelans in 1998 to 2.4 million in 2011.

and allocated $10 billion dollars to set up a nationally controlled IT system. Imperial policy makers had relied exclusively on interventionist strategies with military-intelligence operations and were clearly out of touch with the new configuration of power in Latin America. In contrast, Venezuela consolidated its economic ties with the new regional and global economic power centers, as the foundations for its independent policies.

Washington viewed President Chávez and, his successor President Maduro's regional strategy as a security threat to US hegemony rather than an economic challenge. Venezuela's success in forging bilateral ties, even with US clients like Colombia and Mexico, and a number of English-speaking Caribbean islands, undermined efforts to 'encircle and isolate' Venezuela. Caracas success in financing and backing multi-lateral regional economic and political organizations in South America and the Caribbean, which excluded the US, reflects the power of oil diplomacy over sabre rattling. Venezuela's PetroCaribe program won the support of number of neoliberal and centre-left regimes in the Caribbean, which had previously been under US hegemony. In exchange for subsidized oil prices, medical aid and interest-free loans, these US clients started rejecting Washington's intervention. ALBA brought together several center-left governments, including Bolivia, Ecuador and Nicaragua, into a common political bloc opposing US meddling.

ALBA rejected regime change via coups throughout Latin America and opposed Washington's wars in Iraq, Libya, Syria and elsewhere. Venezuela successfully joined the powerful economic bloc, MERCOSUR, enhancing its trade with Brazil, Argentina and Uruguay. Venezuela's strategic alliance with Cuba (trading its oil for Cuba's medical services) made the massive Bolivarian health program for the poor a great success, cementing Chávez and Maduros' electoral base among the Venezuelan masses. This undermined Washington's well-funded program of NGO subversion in poor neighbourhoods. Venezuela successfully undercut Bush and Obama's efforts to use Colombia as a 'military proxy' when it signed a historic peace and reconciliation agreement with President Santos. Colombia agreed to end its cross-border paramilitary and military incursions and withdrew its support for US destabilization operations in exchange for Venezuela closing guerrilla sanctuaries, re-opening trade relations and encouraging the FARC to enter into peace negotiations with the Santos regime (Petras, 2008). Santos' embrace of Venezuela's trade and diplomatic ties eroded Washington's policy of using Colombia as a trampoline for military intervention and forced imperial policy-makers to turn to its domestic Venezuelan clients through elections as well as internal 'direct action', e.g. the sabotage of power stations and the hoarding of essential food and commodities.

While Washington's imperial rhetoric constantly portrayed Venezuela as a 'security threat' to the entire hemisphere, no other country adopted that position. Latin America viewed Caracas as a partner in regional trade integration and a lucrative market. US diplomacy does not reflect its trade relations with Venezuela: only Mexico is more dependent on the US oil market. However, Venezuela's dependence on the US to purchase its oil has been changing. In 2013 Venezuela signed a $20 billion dollar investment and trade deal with China to extract and export 'heavy oil' from the Orinoco Basin. Venezuela's deep trade ties with the US are in sharp contrast with the hostile diplomatic relations resulting in the mutual withdrawal of ambassadors and Washington's gross interference in Venezuelan elections and other internal affairs. For example, in March 2013, two US military attaches were expelled after they were caught trying to recruit Venezuelan military officers. A few months later, in September, three US Embassy officials were kicked out for their participation in destabilization activity with members of the far right opposition (*La Jornada*, September 30, 2013).

Imperialism's Multi-Track Opposition

US hostility toward Venezuela occurs at three levels of conflict. At the country level, Venezuela marks out a new development paradigm which features public ownership over the free market, social welfare over multinational oil profits and popular power over elite rule. At the regional level Venezuela promotes Latin American integration over US-centered Latin American Free Trade Agreements, anti-imperialism over 'pan-Americanism', foreign aid based on reciprocal economic interests and non-intervention as opposed to US military pacts, narco-military collusion and military bases.[8] At the global-level Venezuela has rejected the US invasions of Afghanistan and Iraq, ignored US trade sanctions against Iran, opposed Washington and NATO's bombing of Libya and the proxy invasion of Syria. Venezuela condemns Israel's colonization and annexation of Palestine. In other words, Venezuela upholds national self-determination against US military driven imperialism.[9]

Presidents Chávez and Maduro have presented a successful alternative to neoliberalism. Venezuela demonstrates that a highly globalized, trade dependent economy can have an advanced welfare program. The US, on the

---

8 Interview, President Chávez Caracas, November 7, 2006.
9 Interview, President Chávez Caracas, November 7, 2006.

other hand, as it 'globalizes', has been eliminating its domestic social welfare programs in order to finance imperial wars. Venezuela has shown the US public that a market economy and large social welfare investments are not incompatible. This paradigm flies in the face of the White House's message. Moreover, US Empire builders have no economic initiatives compete with Venezuela's regional and global alliances. This situation is very different from the 1960s when President Kennedy proposed the 'Alliance for Progress', involving trade, aid and reforms, to counter the revolutionary appeal of the Cuban revolution (Petras & Zeitlin, 1968). Presidents Bush and Obama could only 'offer' costly military and police co-operation and worn-out neoliberal clichés accompanied by market constraints.

Despite its severe diplomatic setbacks, regional isolation, the loss of its military platform, and an economic boom, driven by the high world price of oil, Washington keeps on trying to destabilize Venezuela. Beginning in 2007, imperial strategy re-focused on elections and domestic destabilization programs. Washington's first success occurred when it backed a campaign against new constitutional amendments in December 2007 defeating Chávez by one percent. This happened right after his substantial Presidential re-election victory. The overtly socialist constitution proved too radical for a sector of the Venezuelan electorate (Wilpert, 2011).

Since 2008 Washington has infused large sums of money into a variety of political assets, including NGOs and middle class university students' organization engaged in agitation and anti-Chávez street demonstrations (Golinger, 2007). The goal was to exploit local grievances. US funding of domestic proxies led to extra-parliamentary, destabilization activity, like sabotage, disrupting Venezuela's economy while blaming the government for 'public insecurity' and covering up opposition violence.

The business community started hoarding essential goods in order to provoke shortages and whip up popular discontent. The opposition media blamed the shortages on state 'inefficiency'. Opposition political parties started receiving significant US funding, on condition that they unified and ran on a single slate in contesting elections and questioned the legitimacy of the election results (claiming 'fraud') after their defeat.

In summary, US efforts to restore its hegemony in Caracas involved a wide range of domestic clients from violent paramilitary groups, NGOs, political parties, elected officials and manufacturing and commercial executives linked to the production and distribution of essential consumer goods.

The shifts in Washington's policies, from internal violence (coup of 2002, oil lockout of 2002–03), and cross border military threats from Colombia (2004–2006), returning to internal domestic elections and campaigns of

economic sabotage reflects recent attempts to overcome failed policies without surrendering the strategic objective of restoring hegemony via overthrowing the elected government ('regime change' in the imperial lexicon).

Seven Keys to Imperial Politics: An Overview

Washington's effort to restore hegemony and reimpose a client regime in
Caracas has last over a decade and involves the empire's capacity to achieve
seven strategic goals:

1. Imperial capacity to overthrow a nationalist government requires a uni-
    fied collaborator military command. President Chávez made sure there
    were loyalists in strategic military units able to counter the coup-making
    capacity of imperial proxies.
2. Imperial capacity to intervene depends on not being tied down in
    on-going wars elsewhere and on securing regional collaborators. Neither
    condition was present. The armies of the empire were bogged down in
    prolonged wars in the Middle East and South Asia creating public hostil-
    ity to another war in Venezuela. The plans to convert Colombia into an
    ally in an invasion of Venezuela failed because Colombia's business elite
    were already shouldering significant trade losses due to the cross-border
    skirmishes and Washington had little or nothing in economic compensa-
    tion or alternative markets to offer Colombian exporters and most of
    US 'aid' (Plan Colombia) involved direct military transfers and sales—
    useless to domestic producers.
3. The imperial destabilization campaign wasted its strategic assets through
    premature, ill-calculated and high-risk operations where one failuRe
    seemed to lead to even higher risk interventions in an effort to cover-up
    Washington's bankrupt strategy. The US-backed coup of 2002 was clearly
    based on poor intelligence and a grotesque underestimation of President
    Chávez's support among the military and the masses. Washington did not
    understand how Chávez's astute institutional changes, in particular his
    promotion of loyalist sectors of the armed forces, undercut the capacity
    of its domestic collaborators. Blinded by its racist anD ideological blind-
    ers, Washington counted on its business allies and trade union bureau-
    crats to 'turn-out the crowds' to back the junta and provide a legal cover.
    In the face of serious losses resulting from the subsequent purging of
    client elites in the military and business associations, Washington
    then unleashed its client oil executives and trade union officials to

mount an oil lockout, without any support from the military. Eventually the shutdown of oil production and delivery managed to alienate broad sectors of the business community and consumers as they suffer from fuel and other critical shortages. In the end, over ten thousand US clients among senior and middle management were purged and the PDVSA (the state oil company) was restructured and transformed into a formidable political instrument funding Venezuela comprehensive social welfare programs.

Increases in social spending in turn boosted Chávez's support among voters and consolidated his mass base among the poor. Imperial strategists switched from failing to overthrow Chávez by extra-parliamentary tactics to launching an unsuccessful referendum and suffered a decisive and demoralizing defeat in the face of strong popular for Chávez' social initiatives. To make a virtue of its serial disasters, Washington decided to back a boycott of the Congressional elections and ended up with near unanimous Chavista control of Congress and a wide popular mandate to implement Chávez executive prerogatives. Chávez then used his executive decrees to promote an anti-imperialist foreign policy with no congressional opposition!

4. The US' ill-timed ideological warfare (both the 'neoliberal' and 'war on terror' variants) was launched against Venezuela from 2001 on, just when revolts, uprisings and collaborator 'regime change' were occurring throughout Latin America. The continent-wide rebellion against US-centred free-market regimes resonated with Chávez's nationalist-populism. Washington's ideological appeals flopped. Its blind, dogmatic embrace of a failed development strategy and the continued embrace of hated clients ensured that Washington's ideological war against Venezuela would boomerang: instead of isolating and encircling Venezuela, there was greater Latin American regional solidarity with the Bolivarian regime. Washington found itself isolated. Instead of dumping discredited clients and attempting to adapt to the changing anti-neoliberal climate, Washington, for internal reasons (the ascent of Wall Street), persisted in pursuing a self-defeating propaganda war.

5. Imperial efforts to reassert hegemony required an economic crisis, including low world demand and prices for Venezuela's commodities, declining incomes and employment, severe balance of payment problems and fiscal deficits—the usual mix for destabilizing targeted regimes. None of these conditions existed in Venezuela. On the contrary, world demand and prices for oil boomed. Venezuela grew by double-digits. Unemployment and poverty sharply declined. Easy and available

consumer credit and increased public spending greatly expanded the domestic market. Free health and education and public housing programs grew exponentially. In other words, global macro-economic and local social conditions favoured the anti-hegemonic perspectives of the government. US and clients' efforts to demonize Chávez flopped. Instead of embracing popular programs and focusing on the problems of their implementation and mismanagement, Washington embraced local political collaborators who were identified with the deep socio-economic crisis of the 'lost decade' (1989–1999)—a period of real misery for the Venezuelan masses prior to Chávez ascent to power. Imperial critics in Latin America easily refuted Washington's attacks on the Chávez development model by citing favourable employment, income, purchasing power and living standards compared to the previous neoliberal period Weisbrot & Sandoval, 2008).

6.   Imperial policy makers were way out of step in Latin America, emphasizing its brand of global ideological-military confrontation while leaders and public opinion in Latin America were turning toward growing market opportunities for their commodities. The 'War on Terror', Washington's hobbyhorse for global supremacy, had minimum support among the people of Latin America. Instead, China's demand for Latin American commodities displaced the US as the major market their exports. In this context, global militarism was not going to restore US hegemony; Latin American leaders were focused on domestic and Asian markets, poverty reduction, democracy and citizen participation. During past decades, when Latin America was ruled by military regimes, US global militarism resonated with the elites. Washington's attempt to restore an earlier model military-client rule by backing the coup in Honduras was denounced throughout the continent, not only by centre-left governments, but even by conservative civilian regimes, fearful of a return to military rule at their expense.

7.   The change from a Republican to a Democratic presidency in Washington did not result in any substantive change in imperial policy toward Venezuela or Latin America. It only led to the serving up of 'double discourse' as President Obama touted a 'new beginning', 'new overtures' and 'our shared values'. In practice, Washington continued military provocations from its bases in Colombia, backed the Honduras military coup and supported a violent destabilization campaign in April 2013 following the defeat of its favoured presidential candidate, Henrique Capriles Radonski, by the Chavista Nicholas Maduro. The Obama regime stood isolated throughout the hemisphere (and the OECD) when it refused to recognize

the legitimacy of the Maduro's election victory. In imperial countries, political changes from a liberal to a conservative executive, (or vice versa), does not in any way affect the deep imperial state, its military interests or strategies. President Obama's resort to a double discourse of talking diplomatically while acting militarily as a mode of hegemonic rule quickly lost its lustre and effectiveness even among centrist-post-neoliberal leaders.

Imperialism is not simply a 'policy'; it is a structure based on a defined set of rules. It has a powerful military aid component dependent on strategically placed collaborators and supporters in targeted countries and operating in a favourable (crisis-ridden) environment. Imperialism flourishes when its military and diplomatic approach serves economic interest benefiting both the 'home market' and local collaborators. In the second decade of the 21st century, the dominance of 'military-driven imperialism' bled the domestic economy, destroying and impoverishing the targeted society and shattering living standards. The recent devastating wars in the Middle East have dismantled entire societies and weakened US-client elites.

Latin American and Venezuelan development-oriented leaders took a long look at the destruction wrought by US policy elsewhere and turned to new partners—the newly emerging economic powers with growing markets. These new partners, like China, pursue economic ties, which are not accompanied by military and security threats of intervention. Chinese investments do not include military missions and massive spy networks such as the CIA, DEA, and NSA that pose a threat to national sovereignty.

The Imperial Dynamic and the Radicalization of Venezuelan Politics

Imperial intervention can have multiple and contrasting effects. It can intimidate a nationalist government and force it to renege on its electoral promises and revert to a liberal agenda. It can lead to an accommodation to imperial foreign policies and force a progressive government to moderate domestic reforms. It can lead to concessions to imperial interests, including military bases, as well as concessions to extractive capital, including the dispossession of local producers, to facilitate capital accumulation. Covert or overt intervention can also radicalize a moderate reformist government and force it to adopt anti-imperialist and socialist measures as defensive strategy. Over time incremental changes can become the basis for a proactive radical leftist agenda.

The range of systemic responses illustrates the analytical weakness of the so-called 'centre-periphery' framework, which lumps together (i) disparate political, social and economic internal configurations; (ii) opposing strategies and responses to imperialism; and (iii) complex international relations between imperial and nationalist regimes. The polar opposite responses and political-economic configurations of the US and China (so-called 'centres') to Venezuela further illustrates the lack of analytical utility of the so-called 'world system' approach in comparison with a class-anchored framework.

The imperial dynamic, the drive by Washington to reassert hegemony in Venezuela by violent regime change, had the unintended consequence of radicalizing Chávez' policies, consolidating power and furthering the spread of anti-imperialist programs throughout the region (Ciccariello-Maher, 2013; Ellner, 2009).

In the first years of the Chávez government, 1999–2001, Venezuela pursued largely orthodox policies and sought friendly relations with Washington, while espousing a Bolivarian vision. In this period, Chávez did not implement his vision. He did not try to set up any regional organizations that excluded the US. Nevertheless, Washington retained its ties to the opposition and sought to influence a motley collection of opportunist politicos who had jumped on the Chávez bandwagon while countering the leftists in the coalition government.

The first big break in this Caracas-Washington peaceful co-existence was caused by the Bush Administration's big push for global power via the so-called 'War on Terror' doctrine. Its demand that Chávez support the military offensives against Afghanistan and Iraq or face retaliation provoked the break. Chávez resisted and adopted the position that the 'War on Terror' violated international law. In other words, Venezuela upheld traditional international norms just when Washington had turned to global military extremism. Washington perceived Chávez's policy as a grave threat, an example for other 'recalcitrant' states within Latin America and across the globe to follow in resisting the US bullying. This led to an overt warning from the US State Department that '*he (Chávez) would pay a price*' for not submitting to the US global military offensive.[10]

Washington immediately started to implement plans to overthrow the Chávez government leading to the bloody, but unsuccessful coup of April 2002. If the trigger for US imperial intervention was Chávez's lawful opposition to Washington's global military strategy the defeat of the coup and his restoration to power, led a re-definition of Venezuelan-US relations. Bilateral relations went from co-existence to confrontation. Venezuela began looking for regional

---

10   Interview of a Foreign Affairs official, Caracas, November 6, 2006.

allies, actively supporting left and nationalist movements and governments in Latin America. Simultaneously it pursued relations with imperial rivals and adversaries, including Russia, China, Belarus and Iran. Washington launched its second effort to unseat Chávez by backing the oil bosses' lockout, severely damaging the economy.

The defeat and purge of the US-backed PDVS oil executives led to the radicalization of social policy in Venezuela, with the vast reallocation of oil revenues to working class-based social programs. Chávez appointed nationalists to key economic ministries, selectively nationalizing some enterprises and declaring a radical agrarian reform program, which included the expropriation of un-cultivated land. In part, the radical policies were 'pragmatic', defensive measures in pursuit of national security. They also were in response to the support for the Bolivarian government from the newly mobilized urban and rural poor. Radicalization was also a response to pressures from the nationalist and socialist elements in the newly formed Socialist Party and allied trade union confederations. US imperial efforts to isolate Venezuela in the hemisphere, copying the 1960s blockade of Cuba failed.

There was also a region-wide trend in line with Venezuela: nationalist populist and leftist movements and coalition governments were replacing US client regimes. Washington's policy backfired by regionalizing the conflict under unfavourable conditions: Venezuela gained popularity and support while Washington was isolated, leading to the demise of its plan for a regional free trade agreement.

The threat from the US pushed Chávez to re-define the nature of the political process from 'reform' to 'revolution'; from moderate nationalism to 21st century socialism; from a bilateral conflict to a regional confrontation. Venezuela sponsored and promoted several key alliances including ALBA and PetroCaribe; Chávez later broadened Venezuela's regional ties to include UNASUR and MERCOSUR.

Venezuela's radical rejection of US hegemony, however, was tempered by structural limitations that provided US empire builders and internal clients with access points to power. The 'socialization' program did not affect 80 percent of the economy. Banking, foreign trade, manufacturing and agriculture remained under private ownership. Over 95 percent of the public watched programs from a domestic mass media owned by US-backed private clients (Center for Economy and Policy Research, 2010). Transport, food distributors and supermarkets remained privately owned. Campaigns and elections remained vulnerable to foreign funding by the National Endowment for Democracy and other US conduits. While the mixed economy and open electoral system, secured approval from Latin America's centre-left regimes and neutralized some of the hostile US propaganda, they also allowed the empire to use its local collaborators to commit sabotage, hoard vital consumer goods and create shortages, stage violent street confrontations during elections and permitted the mass media openly call for insurrection.

The confrontation between US imperial aggression and Venezuelan nationalism deepened the revolution and spread its appeal overseas. Venezuela's successful defiance of US imperialism became the defining reality in Latin America.

Imperialism, based on militarism and regime destabilization, led Venezuela to begin a process of transition to a post neoliberal, post-capitalist economy rooted in regional organizations. Yet this process continued to reflect economic realities from the capitalist past. The US remained Venezuela's most important petroleum market. The United States, caught up in Middle-East wars and sanctions against oil producers (Iraq, Iran, Libya and Syria), was not willing to jeopardize its Venezuelan oil imports by means of a boycott. Necessity imposed constraints on even imperial aggression as well as Venezuela's 'anti-imperialism'.

Conclusion

US-Venezuela relations provide a casebook study of the complex, structural and contingent dimensions of imperialism and anti-imperialism. Contemporary US empire building, with its global engagement in prolonged serial wars and deteriorating domestic economy, has witnessed a sharp decline in its capacity to intervene and restore hegemonic influence in Latin America. Throughout Latin America, Venezuela's success in resisting imperial threats, demonstrates how much imperial power is contingent on local client regimes and collaborator military elites to sustain imperial hegemony. The entire process of imperial capital accumulation through direct exploitation and 'dispossession' is based on securing control over the state, which, in turn, is contingent on defeating anti-imperialist and nationalist governments and movements. Imperialist hegemony can be based on either electoral processes ('democracy') or result from coups, lockouts and other anti-democratic, authoritarian mechanisms.

While, historically, economic interests are an important consideration of imperial policymakers, contemporary US imperialism has confronted emerging nationalist governments because of their rejection of its 'global war' ideology. In other words Venezuela's rejection of the ideology and practice of offensive wars and violations of international law is the trigger that set in motion imperial intervention. Subsequent conflicts between Washington and Caracas over oil company expropriations and compensation were derived from the larger conflict resulting from US imperial militarism. US oil companies had become economic pawns and not the subjects of imperialist policymakers.

US imperialist relations in Latin America have changed dramatically in line with the internal changes in class relations. US financial and militarist elites, not industrial-manufacturers, now dictate policy. The relocation of US manufacturers to Asia and elsewhere has been accompanied by the ascendancy of a power configuration whose political pivot is in the Middle East and, in particular, in their own words, 'securing Israel's superiority in the region'. This has had two opposing effects: On the one hand it has led imperial policymakers to pursue non-economic militarist agendas in Latin America and, on the other, to 'neglect' or allocate few resources, investments and attention to cultivating clients in Latin America. Inadvertently, the 'Middle East pivot' and the militarist definition of reality has allowed Latin America to secure a far greater degree of independence and greater scope for cultivating diverse economic partners in the 21st century than was possible for the greater part of the 20th century.

Have US-Latin American relations permanently changed? Has Venezuela consolidated its independence and achieved the definitive defeat of imperial intervention? It would be premature to draw firm conclusions despite the substantial victories achieved during the first decade and a half of the 21st century.

Pro-US regimes and elites still wield influence throughout Latin America. As was evident in the Presidential elections in Venezuela in April 2013, the US-funded opposition candidate, Henrique Capriles, came within two percent of winning the election. And Washington, true to its vocation to destabilize, has refused to recognize the legitimacy of the election. Since then several officials of the US Embassy have been implicated in plots to overthrow the Maduro government. The on-going, intrusive imperial cyber-spying system under the US National Security Agency introduces a new element in colonial intervention reaching into the highest political and economic spheres in the entire region, incurring the wrath of Brazil, the largest country in Latin America. Unrepentant, Washington has affirmed its right to colonize and dominate Brazilians and Venezuelan cyber-space and control all communications between strategic elites.

Obama's affirmation of the US 'right to spy' prompted new anti-imperialist measures, including proposals to end ties to US-based and controlled information networks. In other words, new imperial methods of colonization based on

new technologies triggers new anti-imperial responses, at least for independent states.

The anti-neoliberal governments in Latin America, heading up the struggle
against US hegemony, face serious challenges resulting from the continuing
presence of private banking and finance groups, US based multi-nationals and
their local collaborators in the political parties. Except for Venezuela and
Bolivia, on-going US-Latin American joint military programs provide opportunities for imperial penetration and recruitment.

The high dependence of Venezuela and the other centre-left countries
(Ecuador, Argentina, Brazil, Bolivia, etc.) on commodity exports (agriculture,
minerals and energy) exposes the vulnerability of their finances and development and social welfare programs to fluctuations and sharp downturns in
global export revenues (Petras, 2012a; Wilpert, 2007).

So far world demand for Latin American commodities has fuelled growth
and independence and weakened domestic support for military coups. But can
the mega-cycles continue for another decade? This is especially important for
Venezuela, which has not succeeded on diversifying its economy with oil still
accounting for over 80 percent of its export earnings. The China trade, which is
growing geometrically, has been based on exports of raw materials and imports
of finished goods. This reinforces neo-colonial economic tendencies within
Latin America.

Intra-Latin American trade (greater regional integration) is growing and
internal markets are expanding. But without changes in class relations, domestic and regional consumer demand cannot become the motor force for a definitive break with imperialist-dominated markets. In the face of a second world
economic crisis, the US may be forced to reduce its global military operations,
but will it return to hemispheric dominance? If commodity demand drops and
the Chinese economy slows down do post-neoliberal regimes have alternative
economic strategies to sustain their independence?

Imperial power in Latin America and in Venezuela in particular, has suffered serious setbacks but the private property power structures are intact and
imperial strategies remain. If the past half-century offers any lessons it is that
imperialism can adapt different political strategies but never surrenders its
drive for hegemony and political, military and economic domination.

CHAPTER 11

Dynamics of 21st Century Imperialism

The configuration of 21st century imperialism combines patterns of exploitation from the past as well as new features which are essential to understanding the contemporary forms of plunder, pillage and mass impoverishment. In this chapter we will highlight the relatively new forms of imperial exploitation, reflecting the rise and consolidation of an international ruling class, the centrality of military power, large scale long-term criminality as a key component of the process of capital accumulation, the centrality of domestic collaborator classes and political elites in sustaining the US–EU empire and the new forms of class and anti-imperialist struggles.

Imperialism is about political domination, economic exploitation, cultural penetration via military conquest, economic coercion, political destabilization, separatist movements and via domestic collaborators. Imperial aims, today as in the past, are about securing markets, seizing raw materials, exploiting cheap labour in order to enhance profits, accumulate capital and enlarge the scope and depth of political domination. Today the mechanisms by which global profits are enhanced have gone far beyond the exploitation of markets, resources and labour; they embrace entire nations, peoples and the public treasuries, not only of regions of Africa, Asia and Latin America but include the so-called 'debtor countries of Europe', Ireland, Greece, Spain, Portugal and Iceland, among others.

Today the imperial powers of Europe and the United States are re-enacting the 'scramble for the riches of Africa, Asia and Latin America' via direct colonial wars accompanying a rising tide of militarism abroad and police state rule at home. The problem of empire building is that, given popular anti-imperialist resistance abroad and economic crisis at home, imperial policymakers require far-reaching expenditures and dependence on collaborator rulers and classes in the countries and regions targeted for imperial exploitation.

Any discussion of 21st century empire building—its dynamic growth and its vulnerability—requires a discussion and analysis of the different types and forms of 'collaborator rulers and classes'; the new forms of imperial pillage of entire societies and economies via debt and financial networks; and the central role of criminal operations in global imperial accumulation.

Imperial Pillage of Debtor Countries on the Southern Periphery of Europe

The greatest transfer of wealth from the workers and employees to the imperial banks and state treasuries of the European Union, North America and Japan has taken place via the so-called 'debt crises'. With the political ascendancy FIRE sectors (finance, insurance and real estate) of the capitalist class, the state and the public treasury became one of the key sources of capital accumulation, corporate profits and private wealth. Using the pretext of the crash of speculative investments, the FIRE ruling class extracted hundreds of billions of dollars directly from the public treasury and hundreds of millions of taxpayers. To secure the maximum wealth from the public treasury of the debtor states social expenditures were sharply reduced, wages and salaries were slashed and millions of public employees were fired.

The state took over the private debts in order to restore the profits of the FIRE sector and in the process reduced the average wage and salaries of workers and employees across the entire economy. The centrepiece of this new structure of imperial pillage was the imperial states acting on behalf of the financial-real estate and insurance capital of the EU and North America.

The collaboration of the governing political class and their local financial elites was essential in facilitating the long term, large-scale plunder of the local economy, taxpayers, employees, negotiating the terms and time frame for paying tribute to the imperial states: Ireland, Greece, Spain, Portugal because the site of the biggest suction pump for imperial enrichment in modern history: entire working populations are impoverished to transfer wealth for at least the next generation and beyond. Through onerous debt extraction payments and public pillage imperialism has created the perfect mechanism for imperial enrichment, deepening class and regional inequalities and the dispossession of homes, factories and land. Cheap labour, regressive taxes, open markets, a vast pool of unemployed, are results of imperial financial dictates complemented and enforced by the local collaborator political class (conservative, liberal and social democratic) and justified by a small army of media pundits, academic economists and trade union bureaucrats.

State-Organised Crime as the Highest Stage of Empire Building

Lenin, in his time, wrote of finance monopoly capital as the highest stage of imperialism; since his time a new and more pernicious state has emerged:

organized massive criminality has become the centrepiece for imperial exploitation and accumulation.

One has only to read the headlines of the major financial press to find trillion dollar swindles by the biggest and most prestigious investment banks, financial houses, credit agencies, risk-rating corporations across Europe, North America and Asia. The famous French novelist Honore Balzac once wrote that 'behind every great fortune there is a great crime'. In today's financial world he would have to say that great criminal acts are perpetual and integral to the accumulation by great financial houses. Capital accumulation especially in the dominant international financial sector via criminality is evident in at least three major types of financial activity.

Trillion dollar swindles by all the major banks involve manipulation of the Libor inter-banking interest rates, deliberately puffing up and dumping stocks and bonds, fleecing pension funds and millions of investors of billions of dollars: packaging trillions in worthless mortgages and securities and selling them to small investors; conning Governments into taking over bad debts based on speculative bets gone south. The entire financial system for over two decades has engaged in systematic fraud, extortion of public wealth based on falsified credit and earnings reports—accumulating capital which is re-invested in new, bigger scams on a global level. Adam Smith's *Wealth of Nations* would have to be rewritten to take account of the wealth of swindlers' capitalism.

Complementary to fraud and swindles are the hundreds of billions of dollars that the leading banks accrue through laundering illicit income from billionaire drug cartels, sex slavers, body parts entrepreneurs, corrupt political leaders, tax evaders from five continents. Each year trillions are 'packaged' by Oxford, Cambridge and Harvard educated MBAs employed by Barclays, Citibank, UBS and other financial leaders and dispatched to offshore accounts and 'washed' in upscale real estate in London, Manhattan, the Riviera, Dubai and other high end real estate sites.

Imperial capital's profits and total wealth is enhanced by large-scale illegal international capital flows from 'developing countries'. Between 2001 and 2010 developing countries 'lost' US 5.86 trillion dollars to illicit outflows. During the past decade China's new billionaire capitalists, running the world's biggest manufacturing sweatshops, shipped $2.74 trillion to Western imperial banks, Mexican plutocrats $476 billion, Nigerian corrupt elites pillaged oil wealth and poured $129 billion; India's new and old rich rulers sent out $123 billion in illegal funds to the big banks of England and the Middle East. Obviously we need to update Marx and Lenin to take account of the systematic criminalization of capital as a central element in the process of capital reproduction. As capital becomes criminal, criminals become capitalists—on a world-historical scale.

Imperialism and the Central Role of Domestic' Collaborators

Contemporary Empire building is based on a complex network of overseas class, political and military collaborators who play an essential role in facilitating imperial entry and exploitation, defending its profits and privileges, and extracting wealth. Imperial armies, banks and multi-nationals operate within the framework of compliant clients, trained, selected, protected and rewarded by the imperial powers.

The US and France, together with other NATO powers have established military bases, training missions and special funds to create African mercenary armies to defeat anti-imperialist insurgents and to prop up puppet regimes which facilitate imperial plunder of the natural resources and vast agricultural lands. Imperial military commanders direct African mercenary forces from Ethiopia, Uganda, Kenya, Nigeria, Mali, Libya and elsewhere. Without these mercenary collaborators imperialist politicians would face greater domestic opposition due to loss of their soldiers' lives and higher military expenditures.

Following Euro-American and Gulf States military intervention in Libya—over 26,000 bombing missions—the imperial forces recruited a mercenary army to protect the petrol installations and prepare public firms for privatization. France with its eye on the gold, uranium and other mining resources invaded Mali took political control and established a collaborator regime. Following popular uprisings in Tunisia and Egypt, which overthrew established imperial client dictatorships, Euro-US imperialism endeavoured to establish a new collaborator coalition composed of pro-capitalist Islamists and the security apparatus of the dictatorships.

In Asia, in Afghanistan, Iraq and Kurdistan, imperial rulers despite over a decade of colonial wars are desperately trying to create mercenary armies to sustain client regimes to facilitate the plunder of oil wealth (Iraq and Kurdistan) and sustain strategic military bases facing China (Afghanistan). In Afghanistan after 12 years of war without victory, the US is forced to retreat, hoping to stave off an ignominious defeat by recruiting 350,000 Afghan mercenary soldiers—proven to be of a very dubious loyalty. Despite conquering Iraq and imposing its rule, Euro-American imperialism is left with an unstable regime with growing links to Iran.

In the scramble to plunder African resources, amidst inter-imperialist competition, new imperial-collaborator partnerships have emerged: a new class of corrupt billionaire African rulers has opened their countries to unrestrained pillage. While imperial multinationals extract mineral wealth, the African collaborators transfer hundreds of billions in illegal flows to the imperial financial centres. Africa leads the way in the growth of illicit financial flows—24 percent yearly between 2001 and 2010.

Western imperialism, more than ever, depends on the cultivation, maintenance of collaborator regimes—politicians, military officials, business elite—to open their countries to plunder, to transfer wealth to the imperial financial centers and to repress any popular opposition.

The entire imperial enterprise would collapse in the face of domestic anti-imperialist opposition movements ousting collaborator elites.

In Europe, imperial financial institutions depend on local political collaborators to impose and enforce so-called 'austerity programs', to assume the private financial debts and to transfer tribute to the imperial centres for indefinite time frames. Collaborator regimes are essential to maintaining tributary relations to their imperial rulers.

Imperialism, Militarism and Zionism

If we compare US imperialism to the expansion of Chinese global power, we will observe profound differences in the modes of operation and on-going trajectory. China's overseas expansion is fundamentally economic—large-scale investment in raw materials, markets for its manufactured goods and large-scale infrastructure projects to facilitate the trade flows in both directions. It provides financial incentives, low interest loans and bribes to collaborator elites to propel economic expansion.

US-EU imperialism has emphasized and relied on military intervention, operates over 700 military bases, has military advisors in dozens of countries, is engaged in drone wars against Pakistan, Yemen, Afghanistan, Somalia and elsewhere. Military conquests have enlarged the US military presence but at enormous economic cost, leading to unsustainable fiscal and trade deficits and hundreds of billions of losses for the 'private sector'. The Iraq and Libyan wars and economic sanctions against Iran have undermined billions in oil profits. As the US economic empire declines, Chinese global economic power rises: and their conflict and competition intensifies.

The key to the rise of a military driven empire and the eclipse of the economic component of empire building can be attributed to three inter-related factors: the extraordinary influence of the Zionist power configuration in harnessing US imperial power to Israel's militarist regional goals; the ascendancy of financial capital and its subordination of manufacturing and resource capitalists; the increasing importance of the military-security apparatus in the imperial state as a result of the 'global war on terror' ideology.

The subordination of US imperial power to a small, economically insignificant and isolated state like Israel is unprecedented in world history. As is the fact that US citizens whose primary loyalty is to Israel, have secured strategic policy-making positions in the power structure of the imperial state; including the Executive (White House), Pentagon, State Department and the Congress. The 52 Presidents of the Major American Jewish organizations exercise power via million dollar funding of legislators, parties and electoral campaigns; appointment of Zionist loyalists to strategic government posts dealing with the Middle East; private consultants to the government (housed in Zionist-funded 'think tanks') and their influence in the major mass media outlets.

Although the population identifying as Jews has decreased (the only major denomination to decline by as much as 14 percent over the past two decades), representing less than one percent of the US religious population, the wealth, organization, tribal zeal and strategic institutional location of Israel Firsters has magnified their power several fold. As a result Zionist policymakers played a dominant role in driving the US to war with Iraq, formerly a powerful supporter of the Palestinians, and staunch opponent of Israeli colonial expansion into Palestine. Because of the political power of the Zionist power configuration, Israel extracts $3 billion a year in aid and a total of over a $100 billion over the past 30 years—in addition to having the US military engage in wars against Arab, Islamic and secular regimes which materially support the Palestine national liberation struggle. Never in the history of modern imperialism has the foreign policy of a world power been subject to tributary demands and served the colonial aspirations of a second rate state. This historical anomaly is easily understood through the role of its powerful overseas networks that wield power in the Imperial State at the service of Jewish colonial settlers in Palestine.

In short, US imperialism has sacrificed major economic interests including hundreds of billions in petroleum profits, by engaging in destructive wars against Iraq and Libya and imposing economic sanctions on Iran—a telling statement of the power of Israel in shaping the US imperial agenda. Militarism and Zionism have dictated the direction of US imperial policy, greatly weakening the domestic foundations of empire and hastening its economic decline.

Militarism and Criminality Abroad and the Police State at Home

In the past imperialism was seen as compatible with democracy at home: as long as imperial wars were short in duration, inexpensive to the Treasury, resulted in the successful extraction of wealth and was based on collaborator mercenary armies, the masses enjoyed the constitutional rights and the vicarious pleasures and illusions of being part of a superior race.

Contemporary US-EU imperial expansion has provided neither material nor symbolic gratifications: prolonged wars and occupations with no definitive victories, imperial armies surrounded by overwhelmingly hostile populations and facing daily attacks from fighters blending with the population has led to profound disenchantment among the public, and sadistic and self-destructive behaviour (high rates of suicides) among the imperial soldiers and unsustainable budget deficits.

Unreliable and corrupt collaborators and the bankruptcy of the anti-terrorist ideology have provoked widespread political opposition to overseas military wars. No longer convincing the public via propaganda, the US executive has instituted a raft of police state measures, suspending habeas corpus and culminating in executive decrees claiming Presidential prerogatives allowing for the extra judicial assassination of terror suspects including US citizens: militarism and criminality abroad has spread and infected the domestic body politic.

Imperial Wars by Proxy and Domestic Decay

Imperialism today is profoundly linked to the domestic crises—transferring billions from domestic programs to imperial wars abroad. The bulk of wealth extracted from the pillage abroad is concentrated in the hands of the FIRE ruling class. The 'aristocracy of labour', which Lenin identified as a beneficiary of empire, has shrunken and is largely confined to the upper echelons of the trade union bureaucracy, especially those who sign off on austerity programs, tributary payments and bank bailouts. Imperialism has reshaped the class structured budgets and economies of the neocolonies and tributary states. In the first instance it has proletarianized the middle class, polarized the classes, concentrating income in the hands of a parasitic criminal financial elite of five percent and reducing living standards for the 70 percent of workers, unemployed, semi-employed, public and private employees and self-employed.

Given the deepening global polarization between empire and masses and the tiny minority of beneficiaries, the entire imperial architecture depends on the central role of domestic collaborators to sustain imperial power, administer the transfer of wealth, ensure the extraction of wealth, provide a veneer of electoral legitimacy to the entire criminal enterprise and where necessary apply muscular repressive force.

Faced with prolonged downward mobility, a permanent 'class war from above' and, above all, the near universal recognition that welfarism and imperialism/capitalism are no longer compatible, the working classes have turned to direct action: repeated general strikes have replaced the ballot box for the millions of unemployed young workers, downwardly mobile employees, bankrupt small business people and those dispossessed of their homes in Greece, Spain, Portugal and Italy. Millions of peasants, and artisan workers have shed the plough, the hammer and anvil, and picked up the gun to confront imperial powers and their political collaborators and mercenary armies in South Asia, the Middle East and Africa; Arab revolts, detoured from revolution by Islamic collaborators in the first round, are rising once again: the second round promises more consequential changes.

Imperialism with its powerful bankers and advanced arms, its hundreds of military bases and monstrous expenditures, rests on fragile foundations. Who now believes that the 'war on terror' has replaced the class war? The overwhelming majority of people now recognize that Wall Street, the City of London and Brussels are the real criminals, pillaging billions, laundering illegal financial flows and extracting tribute from the public treasury. Who believes today that capitalism and the welfare state are compatible? Who believes that Israel is anything but a brutal police state administrating the world's biggest open-air concentration camp for Arabs, administered exclusively by and on behalf of its Chosen People?

Today the struggle against imperialism is first and foremost a class struggle against the local collaborators: domestic politicians and business people who extract and transfer the wealth of a people to the imperial centres. Undermining the collaborators worldwide is already a work in progress. Conservatives, liberals, and social democratic collaborators in Europe have lost credibility and legitimacy—the task of the mass movements is to organize for state power.

The imperial offensive in Africa and Asia rests on unreliable mercenary armies and corrupt rulers: as the imperial armies retreat, their collaborator rulers will collapse. And out of the ruins, new anti-imperialist states will eventually emerge.

By defeating the US strategy of imperial military coups, collaborating with the political opposition and staged elections Venezuela has shown that the building of socialism as an alternative to capitalism is still a possibility. In China the socialist revolution lives on in the hundreds of thousands of strikes and protests against imperial capitalists and their millionaire political collaborators. The capitalist counter-revolution is only a detour in the transition to socialism.

CHAPTER 12

Reflections on US Imperialism at Home and Abroad

The world political economy is a mosaic of cross currents: domestic decay and elite enrichment, new sources for greater profits and deepening political disenchantment, declining living standards for many and extravagant luxury for a few, military losses in some regions with imperial recovery in others. There are claims of a unipolar, a multi-polar and even a non-polar configuration of world power. Where, when, to what extent and under what contingencies do these claims have validity?

Busts come and go, but let us talk of 'beneficiaries'. Those who cause crashes, reap the greatest rewards while their victims have no say. The swindle economy and the criminalized state prosper by promoting the perversion of culture and literacy. 'Investigative journalism', or peephole reportage, is all the rage. The world of power spins out of control. As they decline, the leading powers declare that 'it's our rule *or everyone's ruin!*'

Global Configurations of Power Relations

Power is a relationship between and among classes, states and military and ideological institutions. Any configuration of power is contingent on past and present struggles reflecting shifting correlations of forces. Structures and physical resources, concentrations of wealth, arms and the media matter greatly; they set the framework in which the principle power wielders are embedded. But strategies for retaining or gaining power depend on securing alliances, engaging in wars and negotiating peace. Above all, world power depends on the strength of domestic foundations. This requires a dynamic productive economy, an independent state free from prejudicial foreign entanglements and a leading class capable of harnessing global resources to 'buy off' domestic consent.

To examine the position of the United States in the global configuration of power it is necessary to analyse its changing economic and political relations on two levels: by region and by sphere of power. History does not move in a linear pattern or according to recurring cycles: military and political defeats in some regions may be accompanied by significant victories in others. Economic decline in some spheres and regions may be compensated by sharp advances in other economic sectors and regions.

In the final analysis, it is not a question is not 'keeping a scorecard' or adding wins and subtracting losses, but translating regional and sectorial outcomes into an understanding of the direction and emerging structures of the global power configuration. We start by examining the legacy of recent wars on the global economic, military and political power of the United States.

Sustaining the US Empire: Defeats, Retreat, Advances and Victories

The dominant view of most critical analysts is that over the past decade US empire building has suffered a series of military defeats, experienced economic decline, and now faces severe competition and the prospect of further military losses. The evidence cited is impressive. The US was forced to withdraw troops from Iraq, after an extremely costly decade-long military occupation, leaving in place a regime more closely allied to Iran, the US regional adversary. The Iraq war depleted the economy, deprived American corporations of oil wealth, greatly enlarged Washington's budget and trade deficits and reduced the living standards of US citizens. The Afghanistan war had a similar outcome, with high external costs, military retreat, fragile clients, domestic disaffection and no short or medium term transfers of wealth (imperial pillage) to the US Treasury or private corporations. The Libyan war led to the total destruction of a modern, oil-rich economy in North Africa, the total dissolution of state and civil society and the emergence of armed tribal, fundamentalist militias opposed to US and EU client regimes in North and sub-Sahara Africa and beyond. Instead of continuing to profit from lucrative oil and gas agreements with the conciliatory Gadhafi regime, Washington decided on 'regime change', engaging in a war that ruined Libya and destroyed any viable central state. The current Syrian *'proxy war'* has strengthened radical Islamist warlords, destroyed Damascus' economy and added massive refugee pressure to the already uprooted millions from wars in Iraq and Libya. US imperial wars have resulted in economic losses, regional political instability and military gains for Islamist adversaries.

Latin America has overwhelmingly rejected US efforts to overthrow the Venezuelan government. The entire world—except for Israel and Washington—rejects the blockade of Cuba. Regional integration organizations, which exclude the US, have proliferated. US trade shares have declined, as Asia is replacing the US in the Latin American market.

In Asia, China deepens and extends its economic links with all the key countries, while the US 'pivot' is mostly an effort at military base encirclement involving Japan, Australia and the Philippines. In other words, China is more important than the US for Asian economic expansion, while Chinese financing of US trade imbalances props up the US economy.

In Africa, US military command operations mainly promote armed conflicts and lead to greater instability. Meanwhile Asian capitalists, deeply invested in strategic African countries, are reaping the benefits of its commodity boom, expanding markets and the outflow of profits.

The exposure of the US National Security Agency's global spy network has seriously undermined global intelligence and clandestine operations. While it may have helped privileged private corporations, the massive US investment in cyber-imperialism appears to have generated negative diplomatic and operational returns for the imperial state.

In short, the current global overview paints a picture of severe military and diplomatic setbacks in imperial policies, substantial losses to the US Treasury and the erosion of public support. Nevertheless this perspective has serious flaws, especially with regard to other regions, relations and spheres of economic activity. The fundamental structures of empire remain intact.

NATO, the major military alliance headed by the US Pentagon, is expanding its membership and escalating its field of operations. The Baltic States, especially Estonia, are the site of huge military exercises held just minutes from the principle Russian cities. Central and Eastern Europe provide missile sites all aimed at Russia. Until very recently, the Ukraine had been moving toward membership in the European Union and a step toward NATO membership.

The US-led Trans-Pacific Partnership has expanded membership among the Andean countries, Chile, Peru and Colombia. It serves as a springboard to weaken regional trading blocs such as MERCOSUR and ALBA that exclude Washington. Meanwhile, the CIA, the State Department and their NGO conduits are engaged in an all-out economic sabotage and political destabilization campaign to weaken Venezuela's nationalist government. US-backed bankers and capitalists have worked to sabotage the economy, provoking inflation (50 percent), shortages of essential items of consumption and rolling power blackouts. Their control over most of Venezuela's mass media has allowed them to exploit popular discontent by blaming the economic dislocation on 'government inefficiency'.

The US offensive in Latin America has focused on a military coup in Honduras, on-going economic sabotage in Venezuela, electoral and media campaigns in Argentina, and cyber warfare in Brazil, while developing closer ties with recently elected compliant neoliberal regimes in Mexico, Colombia, Chile, Panama, Guatemala and the Dominican Republic. While Washington lost influence in Latin America during the first decade of the 21st century, it has since partially recovered its clients and partners. The relative recovery of US influence illustrates the fact that 'regime changes' and a decline in market shares, have not lessened the financial and corporate ties linking even the progressive countries to powerful US interests. The continued presence of powerful political allies—even those 'out of government'—provides a trampoline for regaining US influence. Nationalist policies and emerging regional integration projects remain vulnerable to US counter-attacks.

While the US has lost influence among some oil producing countries, it lessened its dependence on oil and gas imports as a result of a vast increase in domestic energy production with *'fracking'* and other intense extractive technologies. Greater local self-sufficiency means lower energy costs for domestic producers and increases their competitiveness in world markets, raising the possibility that the US could regain market shares for its exports.

The seeming decline of US imperial influence in the Arab world following the popular 'Arab Spring' uprisings has halted and even been reversed. The military coup in Egypt and the installation and consolidation of the military dictatorship in Cairo suppressed the mass national-popular mobilizations. Egypt is back in the US-Israel orbit. In Algeria, Morocco and Tunisia the old and new rulers are clamping down on any anti-imperial protests. In Libya, the US-NATO air force destroyed the nationalist-populist Gadhafi regime, eliminating an alternative welfare model to neo-colonial pillage—but has so far failed to consolidate a neoliberal client regime in Tripoli. Instead rival armed Islamist gangs, monarchists and ethnic thugs pillage and ravage the country. Destroying an anti-imperialist regime has not produced a pro-imperialist client.

In the Middle East, Israel continues to dispossess the Palestinians of their land and water. The US continues to escalate military manoeuvers and impose more economic sanctions against Iran—weakening Teheran but also decreasing US wealth and influence due to the loss of the lucrative Iranian market. Likewise in Syria, the US and its NATO allies have destroyed Syria's economy and shredded its complex society, but they will not be the main beneficiaries. Islamist mercenaries have gained bases of operations while Hezbollah has consolidated its position as a significant regional actor. Current negotiations with Iran open possibilities for the US to cut its losses and reduce the regional threat of a costly new war but these talks are being blocked by an 'alliance' of Zionist-militarist Israel, monarchist Saudi Arabia and 'Socialist' France.

Washington has lost economic influence in Asia to China but it is mounting a regional counter-offensive, based on its network of military bases in Japan, the Philippines and Australia. It is promoting a new Pan Pacific economic agreement that excludes China. This demonstrates the capacity of the US state to intervene and project imperial interests. However, announcing new policies and organizations is not the same as implementing and providing them with dynamic content. Washington's military encirclement of China is offset by the US Treasury's multi-trillion dollar debt to Beijing. An aggressive US military encirclement of China could result in a massive Chinese sell-off of US Treasury notes and five hundred leading US multinationals finding their investments in jeopardy!

Power sharing between an emerging and established global power, such as China and the US, cannot be 'negotiated' via US military superiority. Threats, bluster and diplomatic chicanery score mere propaganda victories but only long-term economic advances can create the domestic Trojan Horses need to erode China's dynamic growth. Even today, the Chinese elite spend hefty sums to educate their children in 'prestigious' US and British universities where free market economic doctrines and imperial-centred narratives are taught. For the past decade, leading Chinese politicians and the corporate rich have sent tens of billions of dollars in licit and illicit funds to overseas bank accounts, investing in high end real estate in North America and Europe and dispatching billions to money laundering havens. Today, there is a powerful faction of economists and elite financial advisers in China pushing for greater *'financial liberalization'*, i.e. penetration by the leading Wall Street and City of London speculative houses. While Chinese industries may be winning the competition for overseas markets, the US has gained and is gaining powerful levers over China's financial structure.

The US share of Latin American trade may be declining, but the absolute dollar worth of trade has increased several-fold over the past decade. The US may have lost right-wing regime clients in Latin America, but the new centre-left regimes are actively collaborating with most of the major US and Canadian mining and agribusiness corporations and commodity trading houses. The Pentagon has not been able to engineer military coups, with the pathetic exception of Honduras, but it still retains its close working relations with the Latin American military in the form of (i) its regional policing of 'terrorism', 'narcotics' and 'migration'; (ii) providing technical training and political indoctrination via overseas military 'educational' programs; and (iii) engaging in joint military exercises.

In short, the *structures* of the US empire, corporate, financial, military and political-cultural, all remain in place and ready to regain dominance if and when political opportunities arise. For example, a sharp decline in commodity prices would likely provoke a deep crisis and intensify class conflicts among center-left regimes, which are dependent on agro-mining exports to fund their social programs. In any ensuing confrontation, the US would work with and through its agents among the economic and military elite to oust the incumbent regime and re-impose pliant neoliberal clients.

The current phase of post-neoliberal policies and power configurations are vulnerable. The relative 'decline of US influence and power' can be reversed even if it is not returned to its former configuration. The theoretical point is that while imperialist structures remain in place and while their collaborator counterparts abroad retain strategic positions, the US can re-establish its primacy in the global configuration of power.

Imperial 'roll-back' does not require the 'same old faces'. New political figures, especially with progressive credentials and faint overtones of a 'social inclusionary' ideology are already playing a major role in the new imperial-centred trade networks. In Chile, newly elected 'socialist' President Michelle Bachelet and the Peruvian ex-nationalist, President Ollanta Humala, are major proponents of Washington's Tran-Pacific Partnership, a trading bloc that competes with the nationalist MERCOSUR and ALBA, and excludes China. In Mexico, US client President Enrique Peña Nieto is privatizing the 'jewel' of the Mexican economy, PEMEX, the giant public oil company—strengthening the Washington's hold over regional energy resources and increasing US independence from Mid-East oil. Colombian President Santos, the 'peace president', is actively negotiating an end to guerrilla warfare in order to expand multinational exploitation of mineral and energy resources located in guerrilla-contested regions, a prospect that will primarily benefit US oil companies. In Argentina, the state oil company, Yacimientos Petroliferos Fiscales (YPF) has signed a joint venture agreement with the oil giant, Chevron, to exploit an enormous gas and oil field, known as Vaca Muerte (Dead Cow). This will expand the US presence in Argentina in energy production alongside the major inroads made by Monsanto in the powerful agro-business sector.

No doubt Latin America has diversified its trade and the US share has relatively declined. Latin American rulers no longer eagerly seek 'certification' from the US Ambassador before announcing their political candidacy. The US *is* totally isolated and alone in its boycott of Cuba. The OAS is no longer a US haven. But there are counter-tendencies, reflected in new pacts like the TPP. New sites of economic exploitation, which are not exclusively US-controlled, now serve as springboards to greater imperial power.

Conclusion

We began the book with the formulation of ten theses regarding extractivism and imperialism. In regard to the first thesis under recent and still current conditions in the current conjuncture both capitalism and imperialism are increasingly taking an extractivist form, particularly in South America where the growing demand for natural resources and the resulting primary commodities boom has had the greatest impact and echo in the world system.

Some analysts write of a process of reprimarization. We would not go this far in that despite the unfolding of a process of import-substitution industrialization in the era of state-led development most Latin American economies continued to export predominantly natural resources in primary commodity form. This is evidenced in Table 1.1, which shows that the level of primary commodities exports (as a percentage of total exports) for 1990 was higher (66.9 percent) than in 2008 (56.7 percent), when the wave of primary commodity exports began to subside. Nevertheless, in the region overall the share of primary commodities exports as a share of total exports did drop substantially in the 1990s (down 15 percentage points) before rising by five percentage points between 2000 and 2004, the year after the boom was seen to have started, and then rising another 14.7 percentage points over the next six years.

The problem is that there are significant intra-regional variations in this trend. In some countries (Brazil, Colombia, Peru, Venezuela) primary commodities as a share of exports did indeed increase, significantly so in the case of Brazil. But in Argentina, Chile and Bolivia the primary commodities export rate in 2011 was almost identical to 1990, thirteen years before the 'primary commodities boom'. The strongest case for the reprimarization thesis is Bolivia, which evidenced an decrease of 23 percent in this rate from 1990 to 2000 before recovering 14.4 percentage points between 2000 and 2004 and another nine percentage points over the course of the MAS regime led by Evo Morales and Alvaro Linera. Mexico provides an atypical case in evidencing a significant drop (40 percent) in the share of primary commodities in total exports from 1990 to 2000—mostly as the result of the rapid expansion of the maquiladoras in the industrial sector—before evidencing a six-percentage point increase in this share from 2004 to 2011.

Despite this intra-regional variation in the structure of exports there is no doubt that the value of primary commodity exports in south America from 2004 to 2008, the period of the boom in question, rose significantly, providing the countries that responded to the growing world demand for natural resources—mostly in south America—a major boost in fiscal revenues. This boost and the 'inclusionary state activism' associated with it reflect the search in the region for a new model that combines a new social policy (social inclusion, poverty reduction) with an extractivist approach to economic development. It also reflects the new geoeconomics of global capital: the advance of large-scale resource-seeking private investments in the acquisition of land and the extraction of natural resources for the purpose of capital accumulation in the form of both profit and resource rents.

Notwithstanding the resurgence of extractive capitalism and the re-emergence of an extractivist approach to national development—what Cypher views as a 'return to the 19th century' and what Girvan in this book terms 'extractivist imperialism' and neocolonialism—it is evident that imperialism, understood as the exercise of state power to advance the hegemonic interests of capital and the geopolitical interests of the imperial state, is taking multiple forms, including the projection of ideological, market and military power.

But what is also evident is that imperialism, even in its overt and covert military form, is unable to counteract the contradictory features or contain the crisis tendencies of the system. Both world capitalism and US imperialism are in crisis. Not only are the foundations cracking under the weight of the system's contradictions, but the state system which is needed to manage the outcomes of these contradictions and is absolutely vital for the maintenance of the empire, is failing, unable, as Geoff Wood, President of the British Development Studies Association, notes, 'to protect their population from... predatory capitalists within' (Wood, 2014). In addition, the ideological pillars of the system have been eroded to the point that even the guardians of the system, the system's 'senior practitioners' in their annual gathering at Davos, confessed to Wood that the World Economic Forum, an institution charged with the responsibility of safeguarding the world capitalist system, is 'absolute crap'. As Wood puts it, when 'senior participants' of a key institution despair of their futile efforts in safeguarding the system then 'its days [as an institution] are numbered'. And perhaps those of the system as well.

As for the US economy, the major structural pillar of the world system and US imperialism, it has been over-financialized and is stagnant; it has failed to regain momentum because of the State's strategy of imperial war in defence of its geopolitical and economic interests. The inordinate but unavoidably excessive costs of this strategy are placing an unbearable strain on the functioning of both the economy and the political system.

In the Middle East, a major theatre of imperial war, the decline of the US economy and a weakening in the capacity of Washington to politically manage the forces released by the financialization of production and the operations of finance capital has not been accompanied by the ascent of its old rivals. Europe, for example, is in the throes of a deep crisis, with vast armies of unemployed workers, chronic negative growth and few signs of recovery in the foreseeable future. Even China, the new emerging global economic power, has begun to show signs of weakness; the economy is slowing down, the rate of growth falling from over eleven percent for several decades to seven percent in the current decade. Beijing also faces growing domestic discontent as well as protest actions by a growing rural proletariat and millions of super-exploited urban workers in the industrial sector. And India, another 'emerging economy', is following China in liberalizing its financial system, opening it up to penetration by US finance capital and forces that might well lead to the destruction of existing forces of industrial production and associated problems, and end up undermining both the Chinese and the Indian model of capitalism.

Forces of resistance to imperialist exploitation and to capitalism in its neo-liberal form are brewing in Latin America, but the anti-imperialist forces in Asia and Africa are not composed of progressive, secular, democratic and socialist movements. In these regions the empire in these parts of the world is confronted by religious, ethnic, misogynist and authoritarian or reactionary movements with irredentist tendencies. The old secular, socialist voices have lost their bearings, and provide perverse justifications for imperialist wars of aggression in Libya, Mali and Syria. French socialists, who had opposed the Iraq war in 2003, now find their President Francoise Hollande parroting the brutal militarism of the Israeli warlord Netanyahu.

The point here is that the thesis of the 'decline of the US empire'—and its corollary: the 'crisis of the US'—are overstated, time-bound and lacking in specificity. There is no alternative imperial power or anti-hegemonic power bloc on the immediate horizon. While it is true that Western capitalism is in crisis, the recently ascending Asian capitalism of China and India face a different crisis resulting from their savage class exploitation and murderous caste relations. If objective conditions are 'ripe for socialism' as they seem to be, many socialists—at least those retaining any political presence—are comfortably embedded in their respective imperial regimes. Marxists and socialists in Egypt joined with the military to overthrow an elected conservative Islamist regime, leading to the restoration of imperialist clientelism in Cairo. French and English 'Marxists' supported NATO's destruction of Libya and Syria. Numerous progressives and socialists in Europe and North America support Israel's warlords or remain silent in the face of domestic Zionist power in the executive branches and legislatures of the US and European imperial state.

To conclude, if imperialism is on the decline—and it appears to be—so is anti-imperialism. And if capitalism is in crisis the forces of resistance and opposition are in disarray where not in retreat. But if capitalists are looking for new projects and new faces, and different politicians and ideologies, to revive their fortunes, is it not time for the anti-imperialists and anti-capitalists to do likewise?

Bibliography

Abya Yala—Movimientos Indígenas, Campesinos y Sociales (2009), "Diálogo de Alternativas y Alianzas," *Minga Informativa de Movimientos Sociales*, La Paz, 26 de Febrero.

Acosta, Alberto (2009), *La maldición de la abundancia*. Quito: Comité Ecuménico de Proyectos CEP.

Acosta, Albertto (2011), "Extractivismo y neoextractivismo: dos caras de la misma maldición," in M. Lang and D. Mokrami (eds.), *Mas allá del Desarrollo*, Quito: Fundación Rosa Luxemburgo/Abya Yala.

Aggarwal, Vinod and Ralph Espach (2005), "Diverging Trade Strategies in Latin America: An Analytical Framework." http://basc.berkeley.edu/pdf/articles/Diverging%20Trade%20Strategies%20in%20Latin%20America.pdf.

Aggarwal, Vinod, Joseph Tulchin and Ralph Espach (eds.) (2004) *The Strategic Dynamics of Latin American Trade*. Stanford University Press.

Aguirre-Beltrán, Gonzalo (1991), *Obra Antropológica IX. Regiones de Refugio: El desarrollo de la comunidad y el proceso dominical en mestizo América*. México, DF: Fondo de Cultura Económica.

Albrow, M. et al. (eds.), 2008. *Global Civil Society*. London: Sage.

Aluminum International Today (2009), "Bauxite: Global Demand Is up, but Exporting Nations Might Pose Problems," *Journal of Aluminum Production and Processing Aluminum International Today*, August 9.

Altieri, Miguel (2004), *Genetic Engineering in Agriculture. The Myths, environmental risks, and alternatives*. Oakland CAL: Food First Books.

Amin, Samir (1973), "Underdevelopment and Dependence in Black Africa: Their Historical Origins and Contemporary Forms," *Social and Economic Studies*, March. http://thereformcooperative.wordpress.com/2009/05/12/review-african-development-articles.

Araghi, Farshad (2000), "The Great Global Enclosure of Our Times: Peasants and the Agrarian Question at the End of the Twentieth Century," pp. 145–160 in F. Magdoff, J.B. Foster, and F. Buttel (eds.), *Hungry for Profit*. New York: Monthly Review Press.

Araghi, Farshad (2009), "The Invisible Hand and the Visible Foot: Peasants, Dispossession and Globalization," pp. 111–147 in A.H. Akram-Lodhi and C. Kay (eds.), *Peasants and Globalization: Political Economy, Rural Transformation and the Agrarian Question*. London and New York: Routledge.

Araghi, Farshad (2010), "Accumulation by Displacement, Global Enclosures, Food Crisis and the Economic Contradictions of Capitalism," *Review*, 32(1): 113–146.

Arbix, Glauco and Scott Martin (2010), "Beyond Developmentalism and Market Fundamentalism in Brazil: Inclusionary State Activism without Statism," Paper presented at the Workshop "States, Development and Global Governance," University of Wisconsin-Madison, March 12–13.

Arellano, M. (2010), "Canadian Foreign Direct Investment in Latin America," Background Paper, North–south Institute, Ottawa, May.

Auditoría Superior de la Federación (ASF) (2012), *Informe del Resultado de la Fiscalización Superior de la Cuenta Pública 2010.* http://www.asf.gob.mx/Trans/Informes/IR2010i/Grupos/Desarrollo_Economico/2010_0809_a.pdf.

Auty, Richard M. (1993), *Sustaining Development in Mineral Economies: The Resource Curse Thesis.* London: Routledge.

Auty, Richard, ed. (2001) *Resource Abundance and Economic Development.* Oxford University Press. http://www.wider.unu.edu/research/1998-1999-4.2.publications.htm.

Babcock, Bruce (2008), "Breaking the Link between Food and Biofuels," CARD *Briefing Paper 08-BP 53. Iowa Agriculture Review,* Summer, 14 (3), Iowa State University.

Bannon, Ian and Paul Collier (eds.) (2003), *Natural Resources and Violent Conflict: Options and Actions.* Washington, DC.

Bárcenas, Francisco López (2012), "Detener el saqueo minero en México," *La Jornada,* February 28: 31.

Barrett, Patrick S., Daniel Chávez and César A. Rodríguez Garavito (eds.) (2008), *The New Latin American Left: Utopia Reborn.* London: Pluto.

Bartra, Roger (1976), "¡Si los campesinos se extinguen!" *Historia y Sociedad,* No. 8, Winter.

Bartra, Roger (1974), *Estructura agraria y clases sociales en México.* Mexico City: Era.

Bebbington, Anthony (2009), "The New Extraction: Rewriting the Political Ecology of the Andes?" *NACLA Report on the Americas,* 42(5): 12–20.

Bebbington, Anthony (ed.) (2011), *Minería, movimientos sociales y respuestas campesinas. Una ecología política de transformaciones territoriales.* Lima: Instituto de Estudios Peruanos-Centro Peruano de Estudios Sociales.

Bebbington, Anthony and Denise Humphreys (2010), "An Andean Avatar: Post-Neoliberal and Neoliberal Strategies for Promoting Extractive Industries," BWPI *Working Paper* 117. www.manchester.ac.uk/bwpi.

Beinstein, Jorge (2013), "Annus Horribilis. 2013: Punto de inflexión en la larga decadencia occidental," *ALAI-America latina en Movimiento,* 2013-12-04. http://alainet.org/active/69509.

Bernstein, Henry (2010), *Class Dynamics of Agrarian Change.* Halifax: Fernwood; MA Kumarian.

Bernstein, Henry (1997), "Social change in the South African countryside? Land and production, poverty and power. Land reform and agrarian change in southern

Africa," Occasional Paper. No.4, Programme for Land and Agrarian Studies (PLAAS), University of the Western Cape, SA.

Bernstein, Marvin (1964), *The Mexican Mining Industry 1890–1950*, New York: State University of New York.

Berry, Barry (2010), "The Natural Resource Curse in 21st Century Latin America, *Canada Watch*, Fall, pp. 23–24.

Berterretche, Juan L. (2013), "Mujica, discurso en la ONU," Agenda Radical, Boletín informativa, No. 1335, Montevideo, 1° de octubre.

Best, Lloyd (1997), "Independent Thought and Caribbean Freedom: Thirty Years later," *Caribbean Quarterly*, 43 (1/2), March–June, pp. 16ff. http://www.jstor.org/stable/40653983.

Best, Lloyd and Kari Polanyi Levitt (2009), *Essays on the Theory of Plantation Economy*. Mona: UWI Press.

Black, David and Peter McKenna (1995), "Canada and Structural Adjustment in the South: The Significance of the Guyana Case," *Canadian Journal of Development Studies*, VXI(I).

Borras, S. Jr, J. Franco, S. Gomez, C. Kay and M. Spoor (2012), "Land Grabbing in Latin America and the Caribbean," *Journal of Peasant Studies* 39 (3–4): 845–872.

Borras Jr, Saturnnino [Jun], Jenniffer Franco, Cristobal Kay and Max Spoor (2011), "Land grabbing in Latin America and the Caribbean viewed from broader international perspectives," Paper presented at the Latin America and Caribbean seminar 'Dinámicas en el mercado de la tierra en América Latina y el Caribe', 14–15 November, FAO Regional Office, Santiago, Chile.

Borras, S. Jr, and J.C. Franco (2010), "Towards a broader view of the politics of global land grab: rethinking land issues, reframing resistance," The Hague: International Institute of Social Studies (ISS), *ICAS Working* Paper, No. 1.

Borras, S. Jr, P. McMichael and I. Scoones (2010), "The Politics of Biofuels, Land and Agrarian Change: An Editorial Introduction," *Journal of Peasant Studies*, 37(4): 575–592.

Bowles, Paul and Henry Veltmeyer (2014), *The Answer Is Still No: Voices of Resistance to the Enbridge Oil Pipeline Project*. Halifax: Fernwood Publications.

Brazil Exports by Product Section (USD), http://www.INDEXMUNDI.com/trade/exports/Brazil.

Brazil Mining, http://www.e-mj.com/index.php/reatures/850-Brazil-,mining.

Brenner, Robert (2006), "What is and what is not imperialism', *Historical Materialism*, 14(4): 79–105.

Bresser-Pereira, Luiz Carlos (2006), "El Nuevo Desarrollismo y la Ortodoxia Convencional," *Economía UNAM*, 4(10): 7–29.

Bresser-Pereira, Luiz Carlos (2007), "Estado y Mercado en el Nuevo Desarrollismo," *Nueva Sociedad*, No. 210, Julio–Agosto.

Bresser-Pereira, Luiz Carlos (2009), *Developing Brazil. Overcoming the Failure of the Washington Consensus.* Boulder: Lynne Rienner Publications.

Buira, Ariel (2003), "An Analysis of IMF Conditionality," *G-24 Discussion Papers.* UNCTAD.

Burnes Ortiz, Arturo (2006), *El drama de la minería Mexicana. Del pacto colonial a la globalización contemporánea,* Zacatecas: Universidad de Zacatecas.

Cámara Minera de México (2013), *Informe Anual 2013.* México, DF: CAMIMEX.

Cámara Minera de México (CAMIMEX) (2012), *Informe Anual 2012.* México, DF: CAMIMEX.

Campodónico, Humberto (2008), *Renta petrolera y minera en países seleccionados de América Latina.* Santiago: CEPAL.

Canada, House of Commons (2012), *Driving Inclusive Economic Growth: The Role of the Private Sector in International Development.* Report of the Standing Committee on Foreign Affairs and International Development, House of Commons. Ottawa: Public Works and Government Services Canada.

Caribbean 360 (2012), "Guyana gold wealth fleeing across the border," July 23.

Center for Economy and Policy Research (2010), "Private Opposition TV Continues to Dominate in Venezuela," Washington DC: CEPR, December 13.

Centro de Estudios de las Finanzas Públicas (CEFP) (2013), *Indicadores macroeconómicos 1980–2013,* www.cefp.gob.mx/Pub_Macro_Estadisticas.htm.

CEPAL (1998), *Foreign Investment in Latin America and the Caribbean.* Santiago: United Nations.

CEPAL (2010), *La inversión extranjera directa en América latina y el Caribe.* New York: UN.

Chabrol, Denis Scott (2012a), "Bauxite company moves to court to stop arbitration," *Demerara Waves,* March 30.

Chabrol, Denis Scott (2012b), "Chairman of Linden electricity review committee resigns," *Demerara Waves,* October 16.

Chabrol, Denis Scott (2013), "Police responsible for Linden killing; 'shooting' to scare 'hostile' crowd justified," *Demerara Waves,* March 1.

Ciccariello Maher George (2013), *We Created Chávez: A Peoples History of the Venezuelan Revolution.* Durham: Duke University Press.

Collier, Paul and A.J. Venables (2011), *Plundered Nations? Successes and Failures in Natural Resource Extraction.* London: Palgrave Macmillan.

Comisión Nacional de Derechos Humanos (CNDH) (2011), "Recomendación 12/2011 Sobre el caso de V1 y V2, quienes perdieron la vida en el interior de la mina Lulú, en el municipio de Escobedo, Coahuila," *Gaceta,* No. 48, México, pp. 139–162.

Correa, Rafael (2012), "Ecuador's Path," *New Left Review,* 77.

Costa Vaz, Alcides (2001), "Forging a Social Agenda within Regionalism: The Cases of Mercosur and the FTAA in a Comparative Approach," Centre for Mercosur Studies, University of Brasilia. www.robarts.yorku.ca/pdf/vaz.pdf.

Cypher, James (2010), "South America's Commodities Boom. Developmental Opportunity or Path Dependent Reversion?" *Canadian Journal of Development Studies*, 30(3–4): 635–662.

Cypher, James (2013), "Neoextracciónismo y Primarización: ¿la subida y descenso de los términos del intercambio en América del Sur?" Unpublished paper, Estudios del Desarrollo, Universidad Autónoma de Zacatecas, Zacatecas.

Cypher, James and Raúl Delgado Wise (2012), *Génesis, desempeño y crisis del modelo exportador de fuerza de trabajo*. Zacatecas, Mexico: Autónomous University of Zacatecas/Miguel Ángel Porrúa.

Dangl, Benjamin (2007), *The Price of Fire: Resource Wars and Social Movements in Bolivia*. Oakland, CA: AK Press.

Dangl, Benjamin (2010), *Dancing with Dynamite: Social Movements and States in Latin America*. Aukland, CA: AK Press.

Dávalos, Pablo and Veronica Albuja (2014), "Ecuador: Extractivist Dynamics, politics and Discourse," in H. Veltmeyer and J. Petras (eds.), *The New Extractivism: A Post-Neoliberal Development Model or Imperialism of the 21st Century?* London: Zed Books.

Davis, Mike (2006), *Planet of Slums*. London: Verso.

De Echave, José (2008), *Diez años de minería en el Perú*. Lima: Cooperacción.

De Echave, José (2009), "Minería y conflictos sociales en el Perú," pp. 105–129 in J. de Echave, R. Hoetmer and M. Palacios (eds.), *Minería y territorio en el Perú. Conflictos, resistencias y propuestas en tiempos de globalización*. Lima: Programa Democracia y Transformación Global/Confederación Nacional de Comunidades del Perú Afectadas por la Minería/CooperAcción/Fondo Editorial de la Facultad de Ciencias Sociales, Unidad de Postgrado UNMSM.

De Sousa Santos Boaventura (2005), *Crítica de la Razón Indolente. Contra el desperdicio de la experiencia*. Bilbao: Editora Desclée de Brouwer.

Deininger, Klaus and Derek Byerlee (2011), *Rising Global Interest in Farmland: Can It Yield Sustainable and Equitable Benefits?* Washington, DC: World Bank.

Delgado-Wise, Raúl and Rubén Del Pozo (2002), *Minería, Estado y gran capital en México*. México, DF: Universidad Nacional Autónoma de México, Centro de Investigaciones Interdisciplinarias en Ciencias y Humanidades.

Demara Waves (2012), "Guyana halts granting new river mining permits in the wake of massive environmental degradation," July 5.

Deneault, Alain and William Sacher (2012), *Imperial Canada Inc: Legal Haven of Choice for the World's Mining Industries*. Vancouver: Talonbooks.

Domínguez, D. and P. Sabatino (2006), "Con la soja al cuello: crónica de un país hambriento productor de divisas," CLACSO, March.

ECLAC—UN Economic Commission for Latin America and the Caribbean (2009), *Foreign Investment in Latin America and the Caribbean*. Santiago, Chile: ECLAC.

ECLAC (2010), *Time for Equality: Closing Gaps, Opening Trails*. Santiago, Chile: ECLAC.

ECLAC (2012), *Foreign Direct Investment in Latin America and the Caribbean 2012.* Santiago: ECLAC.

ECLAC (2007), *Foreign Investment in Latin America and the Caribbean.* Santiago, Chile: ECLAC.

ECLAC (2002). *Statistical Yearbook for Latin America and the Caribbean.* Santiago: ECLAC.

Ellner, Steve (2009), *Rethinking Venezuelan Politics: Class, Conflict and the Chávez Phenomenon.* Boulder, COL: Lynn Reiner.

Enciso, Angélica (2013). "Minera canadiense en busca de oro y plata pone en riesgo la zona de Xochicalco," La Jornada. August 6. http://www.jornada.unam.mx/2013/08/06/politica/002n1pol.

Engler, Yves (2012), *The Ugly Canadian: Stephen Harper's Foreign Policy.* Vancouver: RED Publishing/Halifax: Fernwood Publishing.

Ericsson, Magnus and Victoriya Larrson (2013), "E&MJ's Annual Survey of Global Mining Investment," *E&MJ News*, January 22.

Esteva, Gustavo (1983), *The Struggle for Rural Mexico.* Greenwood Publishing.

Evans, Peter (1979), *Dependent Development: The Alliance of Multinational State and Local Capital in Brazil.* Princeton, NJ: Princeton University Press.

Familia Pasta de Conchos (2011), *Dime desde allá abajo. V Informe de Pasta de Conchos,* http://www.fomento.org.mx/novedades/5to_PC.pdf (Accessed 20/12/13).

FAO—Food and Agricultural organization of the United Nations (2008), "The State of Food and Agricultur," in *BIOFUELS: Prospects, Risks and Opportunities.* Rome: FAO.

FAO (2011), *Land Tenure and International Investments in Agriculture.* Rome: FAO.

Farah, I. and L. Vasapollo (2011), *Vivir bien: ¿Paradigma no capitalista?* La Paz: CIDES-UMSAH.

Farthing, L. and Kohl B. (2006), *Impasse in Bolivia: Neoliberal Hegemony and Popular Resistance.* London: Zed Books.

Fernandes, Bernardo Mançano and Elizabeth Alice Clements (2013), "Land Grabbing, Agribusiness and the Peasantry in Brazil and Mozambique," *Agrarian South*, April 2013.

Fernandes, B.M., Clifford A.W., E.C. Gonçalves (2010), "Agrofuel Policies in Brazil: Paradigmatic and Territorial Disputes," *Journal of Peasant Studies*, 37(4): 793–819.

Fidler, Richard (2012), "Pipeline Politics: Can Popular Protest Stop the Tarsands Leviathan?" *The Bullet*, E-Bulletin 743, December 11.

Financial Times (2011), Special Supplement "Latin America: New Trade Routes," 4/26/2011.

Financial Times (2011), "China is now Regions Biggest Partner," *Special Report*, 4/26/2011. https://www.yumpu.com/en/document/view/17903286/china-is-now-regions-biggest-partner-financial-times-ftcom.

Foster, John Bellamy (2003), "Ecological Imperialism: The Curse of Capitalism," pp. 186–201 in Leo Panitch and Colin Leys (eds.) *The New Imperial Challenge, Socialist Register 2004.* Halifax: Fernwood Publishing.

Friedmann, Harriet (1987), "International regimes of food and agriculture since 1870," pp. 258–276 in T. Shanin (eds.) *Peasants and peasant societies*. Oxford: Basil Blackwell.

Friedmann, H. and P. McMichael (1989), "Agriculture and the State System: The Rise and Decline of National Agricultures, 1870 to the Present," *Sociologia Ruralis*, 29(2): 93–117.

Fusion, Robert H. (ed.) (1992), *The Log of Christopher Columbus*, Tab Books, International Marine Publishing.

Gaitán Riveros, Mercedes (1986), "Modernización y lucha obrera en la industria siderúrgica," *Momento Económico*, (24), 10–14.

García Linera, Álvaro (2012), *Geopolítica de la Amazonía. Poder Patrimonial y acumulación capitalista*. La Paz: Vicepresidencia del Estado Plurinacional.

García Linera, Álvaro (2013), "Once Again on so-called 'Extractivisim,'" *Monthly Review*, April 29. http://mrzine.monthlyreview.org/2013/gl290413.html.

Garibay, Claudio (2010), "Paisajes de acumulación minera por desposesión campesina en el México actual", pp. 133–182 in Gian Carlo Delgado Ramos (ed.), *Ecología política de la Minería en América Latina. Aspectos socioeconómicos, legales y ambientales de la mega minería*, México, DF: Centro de Investigaciones Interdisciplinarias en Ciencias y Humanidades, UNAM.

Garibay, Claudio, Andrés Boni, Francisco Panico and Pedro Urquijo (2011), "Unequal Partners, Unequal Exchange: Goldcorp, the Mexican State, and Campesino Dispossession at the Peñasquito Goldmine," *Journal of Latin American Geography*, 10(2): 153–176.

Giarracca, Norma and Miguel Teubal (2008), "Del desarrollo agroindustrial a la expansión del agronegocio," in Mançano Fernandes Organizador (ed.), *Campesinato e agronegócio na América Latina: a questao agrária atual*. Sao Paulo: Expressao Popular.

Giarracca, Norma and Miguel Teubal (2010), "Disputa por los territorios y recursos naturales: el modelo extractivista," in *ALASRU*, No. 5, América Latina, realineamientos políticos e projetos em disputa. Brasil Diciembre.

Giarracca, Norma and Miguel Teubal (eds.) (2005), *El campo argentino en la encrucijada*, Buenos Aires, Alianza Editorial Vladimir Gil (2009) *Aterrizaje minero. Cultura, conflicto, negociaciones y lecciones para el desarrollo desde la minería en Ancash, Perú*. Lima: Instituto de Estudios Peruanos.

Giarracca, Norma and Miguel Teubal (2014), "Argentina: Extractivist dynamics of Soy Production and Open-Pit Mining," in H. Veltmeyer and J. Petras (eds.) *The New Extractivism*. London: Zed Books.

Giles, Latoya (2012), "Linden Shootings...Bullets struck two protesters in the heart, one in the back," *Kaieteur News*, July 26.

Girvan, Norman (1976), "Aspects of the Political Economy of Race in the Caribbean and the Americas: A Preliminary Interpretation," *Working Paper*, Mona: Institute of Social and Economic Research, University of the West Indies.

Girvan, Norman (2011), "Is ALAB a New Model of Integration," *International Journal of Cuban Studies*, September.

Glave, Manuel and Juana Kuramoto (2007), "La minería peruana: lo que sabemos y lo que aún nos falta por saber," *Investigación, políticas y desarrollo en el Perú*. Lima, GRADE, pp. 135–181.

Glusing, Jens (2013), "Bow, Arrow, Facebook: Brazilian Tribes Fight for Their Land," *Spiegel Online*, August 22. http://www.spiegel.de/international/business/0,1518,935 801,00.html.

Golinger, Eva (2006), *The Chávez Code: Cracking US Intervention in Venezuela*. Olive Branch Press.

Golinger, Eva (2007), *Bush versus Chávez*. New York: Monthly Review Press.

González Rodríguez, José de Jesús (2011), *Minería en México. Referencias generales, régimen fiscal, concesiones y propuestas legislativas*, Documento de Trabajo No. 121, México, DF: Centro de Estudios Sociales y de Opinión Pública.

Gordon, Todd (2010), *Imperialist Canada*. Winnipeg: Arbeiter Ring Publishing.

Gott, Richard (2005), *Hugo Chávez: The Bolivarian Revolution in Venezuela*. London: Verso.

Government of Guyana (2006), "Enhancing National Competitiveness: A National Competiveness Strategy for Guyana," *Draft Policy Paper* II, Government of Guyana in Partnership with the Private Sector, May.

Government of Guyana (2012), Budget 2012: Remaining on Course, United in Purpose, Prosperity for All, Ministry of Finance, Georgetown, March 30.

GRAIN (2008), *Seized: The 2008 Land Grab for Food and Financial Security*. Barcelona: GRAIN.

GRAIN (2010), *Land Grabbing in Latin America*. Georgetown, Guyana, March 29.

Griffiths, Tom and Lawrence Anselmo (2010), "Indigenous Peoples and Sustainable Livelihoods in Guyana: An Overview of Experiences and Potential Opportunities." Amerindian People's Association, Forest People Program, and the North–south Institute. Georgetown, Guyana, United Kingdom, and Ottawa, Canada, June

Gudynas, Eduardo (2009), "Diez tesis urgentes sobre el nuevo extractivismo. Contextos y demandas bajo el progresismo sudamericano actual', in *Extractivismo, Política y Sociedad*. Quito: CLAES/CAAP.

Gudynas, Eduardo (2010) 'The New Extractivism in South America: Ten Urgent Theses about Extractivism in Relation to Current South American Progressivism'. Bank Information Center. http://americas.irc-online.org/pdf/reports/1001theses.pdf.

Gudynas, Eduardo (2011), "Más allá del nuevo extractivismo: transiciones sostenibles y alternativas al desarrollo," in Fernanda Wanderley (ed.), *El desarrollo en cuestión. Reflexiones desde América Latina*. La Paz: Oxfam/CIDES-UMSA.

Gudynas, Eduardo (2013), "Brazil, the Biggest Extractivist in South America," ALAI AMLAT-en, 13/05/2013. alai-amlatina@alai.info.

Guerra, François-Xavier (1983), "Territorio minado (más allá de Zapata en la Revolución mexicana)," *Nexos*, 6(65), 31–47.

Gustafson, Bret (2013), "Amid Gas, Where Is the Revolution?" NACLA, May 28.

Guyana Bauxite and General Workers Union (2010), "Time to take a stand! Workers' right and laws are under attack in Guyana and the Government, NAACIE, Trade Union Recognition and Certification Board, and RUSAL/BCGI must stop their transgressions," March 13. http://www.thewestindiannews.com/time-to-take-a-stand-workers'-right-and-laws-are-under-attack-in-guyana-and-the-government-naacie-trade-union-recognition-and-certification-board-and-rusalbcgi-must-stop-their-transgressi/.

Haber, S. and V. Menaldo (2012), "Natural Resources in Latin America: Neither Curse Nor Blessing," SSRN *Working Paper*. Oxford Handbook of Latin American Political Economy. http://papers.ssrn.com/sol3/papers.cfm?abstract_id=1625504.

Hardt, Michael and Antonio Negri (2000), *Empire*. Cambridge: Harvard University Press.

Harvey, David (2003), *The New Imperialism*. New York: Oxford University Press.

Higginbottom, Andy (2013), "The Political Economy of Foreign Investment in Latin America Dependency Revisited," *Latin American Perspectives*, 40(3), May 184–206.

Hogenboom, B. (2012), "Depoliticized and Repoliticized Minerals in Latin America," *Journal of Developing Societies*, 28(2).

IBGE—Instituto Brasileiro de Geografia e Estatística (2009), *Censo Agropecuário 2006*. Brasilia, DF.

ILO (2003), Working Paper Globalization and Labour Relations of the Inter-American Research and Documentation Centre of the ILO.

IMF (1998), Staff Country Report No 98/117, October, Washington, DC.

Infante B. Ricardo and Osvaldo Sunkel (2009), "Chile: hacia un desarrollo inclusive," *Revista CEPAL*, 10(97), 135–154.

Isles, Kwesi (2013a) "Increased compensation for Linden dead unlikely—Dr. Luncheon," *Demerara Waves*, March 7.

Isles, Kwesi (2013b), "Linden Commission Inquiry Hearing Compensation Claims," *Demerara Waves*, January 28.

Isles, Kwesi (2013c), "Linden Commission Looking to complete reports by February month end," January 29.

Isles, Kwesi (2013d), "GGMC, Isseneru Village to Appeal High Court Land Ruling," *Demerara Waves*, January 22.

Jank, M.S., M.F.P. Leme, and A.M. Nassar (1999), "Concentration and International of Brazilian Agribusiness Exporters," *International Food and Agribusiness Management Review*, 2(3–4): 359–374.

Kaieteur News (2012a), "2011: A Year Replete with Scampishness, Secret Deals and Downright Skullduggery," Kaieteur News Online, January 1.

Kaieteur News (2012b), "Bauxite workers' dismissal dispute heads to arbitration," March 6.

Kaieteur News (2012c), "Indian Coffee Company Ships Out 50 Containers of Logs in 2 Months," Kaieteur News Online, April 5.

Kapstein, Ethan (1996), "Workers and the World Economy," *Foreign Affairs,* 75(3).

Kapur, Devesh and Richard Webb (2000), "Governance Related Conditionalities of the International Financial Institutions," UNCTAD, G-24 Discussion Paper 6, August.

Karl, T.L. (2000), "Economic Inequality and Democratic Instability," *Journal of Democracy,* XI(1), 149–156.

Katz, Caludio (2011), "Clases, estados e ideologías imperiales," *ARGENPRESS.info,* 26 de agosto.

Kautsky, Karl (1988), *The Agrarian Question.* London: Zwan publications.

Kay, Cristóbal (2006), "Rural Poverty and Development Strategies in Latin America," *Journal of Agrarian Change,* 6(4): 455–508.

Kay, Cristóbal (2009), "Development Strategies and Rural Development: Exploring Synergies, Eradicating Poverty," *Journal of Peasant Studies,* 36(1): 103–138.

Kay, Cristóbal and Jenny Franco (2012), *The global water grab: A primer.* Amsterdam: Transnational Institute.

Keenan, K. (2010), "Canadian Mining. Still Unaccountable," NACLA, May/June.

Kingstone, Peter (2012), "Brazil's Reliance on Commodity Exports threatens its Medium and Long Term Growth Prospects." http://www.americasquarterly.org/kingstone.

Klein, Emilio and Victor Tokman (2000), "La estratificacion social bajo tension en la era de la globalizacion," *Revista CEPAL* 72, Deciembre: 7–30.

Konold, Mark (2013), "Commodity Supercycle Slows Down in 2012," Worldwatch Institute, October 10.

Leff, Enrique (1996), "Ambiente y democracia: los nuevos actores del ambientalismo en el medio rural mexicano," pp. 35–64 in Hubert de Grammont and Héctor Tejera Gaona (eds.), *La sociedad rural mexicana frente al nuevo milenio. Los nuevos actores sociales y procesos políticos en el campo.* Mexico: Plaza y Valdez Editores.

Lewis, Arthur W. (1978), *Growth and Fluctuations: 1870–1913.* London.

López Bárcenes, Francisco and Mayra Eslava Galicia (2011), *El mineral o la vida. La legislación minera en México.* México, DF: Centro de Orientación y Asesoría a Pueblos indígenas/Pez en el Árbol/Red Interdisciplinaria de Investigadores de los Pueblos Indios de México, A.C.

Lorenz, Andres (2013), "The global land grab: The new enclosures." www.resilience.org/stories/2013-05-09/the-global-land-grab-the-new-enclosures 5/8.

Lust, Jan (2014), "Peru: Mining Capital and Social Resistance," in H. Veltmeyer and J. Petras (eds.), *The New Extractivism: A Post-neoliberal Development Model or Imperialism of the Twenty-first Century?* London: Zed Books.

Luxemburg, Rosa (2003 [1913]), *The Accumulation of Capital*. London and New York: Routledge.

Magdoff, Fred (2013), "Accumulation by Agricultural Dispossession," *Monthly Review*, December.

Martin Khor, Martin (2012), "The Emerging Global Crisis of Investment Agreements," *South Centre Bulletin*, Issue 69, 21 November.

Martínez Alier, Joan (1997), "From Political Economy to Political Ecology," in R. Guha and J. Martinez-Alier (eds.), *Varieties of Environmentalism*. London: Earthscan.

Martínez Alier, Joan (2009), *El ecologismo de los pobres, veinte años después: India, México y Perú*. Mexico City: CEIICH-PUMA/UNAM.

Martínez, Maria (2010), "El minero vengador," *Expansión*, July 28, pp. 77–80.

Marx, Karl (1979), *Capital*, vol. 1. New York: International Publishers Co.

Marx, Karl (1967). *Writings of the Young Marx on Philosophy and Society*. New York: Doubleday & Co.

McMichael, Philip (2009), "A Food Regime Genealogy," *Journal of Peasant Studies*, 36(1): 171–196.

Metals Economics Group (2011, 2013), *Worldwide Exploration Trends 2013*. http://www.metalseconomics.com (consulted 15/03/13).

Meyer, P.M., P.H. Rodrigues and D.D. Millen (2013), "Impact of biofuel production in Brazil on the economy, agriculture, and the environment," *Animal Frontier*, 3(2), April: 28–37.

Mining Association of Canada (2012), *Facts and Figures of the Canadian Mining Industria 2012*, http://mining.ca/node-46-document.

Moraes, M.A.F.D. (2007), "Indicadores do Mercado de Trabalho do Sistema Agroindustrial da Cana-de-Açúcar do Brasil no Período 1992–2005," *Estudos Econômicos*, 37(4), 28.

Morales, Evo (2003), "La hoja de coca, una bandera de lucha," Interview with *Punto Final* [Santiago], May.

Morales, Josefina (2002), "Transnacionalización del capital minero mexicano," pp. 51–81 in Atlántida Coll-Hurtado, María Teresa Sánchez-Salazar and Josefina Morales, *La minería en México* México, DF: Instituto de Geografía, UNAM.

Morganthau, Tom, with Mary Talbolt (1991), *Slavery. How It Built the New World*. http://faculty.lacitycollege.edu/moonmc/html/slavery.html.

Moyo, Sam and Paris Yeros (2005), *Reclaiming the Land: The Resurgence of Rural Movements in Africa, Asia, and Latin America*. London: Zed Books.

Muñoz Ríos, Patricia (2013a), "Denuncian sindicatos canadienses abusos laborales de mineras de su país en México," *La Jornada*, April 17.

Muñoz Ríos Patricia (2013b), "Reconoce el gobierno de Peña el liderazgo de Gómez Urrutia," *La Jornada*, July 4.

Muñoz Ríos Patricia (2013c), "Se ampara minera contra rescate de cuerpos en Pasta de Conchos," *La Jornada*, October 28.

Neves, M.F. and M.A. Consoli (2006), "Mapeamento e quantificação da cadeia do leite: relatório final," *Projeto* PENSA, *Workshop do Sistema Agroindustrial do Leite*, 1, 10.

Novo, A., K. Jansen, M. Slingerland and K. Giller (2010), "Biofuel, Dairy Production and Beef in Brazil: Competing Claims on Land Use in São Paulo State," *Journal of Peasant Studies*, 37(4): 769–792.

Nun, José (2001), *Marginalidad y exclusion social*. Fondo de cultura Económica.

Nun, José (1969). *Marginalidad y exclusion social*. Mexico: Fondo de Cultura Económica.

Otero, Gerardo (1999), *Farewell to the Peasantry? Political Class Formation in Rural Mexico*. Boulder VCO and Oxford: Westview Press.

OXFAM (2008), "Another Inconvenient Truth: How Biofuel Policies Are Deepening Poverty and Accelerating Climate Change," *Briefing Paper*. Boston: OXFAM International.

Paiva, Paulo and Ricardo Gazel (2003), "Mercosur: Past, Present, and Future," *Nova Economia*, Belo Horizonte, 13(2), julho–Dezembre: 115–136.

Panfichi, Aldo and Coronel Omar (2011), "Los conflictos hídricos en el Perú 2006–2010: una lectura panorámica," pp. 393–422 in R. Boelens, L. Cremers and M. Zwarteveen (eds.) *Justicia Hídrica. Acumulación, conflicto y acción social*. Lima: Instituto de Estudios Peruanos/Fondo Cultural PUCP.

Pérez, Matilde (2009), "Falta voluntad al gobierno: campesinos," *La Jornada*, 24 de Febrero.

Pérez Ruiz Abel and Sergio Sánchez Díaz (2006), "De Pasta de Conchos a 1 de mayo. La Coyuntura de una movilización obrera," *El Cotidiando*, 21(138), julio-agosto, pp. 101–108.

Perry, Jeffrey B. (2013), The Invention of the White Race. http://www.counterpunch .org/2013/05/21/the-invention-of-the-white-race.

Petras, J. (2012a), "Beyond President Chávez Electoral Victory," Socialism in a Rentier State," *JPetrasLaHaine*, 10/26/12.

Petras, James (2005), *Brasil e Lula – Ano Zero*. Blumenau: EdiFurb.

Petras, James (2006), "US-Latin American Relations: Ruptures, Reaction and Illusions of Times Past," *JPetrasLaHaine*, 11/2/06.

Petras, James (2008), "President Chávez and the FARC: State and Revolution," *JPetrasLaHaine*, 7/3/2008.

Petras, James (2010a), "Rethinking Imperialist Theory," *JPetrasLaHaine*, 12/21/2010.

Petras, James (2010b), "US-Venezuelan Relations: Imperialism and Revolution," *JPetrasLaHaine*, 1/5/2010.

Petras, James (2011a), "Chávez Right-Turn: State Realism versus International Solidarity," *JPetrasLaHaine*, 6/13/2011.

Petras, James (2011b), "Networks of Empire and Realignments of World Power," *JPetrasLaHaine*, 1/2/2011.

Petras, James (2012b), "Venezuelan Elections: A Choice and Not an Echo," *JPetrasLaHaine*, 10/4/12.

Petras, James (2013a), "Beyond President Chávez Electoral Victory: Socialism in a Rentier State," *JPetrasLaHaine*, 10/26/2013.

Petras, James (2013b), "Surgimiento y muerte del capitalismo extractivo," *Observatorio del Desarrollo*, Vol. 2, No. 7.

Petras, J. and H. Veltmeyer (2001a), "Are Latin American Peasant Movements Still a Force for Change? Some New Paradigms Revisited," *Journal of Peasant Studies*, January–March, 28(2), January.

Petras, James and Henry Veltmeyer (2001b), *Globalization Unmasked: Imperialism in the 21st Century*. London: ZED Press/Halifax: Fernwood Publishing.

Petras, James and Henry Veltmeyer (2003), *Cardoso's Brazil: A land for Sale*. Lanham, Maryland: Rowman and Littlefield.

Petras, James and Henry Veltmeyer (2004), *Las dos caras del imperialismo*. Mexico, DF/ Buenos Aires: Grupo Editorial Lumen.

Petras, J. and H. Veltmeyer (2005a), *Empire with Imperialism: The Globalizing Dynamics of Neo-liberal Capitalism*. London: Zed.

Petras, J. and H. Veltmeyer (2005b), *Social Movements and the State. Argentina, Bolivia, Brazil, Ecuador*. London: Pluto Press.

Petras, J. and H. Veltmeyer (2009), *What's Left in Latin America*. London: Ashgate.

Petras, James and Henry Veltmeyer (2011), "Rethinking Imperialist Theory and US imperialism in Latin America," *Proyecto Socialista: anuario de crítica, análisis y alternativa*," UNAM, Centro de Investigaciones Interdisciplinarias en Ciencias y Humanidades; Historia Actual Online (HAOL), Núm. 26 (Otoño, 2011), 103–114.

Petras, James and Henry Veltmeyer (2013a), *Imperialism and Capitalism in the 21st Century*. London: Ashgate.

Petras, James and Henry Veltmeyer (2013b), *Social Movements in Latin America; Neoliberalism and Popular Resistance*. New York: Palgrave/MacMillan.

Petras, James and Maurice Zeitlin (1968), *Latin America: Reform or Revolution*. New York: Fawcett.

Petras, James, et al. (1977), *The Nationalization of Venezuelan Oil*. New York: Praeger.

Phillips, Nicola (2002), "Reconfiguring Subregionalism: The Political Economy of Hemispheric Regionalism in the Americas," IPEG Papers in Global Political Economy No. 4, April 2002, British International Studies Association. https://www .chathamhouse.org/sites/files/chathamhouse/public/Research/Americas/phillips _paper.pdf.

Polanyi Levitt, Kari (2013), *From the Great Transformation to the Great Financialization: Essays on Karl Polanyi*. Fernwood Press.

Portes, A. and Hoffman K. 2003. Latin American Class Structures: Their Composition and Change during the Neoliberal Era, *Latin American Research Review*, 38(1).

Porzecanski, Arturo (2009), "Latin America: The Missing Financial Crisis," ECLAC Studies and Perspectives series, No. 6, ECLAC, Washington.

Prebisch, Raúl (1950) *The Economic Development of Latin America and Its Principal Problems*. New York: United Nations.

Quijano, Anibal (1974), "Marginal Pole and Marginal Labor Force in Latin America," *Economy and Society*, (1).

Ram, Christopher (2012), "The economics of Linden and electricity rates: Region Ten Is Not a Burden on, but a Contributor to the State," *Stabroek News*, July 29.

Rambla, José Manual Rambla (2013), "La agonia de los pueblos indigenas, buera de la agenda reivindicativa de Brasil," rebellion.org/notice, 5/7/13.

Red Mexicana de Afectados por la Minería (REMA) (2009), *Agenda Legislativa ante el modelo y la política de la minería devastadora e inconstitucional*. http://rema .codigosur.net/leer.php/8487628. (consulted 25/05/11).

Ribeiro, Silvia (2006), "From food to biofuel production," *La Jornada*, November 23.

Ricci, R., F.J. Alves and J.R.P. Novaes (1994), "Mercado de trabalho no setor sucro-alcooleiro do Brasil," *Estudos de Política Agrícola*. Brasília. Instituto de Economia Agrícola Aplicada.

Richards, Cathy (2012), "Bauxite talks collapse," *Stabroek News*, November 27.

Robinson, William (2010), "Beyond the Theory of Imperialism. Global Capitalism and the Transnational State," pp. 61–76 in Alexander Ancevas (ed.), *Marxism and World Politics: Contentesting Global Capitalism*. New York: Routledge.

Rodríguez García Arturo (2013), "El millonario negocio de las minas y su macabro saldo: 159 trabajadores muertos", *Proceso*, March 19th http://www.proceso.com .mx/?p=336653 (consulted 26/11/13).

Rostow, W.W. (1960), *The Stages of Economic Growth: A Non-communist Manifesto*. Cambridge University Press.

Ruiz-Dana, Alejandra, Peter Goldschagg, Edmundo Claro and Hernán Blanco (2007), *Regional Integration, Trade and Conflict in Latin America*. Winnipeg: ISSD.

Sachs, J. and Warner (2001), "The Curse of Natural Resources," *European Economic Review*, 45, 827–838.

Sacristán Roy, Emilio (2006), "Las privatizaciones en México," *Economía UNAM*, 3(9), 54–64.

Sankey, Kyla (2014), "Colombia: The Mining Boom: A Catalyst of Development or Resistance?" in H. Veltmeyer and J. Petras (eds.), *The New Extractivism: A Post-neoliberal Development Model or Imperialism of the Twenty-first Century?* London: Zed Books.

Sariego, Juan Luis (2011), "La minería mexicana: el ocaso de un modelo nacionalista," *Apuntes*, XXXVIII(68), 137–165.

Sariego, J.L., Luis Reygadas, Miguel Ángel Gómez and Javier Farrera (1988), *La industria paraestatal en Mexico: El estado y la minería mexicana. Política, trabajo y sociedad durante el siglo XX*. México, DF: Fondo de Cultura Económica.

Schneider Ross Ben (2002), "Why is Mexican Business so Organized?" *Latin American Research Review*, 37(1): 77–118.

Secretaría de Economía (2005), *Anuario Estadístico de la Minería Mexicana, 2004*. México, DF: Coordinación General de Minería.

Secretaría de Economía (2012), *Anuario Estadístico de la Minería Mexicana, Ampliada 2011*. México, DF: Coordinación General de Minería.

Secretaría de Economía (2013), *Reporte de coyuntura de la minería nacional*, No. 72. http://www.economia.gob.mx/files/comunidad_negocios/industria_comercio/informacionSectorial/minero/reporte_de_coyuntura_mineria_nacional_0713.pdf (consulted 25/11/13).

Secretaría de Energía, Minas e Industria Paraestatal (SEMIP) (1993), *Anuario estadístico de la Minería Mexicana 1993*. México, DF: SEMIP.

Sena-Fobomade (2011), Se intensifica el extractivismo minero en América Latina," *Foro Boliviano sobre Medio Ambiente y Desarrollo*, 03–02. http://fobomade.org.bo/art-1109.

Serra, José (1973), "The Brazilian Economic Miracle," pp. 100–140 in James Petras, ed. *Latin America from Dependence to Revolution*. New York: John Wiley.

Shepard, Daniel, with Anuradha (2009), *The Great Land Grab: Rush for World's Farmland Threatens Food Security for the Poor*. Oakland, CA: The Oakland Institute.

Sibaud, Philippe (2012) "Opening Pandora's Box: The New Wave of Land Grabbing by Extractive Industries and the Devastating Impact on Earth," Commissioned by The Gaia Foundation, London.

Silva, Letizia (2010), "Implicaciones sociales en la legislación ambiental. El proceso de evaluación de impacto ambiental de Minera San Xavier," pp. 213–249 in Gian Carlo Delgado Ramos (ed.), *Ecología política de la Minería en América Latina. Aspectos socioeconómicos, legales y ambientales de la mega minería*, México, DF: Centro de Investigaciones Interdisciplinarias en Ciencias y Humanidades, UNAM.

Smeets, E.M. (2006), *Sustainability of Brazilian bio-ethanol*. Utrecht: Utrecht University.

Smith, Richard (2013), "Capitalism and the Destruction of Life on Earth: Six Theses on Saving Humans," *Real-World Economics Review*, No. 64.

SOBEET (2011), Boletim No. 77, Sociedade Brasileira de Estudos de Empresas Transnacionais e da Globalização Econômica, Sâo Paulo, 25 de enero.

Solanas, F. (2007), "El despojo de los metales argentinos (Parte IV)." *Rebelión*, July 31: 1–9. http://www.rebelion.org/seccion.php?id=9.

Sosa, Milagros and Margreet Zwarteveen (2012), "Exploring the Politics of Water Grabbing: The case of large mining operations in the Peruvian Andes," *Water Alternatives*, 5(2): 360–375.

Spiegel Online (2013), Land Grabbing: Foreign Investor s Buy Up Third World Farmland. http://www.spiegel.de/international/business/0,1518,935801,00.html.

Stabroek News (2009), "Expelled Brazilian Rice Farmer Looking to Shift Operations to Guyana," Georgetown Guyana, May 14.

Stefanoni, Pablo (2012), "Posneoliberalismo cuesta arriba: Los modelos de Venezuela, Bolivia y Ecuador en debate," *Nueva Sociedad*, No. 239, Mayo-Junio.

Stijns, J.-P. (2006), "Natural Resource Abundance and Human Capital Accumulation," *World Development*, 34(6), June, 1060–1083.

Svampa, Maristella (2012), "Consenso de los commodities y megaminería," pp. 5–8 in *América Latina en movimiento. Extractivismo: Contradicciones y conflictividad.* Quito: Agencia Latinoamericana de Información (ALAI).

Tellez, Juan (1993), "TheChallenge for a Multi-ethnic Approach to Development: The Case of Bolivia," MA Thesis, IDS. Halifax: Saint Mary's University.

Tellez, Juan (2013), "Prácticas y Agentes en la Extracción Minera en el Desarrollo de Bolivia," Universidad Autónoma de Zacatecas-Unidad de Doctorado en Estudios del Desarrollo, Marzo.

Tetreault, Darcy (2013), "Los mecanismos del imperialismo en el sector minero de América Latina," *Estudios Críticos del Desarrollo*, III(4).

Tetreault, Darcy (2014), "Mexico. The Political Ecology of Mining," pp. 172–191 in H. Veltmeyer and J. Petras (eds.), *The New Extractivism*, London/New York: Zed Books.

Teubal, Miguel (1995), "Internacionalización del capital y complejos agro-industriales: impactos en América Latina," pp. 45–79 in M. Teubal, *Globalización y Expansión Agroindustrial: ¿Superación de la Pobreza en América Latina?* Buenos Aires: Ediciones Corregidor.

Teubal, Miguel (2001), "Globalización y nueva ruralidad en América Latina," in N. Giarracca (ed.), *¿Una nueva ruralidad en América Latina?* Buenos Aires: CLACSO-ASDI.

Teubal, Miguel (2006), "Expansión del Modelo Sojero en la Argentina. De la Producción de Alimentos a los Commodities," *Realidad Económica*, No. 220.

Teubal, Miguel (2009), "La Lucha por la Tierra," pp. 205–229 in N. Giarracca and M. Teubal (eds.), *La Tierra es Nuestra, Tuya y de Aquel: Las Disputas por el Territorio en América Latina.* Buenos Aires: Antropofagia.

Teubal, Miguel and Tomás Palmisano (2012), "Acumulación por desposesión: la colonialidad del poder en América Latina," in *Renunciar al bien común. Extractivismo y (pos)desarrollo en América Latina.* Buenos Aires: Edición Gabriela Massuh, Mardulce.

Teubal, Miguel et al. (2005), "Transformaciones Agrarias en la Argentina. Agricultura Industrial y Sistema Alimentario," pp. 37–78 in N. Giarracca and M. Teubal, eds., *El Campo en la Encrucijada. Estrategias y Resistencias Sociales, Ecos en la Ciudad.* Buenos Aires: Alianza Editorial.

The Tripoli Post (2009), "Libya to Boost Agriculture Ties with Guyana," March 7.

Toledo, Víctor (2000), "El otro zapatismo: luchas indígenas de inspiración ecológica en México," in Víctor Toledo (ed.) *La paz en Chiapas: ecología, luchas indígenas y modernidad alternativa.* Mexico City: Ediciones Quinto Sol.

Toledo, Victor (2002), "Biodiversidad y pueblos indios," *Biodiversitas*, No. 43, pp. 1–8.

Trasviña Aguilar Juan Ángel (2013), "Baja California Sur. Breve historia del movimiento contra la minería tóxica," *La Jornada del Campo*, April 20th, No. 67.

UNCTAD (1998), *World Investment Report 1998: Trends and Determinants.* New York and Geneva: United Nations.

UNCTAD (2009), *World Investment Report 2009. Transnational Corporations, Extractive Industries and Development.* New York and Geneva: United Nations.

UNCTAD (2010), *Informe sobre las inversiones en el mundo 2010.* New York and Geneva: UNCTAD.

UNCTAD (2011), *World Investment Report 2011* New York: United Nations.

UNCTAD (2012a), "Investment Trend Monitor," No. 8, New York, United Nations, January 24.

UNCTAD (2012b), *World Investment Report 2012. Towards a New Generation of Investment Policies.* New York and Geneva: United Nations.

UNDESA—United Nations, Department of Economic and Social Affairs (2005), *The World Social Situation: The Inequality Predicament.* New York: United Nations.

UNDP (2010) *Regional Human Development Report for Latin America and the Caribbean 2010.* New York: UNDP.

United Nations (2011), General Assembly. Report of the Special Rapporteur on the Rights of Indigenous Peoples, James Anaya: Extractive Industries Operating Within or Near Indigenous Territories, July. A/HRC/18/35.

United Nations Secretariat (2008), *An Overview of Urbanization, Internal Migration, Population Distribution and Development in the World.* New York: United Nations, DESA [UN/POP/EGM-URB/2008/01].

U.S. Department of State (2012a), *Investment Climate Statement – Guyana.* Washington, DC.

U.S. Department of State (2012b), *Trafficking in Persons Report 2012.* Washington, DC, June.

UNU-IHDP-UNEP (2012), *Inclusive Wealth Report 2012. Measuring Progress toward Sustainability.* Cambridge: Cambridge University Press.

Urías, Homero (1980), "¿Quién controla la minería mexicana?" *Comercio Exterior,* 30(9): 949–965.

Veltmeyer, Henry (1983), "Surplus Labour and Class Formation on the Latin American Periphery," In Ron Chilcote and Dale Johnston (eds.), *Theories of Development.* Beverly Hills CA: SAGE Publications.

Veltmeyer, Henry (1997), "New Social Movements in Latin America: the Dynamics of Class and Identity," *The Journal of Peasant Studies,* 25(1), October.

Veltmeyer, Henry (2010), "Una sinopsis de la idea de desarrollo," *Migración y Desarrollo*, No. 14, Primer Semestre, pp. 9–34.

Veltmeyer, Henry (2012) "The Natural Resource Dynamics of Post-Neoliberalism in Latin America: New Developmentalism or Extractivist Imperialism?" *Studies in Political Economy*, 90(Autumn): 57–86.

Veltmeyer, Henry (2013), "The Political Economy of Natural Resource Extraction: A New Model or Extractive Imperialism?" *Canadian Journal of Development Studies*, 34(1), March: 79–95.

Veltmeyer, Henry and Darcy Tetreault (eds.) (2013), *Poverty in Latin America: Public Policies and Development Pathways.* Kumarian Press.

Veltmeyer, Henry and James Petras (2014), *The New Extractivism in Latin America.* London: Zed Books.

Wagner, Sarah (2006), "Summit in Venezuela: Accelerate South American Union," *Venezuelaanalysis.com,* 30 March 2005, 2 February 2006, http://www.venezuelanaly sis.com/news.php?newsno=1564.

Walton, Timothy (2002), *The Spanish Treasure Fleets.* Pineapple Press.

Webber, Jeffery (2010), *Red October: Left Indigenous Struggle in Modern Bolivia.* Leiden: Brill Academic Publishers.

Webber, J.R. (2011), *Rebellion and Reform in Bolivia.* Chicago, IL: Haymarket Books.

Weisbrot, Mark and Luis Sandoval (2008), *The Venezuelan Economy in the Chávez Years.* Washington, DC: Center for Economics and Policy.

Weismann, Robert (2003), "The U.S. Meets Defeat: Thwarted in the FTAA Negotiations, The U.S. Looks to Smaller Trade Deals," *Multinational Monitor*, 24(12), December.

Westra, Richard (2012), *The Evil Axis of Finance: The US-Japan-China Stranglehold on the Global Future.* Clarity Press.

White, B., S. Borras, R. Hall, I. Scoones and W. Wolford (2012), "The New Enclosures: Critical perspectives on Corporate Land Deals," *Journal of Peasant Studies,* 39(3–4): 619–647.

Wikipedia Vale. http://en.wikipedia.org/wiki/Vale_(mining_company).

Williamson, John (1990), *Latin American Adjustment: How Much Has Happened?* Washington, DC: Institute for International Economics.

Wily, Liz Alden (2013), "The Global Land Grab: The New Enclosures," in David Bollier and Sike Helfrich (eds.), *The Wealth of the Commons.* The Commons Strategy Group.

Wilkinson, Bert (2010), "Guyana: Pro-forest Measures Anger Miners," IPS, February 12.

Wilkinson, Bert (2012), "Runaway Gold Prices Spark Major Headaches for Guyana," IPS, May 29.

Wilkinson, Bert (2012a), "Young Child Rescues from Guyana Gold Camp," AP, November 6.

Wilkinson, J. and S. Herrera (2010), "Biofuels in Brazil: Debates and Impacts," *Journal of Peasant Studies,* 37(4): 749–768.

Wilpert, Gregory (2007), *Changing Venezuela by Taking Power: The History and Policies of the Chávez Government*. London: Verso.

Wilpert, Gregory (2011), "An Assessment of Venezuela's Bolivarian Revolution at Twelve Years," Venezuelanalysis.com, 2/2/2011.

Wise, Timothy A (2009), "Promise or Pitfall? The Limited Gains from Agricultural Trade Liberalisation for Developing Countries," *Journal of Peasant Studies*, 36(4): 855–870.

Wood, Ellen Meiksins (2003), *Empire of Capital*. New York: Verso.

Wood, Geoff (2014). "President's Message," *DSA Bulletin*. February. p. 1. http://www.devstud.org.uk/downloads/530ca428d797c_february2014newsletter.pdf.

World Bank (1991–2001), *World Development Reports*. Washington, DC.

World Bank (2005), *Extractive Industries and Sustainable Development. An Evaluation of World Bank Group Experience*. Washington.

World Bank (2008). *World Development Report 2008: Agriculture for Development*. New York: Oxford University Press.

World Bank (2010), *Rising Global Interest in Farmland: Can It Yield Sustainable and Equitable Benefits?* Washington, DC: World Bank.

World Bank (2011), *The World Bank Group in Extractive Industries. 2011 Annual Review*. Washington, DC.

Zapata Schaffeld Francisco (2006), "Las huelgas mineras de 2005–2006. Del corporativismo a la autonomía syndical," http://www.sjsocial.org/crt/articulos/758_zapata.htm (consulted 26/11/13).

Zapata Schaffeld Francisco (2008), "De Cananea y Río Blanco a La Caridad y las Truchas. Un siglo de conflicto laborales en México (1907–2006)," *Revista de Historia, Sociedad y Cultura*, 6(12), 113–138.

Zibechi, Raúl (2012), La nueva geopolítica del capital," ALAI, América Latina en Movimiento, Abril 19. *Le Monde Diplomatique* Colombia, abril).

Zibechi, Raúl (2013), "El fin del consenso lulista," *Rebellion* 7/7/13.

Zorrilla, Carlos (2009), *Protegiendo a su comunidad contra las empresas mineras y otras industrias extractivas*. Boulder, CO: Global Response.

Index

CPSIA information can be obtained
at www.ICGtesting.com
Printed in the USA
LVOW13s1135110117
520560LV00010B/64/P

9 781608 464944